91100000039730

D1756353

Kenisha

T

BRENT LIBRARIES

Please return/renew this item
by the last date shown.
Books may also be renewed by
phone or online.
Tel: 0115 929 3388
On-line www.brent.gov.uk/libraryservice

Dedicated
To all the Members of the Former Evangelical Church of Eritrea
and the Present Members of the Evangelical Lutheran Church of Eritrea.

THE RED SEA PRESS
541 West Ingham Avenue | Suite B
Trenton, New Jersey 08638

SEM, S-751 70 Uppsala, Sweden
Phone +46 18 16 98 00
E-mail: efs@efs.nu
www.efs.nu

Copyright © 2011 SEM/EFS
First Printing 2011

Book Design: Martin Nilsson
Pictures on Front Page: See pages 129, 163, 269, 311, 327, 504

Library of Congress Cataloging-in-Publication Data

Lundström, Karl Johan, 1927-2003.
Kenisha : the roots and development of the Evangelical Church of Eritrea (ECE), 1866-1935 / by Karl Johan Lundström ; edited by Ezra Gebremedhin.
   p. cm.
Includes bibliographical references (p.   ) and index.
ISBN 978-1-56902-350-1 (pbk.)
1. Evangelical Church of Eritrea–History. 2. Eritrea–Church history.
I. Gebremedhin, Ezra, 1936- II. Title.
BX8063.E65L86 2011
284.1'63509034–dc22

               2011005484

Already in 1871, the SEM periodical published these three illustrations of a woman who is spinning, a man who is ploughing and some tools that were in use. The artist was Mrs. Gustava Lundahl, the wife of missionary Bengt Peter Lundahl. The drawings were prepared in response to questions from Swedes about the life-style of the people among whom the Gospel was being preached.

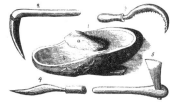

1. Cwarn (a den sten som föres med handen, b den sten som står på marken.) 2. Jordhacka. 3. Stara. 4. Knif. 5. Yxa.

1. Hand-grinder of stone, 2. A hoe,
3. A sickle, 4. A Knife, 5. An Axe.

A woman spinning cotton.

A man ploughing in the Geleb region, with the mountain "The Princess", in the background.

ፈን፡ክእፅም፡ጓፎፅም፡ፍ፡ሶብ፡ሐጸር፡በብር ኸስየ፡እ ንነብር፡ኢ
ፍ፡ዝነበርፍ፡ሃብኣም፡እንደልዮ፡ኣይነበረፍ ን፡፡ግንዘብ፡ይህሉ
ኣዮም፡ዚብሃል፡ወሬ፡ድዐ፡ኣይተሰምዔን፡ እንተኾ ነ፡ብኣዮ፡ፍ
ሳይ፡፲፰፻፳፫፡እተሐነ ሙ፡መጸሐፍቲ፡ብቖገፁ፡ እዮሐራ፡ቌ ወይ፡ዘ
ልኣለም፡ይህ ንነት፡የዐ መስይ፡መ ንገይ፡፪ መግለጫ፡፫ ክርስቶ
ስ፡ሁሉ፡በሁሉዎ፡ነው፡ዚብሃሉ፡መጸሐፍቲ፡እናእ ምበብ ፍ
ፍ ጡ ን፡ግሬ ሁት፡ነበር ፍ ፡ኣ ም በር፡ድሌት፡ግ ን ዘ ብ ፡ ኣ ደ ነ በ
ሬፍ ፍ ፡ ሾ ሁ ፡ ድ ዐ ፡ እቶ ም ፡ ፈ ረ ን ጀ ፡ ግ ን ዘ ብ ፡ ዚ ህ ብ ዎ ፡ ሶ ብ
ኣ ደ ነ በ ረ ፍ ፡ ካ ባ ነ ዉ ን ፡ ግ ን ዘ ብ ፡ ዚ ቅ በ ል ፡ ኣ ደ ነ በ ሬ ን ፡ በ ቲ ፡ ጊ ዜ
ቲ፡ድዐ፡ሳዮም ኣ ደ ነ በ ሬ ን፡፡

ክንብል፡ክንብል፡ግ ፍ፡ ም ስ ት ም ፡ ለ እ ኛ ት ፡ ወ ን ገ ል ፡ ሾ ፀ
ድ ን ፡ ኣ ት ፡ ባ ግ ሬ ፡ ሃ ደ ፡ ፡ ን ስ ት ር ዮ ፡ ተ ፈ ለ ጥ ፍ ፡ ብ ፍ ቃ ድ ፡ ዐ
ጀ ዘ ወ ግ ፍ ፡ ግ በ ሬ ፡ ን ሁ ሬ ፡ ኢ ድ ፡ ድ ሐ ር ፡ ወ ክ ሾ ም ፡ ዘ በ ሉ ፡ ፍ ብ
ዘ ለ ዛ ፡ በ ሬ ር ም ፡ ነ በ ሬ ም ፡ ኣ ብ ፡ ጸ ዓ ዘ ጋ ፡ ደ በ ጁ ሑ ን ፡ ነ በ ሬ ን ፡ ን
ሐ ፡ ክ ኣ ፡ ብ ፍ ቅ ሬ ን ፡ ቅ በ ሉ ም ፡ ነ በ ር ፍ ፡ እ ን ተ ኾ ነ ፡ ጸ ነ ኹ ቲ ፡ ወ
ን ጓ ል ፡ ብ ኽ ፍ ኣ ቶ ም ፡ እ ና ክ ስ ኹ ፡ ን ኹ ሉ ፡ ሰ ብ ፡ ኣ ህ ግ ር ግ ር ዮ
ክ ም ዚ ፡ እ ና ኹ ፡ ስ ለ ስ ቴ ፡ ዓ መ ት ፡ ዚ ኽ ክ ል ፡ ጸ ና ሕ ፍ ፡ ድ ሐ ር ዚ ፡ ስ ደ
ት ፡ ዮ ስ ፡ ኮ ፤ ፡ ብ ፍ ቅ ሬ ፡ ተ ቀ በ ሉ ፍ ፡ እ ዮ በ ር ፡ ቅ ደ ም ፡ ዝ ስ ፡ ዝ ገ በ
ሬ ል ፍ ፡ ነ ገ ር ፡ የ ል ቦ ን ፡ እ ቲ ፡ ብ ፍ ቅ ሬ ፡ ም ቅ በ ሉ ም ፡ ግ ፍ ፡ እ ን ተ ሐ
ሰ ብ ና ዮ ፡ ዘ ደ ን ቅ ፡ ነ ገ ር ፡ እ ዩ ፡ እ ቶ ም ፡ ኣ ሕ ወ ት ና ን ፡ ኣ ኅ ዐ ድ ና ን ፡
ኪ ጸ ል ኡ ና ን ፡ ኪ ሶ ጉ ና ን ፡ ኀ ዘ ም ፡ ብ ሥ ጋ ፡ ዘ ደ ዘ መ ደ ን ፡ ብ ሀ ገ
ር ፡ ዘ ደ ን ፈ ል ጥ ፡ ግ ፍ ፡ ካ ብ ፡ እ ዝ መ ድ ፡ ን ፡ ነ ብ ፡ ወ ለ ድ ፡ ና ን ፡ ዘ በ ሰ ዱ
ሾ ኑ ፍ ፡ እ ዚ ፡ ዘ ጋ ጠ መ ፍ ፡ ዚ ደ ገ ት ፡ መ ስ ቱ ን ክ ር ፡ ዘ ኮ ፤ ፡ ነ ገ ር ፡ ፍ
ቅ ሬ ፡ ካ ር ስ ቶ ስ ፡ ፈ ፡ ወ ን ገ ሉ ን ፡ ጥ በ ሁ ፡ ለ ው ሃ ቱ ን ፡ እ ዩ ፡ ን ኡ ፡ ም
ስ ጋ ፍ ፡ ነ ቅ ር ብ ፡ ኣ ሎ ፍ ፡፡

በ ቲ ፡ ጊ ዜ ፡ እ ቲ ፡ እ ብ ፡ ግ ራ ት ፡ እ ተ ሐ ብ ኤ ፡ መ ዘ ገ ብ ፡ ዝ ሬ ኸ በ
እ ም ፡ ብ ታ ሕ ጊ ስ ፡ ነ ፓ ፡ ግ ራ ት ፡ እ ቲ ኣ ፡ ክ ም ዚ ሾ የ ጥ ፡ ግ ሁ ና ፡ ድ ዐ ፡
ተ ሾ የ ጥ ና ዮ ፡ ዐ ሃ ቱ ፡ ፲ ፰ ፡ ሙ ፡ ፬ ፡ እ ገ ሃ ፡ ክ ሳ ዐ ፡ ሱ ም ፡ ሥ ሳ ን ፡ እ ሳ ፡ ነ ፓ
ም ፡ እ ሳ ቀ በ ሉ ፍ ፡ ድ ዐ ፡ ፪ ም ኣ ም ፡ ካ ብ ፡ እ ግ ዚ እ ብ ሄ ር ፡ ብ ብ ዙ ሕ
በ ሬ ኸ ት ፡ ደ ክ ፈ ሉ ፍ ፡ እ ሬ ፡ ን ም ዐ ል ፡ ክ ሶ ዐ ፡ ዘ መ ዉ ት ክ ቶ ፡ ኣ ደ ሐ
ደ ገ ን ፡ ብ ጸ ሶ ተ ደ ወ ን ፡ ኣ ደ ር ስ ዖ ን ፡ እ ብ ፡ ስ በ ይ ፡ ፤ ሁ ር ፡ ኢ ፈ ፡

This text from ca 1933 is an example of many striking glimpses into the lives of the fathers of the Kenisha. It is a narrative about the life of one of the pioneers of the Evangelical Church of Eritrea, Qeshi Zer'a-Tsion Musé, for the period between 1850 and 1933. The narrative must have been written in or around 1933. Qeshi Zer'a-Tsion states that he was 83 at the time of writing.

The Story of My Life – In Brief

... We were individuals with our families and lived independently, according to our means. We didn't expect anything from them ['the *ferendji*', i. e. Europeans]. Neither were there any rumours to the effect that they [the *ferendji*'] doled out money. However, we became diligent and were granted openness as a result of our reading of some books in Amharic, printed by Otto Flad in 1875. The titles of these books were: *Wädä zel'aläm dähninät yämiwäsd mängäd* (A Way Which Leads to Eternal Salvation), *Mäglächa* (Explanation), *Kristos hulu bähulum näw* [Christ is All in All]. We had no craving for money. At that time there was no one to whom the ferendji doled out money. Neither was there anyone among us who received money. And at that time there was no lamba (kerosene).

But in the course of time, we became acquainted with the Swedish missionaries of the Gospel, Mr. Lager [1837-1876]) and Mr. Hedenström [1844–1904]. These two had settled in Beleza with the permission of *Niburä Id* (later Waqshim) Gäbru. The two [missionaries] used to visit us in Tseazzega, and we used to receive them with love. However, enemies of the Gospel kept accusing us maliciously and caused turbulence among all the people. Three years passed in this state of turbulence, after which a time of persecution began. Then, the missionaries received us in love. Prior to that, they hadn't done anything on our behalf or for us. However, the fact that they received us with love is a source of wonder. While our brothers and relatives hated us and persecuted us, these people, who were not related to us biologically, became closer to us than our relatives and parents. This most wonderful and astonishing experience is a result of the love of Christ and his Gospel, his wisdom and his bounty. We render him our praises.

At that time we did that which has been narrated in Matthews 13: 45-46, "The kingdom of heaven is like a merchant looking for fine pearls. When he found one of great value, he went away and sold everything he had and bought it." We too bought the treasure [i.e. the Gospel of Grace], and this treasure is with us until this very day. May God richly reward those who once received [welcomed] us. I shall not cease to say so until the day of my death. Neither shall I forget it [this favour] in my prayers. It is in my heart to stay. ...

For the full text of this story see Appendix V, page 464.

Table of Contents

CHAPTER NINE 180

Probing While Waiting on the Coast 1870–1890

Introduction [180] • A new Beginning [181] • Stay on the Highlands [182] • Lager's and Hedenström's Ministry at Ailet [184] • Lager and Lundahl: Divergent Views on Relations to Different Power Constellations [186] • The Death of Lager and a new Period of Hiding [187] • Mensa 1879–1880 [188] • New Challenges: Pondering the next Move [189] • The Beginning of the Oromo Expeditions. The First Oromo Expedition [191] • Nigusé Advances to Gojjam [193] • The Second Oromo Expedition [194] • The Third Oromo Expedition [195] • The Fourth Oromo Expedition [196] • The Fifth Oromo Expedition –A Breakthrough (1897–1898) [197] • In Closing [200]

CHAPTER TEN 202

Mission under a Colonial Master – A Blessing in Disguise?

Introduction [202] • SEM in the Midst of a Struggle for Control of Territory [206] • A Divided Italy Rallies under Giuseppe Garibaldi [207] • The Acceleration of Italy's Ambitions at Home and Abroad [208] • Eritrea: What kind of Colony? [208] • Growing Vitality in the Catholic Church [210] • The Waldensian Church – A Protestant Minority in Catholic Italy [211] • The Waldensian Church to the Aid of the SEM [212] • The First Decade of the SEM in Italian Eritrea, 1890–1900. The Scourge of Drought, Locusts and Cattle Diseases [213] • Medical Care, Evangelism and Diaconal Activities [214] • Land Rights and Land Policies in Colonial Eritrea [216] • Returning Kenisha in Conflict with their Traditional Home Regions [216] • Ambivalence and Irritation of Colonial Authorities Towards the Kenisha [218] • Amharic or Tigrinya? The Language Issue [219] • In Closing [220]

CHAPTER ELEVEN 222

Return to Mensa 1889

Introduction [222] • A Station Reopened [223] • Serving the Community [224] • Evangelism [226] • Disagreement on Choice of Tigré Language Forms [228] • Itinerant Mission to Marea and Bogos – Sundström and Alazar [231] • Mediation on Issues of Language [232] • The Dilemma of Placing two Missionaries [234] • Other Labourers in the Vineyard [236] • In Closing [238]

CHAPTER TWELVE 240

Return to Kunama (I): Reunion and Resumption of Activities 1897–1915

Introduction [240] • Re-Establishing a Mission [242] • August Andersson. His Call, Preparation and Start as a Missionary [244] • Jack-of-All-Trades: Builder, Scholar and Healer [245] • Marriage and Short-lived Bliss [246] • Peter and Emma Andersson in Kunama. Peter – A Meticulous Missionary [247] • The

Placement of Medical Personnel [306] • The Efforts of De Pertis at Expanding Medical Work. Ivarson's Worries [308] • De Pertis Heavily Engaged as Planner and Healer [310] • Deaconesses Graduate [312] •The Training of Teachers [312] • Ato Bairu Uqbit [314] • Ato Tedla Bairu [315] • Overall Picture on Educational Activities [316] • The Production of Literature [316] • In Closing [320]

Highland Centres of Evangelical Christianity – Tse'azzega

Introduction [324] • A Place with a Character of its Own [326] • 'Father' Svensson and Gebre-Le'ul [328] • A Eulogy to A. Kolmodin – A Credit to Svensson [328] • Implications of Mission among the Orthodox [329] • Providing for the Spiritual Care of Evangelical Christians [330] • Svensson – Patriarch of Tse'azzega and Master of his own House [332] • Tse'azzega – The first Parish to Send Eritrean "Missionaries" [336] • Sigrid Berggren – Champion of Work among Women and a Promoter of Missionary Outreach [338] • Svensson, His Eritrean Family and His Protégés [340] • A Leadership Crisis in Tse'azzega [340] • Iwarson Critical of Svensson [341] • A Final Visit to Sweden [341] • A Patriarch Passes Away [341] • A Painful Development [342] • In Closing [343]

Mission in the Context of Catholic Priorities (I)

Introduction [346] • Tug of War between the Colonial Government and the SEM after 1915 [349] • Signs of Colonial Hospitality [350] • Historical Background to the Catholic Presence in Eritrea [352] • Renewed Catholic Contacts with Ethiopia [353] • Mgr. Giustino de Jacobis Arrives in Tigrai [354] • On to Massawa and Halai [354] • Catholic Mission into new Areas in the North [355] • Ambivalent Relations with Colonial Authorities [356] • In Closing [356]

Mission in the Context of Catholic Priorities (II)

Introduction [358] • State and Church Come Closer in Italian Politics [359] • Italian Colonial Policy towards Muslims and Orthodox Christians [360] • Vigorous Catholic Outreach Under Mgr. Carrara. Approach to "Copts" (Orthodox Tewahdo) [361] • Outreach among the Kunama [364] • Work among the Mensa [364] • Restrictive Stance under Salvago Raggi [365] • Expulsion of Missionaries and the Challenge of other Constraints (1915–1925) [365] • Further Restrictions Under Governor Gasparini [366] • Increased Cost of Living [369] • In Closing [370] • Caution and Restrictive Measures [370]

Persisting in Mission in Spite of a Gathering Storm

Introduction [372] • Changes for the Better [373] • Missionaries Under Severe

Abbreviations

BFBS	British and Foreign Bible Society
BV	Bibeltrogna Vänner (Bible-True Friends)
BY	Birhan Yikun
CMS	Church Missionary Society
CSA	Church of Sweden Aid
CSM	Church of Sweden Mission
DAM	Deaf Africa Mission
DB	Debre Bizen
EAE	Encyclopaedia Aethiopica
EECMY	Ethiopian Evangelical Church Mekane Yesus
ECE	Evangelical Church of Eritrea
EFS	Evangeliska Fosterlands-Stiftelsen (SEM)
ELM-BV	Evangelisk luthersk mission – Bibeltrogna Vänner (Evangelical Lutheran Mission – Bible-True Friends)
EOC	Ethiopian Orthodox Church
EOTC	Ethiopian Orthodox Tewahdo Church
ELCE	Evangelical Lutheran Church of Eritrea
EMML	Ethiopian Monastic Manuscript Library
HMML	Hill Monastic Manuscript Library
K. J.	Karl Johan Lundström
LCE	Lutheran Church of Eritrea
LWF	Lutheran World Federation
M-B	Maj-Britt Lundström
MSS	Manuscripts
MT	Missions Tidning (Mission Periodical)
NIV	New International Version of the Bible
OH/ OHD	Olle Hagner/ Olle Hagner's Diaries
OHD/K.J.S.	Olle Hagner's Diaries/K.J.'s Summary
OTC	Orthodox Tewahdo Church
RSE	Rassegna Di Studi Etiopici
SEM	Swedish Evangelical Mission
SEM/MT	Swedish Evangelical Mission/Missions Tidning
SEM/MTBB	Swedish Evangelical Mission Periodical in combination with both Missions Tidning and Budbäraren from 1928
U14	Stockholm Archives. Special Archives. U14

Acknowledgements

It is difficult to mention the names of all individuals and organizations that should be thanked for helping Karl Johan (1927–2003) and Maj-Britt Lundström (1915–2010) in the collection of material and the editing of the texts for this book. Since I shall mention Maj-Britt's unique role later on I won't say more about her in this connection.

This work owes a sincere debt of gratitude to the Swedish Evangelical Mission (SEM), which not only approved and financed it, but also contributed office-space and technical support towards its actualization. The leadership of the Evangelical Church of Eritrea (ECE) has followed the project with its blessings and support, a stance which was a source of encouragement for the Lundströms and the editor. The Lundströms were highly appreciative of the cooperation that they enjoyed with the late Yosef Gebre-Woldi, a person who was deeply interested in the history of the ECE.[1]

Pastor Bruno Tron has been a source of very great help to the Lundströms and to the editor in the process of the production of this book. A son of the revered missionary from the Waldensian Church to Eritrea, Pastor Alessandro Tron, Bruno was born and brought up in Eritrea. After receiving his theological education in Italy and Germany, he served for many years as a missionary and pastor within the ECE, before he and his wife Paola returned to Italy. As far as the material related to the Italian colonial period and Catholic missions in Eritrea is concerned, Bruno's editorial contributions have been indispensable.

---

1   *Yosef* is sometimes spelt as *Yosief* or *Joseph*. In his B.A. thesis in the field of Education (1972) the author spells his forename as Joseph.

He has also made many relevant suggestions on both the content and the language of the book. I have inserted several of his suggestions, into the body of this book, albeit in modified forms.

I would like to thank *Qeshi* Asfaha Mehari, President of the ECE until early 2010 and *Qeshi* (formerly known to most of us as *Memhir*/Teacher) Musa Aron for suggestions on certain formulations in the chapter on Mensa as well as Mr. Wolde-Yesus Elisa, Mr. Selomon Dawit, Mr. Samuel Adem, Pastor Sture Normark and Pastor Bertil Holmgren for helping me in editing the material on Kunama. Pastor Gunnar Svensson, Pastor Nils Rönnbäck and Pastor Inge Rönnbäck, all of whom are former missionaries to Eritrea, have shared their views with me on different aspects of the work. I thank them for the suggestions they have made and for the encouragement they have given me.

I am indebted to my paternal uncle, *Qeshi* Elias Habte-Egzy, as well as to *Qeshi* Asfaha Mehari, and *Qeshi* Musa Aron for help with the spelling of names of persons and places and for identifying a good number but not all of the surnames of the Kenisha named in this book. A more widespread and concentrated search would have certainly led to better results. The difficulties into which I have run in this regard underline, once more, the urgency of recording the history of the ECE before more old people die and more memories grow dim.

Dr. Tesfa-Yesus Mehari, Associate Dean of Academic Affairs at the College of Business and Economics, in Asmara, Professor Tekeste Negash, Uppsala, Docent (Assistant Professor) Agne Nordlander, Uppsala, and Professor Asmarom Legesse, Asmara, have all contributed to this work with editorial comments and suggestions. I am sincerely grateful to all of them.

I owe Professor Asmarom a special debt of gratitude for providing me with a number of valuable suggestions on the content and formulation of the narrative in this book and for sharing with me some interesting facts on his great grandfather, *Qeshi* Zer'a-Tsion Musé. Furthermore, he took upon himself the painstaking task of working out an index to this work. Our modified version is based on the detailed version of his index. Docent (Assistant Professor) Bereket Yebio, Lund, who was kind enough to go quickly through a late version of this book, gave me some useful suggestions as to how to relate the work that had been done to date with the history of the Bible-True Friends (BV) and the Lutheran Church of Eritrea for the period after 1911. He also indicated further sources for a history of the Evangelical Lutheran Church of Eritrea (ELCA). I am sincerely grateful to him.

At a late stage in the process of the editing of this work, Gianni Dore, Associate Professor at *Università Ca' Foscari di Venezia*, Italy, visited Uppsala in connection with a teaching and research assignment. He was of great help in enlightening me on a number of issues in the chapters related to Kunama. I am sincerely grateful to him.

Martin Nilsson, Uppsala, Information Secretary for EFS/SEM has laboured for a number of years in making this book ready for publication. The list of Swedish missionaries and their Eritrean and Ethiopian colleagues in Appendix V and VI, as well as the search for appropriate pictures, are basically a fruit of his labours. I am deeply grateful to him. Ruth Normark, Uppsala, a former missionary to Eritrea and one of the actors in the planning and implementation of this project and her husband Sture Normark, came forward with valuable suggestions not only on aspects of the content of the book but also on the choice of pictures. Both SEM and I are sincerely grateful to them. Olle Hagner Jr., the son of missionary Olle Hagner, allowed me to use the five small books of diaries kept by his father during the war years and the early stages of the British occupation of Eritrea, from 1939 to 1943. I am very grateful to him for this act of kindness.

During some wintry days in January 2010, in Spring Field, Maryland, USA, my brother Naigzy Gebremedhin took time to read an almost final draft of this book with intense care and interest. Dr. Eskil Forslund, former missionary to Ethiopia, went through the final text with great thoroughness. I am deeply grateful to both of these persons.

Mr Kassahun Checole and The Red Sea Press have not only received us with open arms but also encouraged us in the fulfilment of our project and given us wise counsel.

Finally, I would like to thank my wife Gennet Awalom for encouraging me in the pursuit of this assignment and for her patience with the persistent claims of this present task and its invasions into the early years of our retirement.

December 2010, Uppsala, Sweden
Ezra Gebremedhin
Editor

The Assignment

Ezra Gebremedhin

The Product of a Team of Two

This work is, essentially, a fruit of the labours of the late Dr. Karl Johan Lundström. Having said so, I would like to add an important qualification. His wife Maj-Britt was with him from the beginning of this project and his research-related trips in Sweden, Italy and Eritrea. She helped not only in sorting out the material that was collected but also in typing out the texts born out of the material. Even though the proper place to mention her name would be in the section for acknowledgements, I feel that her special role in the creation of this book justifies her being named already in this chapter. She is, in a sense, a co-author of this book.

Contact with the Leadership and Members of the ECE

The Lundströms came to Eritrea in February, 1952 and left in 1964, after 12 years of missionary service. K. J. had been called to become the Field Director for the SEM mission field in the whole of Ethiopia which, after the end of the Federation in 1962, included also Eritrea. The Lundströms were in Ethiopia during some of the years of the Marxist regime. They moved on to (Southern) Sudan in 1979, and were there during most of the nineteen-eighties. Towards the end of the nineteen-eighties they moved to Nairobi, Kenya, where K. J. had previously had assignments connected with LWF-related radio work

Maj-Britt and Karl-Johan Lundström at work on this book at the library of Johannelund Theological University College in Uppsala. Picture from ca 2002.

based in Kenya. During the latter part of the stay of the Lundströms in Nairobi, K. J. worked as a lecturer at Day Star University, a Christian institution of learning that specialized in Communication. M-B acted as the representative for SEM in Kenya. The Lundströms had made it a point to keep in touch with Eritrea and Eritreans, even when they served in the Sudan and Kenya. They were in Eritrea in December 1991, in 1992, 1996 and 1998. The couple visited Eritrea again in 2001, this time for a period of two months.

Contacts with the Evangelical Church were maintained and intensified when *Qeshi* Asfaha Mehari became president of the ECE. K.J.'s last visit to Eritrea, in 2002, had an even broader goal. He was a member of a delegation from the SEM to the ECE on a mission intended to renew and strengthen the old ties between the two bodies. He is reported to have greeted the congregation in Asmara with emotion. I was told that he collapsed on one occasion during this trip to Eritrea. This was not a good sign, but his family and friends did not fear the worst. I remember a telephone conversation with him just at that point of time. His report on this medical condition was not serious. Soon however, K. J. received a far more disturbing diagnosis. In a year, he was called to his Lord.

K. J. Lundström began the task of writing the history of the ECE in late 1997 upon the recommendation of the Rev. Dr. Gustav Arén. Gustav had written the history of the EECMY, in two volumes.[2] In the preface to *Envoys of the Gospel in Ethiopia,* he wrote,

> I do regret that I have not been able to include an account of developments in Eritrea during the same period (i.e. ca 1913–1952). The defunct Marxist regime obstructed all proper research. Today there are hopes that a scholar of long experience in Eritrea will fill this gap.

The last sentence is a reference to K. J. By experience, mentality and academic equipment, he was qualified for the task. He had been a missionary to Eritrea and had access to the Swedish material on the country. He and M-B had worked in Eritrea in their days of strength and knew many of its people intimately. K. J. spoke not only Tigrinya but also Italian, a language that is important for any one who intends to write on Eritrea and the ECE.[3]

Correspondence with the Leadership and Members of the ECE

When the Lundströms visited Eritrea in 1998, their express purpose was to begin the collection of material for the history of the ECE. In 2001, K. J. wrote to two of the leaders of the ECE, *Qeshi* Oqbarebi Hibtes, the President of the Church, and *Qeshi* Zerit Yohannes, the General Secretary, on his and M-B's behalf. He stated that the couple intended to arrive on November 3 and that they would appreciate help in acquiring accommodations. K. J. adds that he and M-B would appreciate "this chance of meeting all of you and renewing the contacts that we have had over almost half a century (we arrived the first time in Eritrea on the 8th of March 1952)." During their last working trip to Eritrea, K. J. and M-B lived with Eritrean relatives in a small house near the Idaga Hamus Mosque, in Asmara.[4] Contacts were maintained and intensified

2 *Evangelical Pioneers in Ethiopia*, 1978 and *Envoys of The Gospel in Ethiopia*, 1999.
3 Not only did the region where the SEM had started and consolidated its work become an Italian colony, but SEM too started cooperating with a church from Italy, the Waldensian Church, in its missionary activities in Eritrea. (Ed.)
4 The couple have two adopted children from Eritrea, Sennait and Hagos. Sennait, a midwife, and her Danish husband Eric, an orthopaedic surgeon, are missionaries within the EECMY. Hagos, a Forest Engineer, and his family (his wife Eva is a native Swede) live in Uppsala, where Eva is regional Chief Prosecutor. (Ed.)

through *Qeshi* Asfaha Mehari and *Qeshi* Yosef Araya.

Olle Hagner's Diaries

In February 2003, K. J. had started and was looking forward to working on the material in the Eritrea diaries (five small notebooks of hand-written notes) of Pastor Olle Hagner (formerly Olle Andersson) for the period between 1939 and 1943. It is regrettable that K. J. was not able to write on this highly interesting material, which I too have had a chance to examine, albeit rather quickly and not in any depth. I have used a very limited part of these diary entries in this book. In the future someone must incorporate the material in the diary into a continuation of the history of the ECE.

Olle Hagner's diary entries should be taken for what they are – observations and impressions from a period of transition, uncertainty and unrest in the life of the colony of Eritrea and of the Kenisha. Olle was in Eritrea on a specific mission: to negotiate about the disposal of the property of the SEM and to secure due compensation for mission property confiscated by the colonial authorities.

In the absence of ready access to other written sources (if such sources are indeed available) by either expatriates or Eritreans, on this period of unrest and uncertainty, we cannot draw final conclusions on the critical comments made or the judgments passed by Hagner on individuals and church-related issues. However, the excerpts from OH's diary (made by K. J.) have their rightful place in this work, even though we can only mention them in passing. In the first place, K. J had gone through Olle Hagner's five notebooks, (some sections of which are difficult to read), laboriously and extracted material which covers 80 type-written pages. I have given this summary the designation OHD/ K.J.S., meaning *Olle Hagner's Diaries, Karl Johan's Summary*. The following words of K. J. indicate the specific intention behind his choice of the extracts,

> I have made excerpts from them, choosing mainly material which throws light on the work of the mission and of the church, and on those factors which have influenced Olle's evaluation, opinions and views.

On the basis of these words I have taken some limited selections from these diary entries and used them, mainly as footnotes. I have abstained from using entries which contain evaluations of and judgments on specific persons. The sifting and evaluation of this material must await a study of the history of the ECE after 1935.

In a letter dated February 5, 2003, K. J. writes,

> Things don't move so quickly, but they are in fact moving. Thus far I have access to most of the material for the period up to 1943. But I must then begin searching for more material from the archives in Uppsala and Stockholm. The plans are that the period between 1952 and 1970 would be treated in the manner of a survey.

These are the words of a person who knew that he had more work waiting for him.

K. J.'s book on the history of the ECE does not cover all phases of the subject under consideration. Neither does it cover the entire stretch of the history of the ECE so far. Nevertheless, it is the most comprehensive treatment of the subject to date.

My Views on the Character of the Work at Hand

It is not easy to take over and complete a task started by someone else, especially if the person in question was a close friend. How much can a work be modified and still remain the work of the one who began it? Answers of different kinds and intensity have been given to this question by different readers. Friends whom I respect have firmly maintained that I should not add to or subtract from a work left by a deceased author.

I fully understand their standpoint. However, to have become content with the function of a mere proof reader of the material left by K. J. would have been tantamount to being guided by the letter rather than by the spirit of his plea that I bring his work to completion. I do hope that the editorial work that I have done is a genuine expression of loyalty both to K. J. as a person and friend and to the main intention behind his work. The Swedish Evangelical Mission, which gave K. J. the original mandate to write a history of the ECE, has given me all the help that I have needed in my work as editor. I regard this gesture as a confirmation of the mandate given to K. J.

At a late stage in the course of my editorial work, I discovered some diary notes that I had made after a telephone conversation with K. J.

on September 15, 2003 and at which I now looked more closely. As a paraphrase of what K. J. had said on the phone, I had written, "He had done what he could with the writing of the history of the ECE. Bruno Tron was going to check some chapters. But would I be willing to take care of the concluding period, as it were, and do the editorial work?"

What did "the concluding period" mean?' Was K. J. referring to the time from 1935 to 1947, as he had indicated in his notes, or the period up to 1970, or simply the material began in the last chapter (which deals with 1935)? I still have no conclusive answer to this question.

In the course of my work with this book, I have acquired a good deal of new knowledge about the history of the SEM and its mission in Eritrea, and of the "prehistory" of the Evangelical Church of Eritrea. This is particularly true of K. J.'s material on the history and culture of Kunama and Mensa. Furthermore, I have been impressed by K. J.'s contributions to our knowledge of the involvement of the Italian colonial powers, the Catholic Church and Catholic mission activity in the life and work of the SEM and the Evangelical community. The accounts on the roles played by missionaries from the Waldensian Church in Italy in the work of the SEM and the ECE have also been very enlightening. Finally it has been most revealing for me to read about some highly gifted, dedicated but stubborn Swedish missionary personalities on the mission field![5]

Dependence on Material from Gustav Arén's Books

Several sections of this book build on material from Gustav Arén's *Evangelical Pioneers in Ethiopia* (1978) and, to a lesser extent, his *Envoys of the Gospel in Ethiopia* (1999). This is not surprising. The book must begin with an introduction into the historical background of the ECE. Not all future readers of the present book would have read Arén's two books. Furthermore, the material taken from Arén is particularly appropriate for Eritrea and the ECE, though Gustav Arén used the same material as a prelude to the history of the Ethiopian Evangelical Church Mekane Yesus.

---

5   I am now thinking of the tension that existed between Rodén and Sundström in the Mensa area and between Winqvist and Nyström in Beleza. More on this question. (Ed.)

Editorial Adjustments

The manuscript that was placed in my hands was in a very preliminary state of readiness. Most of the raw material envisaged for a book which was to cover the period ending in 1935 was, however, in place. On the basis of my knowledge of K. J.'s way of working and my grasp of his wishes (I never received a job description.) I have taken it upon my self not only to edit his text but also to expand it wherever I have felt that this could be done for the benefit of the readers that K. J. had in mind in the first place, the Kenisha. However, where I have done so, I have clearly indicated what my additions are.

And still, the reader is likely to notice differences and discrepancies in style. After all, this book is a reflection of the work of two people. Let me first state that I have tried to reinforce the boundaries of the original text from K. J. with the help of introductions and summaries. I have also tried to restructure and/or divide most of the chapters, whenever I have felt that such a division would serve the cause of further clarity and limitation of subject matter. In its final form, the text abounds in editorial notes, mostly in the form of footnotes. I say *editorial*, because I have made a sincere effort to preserve and pass on the core of K. J.'s material intact. In the text itself, I have clearly indicated my additions. Texts which are from the pen of the editor end with the letter combination (Ed.)

Maj-Britt Lundström had made it clear to me, on several occasions, that it was K. J.'s and her wish that the present book should be regarded as a gift to all members of the ECE, a story told in a manner which members of the ECE on all levels could understand and recognize as their own. My editorial work has been guided mainly by this wish of the Lundströms. I have tried to enhance the narrative character of K. J.'s work. We hope that this story, narrated by two insiders, as it were, is nevertheless marked by the kind of objectivity that can stand the scrutiny of the generous reader and that it breathes a sufficient measure of sobriety.

In the original draft of this work, K. J. took up the Kunama, Mensa and the Orthodox Tewahdo Church as cradles of the ECE in one and the same chapter. I have devoted a separate chapter to each. Furthermore, I have expanded and thoroughly reorganized K. J.'s material on the Tewahdo Orthodox Church as one of the cradles of the ECE, since I felt that it should be augmented by historical and cultural material comparable to the material which was incorporated into the chapters on Kunama and Mensa. Two chapters are devoted to the Tewahdo. I have written by far the greater part of these chapters and have therefore indicated both my name and K. J.'s name at the top of the chapters. My name appears in combination with the name of K. J. also at the heads of other chapters to which I have contributed a substantial amount of material.

In view of the impact of certain places as symbols in the lives of religious communities, I have pulled together the material that K. J. had collected on the three centres of Evangelical Christianity on the highlands of Eritrea (i.e. Beleza, Asmara and Tse'azzega) into three separate chapters. My purpose has been to build narratives around them, with building material taken from K. J., instead of leaving the names to crop up in a rather disparate variety of contexts.

This, I feel, is the kind of editorial work that the K. J. whom I knew would have accepted. My adjustments have to do primarily with the reduction, extension or redistribution of existent material in the interest of balance. I have also created a chapter entitled *The Price They Paid* in which I have pulled together K. J.'s material on some of the few glimpses into stories on persecution and martyrdom among the Kenisha. The material in these four chapters has therefore the character of compilations of texts pulled together from different chapters left by K. J., and supplied with connecting comments. Furthermore I have written an epilogue.

Appendix II, which bears the title "Sources for a History of the ECE" is the result of an attempt to provide a survey of the main written sources which deal with the activities of the Swedish Evangelical Mission in Eritrea and the Evangelical Church of Eritrea. I have tried to produce a chapter which can be of use to both men and women of research and to the lay person who is at home in Swedish, English and Tigrinya.

The narrative in this book follows basically a chronological order. However, at times the thematic scheme takes over. Such a shift entails a certain measure of repetition of or a return to items which have already been taken up under the chronological scheme. The reader should therefore not be surprised if a person already declared dead in a given chapter under the chronological scheme reappears as an actor in a chapter dealing with a specific theme. This story will involve a good deal of hopping back and forth.

Scope of the Assignment

There is the question of the time span that was originally envisaged for this work. A letter dated August 26, 1997 and addressed to Ruth Normark of the SEM envisages the treatment of the period 1913–1945. In another letter, this period was extended to 1952. Yet another outline in a sketchy form (under the title "ECE Headings"), contains six sections, the first of which (entitled *The Beginning*) covers the period between 1866 and 1890 and a sixth section (entitled *Church and Sister Churches*) covers the period between 1946 and 1970. However, the present work stops at 1935, after a short treatment of the few years leading to this crucial year. K. J. did, however, leave a chapter that gives a survey of the history of the ECE, up to 1991.

I have decided to exclude this survey altogether. In the fist place the survey is, for the most part, a drastically shortened repetition of material already presented in his draft for the book. Furthermore I felt that the history of the ECE after 1935, a period seething with political and social events of great consequence for Eritrea, deserved more than a quick summary that only a few paragraphs could provide in a general survey of the history of the ECE.

The Title 'Kenisha'

The word Kenisha is of Semitic origin and is related to the word *kanisa* (the commonest word in Arabic for *church*) and the Hebrew *knesset* (a place for gathering). The latter word goes back to a verb that means *to assemble*. Interestingly enough, the Evangelical Lutheran Church of Tanzania is known, in Kiswahili, as *Kanisa la Kiinjili la Kilutheri Tanzania*. We don't know when the term was used first for the ECE.

The title chosen for this book by Karl Johan is, *Kenisha. The Roots and Development of the Evangelical Church of Eritrea. (ECE) 1866–1935*. However, several persons whom I have consulted on the subject have questioned the advisability of using the term *Kenisha* in the main title. The first person to question the title of the book was Professor Tekeste Negash, Uppsala. His objection was that the term Kenisha referred to a specific category of people in Eritrea, whereas the stated goal of the book was to narrate the history of a *church*. According to this reasoning, a title consisting solely of the term Kenisha would be clearly misleading, by promising to deal with the *people* known by this name, and not with the Evangelical Church of Eritrea as such.

We don´t know when the term *Kenisha* was used first for Lutherans in Eritrea. Memhir Meles Sahle maintains that the name Kenisha was, originally, a derogatory label flung upon Evangelical Christians in Eritrea, not a name willingly chosen by them. This is also the view of Professor Asmarom Legesse. A member of the ECE, originally from Kunama but now residing in Sweden, pointed out to the editor that the term Kenisha was a late-comer on the scene of the history of the ECE. In his view, the term was a highland phenomenon as far as Evangelical Christianity in Eritrea was concerned. The "Evangelicals" among the Kunama, he maintained, were referred to as *asvedés*, implying "those who belong to the Swedish Mission."

It has been argued, further, by Iyasu Tesfay, that the designation Kenisha is unfamiliar to the vast majority of non-Eritrean readers, especially in the Anglo-Saxon world, where this book has, hopefully, its biggest potential readership. If the designation is to be used as a title, it cannot, he argues, stand alone. It must be accompanied by some additional word which would indicate that it is a concept related to Eritrea.

Although all these arguments are weighty, I have found it difficult to change the title chosen by the late Karl Johan Lundström. In the first place, the person who stood closest to him, his wife Maj-Britt, has maintained consistently that the title chosen by her late husband should be respected. Neither former Swedish missionaries to Eritrea, whom I consulted (about seven of them), nor Pastor Bruno Tron of the Waldensian Church in Italy, a former missionary to his country of birth, Eritrea, have objected to the use of this title.

Many respected members of the Evangelical community in both Eritrea and the Diaspora have maintained that keeping the title chosen by Karl Johan was a matter of integrity, an ethical obligation. The argument that the designation Kenisha is unfamiliar to the vast majority of the potential readership of this book, and that it should perhaps appear in a subtitle instead, is cogent. Nevertheless, even a subtitle intended to clarify the connotation of the word, (for example a title like *the Kenisha of Eritrea*) runs the risk of marginalizing non-Eritrean (i.e. Swedish and some Ethiopian) actors who are an integral part of the history of the ECE.

I find myself in the position of a steward whose main duty is to preserve and pass on property entrusted to him. It is true that a steward is sometimes expected to trade with the goods entrusted to him and make a profit on the trade. I have tried to do so through my editorial contributions to this work. However, I feel that there is a limit to the freedom of a steward. He or she can not change the trademark of a master's goods. In short, I have come to the conclusion that the simple and unadorned term Kenisha is, when all is said and done, our best option for a title.

Maps, Memory Aids and Uncertain Sources

The main map used in this book is a copy of a Swedish map printed in 1922 by *Generalstabens Litografiska Anstalt* (The Cartographic Institution of the Chief of Staff). The map is being used simply as a *tidsdokument*, (to use a Swedish word which means, literally, *a time document*), i.e., a contemporary record from a part of the period with which we are dealing. We are using the map to help the reader localize places mentioned in our narrative, and not to prove or disprove the location of specific geographical areas. We have also inserted some datelines and memory aids, short summaries on some topics which can be of interest for those who want to find records of facts and events quickly.

The purpose of these memory aids is to give a birds-eye-view of the origins, highlights and development of events connected to the Christian faith and the activities of the Swedish Evangelical Mission, in the context of wider political and social religious realities. Among the topics taken up under the category of memory aids are Important Dates in the History of the Church (Gregorian Calendar), and Important Dates in the History of the SEM and the ECE. (Ed.)

Transliteration

For the sake of simplicity, I have decided to follow the system of transliterations used by Gustav Arén in his two books. However, where I have felt that the use of the letter *a*, (corresponding to the vowel of the very first form of the letters of the Ge'ez alphabet), can lead to a wrong pronunciation, I have replaced such an *a* by an *ä* (*a* with two dots on top). An apostrophe facing left (e. g. Ra'si) represents a normal vowel sound while one facing right (e. g. Tse'azzega) indicates a

This map was published by The Publishing House of SEM in 1922. In this book we shall use only the section which deals with Eritrea. The original map can be ordered from SEM, Uppsala, Sweden.

guttural vowel sound. I have spelt the common Tigrinya word for *region* or *country* with two *d'* s (i.e. as *Addi*), since a doubling of the consonant *d* does more justice to the native pronunciation of the word than does the single *d* in the older form, *Adi*! I have tried to apply this rule even in other, similar connections.

How I Came into the Picture

Some three months before his death in December 2003, Karl Johan called me in Uppsala to tell me of the state of his health and to ask me to take over and complete the task of recording the history of the ECE. I couldn't believe my ears when he told me that the doctors had diagnosed an advanced state of cancer. I visited K. J. and M-B at their home in the small community of Eksjö in the province of Småland. My intention was to see him in person and to receive some more specific information and directions on the work he had started, before he became too weak to share information with me. Though he looked somewhat emaciated, he was in good spirits.

Even though he showed me some chapters of the emerging history of the ECE and some of the notes on which he had based his work, he felt that there was no need for any special hurry on specific directives to me. I continued my journey to Uppsala and never saw Karl Johan again. In hindsight, I must admit that the lack of a clearly defined mandate has led to uncertainty and unnecessary delays.

After my visit to Eksjö, K. J.'s health grew worse steadily. Some months later he and M-B moved to a flat in Uppsala, whose purchase, I understand, had been expedited by the Lundström children (Sennait and Hagos and their families). Though his sickness was terminal, K. J. wanted to see the flat where his life-long companion, M-B, was going to live. He stayed in the flat for a couple of days but then had to be hospitalized at the University Hospital in Uppsala. He never returned to the new flat. He passed away on December 9, 2003.

His family requested me to perform his funeral, a request that I took as a great honour.

Bible-True Friends (BV) and the LCE

The history of Bibeltrogna Vänner (Bible-True Friends), now known as Evangelical Lutheran Mission Bible-True Friends (ELM-BV), and the Lutheran Church of Eritrea (LCE) has only been touched upon marginally in this book. This fact does not imply that these two organizations don't have a history worth our attention. Some of the missionaries who laboured with BV in Eritrea (the Karl Nyström family and the female missionary Augusta Henriksson), and some of the Eritrean pastors of the LCE (*Qeshi* Marqos Girmai, *Qeshi* Gebre-Hawariat Tesfa-Lidet, *Qeshi* Abraha Ristu and *Qeshi* Habte-Sillassie Gulbot), were all men of stature, both as individuals and shepherds of souls. They and many humble members of the LCE have played important roles in the moulding of Kenisha spirituality in Eritrea. The mandate for the writing of this book was given to K.J. before the Evangelical Church of Eritrea (ECE) and the LCE entered a union in 2006. This explains the book's concentration on the ECE. A continuation of the history of the Kenisha must naturally pay attention to the role of BV and the LCE in the evolution of Evangelical Lutheran Christianity in Eritrea.

In this regard, Dr. Bereket Yebio has pointed out the importance of private archives, among which we have Axel B. Svensson's papers, stored at the Landsarkivet in Lund.

A Plea for a Continuation

To say that the history of the ECE for the period *after* 1935 should be recorded as soon as possible is to state the obvious. However, this obvious fact must be strongly underlined. Time is flying. Old Eritrea missionaries and pastors, as well as members of the ECE and LCE are dying off. Fragile records run the risk of falling apart or disappearing. Delay or procrastination in this respect can be costly, in more than one sense, for the present ELCE and for other parties interested in its history.

Above all, a Human Being

The request of the dying is sobering. The implementation of the task given to me on the threshold to Karl Johan's death has been greatly delayed. I feel sad about this fact. I think, however, that K. J. would have understood me. He too was pulled in many directions by a multiplicity of assignments. K. J. was a missionary, a teacher and an administrator. He was, above all, a human being, a person with humour, energy, a twinkle in the eyes, a generous and warm smile! May God bless this written testimony left by a devoted missionary, a loyal friend of Eritrea and a trustworthy companion of those who knew him closely.

In Closing

The telling of stories is a personal act. And those who have experienced events and developments first hand are specially qualified to account for these. A Tigrinya saying runs, *Ziwä'alä yingerka; i'tägagäyä yimkärka* (*Let a first hand witness narrate for you; let the one who has learned from his mistakes counsel you!*) Karl Johan and Maj-Britt were witnesses to many of the events that became the latter part of the history of the ECE. They had their own personal stories to tell on Eritrea. K. J. didn't have a chance to write a final preface or an epilogue to this book. I am sure that he would have given us glimpses into some personal experiences and feelings, had he had the opportunity to do so.

At the beginning of this book, in the chapter entitled *Flashback – The Evangelical Church of Eritrea,* I have included personal impressions from the years that the Lundströms spent in Eritrea.

Flashback

The Evangelical Church of Eritrea

Introduction

Many a book (not to say many a film) begins at the end or at an advanced stage of the sequence of its narrative, to then jump back to the actual beginning of the story. Such a technique is known as a flashback. We shall avail ourselves of a variant of this device to introduce the subject of this book. This flashback is based on articles and notes by Karl Johan and Maj-Britt Lundström.

Glimpses from the Last Working Visit to Eritrea, 2001

The Lundströms were in Eritrea in November 2001, to collect material for their history of the Evangelical Church of Eritrea (ECE) and to interview friends and former co-workers among the Kenisha. Both kept notes on some of their impressions. We shall first take a sample from K. J.'s notes,

> Early one Sunday morning we journeyed down to a place in the south-western part of Eritrea, the area where there was fighting with Ethiopia one and a half years ago. The peace-keeping forces had camped close to the border. The Eritrean forces which had been mobilized pending the

Servants of the Gospel, 1903: Front row, from left to right: Alazar, Kiflé, Uqbazgi, Timoteos, Gebre-Yesus Tesfai, Naffa and Girma-Tsion.
Middle row: Tekle-Haimanot, Gebre-Sillassé Abba Ma'asho, Qeshi Selomon Atsqu, Mihtsintu, Qeshi Zer'a-Tsion Musè, Segid, Wolde-Tinsaé, Gebre-Mikael, Bihil.
Top row: Tewolde-Medhin Gebre-Medhin, Yishaq, Teklé, Debbas, Natnael, Gebre-Le'ul, Gebre-Sillassé Gebre, Birru, and Begashet.

signing of the peace treaty, had their positions further inland. There are a number of Evangelical congregations in the area. The biggest congregation had promised to get in touch with us.

At noon time we arrived at the town of Mai Dema, down in the hot lowlands. We went to a home where we found no less than twelve elders, with the church register for the district. These elders had come from Addi Gaba, a place we used to visit often when we worked in Eritrea. It was forty years since we had met last. They looked at me and commented: "Why have you become so old and grey-haired?" And my counter-question was, naturally, "You who ran with me once when we were out hunting, why is your beard so white?" And then we sang, prayed, and ate together. The church registers were brought forward and we read names beginning with the early years of 1900. Soon stories started flowing, in quick succession – stories about the one person after the other. People who had worked for the congregation, those who had been cast into prison because they belonged to the Evangelical Church, those who had moved away and, not least, the young who had now started taking over. We sat there for hours and reminisced.

What was the stuff of this reminiscence? Let us touch upon some highlights.

The Trip to Eritrea

The Lundströms first came to Eritrea in March 1952. One of their first letters from Asmara was written on April 12, 1952. On their journey to Eritrea, they had visited the Italian–African Museum in Rome, where they could acquaint themselves with the land that would be their destination. The Federation with Ethiopia was now a fact. The boat that took them through the Suez Canal and down the Red Sea was the *Tripolitania*. The name reminds one of the years during which thousands of Eritrean recruits into the Italian colonial army had travelled in the opposite direction to battles on the sands of Tripolitania and Cyrenaica, the two provinces which were combined into the Italian colony of Libya.[6] There were Kenisha among these recruits. Writing about the journey in 1952 K. J. states,

> To travel to Africa is no longer the same adventure that it was before. The journey, which once took half a year, can now be covered in twenty-four hours. However, the speedy journeys of our times are much poorer in providing impressions and experiences.
>
> Our trip was of the slower variety–it took three weeks–but we were compensated by the experiences that the trip offered.[7]

K. J. continues with a description of Massawa and Imkullu, an account that takes our thoughts back to the history of the very first missionaries of the SEM and the Kenisha on the coast,

> In Massawa, which is regarded as one of Africa's hottest seaports, it was the season of rains, a fact that made it possible for us to stand the heat. About five kilometres outside Massawa lies Monkullo – once a big mission station and the centre for our East African Mission – now a

6   Mockler 1984, 22; There is a novel entitled *The Story of a Conscript* written in Tigrinya in 1927 about the Libyan campaign by a certain G. Hailu. It is reputed to be the first novel in Tigrinya. See Ghirmai Negash, 1999, 132–136. (Ed.)

7   Letter written in 1952 to Piteå-Tidningen by K. J. Text supplied by M-B.

The railway line between Massawa and Asmara (completed in 1911) creeps, like a snake, along the edges of precipitous descents.

The harbour of Massawa in the nineteen-eighties.

mere heap of ruins. At the mission graveyard we found the names of some of our former missionaries. Together with a couple of Eritrean Christians, we paused to pray beside a dislodged cross lying on the ground, carrying the name of B. P. Lundahl, perhaps the foremost figure in the history of our mission.

The last stretch of our journey took us up to the highlands. Along the 120 kilometre long road, the land rises to an altitude of 2 300 metres! The road ascends by way of hairpin curves and sharp climbs. A mountain wall on one side and a precipitous fall of several hundred metres on the other! And so we came from the rainy season of the coast to the dry season of the highlands. Soon we are in Asmara — and are met by the sight of a town with European features at the centre and a view over an adjacent town for the indigenous people. We stop at the border between these two – here lies the Swedish Mission, the end of our journey.[8]

To a Country with Contrasts

When the Lundströms arrived in Eritrea in March 1952, they had left a country with snow-covered heights, thick forests and an abundance of rivers and lakes. They left a country where the days were short and dark in winter and long and light in the summer time. They came to a part of East Africa where the only variety of *snow* that people knew was frost on a December morning, or hail stones in July. They came to a country where there were, according to tradition, forests, lions and elephants once upon a time, but where there were hardly any signs of thick forests or elephants or lions in 1952. They arrived in a country where the supply of water was scarce and unpredictable. They came to a part of the world where day and night were almost equally long, year in and year out.

Maj-Britt's father was a station master for the Swedish Railways. She was trained as a nurse and had become an instructor of nurses. K. J.'s father was a schoolteacher. K. J. too was trained as a teacher. Between these Swedish parents and their children, there was no yawning gap in matters of levels of education.

Yet the Lundströms came to a country where, in the words of K. J.,

It is not at all unusual to find families in which one member has a

8   A letter or article in Swedish, supplied by M-B.

well-paid job, which makes it possible for him to buy a car, live well and maintain a high standard of living. In the same family, the father can be a farmer and cultivate his land in the same manner in which his ancestors had done so many centuries ago [...] Eritrea is a country of contrasts! [9]

As Teachers to a Land Hungering for Knowledge

As trained teachers working within the ECE, a church that has always given priority to the education of both boys and girls, the Lundströms went into their callings with enthusiasm. They had to grapple with limited financial means, a matter that seems to have been a cause for concern throughout the history of the SEM in Eritrea. M-B writes,

> Our time in Eritrea was taken up mostly by schoolwork. For many years, K. J. travelled to the various village schools, to organize the activities of these schools and help the teachers. When we lived in Tse'azzega, I used to sit on the doorstep of our house of stone, when the sun started going down, looking out for the lights of an approaching motorcycle, conscious that this was the time when *shifta* (robbers) began to attack wayfarers. He (K. J.) conducted courses and wrote an ABC book with *Memhir* (Teacher) Musa Aron, a book that I helped to illustrate. When the time came to open a Teacher Training School, he became the director. I believe that we had the words, "To learn to know each other and to learn from each other" as our motto throughout our stay in Eritrea. We experienced the truth of this motto on many occasions.[10]

The Training of Deaconesses

Maj-Britt's main responsibility during the first five years of her missionary duties in Eritrea was conducting a course for would-be deaconesses. The course, which lasted for three years, was intended to give the candidates skills in health and soul care, among other things. M-B has a moving experience from this period. Let her tell her own story,

---

9   A Swedish article from 1957, supplied by M-B.
10   M-B in a talk held at Löten Church in Uppsala, Sweden, on December 9, (the date of K. J.'s death a year earlier), 2004, on the subject *From Letters to the Family and from Newspaper Clippings. Narratives from the Sundry Events of My Life*. (Ed.)

In Eritrea I experienced what was perhaps my most cherished memory as a missionary. I would like to share the story. Among the students in the course for deaconesses, there was a girl from Geleb. She belonged to the Mensa tribe that spoke Tigré. Her name is Marta Joel and she is still (2003) alive, having now retired. Her school background was below standard for her to qualify for training as a deaconess. But she was intelligent and ambitious. We felt that we would like to make an extra effort to help her, both to encourage her but also to enable her to be equipped for fruitful service in her congregation.

Here in Sweden, a day known as Women's Prayer Day is observed every year around the beginning of spring. It is a day on which offerings are taken for the purpose of providing scholarships for young women on our mission field. Such scholarships could be used towards augmenting the knowledge of women already working in a congregation. We applied for such a scholarship on Marta's behalf and succeeded in getting one. We sent her to a one-year course at the fine children's clinic run in Addis Ababa.

After her return from the course she came to me. I could see that she was very worried. At the end of her course in Addis Ababa, the administration of the school had offered her a job, at a higher salary than the one she had already. The offer became a source of a severe temptation for Marta. I could very well understand the reactions of relatives and friends, who would retort, "It would be foolish to forgo this offer. Go back to Addis. What a chance!"

I remember saying to Marta, "You know what you promised your church when you got the scholarship. You also know how much we have talked about the meaning of serving. I think you are now facing the most crucial decision in your life. Wait for fourteen days before you decide and then come to me, so that we can try to find out whether you should answer *Yes* or *No*". Marta went away and returned after fourteen days, something that I had hardly expected! She was a transformed person as she told me, *I shall stay.*

And even in her retirement she goes around visiting the old and sick in the congregations in Asmara.[11]

11   M-B in a talk held at Löten Church in Uppsala, Sweden, on December 9, 2004.

Shortage of Pastors
– A Recurring Problem in the History of the ECE

It is remarkable how persistent some problems can be in the history of a church. One of these is the almost chronic shortage of pastors within the ECE. This problem was discussed long before K. J. and M-B came to Eritrea. On May 11, 1952, they wrote,

> The day before yesterday there was a conference for pastors here in Asmara. Meeting these pastors was a source of joy but also something depressing. Among those who were present most were around 60 years of age. In our entire mission field in Eritrea, there is no pastor who is younger than 50. And the old pastors have experienced great problems, persecution and distress during the time when the missionaries were away. They are exhausted and somewhat disheartened. They remember the time when there were 30 missionaries – 17 Eritrean pastors and over 50 Eritrean teachers. Now there are 13 missionaries, and the number of pastors and teachers has shrunk. The resignation of the pastors, or at least of some of them, has affected the congregations. Some of the pastors have not received their salaries since October. What is now a necessity, indeed a matter of life and death for our Eritrea mission, is that steps be taken to begin the education of pastors. We hope to start such an education next year.[12]

These words, uttered in 1952, could have been said of the state of the ECE in 2002. The passage of time has not solved this problem of shortage of pastors, although steps are now being taken to remedy the situation. The seminary at Beleza is a first step in a long-range plan to meet this need.

Qeshi Wolde-Yesus
– A Mentor in Things Spiritual

K. J. and M-B had the good fortune of becoming acquainted with *Qeshi* (Pastor) Wolde-Yesus, a former Orthodox priest, a man with experience and a soft heart. He became a mentor for K. J. on matters of contacts with the community where Wolde-Yesus carried out his pastoral duties. M-B writes,

12   An article in Swedish in the possession of M-B.

During our years in Eritrea there was an experienced pastor by the name of Wolde-Yesus. He had a number of congregations to take care of and moved from congregation to congregation on his mule, visiting his fold. He told us that this was the right thing to do. Karl Johan has told me that they once came to a village where a member of the Evangelical congregation had died. When they had both alighted from their mules, *Qeshi* Wolde-Yesus gave the young missionary the following piece of advice: "Now, *Memhir* (i.e. Teacher) Lundström, we shall go into those who are in the tent, where they sit, mourning. Do exactly what I do and say exactly what I say. Things will surely work out well!"

Causes of Food Shortage

Another old and recurrent problem in Eritrea was shortage of food. For centuries, drought or swarms of locusts have alternated in creating food shortage, hunger and flight from home and hearth. Imkullu received hungry, tired and sick refuges from both the Eritrean highlands and from Tigrai at different times. In an article which breathes sadness and a measure of desperation, K. J. writes on the subject of *anböta*, locusts.

[*Anböta* = locusts or grasshoppers or, more correctly, the grasshopper, are innumerable or immeasurable, like the sun and the rain. Therefore the word has no plural form.] (Author)

Anböta

There is surely no word in the Tigrinya language of which I am so tired of hearing as the word *anböta*, i.e. locusts.

• Hallo! How are you? –O well, except for *anböta*.

• Why is school closed?

• *Anböta!*

• Have you paid your church taxes?

• No, *anböta!* Haven't you heard that *anböta* has eaten a baby in Kunama?

The whole thing began sometime in July. We heard rumours that massive swarms of locusts had been hatched in Agordat, in the lowlands in the west. But the international locust control would surely eradicate

Drought and locusts were the two great enemies of food sufficiency in Eritrea.
The small picture, bottom right, shows a locust on the palm of a hand.

them. They have three aeroplanes [Desert Locust Control –DLOC].

In August the harvest looked more beautiful than it had been for many a year. People were happy. Two years of crop failure made people place their hope on this harvest. They said that there would be a bumper crop, if only *anböta* didn't come.

In September a statement came from the government; "Hurry and harvest your corps, because this year will be a difficult locust year." After that, no two people could meet without talking about locusts. There was no traveller who wouldn't be stopped and asked, "How far has *anböta* come?"

The answer would be "Yesterday it spent the night at Addi Ni'amin."

At the end of September people began harvesting their crops in panic, even though the fields were still green. One evening, a man came past the mission station and cried out, "The locusts have reached the place of Gebre-Yesus. They have eaten there today. Tomorrow they will eat here."

That night there was moonlight. All villagers who had arms took their sickles and went out into the field. After all, things were getting serious! During the two years when the crops had failed, people had acquired goods from the local merchant on credit (literally by signing with the crayon or chalk!). Where were they to turn now? It was now a matter of life and death: neither more nor less. And people went at the task of cutting grain for four days, day and night. And then the locusts arrived. People didn't need to cut any longer. The locusts ate everything that was left. They ate grass and leaves. They ate their way through the thick leaves of the American aloe. In the garden of the mission, they even got at the radishes!

They came back, again and again, during the whole of October. To the west Kunama had been eaten clean. The same was the case with Mensa. And then it was the turn of Southern Eritrea.

When their grain containers were empty and they had nothing to eat, people said, "It is the will of God." Those who wanted to win the sympathy of the mission said, "This has befallen us because of our sins!"

The government has promised food and work, as they have done for a number of years. Some of the people who have the energy to do so move southwards to the border with Ethiopia. Death awaits the old and sick.

The Lord have mercy on Eritrea's people![13]

One can very well understand the implications of the words of the prophet Joel, after one has read what K. J. has written about the scourge of locusts in Eritrea. The prophet announces God's promise,

I will repay you for the years the locusts have eaten (Joel 2:21).

Humour in the midst of Serious Business

In an article written about a visit to Addi Gaba in the late nineteen fifties. K. J. gives us glimpses into the sundry demands made on a missionary, whether he or she was qualified to render the type of service required of them or not. Lundström writes,

On the evening of our arrival [at Addi Gaba], I told *Qeshi* Zecharias that I had some medicine. After that I had full time work from morning

13   Article in Swedish, supplied by M-B.

to noon, taking care of sores and giving information on the types of sickness that were found in the village and the surrounding villages. I tried, in vain, to explain to them that I was a teacher and not a doctor. "But", they asked, "why then do you have that box", pointing to my medicine box. It was obvious that the white man must be a doctor. I could manage to clean sores, apply penicillin ointments to festering eyes and even give some injections to the boy who was down with fever. But there was one with *water* in the foot, another one with water in the knee, a third one with water in the stomach and an old woman with water in the head. They felt that it was a poor show on my part to refer them to the hospital.[14]

On the State of Security in Eritrea – 1957

By 1957, the Federation between Ethiopia and Eritrea had been in force for five years. The experiment was not working very well. And there were dark clouds on the horizon. Answering questions put to him by the Swedish paper, Piteå-Tidning, on Eritrea, K. J. answers,

> There is no civil war. In fact things have been calm. But there are still bandits and robbers around. It does happen that roads are blocked with boulders. In such cases one knows what to expect. We were out one evening and happened to come upon such a roadblock. However, we saw it in time and turned back quickly on the road that we knew led to the police station.[15]

Though they don't say so in so many words, the Lundströms must have felt creeping anxiety on the political scene in Eritrea.

Missionaries and Parents

The Lundströms were teachers, providers of medical care and evangelists. They also became parents in Eritrea. In 1958 they adopted two Eritrean children, Sennait and Hagos, when their mother died. When the children visited Piteå in northern Sweden for the first time in the summer of 1963, they are reported to have said, "O! How warm it is! "By then these children had experienced the warmth of the parental love of the Lundströms for some years, in Eritrea. The Lundström were soon to move to Ethiopia.

14   Article in Swedish, supplied by M-B.
15   Interview in Piteå-Tidningen in 1957. Text supplied by M-B.

Back to 2001

Maj-Britt Lundström too has written about some of her own impressions from the trip to Eritrea in 2001. We shall let her words bring our flashback to a close,

> We flew from Arlanda on the forenoon of November 3, 2001. Changed flight in Frankfurt, landed in Jidda and came to Asmara soon after midnight. After all the terrible things which had taken place in the world during the autumn [World Trade Center, 9/11], I felt shaken. All the hate in the world! Just then something happened. While we were waiting to take off I went to the women's room. There [in Frankfurt] I met a woman with her two children and I thought, "She must be Arab." She told me that she lived in England but that she was on her way to Mecca [...] We believe that they spoke Urdu with each other and that they were originally from Pakistan. [...] When they disembarked in Jidda we waved to each other happily. And I felt liberated. Imagine feeling a spontaneous human contact even if we came from such different backgrounds!

> This experience was like a joyous prologue to our stay of two months in Eritrea – an experience which turned out to be far beyond our dreams. All the love and care which we experienced carried us through the days of our stay, which we filled with impressions, encounters, work, interviews, visits to graves and houses of mourning, chats with deaconesses whom I had helped to educate in the nineteen-fifties. Students who have now aged! We had the opportunity to share both problems and joys with the members of our Sister Church [meaning the ECE].

> We lived in the part of Asmara which was the centre of town when we worked there. A walking distance from the Evangelical Church. Small shops, small but pleasant. Patisseries where we had our afternoon coffee. Shoe-shine boys around the corner. Being awakened around five every morning by the prayer-announcer of the mosque across the street. Taxi outside our door. Ramadan was celebrated during our stay in Asmara and our Muslim neighbours, who were not allowed to eat before sunset, came to us often with small tidbits in the evening. We shared the experiences that all others in this part of town shared, and we felt good about the whole thing.

> Once again I was reminded, as on many previous occasions, about what people remembered. Alganesh, who helped us when our children were small, dropped in several times, and we talked about incidents which

The New Evangelical Church in Asmara after its completion in 1989.
Photo: Ruth Normark

she remembered from her past. "Do you know" she said, "there is one thing which I have remembered often these past years. Before you went to bed in the evening, you used to come and stand at the entrance of the door and say, 'Alganesh, thank you for today. Sleep well'. You said that every evening. I haven't forgotten that."

This is a book about a historical heritage which is common to all Eritreans: Christians, Muslims and others. Indeed it is a story which embraces Swedes, Italians, Ethiopians and Eritreans. And it has been written so that we too may not forget.

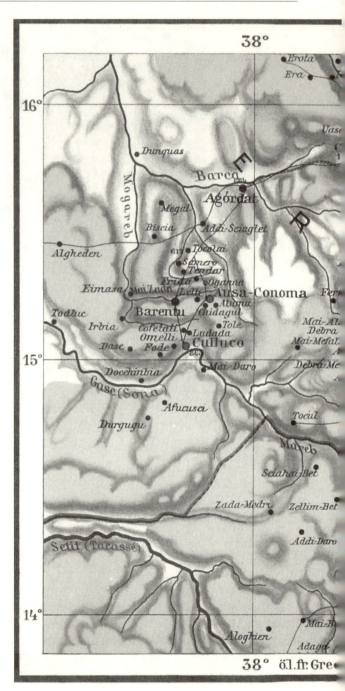

This map was published by The Publishing House of SEM in 1922.

Note that the type of spelling of words used in this map sometimes follows the Italian style.

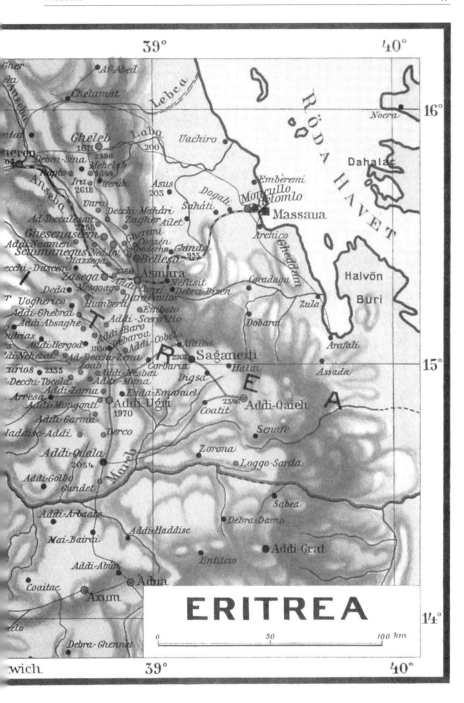

Prologue

Kunama – A Meeting Place for Religions and Contenders for Colonial Territory

Introduction

Already when the *Peloro* cast anchor in the harbour of Massawa at 2 a.m. on October 16, we were met by two of our dear co-workers, Pastor J. M. Nilsson from Kunama and Hj. [Hjalmar] Wirén from Asmara, as well as by two native church members from Hamazén [Hamasen]. At 6 a.m. two more of our faithful comrades, the director of the mission conference, Pastor A. Svensson and Pastor K. Rodén as well as some native church members from Geleb, among them the teacher Natnael [Negasi] came. They were, in other words, representatives from our three mission fields on the highlands: the *Tigrinya*, *Tigré* and *Kunama*."[16]

These are the words of Professor Adolf Kolmodin who was received by representatives of the three regions mentioned above upon his arrival in Massawa on October 16, 1908 for a visit of the Swedish mission field in Eritrea.

In the middle of the nineteenth century, Kunama found itself at a unique juncture on the Horn of Africa, a place where religious and

16   A. Kolmodin 1909 31. (Ed.)

political powers met. It had, in fact, been in that position for several hundred years. There was an ancient Christian Church that spread from Egypt down to Ethiopia.[17] Although Egypt had been overrun by Muslim forces in the 7th century and lost its political hegemony, it still survived under Muslim rule. The Christians of Nubia, south of Egypt, were once a vigorous community. However, in the 13th century they had come under increasing pressure from Islam. Two hundred years later they were more or less extinct as a religious group. Muslims were now in control of the North.

The Christian Kingdom of Ethiopia

In the early sixteenth century, the fury of an overwhelming Muslim onslaught subjected the once well established Christian kingdom of Ethiopia to almost total rout. These were the days of Imam Ahmad ibn Ibrahim al-Ghazi, also called Ahmad Grañ (the left-handed). From his home base in south eastern Ethiopia he had set out to fulfill the task he felt called to, namely the conquest of Ethiopia. As witnessed by the book *Futuh Al-Habasha (The Conquest of Abyssinia) [16th century]*, the campaign was speedy and devastating. Only with the help of Portuguese forces could Ethiopia turn the tide of this nightmare after Grañ fell in battle in 1542.[18]

Axum was the most venerated city of the empire, with the holy Temple of St. Mary, housing the Holy Ark that, according to tradition, had reached Ethiopia miraculously. There was a strong Jewish element in this Christian culture that the envoys of the Patriarch of the Coptic Church (which supplied metropolitans to Ethiopia up to the early nineteen fifties) did their best to uproot, but to no avail.

The northern areas of the Christian Kingdom in particular upheld their traditional culture. These included many Jewish practices, such as the observation of Saturday as Sabbath (in addition to Sunday) as well as most of the Jewish dietary laws and laws of purification.[19]

17 The use of the designations Abyssinia and Ethiopia tends to generate lively discussions. The great majority of the books written about the country prior to the Second World War use the term Abyssinia. There are however exceptions to this practice. (Ed.)

18 See Husein Ahmed in *EAE*, 3, 2007, 204–205, Trimingham, 1952 85–89 and F. Gurmessa 2009, 54–57. For Futuh Al-Habasha, see Paul Lester Stenhouse (translator), 2003.

19 Tamrat 1972, 206–211, 218; Ullendorff, 1973 100–101 (Ed.)

By the middle of the 19th century, however, Egypt's ruler, Viceroy Muhammed Ali, had begun taking moves to expand Egypt's sphere of influence. His local envoy founded Kassala at the northern end of Kunama territory in 1840. In 1846 he leased the port of Massawa. [20]His successor, Khedive Ismail, was determined to create a vast Egyptian Empire.[21]

One of the first steps that he took was to attempt to snatch the right of taxing the Kunama from the Governor of Adiabo, in present-day Tigrai.[22]

Kunama Traditional Religion – The Third Force

Kunama stands for traditional African Religion, "the third force", in the scheme we have chosen to describe the main religious groups in Eritrea. The place of origin of this strand of religious tradition is the southwest of the region. The Kunama had lived, in all probability, close to other Nilotic people, but had now practically lost contact with these groups. However, their ties with their traditional faith were very strong. Other neighbouring groups had been converted to Islam, but the Kunama clung to their traditional faith and culture, with the exception of the Bitama and Elit, who had embraced Islam.

When three Swedish missionaries landed on the coast at Massawa in the spring of 1866, they had no intention of heading in the direction of Kunama. Their goal was to reach the Oromo in western and southern Ethiopia. However, the route from the coast to the interior of Ethiopia was closed to them due to political and social unrest in the country.[23]

The roots of the Evangelical Church of Eritrea (ECE) go back to individuals and small communities that once belonged to the following three religious groups: the "Animist" Kunama, Tigré speaking Muslims and mainly highland population groups who belonged to the Orthodox Tewahdo Church and who spoke mainly Tigrinya.

Since the backgrounds of these populations categories vary considerably, the evolution of their histories, their ways of life, their

20   Trimingham 1952, 116, Rubenson 1976, 57.
21   Collins 1962, 68, Rubenson 1976, 290 ff. See also Miran 2005, 188–191.
22   See Rubenson 1976 289–292, Arén 1978 132, 135–136.
23   Bahru Zewde writes, "Internal opposition to Teodros's authority had started as early as 1855. Teodros was to spend most of his time moving in haste from one province to the other, faced with a fresh outbreak of rebellion before he had succeeded in putting down the previous one." Bahru Zewde 2002, 39–40. Rubenson 1966, 79 ff.

Illustration of a village in Kunama. Published in 1903 in the Mission Periodical, Varde Ljus (Let There Be Light!).

beliefs and their relationships to other groups of people must be presented separately.

We shall begin with the Kunama whose home lies on the lowland planes in what are now Southwest Eritrea, Northwest Ethiopia and the area bordering on Eastern Sudan. We shall then proceed to an exposé of the Tigré-speaking people of North-Central Eritrea and finally cover the Tigrinya-speaking people of the Eritrean highlands.[24]

Highlanders in Kunama. Front row from left: An orthodox woman, Lete-Hiywet Gustavo with the child Franco and her cousin Meraf. Second row: Woldeab Woldemariam, Gustavo Mensa and Sahle Ande-Mikael. Picture taken in 1934.

24   Basic material on the histories and cultures of these three categories of people is available in the following works: August Andersson's two books *På gamla återställda stigar* (On Old, Restored Paths, vol. 1 and 2, 1947 and 1948), on Kunama; K. G. Rodén's work *Le Tribù dei Mensa* (1913) on the history, laws and customs of the Mensa; Alberto Pollera's *Le Popolazioni Indigene Dell' Eritrea*. 1935; G. K. N. Trevaskis' *Eritrea. A Colony in Transition 1941–1952* (1960) 1–17, and Redie Berekteab's *Eritrea. The Making of A Nation* (2000), 62–86, on all three categories of people. (Ed.)

A map of Kunama and environs, with some of the places named in the following chapter: Awsa Konoma, (Ausa Conoma), the Gash River (Gasc [Sona]), Algeden (Algheden), the Barka River (Barca).

Chapter One

Roots of the ECE
The Kunama

Introduction

He was born in 1905 and started school late, having spent his early years as a boy tending his father's cattle in a highland village in Eritrea. However, when he did start studying he made fast progress. Eventually, he attended the Teacher Training School of the Swedish Mission at Beleza from 1927 to 1930. After serving the mission in Asmara until 1932, he was sent to Kunama where was to work as a teacher until 1935. Those years brought him close to Kunama soil, where he almost died of the type of Malaria that attacks the brain. In the same year, he writes the following in a personal report on a Confirmation ceremony that he had attended in Awsa Konoma:

> The mission field in Kunama has thus far been regarded as the most difficult and the least fruitful. Its history, about which I have had occasion to learn more closely in recent days, has been dark. [...] but I only want to say that I have admired and still admire those people who struggled and died victorious, in spite of the fact that they never saw victory.[25]

The faith of the writer of these words was a part of the basic motivation for all that he did. Only a decade after he had written the words quoted above, he was to enter a struggle for the moulding of the future of Eritrea, a venture which almost cost him his life.

His name was Woldeab Woldemariam.

Woldeab was in Kunama in the company of his close friend Sahle Ande-Mikael (later commonly addressed as *Memhir* Sahle). The two were part of a working team led by an energetic, widowed Swedish missionary by the name of Signe Berg.[26]

Woldeab experienced a sense of awe and admiration in the face of what the very first Swedish messengers of the Gospel had met in Kunama, "the land of blood and tears". But who were the Kunama who had captivated the hearts of Swedes and Eritreans alike? Why did they attract such attention?

For answers to these questions we shall now turn to K. J. Lundströms study on their history and culture. It has been pointed out to the editor by people knowledgeable in Kunama history, that what K. J. has written on the culture of the Kunama in this chapter builds, in some respects, more on old Kunama tradition than on present day realities.

25   Woldeab Woldemariam 1935, 25. These words are being quoted simply to underline the impact made on Woldeab by the first missionaries in the area, not to indicate the merits of Woldeab's missionary work in Kunama as such. He did play a vital role in the life of the ECE during the war years 1935–1943, in concert with several colleagues, among whom were Sahle Ande-Mikael and Negasi Kahsai. Olle Hagner's diary entries for these years give ample evidence of this fact. (Ed.)

26   In 1931, Signe, who had bought Olle Andersson's Ford (which had a capacity of 40 hp), writes that Woldeab was not a practical person and that it was Sahle who helped her with her vehicle, "a clever, kind and trusted driver", as she describes him. She also writes that Sahle and Woldeab fitted in very well with the Kunama, just like brothers". Signe Berg, U 14. Signe Berg's Correspondence.

The war for self-determination in Eritrea resulted in the disruption of small, traditional Kunama villages and the forcible setting up of bigger settlements by the Ethiopian Army. It has been pointed out that such big settlements led to the weakening of traditional practices. With this qualification in mind, we shall now proceed to K. J.'s text, which follows. (Ed.)

The People of Kunama and their History

Geography, Flora and Fauna

Not much is known about the early history of the Kunama. Some have suggested that the people were early inhabitants of the Eritrean highlands who were later pushed down towards the western lowlands. However, most scholars today maintain that the Kunama and their neighbours are, in all probability, remnants of tribes that were once widespread in the lowlands. They had settled as far west as the point at which the River Atbara flows into the Nile, but were gradually pushed back into their present day home by the Beja in the north.[27]

The main area of settlement of the Kunama was, and still is, between the Gash and Setit rivers. However, a certain section of the population lives to the north and to the south of this area.

Those of us who have read about the trials through which the first Swedish missionaries went in Kunama are tempted to come to the conclusion that even the geographical area known as Kunama was wild, arid and desolate. It is therefore interesting to note the enthusiasm with which a Kunama missionary, Olle Andersson (later known as Olle Hagner), describes the Kunama landscape as he knew it. He writes,

---

27 Longrigg 1945, 38–40. Leo Reinisch's *Die Kunama-Sprache in Nordost-Afrika (I)*, Wien, 1881, pp. 1–15 provides a good, general, historical background. August Andersson writes, "The land of Kunama lies north-east of Abyssinia [...] about 400 kilometres from Massawa. To the east it borders on the Abyssinian region of Dembelas and Adiabo, to the south on Walkayit, to the west on the homes of the Suderat and Algeden and to north on the land of the Barea. [...]" A. Andersson, 1947, 9–10. See also Redie Bereketab 2000, 63. For an up-to-date survey see Gianni Dore's article "Kunama Ethnography" in *EAE* Vol. 3, 2007, pp. 453–55. (Ed.)

August Andersson, who served in Kunama 1898–1915, rides across the River Gash on a horse, a gift from supporters of the SEM in the province of Dalarna, Sweden. Published in 1903 in the Mission Periodical,Varde Ljus (Let There Be Light!).

The south-west corner of Eritrea, Kunama land, constitutes, without the slightest doubt, the most interesting part of the country. Here we come to a completely new world. The altitude above sea level varies between 600 and 1000 metres. Nevertheless, in spite of this fact, the heat is oppressive. The landscape consists of wide, fertile plains, dotted by low hills here and there, but also separated by low chains of mountains. Everywhere one comes across an unusual wealth of flora and fauna. The mountains are clothed with gum trees (Eucalyptus), which appear far apart. The resins of these trees give us *Gum Arabic*. On the planes, a rich variety of acacia, mimosa and baobab trees grow, as we have indicated earlier. Ebony is so common that we have used this wood, which is so expensive in Europe, for our ovens.[28]

28   Olle Andersson 1947 16. (Ed.) The Tigrinya name for Gash is Mereb and the Kunama name is Sona. Amharic uses the name Tekezé. In the Sudan this river is called Atbara and drains into the Nile at Atbara town, some 300 kms north of Khartoum.

Incursions by Foreign Powers

By the middle of the nineteenth century the Egyptians had begun to exert increasing pressure on the Kunama and other ethnic groups in the region. The Viceroy of Egypt, Muhammed Ali, extended his area of control to Sudan soon after he had assumed power in Egypt in 1820. In the following two years he brought Funj, Doggola, Sennar as well as Butana and Kordofan under his rule, and founded Khartoum in 1830. He invaded Ethiopia in 1838 and reached the vicinity of Gondar, causing panic in this ancient town.[29] Egyptian interests extended further east. The Bani Amir accepted Egyptian suzerainty and Kassala was founded in 1840 as the capital of Taka Province, whence raids were organized against the isolated Christian tribe of Bilén, to take one example. Kufit [and Amideb], east of Kassala, were maintained as frontier forts during the period extending from 1852 to 1857. The Kunama were subjected to repeated attacks.[30] According to Trimingham, the Bilén started shifting their allegiance from Christianity to Islam around this period.[31]

Ottoman Turkey had taken control of Massawa and established a centre called Hirgigo on the mainland, as early as 1557. Its forces then proceeded further inland. Eventually they lost their inland positions but managed to retain their hold on Massawa and Hirgigo, the latter only for a short period. Seeing that their power was on the decline, they decided to lease Massawa to Muhammed Ali in 1846.[32] In 1861 the Baria were attacked by the Abyssinians of Adiabo who burned Mogolo. Consequently, the people in the area were made to pay tribute to both the Abyssinians and the Egyptians.[33]

According to other sources, the Kunama were subjected to almost complete annihilation in 1585 and in 1692. A third attack in 1845 is believed to have reduced the number of Kunama from 200,000 to 15,000. However, according to Brigadier S. H. Longrigg, author of *A Short History of Eritrea* (1945), the figure of a population of 200,000 in Kunama in 1845, is an exaggeration.[34]

29   Trimingham 1952, 115. See also Sven Rubenson 1976 69–70.
30   Trimingham 1952, 116. See Reinisch (I), 1881, pp. 4–5, and Dore's article in *EAE* Vol.3, 2007, p. 454.
31   Trimingham 1952, 113. See also W. Smidt's article on "Bilin", *EAE*, Vol.1, 2003 p. 587
32   Trimingham 1952, 116. Bahru Zewde 2002, 26 and Rubenson 1976, 57, 108, 115–117
33   Trimingham 1952, 218. See Reinisch 1881 4, Dore *EAE* Vol.3, 2007 454 and Beskow 1884, 74–75.
34   Normark 1972, 5. See also Longrigg 1945, 82–83.

The Kunama Language

The Kunama language has been classified under the Nilo-Saharan group of languages. It is a tonal language and the tones determine meaning.[35] While the language of the Baria or Nara is classified under the Eastern Sudanese group of languages, Kunama is regarded as a separate group under the category of Cheri-Nile languages. The chart below can give the reader some orientation on the subject.[36]

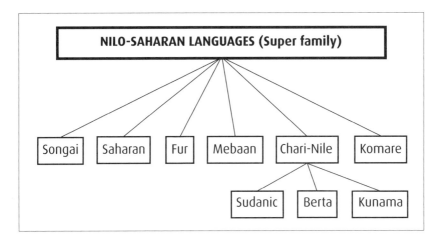

Social Organization

The Kunama share many cultural characteristics with other Nilotic people, who also make use of totem symbols. The Shua, who speak Marda, use the Rhinoceros as a totem symbol, the Gumma, who speak Barka, use the Elephant, the Karawa, who speak Tika, use the

---

35 See Leo Reinisch's *Die Kunama-Sprache in Nordost-Afrika* (1881) in 4 vols. See also M. Lionel Bender's article *Kunama Language* in *EAE*, Vol. 3, 2007, pp. 451–453, and John Abraha's article "Kunama Dialects and Morphology" in *Journal of Eritrean Studies 2005*, Vol. IV, 1&2, pp. 28–44. (Ed.)

36 Nowadays, the official name of the tribe is Nara. See Paice: *Guide to Eritrea* 1996, 148–149. A. Andersson writes, "It is certain that the main part of the population came from the south or from the south-east and that they are related to the Bantu tribes. This also seems to be the case with their language. Thus, for example, I recently read a story that children in the Congo say "O, yaya!" (O, Mother!)", in the same way that children in Kunama do. "A. Andersson 1947, 12–13. A. Andersson admired the sharp memory of those Kunama with whom he was acquainted. (Ed.)

Moon, and the Sogodak, who speak Semma, use the buffalo.[37] There was limited contact among the clans and each considered itself to be superior to the others. August Andersson writes,

> The Kunama themselves divide their tribe into four families. The most prominent one is called "Karawa". Those who belong to this family claim that they are related to thunder and rain. The "Shoa" family claim kinship with fire and the sun. The "Serma" regard the bee as their relative and the fourth, the "Gurma" family, consider themselves relatives of the elephant and a bird. They maintain that all human beings belong to these families and that these kinships are to be found among all races. They ask us, missionaries, to which family we belong.[38]

The feeling of affinity was primarily limited to the nuclear family but could, in special cases, extend to a wider circle.

In 1864 Werner Munzinger wrote of a social system in which the woman played a dominant role in the family, existed among the Kunama.[39] The system was, however, not a form of matriarchy in which the woman was the head of the family, but rather one based on matrilineal kinship. Inheritance followed the mother's lineage, but the dominant personality was the mother's brother, i.e. the maternal uncle. Thus the women played a crucial role in Kunama society as bearers of tradition and spiritual life.[40]

Cohesion within the lineage was firm, but not as important as it was among the neighbouring peoples such as the Bani Amir. The

---

37   Pollera 1935, 239–240. Dore writes: 'Kunama groups are the Marda, Barka, Taguda, Aymasa, Tika and the geographically and linguistically separated Ilit and Sokodas.' Dore *EAE* Vol.3, 2007 453. (Ed.)

38   A. Andersson 1947, 13. Gianni Dore maintains that different combinations of relations can in fact lead to a count of about 18 clans.

39   Normark 1972, 10. The line goes from the maternal uncle to the son of his sister. August Andersson writes, "The Kunama woman is free and is aware of her freedom. [...] The tradition of the fathers is law and protects marriage." A. Andersson 1947, 19. Girls were given full freedom to choose the one they would marry. Andersson continues, "Separation or divorce occurs very rarely, and when it does occur, it is almost always the woman who leaves the man. In this respect, practice is the very opposite of that which prevails in neighbouring Abyssinia. When a woman leaves her husband, the husband has the right to reclaim the bride price given by him to his father-in-law on the day of the wedding." A. Andersson 26. Werner Munzinger (1832–1875) had come out as an independent Swiss linguist and Ethnographer. He ended up becoming Governor General under the Egyptians, after having served as official consular representative for both France and Britain at Massawa. (Rubenson 1976, 17). (Ed.)

40   Normark 1972, 10, Pollera 1935, 241–244. Reinisch 1881 (I), 11, Dore 2003 (2009) 79.

Kasa Marda – a Kunama chief in the village of Ouganna. He became almost 100 years old.

traditional Kunama village consisted of some 25 families. The huts were built close to each other, usually on hills or slopes. The society was very egalitarian and the village was seen as a unit. An attack on a single member was considered as an attack on the village. Every village had a council whose members were called *Andai*, the Great Ones. These elders consisted of all married men in the village. As a sign that they had assumed this role, the men cut their hair and received the title *Anda*. To assume this role, young men had to undergo the *ana-ila* ceremony between the ages of 15 and 18. Marriage was a requirement.[41]

The older a man, the greater his influence. The elders met regularly on the *dibba*, the site of the council, usually located under a big tree. In the deliberations that were held, the younger members of the council spoke first, followed by the older ones, who also had the right of final

41 See Normark 1972, 12, Pollera 1935, 243–244. As a sign of this coming of age, the person in question was allowed to let his hair, which he used to shave, now grow. Reinisch (I) 1881, 6. (Ed.)

say, on the basis of a general consensus (*gomata*).

A stranger could become a member of the village even if he didn't have any relatives in the village.[42]

If a Kunama broke the *faneda* –the manners and customs–he would find himself isolated. This was the worst possible punishment that could be meted out to a Kunama.[43] Kunama society was acephalous, i.e. it had no central ruler or chief. Every village was legally and politically independent, at least on the home level. The absence of a centralized, leadership, however, had some negative consequences. The absence of a common defence organization left the Kunama open to attacks by robbers and to other kinds of harassment. A new office came into being when the Kunama came under the rule of Egyptians and Abyssinians, who forced them to pay tribute. The new masters selected a person from the ranks of the people, and commissioned the same to be the Kunama *Chief*. This office remained in force and was inherited by the same lineage, following a matrilineal descent, but the chief was not regarded as a Paramount Chief. His main task was that of collecting tribute.

Economy

Every nuclear family had its own small farm, which consisted of:

a) An area round its abode, where the family planted maize and a limited variety of vegetables,

b) One or more *bisa* i.e. larger, cleared and swidden [scorched] areas, usually found on the planes around the village.[44] Sorghum and millet were the crops that were cultivated most frequently. Sorghum is the most important grain used in the performance of different rites.

Farming took place mainly during the period between May and November. The men did the clearing and burning of the bushes on the savannah. They also made fences around the fields (at harvest time) and were responsible for ploughing and sowing.[45]

---

42 Normark 1972, 14.
43 Normark 1972, 13.
44 A more correct spelling of *bisa*, according Pastor Bertil Holmgren, would be *Bisha*. (Ed.)
45 Normark 1972, 20. Andersson writes, "The people have a sizeable side income from the sale of honey and Gum Arabic. In times of good harvests, they sell their grain and tobacco towards the payment of taxes, or they exchange these products for cloth, thread, needles and articles of metal." A. Andersson 1947, 17. (Ed.)

Kunama shepherds
at a water well.

The women were responsible for preparing and cultivating the area around the hut and for caring for these gardens. They would also have to assist in the work on the fields, weeding them as well as threshing and grinding the harvested grain.

Children and youth were responsible for guarding the fields, particularly against birds that could cause damage to the harvest. The young men would also assist in the threshing of grain.[46]

Cattle were usually handed over to a group of shepherds who took

46   Andersson writes, "Children learn to work at an early age. Daughters are under the tutorship of their mothers and help as much as possible. Boys help to herd cattle and to aim well with stones and spears." A. Andersson 1947, 25. (Ed.)

care of all the cattle in the village. The shepherds would herd them over large areas and the villagers would pay a small fee for this service. Sheep and goats were usually taken care of by the young.[47]

Owning cattle was a sign of wealth and these were slaughtered only for special rites. Only in emergency situations were cattle slaughtered for food, weddings being such occasions. Bride-price (*digina malé*) was given in the form of cattle. Hunting used to be an important source of food for the Kunama and game was plentiful in the area. So was the gathering of berries, gum, honey and fruits along the riverbeds.[48]

Land

Every person had a right to land, but there was no individual land ownership. A person could not buy or sell land.

As long as a villager made use of a piece of land he had the right to keep it. If he, however, would abandon it for a longer period of time, a neighbour could take it over, upon the approval of the maternal uncle of the delinquent party.

Traditionally, Kunama did not amass wealth. Such a practice would be frowned upon and could lead to expulsion from the community.[49] This however is no longer the case. A person who received the assistance of other villagers in a private undertaking would be required to furnish them with food and beer. Reciprocity was the unwritten law.

Most of the work was done by the nuclear family. However, the village participated collectively in certain tasks requiring tedious labour, especially at harvest time. In such cases too the holder of the land would be expected to supply the workers with beer and food. [50] All important functions connected with land were carried out by men.

Religion

Some scholars regard the worship of one God, *Anna*, as a late development in Kunama religion, probably a result of the influence of Christianity and Islam, the monotheistic religions in the surrounding

47   Normark 1972, 21. See also A. Andersson 1947, 16–17.
48   Normark 1972, 21. See also A. Andersson 1947, 17.
49   Normark 1972, 22.
50   Normark 1972, 23. See also A. Andersson 1947, 18–19.

areas.[51] However, A. Pollera and E. Cerulli maintain that *Anna* was regarded as the one God, the Creator of all, among the Kunama.[52] This was also the case among many, if not all, of the Nilotic peoples.[53]

The first people to be created were Adam and Aua (or Hawa), the original parents of the first Kunama. The names may have been added later as these words occur both in the Jewish-Christian and Muslim traditions.[54] In cultures akin to those of the Kunama, changes may be introduced in the names of deities, while the basic faith in the deity remains the same.[55] The Kunama addressed their prayers not only to God but also to their ancestors.[56] In their religion there were clear signs of a hierarchical structure. Highest in this hierarchy was the Creator, *Anna*, and below him/her came the hierarchy of ancestors, which constituted the various lineages.[57]

The society also had bearers of religious heritage, people who were recognized as specialists in various aspects of religious practice. These assumed both secular and spiritual functions. Among such specialists – called *Manna*, are the

Aula Manna	who brought or withheld rain
Ula Manna	who provided protection from locusts
Sciurka Manna	who provided protection from birds[58]
Bia Manna	who protected especially durra (sorghum) from the scourge of worms,
Attana Manna	who provided protection from flies and insects.

These office-bearers were usually men, co-opted for service by the village community, from specialized matrilineal lineages.[59]

---

51 Reinisch (I) 1881, 8. See also Dore 2003 (2009), 82–83.
52 A. Pollera 1913, 80–81. A. Andersson maintains, "They have several names for God. They call him *Anna* or *Anna baddi shinda*, i.e. the origin of everything and the creator of the first human beings *Adam* and *Haoa*. They even call him *Kas'anda*, which in fact means *big stomach*, whereby the deity's capacity to bestow gifts like children, cattle, and a good harvest is symbolized." A. Andersson 1947, 27–28. (Ed.)
53 Lundström 1990, 70–71. See also Reinisch (I) 1881, 8–9.
54 In Arabic *Adam* and *Hawa*, in Ge'ez *Adam* and *Hewan*.
55 See the names of God among the Lotuho in Southern Sudan. Lundström 1990, 71.
56 Normark 1972, 30. Dore writes, "Furda is a key concept, meaning ceremony, ritual, ancestral heritage." Dore *EAE* Vol. 3, 2007, 453.
57 On the prophetic figure, *Dungul*, among Marda, see Dore's article, 2007 86–88.
58 Another variant of this spelling is *Shurka*.
59 Pollera 1935, 244. See Dore's study "Chi non ha una parente Andinna? [...] (Online), on possession among Kunama women. Dore 2007, 52–62. (Ed.)

The office-bearers were highly respected and were given gifts of various kinds to perform their services. Their power was not questioned. Lack of performance on their part was interpreted as a sign of their desire for more gifts, not as an indication that they were unable to act. If people were convinced that they were unreasonable, it sometimes happened that the office-bearers were punished and even killed by stoning.[60] The same phenomenon appears among the Nilotic groups in Southern Sudan.[61]

The *Manna* were male. There was, however, another group of female actors in the realm of religious rituals. These were called *Asirmina*.[62] It was believed that the spirits of the ancestors possessed them. The possession lasted usually for some ten days, after which the women went through a cleansing ceremony at which they were de-possessed and returned to their daily duties at home. In their state of possession they spoke a language which was interpreted by apprentices (*gilae*) who accompanied the women on their travels.[63]

The Kunama too attach great importance to the presence of spirits. The world is a unit of the living and the dead, Good Beings and Evil Ones. Life continues beyond the grave and the spirits of the deceased are present in the minds of the Kunama. The spirits, usually representing someone from about a generation ago, assume a human shape by becoming a *Manna* and *Asirma*. These spirits would identify themselves.

Another practice, which united the world of the living with the world of the dead, was the offering of first fruits on the graves of the deceased. The head of the family narrated matters regarding the harvest, events in the life of the family and other news that might be of interest to the deceased. At the end, the living took a meal together with the dead.[64]

---

60   See Reinisch 1881 (I), 11. Dore questions the statement. (Ed.)
61   Lundström 1990, 65–68.
62   Here again Bertil Holmgren suggests Ashirmina. See Gianni Dore's recent and highly interesting study on possession among Kunama women. Dore 2007, especially pp. 56–62. *Ashirma* means "ghost" and *andinnä* means "possessed".
63   Dore, Idris and Nati established that ca thirty percent of the glossolalia [language] consisted of Tigré, with Arabic words interspersed. Dore 2007, 59. (Ed.)
64   A. Pollera 1913, 81. See also Andersson 1947, 34–36.

Rites of Passage

Circumcision

Through circumcision a Kunama child becomes a full-fledged human being. The child gets a new name, a new dress and returns to his or her family as reborn. Both boys and girls are circumcised. Circumcision is celebrated through a common rite through which children who belong to a specific age group undergo the first stage of an initiation into the world of adults. This happens usually between the ages of 8 and 10.[65]

Transition to Adulthood

For girls, physical changes (maturing breasts, female circumcision) were considered as clear signs of the transition from girlhood to womanhood. The rite *Ana-ila* was conducted somewhere in the forest with a group of boys of the same age. In earlier times this was done between the ages of 13 and 18. The hair of the youth was cut and water was sprinkled on it three times. Through this rite, the youth were given access to adult life and its responsibilities. This included the right to get married.[66]

Marriage

A wedding is regarded as an initiation rite through which the husband and the wife would enter a new life. At the same it must be pointed out that marriage is not only a rite through which the husband and wife enter a new life but also an act that implies the union of the two families, matrilineal descent groups, etc. The unmodified, age-old social regulations of Kunama society exert a greater influence on the institution of marriage than the freedom implied in the voluntary matrimonial union of two individuals.[67] Only when one is married is one considered to be *abishà*, a full man. Marriage with bride-price or bride–wealth (*digina malè*), was forbidden in both the Catholic and Protestant communities.

---

65   Old men choose the appropriate day for the boys and old women for the girls. A. Andersson writes, "The circumcision of children takes place within a specific period after the ages of two or five or ten. Several families unite to share the cost of such a feast. Almost all Kunama feasts are celebrated for two days. This applies also to circumcision." A. Andersson 1947, 24–25. (Ed.)

66   For this section I am indebted to Pastor Bertil Holmgren. (Ed.)

67   See also A. Andersson 1947, 20 ff. Andersson points out that though the Kunama loved children they regarded twins as a sign of ill omen and, in his days, buried them alive. A. Andersson 1947, 29. (Ed.)

Funerals

These are regarded as rites of transition from the present life to a new one. However, there is no line of separation between the living and the dead. There is always a mysterious communication between them. [68]

In Closing

In his book *Nåden och Världen* (Grace and the World), the Swedish theologian and novelist Christian Braw writes,

> [...] the narrative of God's ways with us is the innermost structure of the history of each and every people. The history of every nation is, in this sense, an Old Testament, a witness about God, an experience of God, and a possibility of arriving at a knowledge of God already before the proclaimers of the Word arrive. Every nation has, in other words, a holy history, a history linked with God, long before the day on which it hears the Word about Jesus. The Word is always there before the missionary.[69]

Braw has borrowed this line of thought from the famous Swedish churchman J. A. Eklund (1863–1945). The idea implies that there can be an initial light, the makings of a prehistory of the Christian faith, a *preparatio evangelica* (a preparation for the Gospel), in every culture.

Can one say that of the cultural and religious history of Kunama presented by K. J.? August Andersson writes,

> Frut had died and had already been taken to the grave. We rode towards it. The grave was open and an animal had already been sacrificed. The blood of the animal had been collected in a bowl and I arrived just in time to see the man who led the burial ceremony dip his finger in the blood and make the sign of the cross on the naked chest of the deceased. I asked, "Why do you do so?" He answered, "We don't know. Our fathers have done likewise." That gave me the text for a funeral sermon on the blood of Jesus which was shed on Golgotha.[70]

That the Kunama attached great importance to the presence of spirits has been pointed out by K. J. He also mentions Kunama women who, in a state of possession, spoke a strange language, which was interpreted by someone who accompanied the women on their travels. Can this

68   Normark 1972, 33. *Andinna* are mediators between the living and the dead. A. Andersson 1947, 41. Dore deals with this in detail. Dore 2009, 71–73. (Ed.)
69   Braw 1993, 58. Andersson likens Kunama religion to Shamanism. Andersson 1947, 27.
70   Andersson 1947, 33–34.

Graduation of candidates from the Teacher Training School in Beleza in 1932.
Front row, from left to right: Jonas Iwarson, Alessandro Tron, Rosina Holmer, Mikael Holmer, Samuel Manna and Valdo Tron.
Second row: Mrs. Louise Iwarson, Mrs. Velia Tron and Habte-Ab Woldemariam.
Third row: Tekletsen Debbas, Almaz Selomon, Unknown, Woldeab Woldemariam and Mrs. Agnes Nyström.
Top row: Unknown, Mihretu Tewolde-Medhin, Embaye Habte-Egzy and Ande-Mikael Wolde-Merqorios.

be regarded as a distant forerunner of the charismatic phenomenon known as speaking in tongues, found in the early church (e.g. First Corinthians chapters 12–14), and in our days? If so, did the proclamation of the Gospel by Swedish missionaries and their Eritrean co-workers use these cultural and religious phenomena among the Kunama as points of contact, as bridges in the proclamation of the Gospel?

It would be interesting to examine the sermons and the teaching of the many Kunama missionaries and the Kenisha pastors in general, to see if attempts were made to establish links between Kunama history, culture and religious concepts and the proclamation of the Gospel. Such an inquiry would probably demonstrate the character of mission as a living encounter with other religious traditions and not only as a one way traffic. (Ed.)

A close-up of a part of the Mensa area with some of the places named in the following chapter: Geleb (Gheleb), Mihlab (Mehelab), the River Laba, the River Wakiro (Uachiro).

Chapter Two

Roots of the ECE
The Mensa

Introduction

I met him in Addis Ababa after my ordination in 1964, though he was then a resident of the town of Dessie, where he ran a restaurant and guesthouse.

He was short of stature and spoke Amharic with a special accent. I had heard that he gathered people at his home for Bible reading

Ato Gustavo Be'alged Maybetot (1908–1987)
A Kenisha from Mensa, Eritrea, who combined
the role of a hotel-owner and a witness for Christ
within the Ethiopian Evangelical Church Mekane
Yesus from his base in Dessie, Ethiopia.

and prayer. He used to come up to Addis Ababa for different meetings related to the Ethiopian Evangelical Church Mekane Yesus (EECMY). At one working session during a church conference, a certain individual objected to the use of the word *Lutheran* in connection with the name of the EECMY. This Kenisha from far away Eritrea objected to the objection. He told me that he was proud to be known as an Evangelical Lutheran Christian and said so unequivocally.

His name was Gustavo Be'alged Maybetot.[71]

In his book *Envoys of the Gospel in Ethiopia*, Gustav Arén writes,

> A convert from Islam, Ato Gustavo Bealged Maybetot (1908–1987), went in 1927 from Geleb to Asmara to seek employment. "On my arrival there a circular had been distributed to all companies and government offices which forbade employment of members of the [Evangelical] Church", stated Ato Gustavo in his [Yä] Hiywot Tarik, his 12-page autobiography in Amharic.[72] After much difficulty he managed to obtain a very

---

71 Long after I had written these words, I found further information on this subject among Olle Hagner's diary entries (Book V) for January 1943. Hagner writes,
"In Dessie we have several of our boys from the Mission. Among others Mensa youth. One of them is Gustavo Belget [Be'alged], who owns Hotel 'Ciao', the biggest and finest hotel in the whole of Dessie. [...] It became late before our car was ready but we used the time for a simple gathering for our people in the small, inviting room for prayer, which Zeré Bekhit had provided when he was once in Dessie for a longer period. Our people gather here every Sunday and for the bigger festivals, to read their Bibles, sing and pray." (OHD/K.J.S. Book V, p. 72).

72 Gustavo Be'alged 1980, 2.

subordinate job at a Greek firm. Later he founded the Mekane Yesus Congregation at Dessie and was a member of the Board of the Wollo-Tigré Synod of the EECMY.[73]

Two things struck me about Ato Gustavo. The first was his forename. It was neither Eritrean nor Italian. Is it possible that the name was given to him by a Swedish missionary, or taken by him in appreciation of a Swedish missionary by the same name? The second thing that struck me about him was his loyalty, his perseverance in his Evangelical faith, in spite of the fact that he lived far from his home in Eritrea.

Why mention Ato Gustavo? In the first place, he was a fervent witness to the Evangelical faith he had received. Secondly, he belonged to the category of people known as Mensa (pronounced with a guttural vowel at the end!). Who were the Mensa? What can we say of their history and culture? In what way did they come in touch with the Swedish Evangelical Mission?

Karl Johan Lundström has given us a short but comprehensive survey of their history. His text follows. (Ed.)

The Mensa and their History

When the first Swedish Missionaries arrived in Massawa, Consul Werner Munzinger, now representing France, advised them against advancing to the Oromo through Abyssinia. He suggested instead that they begin work among the Mensa who, according to him, were pagan and lived just a few days walk from Massawa. However, he soon ran into a problem. Catholic missionaries, who had initiated mission among the Bilén, not far from the Mensa, protested against his proposal. He therefore changed his mind and recommended Kunama as the most suitable region for pioneer missionary work by the Swedes.[74]

Professor A. Kolmodin, who visited Mensa at the end of November 1908, has left us a lyrical description of the scenery between Mihlab and Geleb. He writes,

> On Friday November 27 we started from Mehelab. The way up to Geleb is the most beautiful stretch of country through which one can travel. For a good part of the way we followed the bed of the River Godmer, now dry. We moved now to the right, now to the left and now again along the

---

73   Arén 1999, 221.
74   Arén 1978, 133. A. Kolmodin 1909, 133. Tafvelin-Lundmark 1974, 57–58. (Ed.)

Mensa warriors.

middle of the river bed, and across the river itself. The mountains kept rising, to the right and to the left. Here and there, out of the crevices of the mountains, big trees emerged. Among them was the beautiful candelabra tree. How these trees could cling to the almost sheer faces of the mountains was a source of wonder for me. Often, giant trees cast their shadows on our way.

My attention was drawn to a special tree with fruits half a cubit long and the size of a fist, hanging from branches on vines, thin and long. At times our path went through what appeared like a rich green park. Add to this the songs of all kinds of strange birds, reaching us from different directions. Imagine how it feels when even streams and rivers begin to sing. No, I must abstain from any further descriptions. I could only say to my fellow traveller, Pastor Svensson, that Rodén's country [meaning Geleb or Mensa], with its variations, its wealth of trees and flora, as well as the songs of birds, was much more beautiful than his country [meaning Tse'azzega or Hamasen].[75]

75   See Rodén 1907, 5–7. A. Kolmodin 1909, 133. Professor Asmarom, who visited the area in 1991, recognized the gorgeous scenes in this description. (Ed.)

In 1873, Munzinger, who by then was in Egyptian service, was still urging the missionaries to do something for the Mensa. In December 1873 a missionary by the name of E. E. Hedenström (1844–1904) moved up to the area, settling at Geleb.

In Geleb the missionaries met still another culture. The people were not, as Munzinger had first stated, pagans but bearers of a mixture of Muslim and Christian cultures.[76] Mensa tradition claims that the people originated from Arabia. The Swedish missionary K. G. Rodén writes,

> Their forefathers were two brothers, Tsed and Tsebed, descendants of Kerosh and Maaneja, who lived in Arabia. Later on they separated: Tsebed remained in his country of origin, while Tsed crossed the Red Sea, landed on African soil and settled on Buri, a peninsula south of Massawa. From him were born Haranreway, Hatsotay, Toray, Schiahai, Adalie (Adaglie), Mensaay, and Mareyay. The first of these formed a branch called Haranrewa; the others a second branch with the names of six people: Haso, Tora, Schiahay, Adallye, Mensaay and Mareya.[77]

The new settlers were Saho who had migrated from the coast to Haigat. A migration led the same groups of Saho to the plateau where they took up Tigrinya or Tigré as their language. The story continues to narrate how the *Mensa* and *Marya* left their brothers and moved towards the area where the sun sets and then moved up to Haigat.[78] There they went in different directions. Mensaay settled at Haigat and his descendants were called Mensa, while the Mareyay settled at Erota and his descendants were called Marya.[79]

The existing population, called Tigré, was subdued and Mensa and Marya became the ruling classes in the area.[80]

Other related groups, such as the Bait Juk, settled north of the Mensa.

The Mensa, who "inhabit the country adjacent to the town of Kärän and about 50 km north-west from the Red-Sea port of Massawa which

76   Arén 1978, 204. A. Pollera 1935, 175–176 and K. Volker-Saad 2007, 735–736.
77   Rodén 1913, 3. On claims to Arab origins, Trimingham writes, "An important element in the spread of Islam in Africa has been Arab pride of race. The islamization of tribes throughout the whole region is linked with legends of saints coming from Arabia who gave the leading families an aristocracy of Arab blood and thus exposed the whole tribe to the appeal of Islam [...] In most cases the authenticity of these genealogies is extremely dubious [...]. Trimingham, 1952 141. (Ed.)
78   Pollera 1935, 171. *Qeshi* Asfaha recommends Mareyat (instead of Mareya). (Ed.)
79   Rodén 1913, 5. Pollera 1935, 171, and Littmann *Preliminary Report...* 1906, 7.
80   Pollera 1935 170–171, Volker-Saad 2007, 736.

Two camel drivers from Mensa sharing a meal.

embraces the territory of the 'Northern Hills' [...]."[81], use Tigré as their language. Enno Littmann, who was the leader of the Princeton University Expedition to Abyssinia (1905), writes,

> Among the languages spoken in the Colonia Eritrea the Tigré language is the most important for several reasons. First, the people using it as their mother tongue are more numerous than any other linguistic community within the Italian possessions; secondly, it is spreading very rapidly to tribes of different nationalities and takes, in a way, the place of a lingua franca, competing in this respect with the Arabic in those regions; thirdly, it is of great philological interest, since it is the most archaic of the present Semite-Abyssinian languages and, although not a direct descendant of the ancient Ge'ez, resembles the later more than the Tigriñja [...][82]

81   Volker-Saad, *EAE*, Vol 3, 2007, 735, Rodén 1907, 5.
82   Littmann 1907, 5.

Social Organization

The social organization of the Tigré-speaking peoples consisted of ethnic federations composed of both a ruling caste and a serf caste. These were organized as sub-clans and kinship-groups linked together in a very loose fashion. Most of them were Muslims and earned their livelihood as nomadic herdsmen. Since the nomadic organization was one characterized by great fluidity, a continual process of exchange took place among the members and sections of these groups. The ruling caste was called *Shimagilé*.[83] The serfs, called *Tigré*, were the original inhabitants.[84] They were descendants of various peoples upon whom a more powerful group had imposed itself, or who, in order to gain protection or economic advantages, had allied themselves to a strong tribe, to which they would adhere by common political association. These serfs received protection and the right to use the master's land and livestock in return for services rendered. This system worked for centuries.[85] In addition to these two classes there were slaves. Both the *Shimagilé* and the *Tigré* owned slaves.[86]

The Mensa were divided into two groups: The Beit Abrehé, with their main centre at Habna (Geleb) and Biet Eshhaqan, with their centre at Mihlab. Each group had a headman called Kentiba.[87] The Mensa were independent until the reign of Fasilidas (1632–1667), when they were incorporated into the Abyssinian sphere of influence.[88] As the Abyssinian monarchy declined, Mensa came more and more under the rue of local chieftains, examples being the Naib of Hirgigo or, later on, the *Ra'si* of Tigrai. After 1874, the area came under Egyptian rule.[89]

---

83   Asfaha recommends the spelling *Shimagelé*. See Rodén 1907, 8–10.
84   Trimingham 1952, 159, Rodén 1907, 10.
85   Trimingham 1952, 13.
86   Rodén 1913, 177.
87   *Qeshi* Asfaha Mehari recommends the spelling *Kentabay*.
88   Rodén 1907, 10. *Qeshi* Asfaha Mehari writes, "The centre of Mensa Biet Abrehe is / Geleb. Some of the Mensa chiefs, because of their internal restlessness, created some sort of relation with Fasilidas, the ruler of Gondar in today's Ethiopia, in order to play a dominant role among their subjects." Rodén, however, writes, "Mensa have, generally speaking, been under the influence of the emperors of Ethiopia or of a paramount chief in Arkiko, near the Red Sea." Rodén 1907, 29. (Ed.)
89   Trimingham 1952, 120–121, Rubenson 1976, 310 ff.

Camels being loaded on the riverbed of Bacchacheya, in the lowlands of Mensa.

Economy

The population in the Mensa area was dependent on agriculture for its livelihood. Rainfall was low and crops of sorghum and maize would often fail. However, people could make up for this loss by a second harvest in the lowland area of Schi'ib, along the Laba River which flows from the highlands down to the coastal plain where it drains into the River Wakiro and, finally, into the Red Sea.[90] The population was also dependent on cattle and camels as well as goats and sheep.

On the conditions which prevailed at the turn of the twentieth century (1905) Enno Littmann writes,

> The Mänsa' are semi-nomads: they till the soil and have certain villages where they have their homes and where they spend only a few months: during the larger part of the year, however, they stay on their fields, i.e. in the winter in the lowlands, in the summer in the highlands, according to the natural conditions of the country. [...] Being nomads,

90 Rodén 1907, 7. Naigzy Gebremedhin comments: "An important and possibly unique form of irrigation used in these parts is called *Spate Irrigation*. This consists of creating shallow embankments from earth, stones and wood, and flooding the area before planting".

they have naturally a great many camels, scarcely any cattle, and no chickens at all. Now it is a religious law with the Abyssinian Christians not to drink camel's milk, and this is one of the reasons why the people that are driven to a nomadic life, embrace the Muhammedan faith.[91]

Some game, especially the Greater Kudo, was available in the area, and it provided meat for feasts. Later on, the fruits of *bäläs* (fruit of Cactus), became an important source of food during the pre-harvest season.

Religion

For a long period, sections of the population in the area were Christians of Orthodox Tewahdo persuasion. Towards the north, other groups who had been considered as pagans, had turned to Islam. Most of the serfs, the Tigré, too were Muslims.

It is Trimingham's contention that Christian groups, like the Mensa, the Ad Tamariam, Ad Taklés and Hibtés, had enjoyed the protection of the Ethiopians, especially the leaders of the northern part of Tigrai in the latter part of the nineteenth century. There were close contacts between the holy centres of Ethiopian Christianity in the North, particularly Axum and monasteries like Debre Sina, which lay close to the Mensa area. These population groups held their ground in the face of the onslaught of the Muslim forces of the Ottoman Empire, even though the Turks had been able to maintain their control of Massawa. However, after the middle of the 18th century, the central power of the Ethiopian Empire had started diminishing. Although the local leaders of Tigrai tried to maintain contact with the North, they were not able to do so.[92]

With the introduction of a new political and military power in Egypt and Sudan, which also took control of certain parts of what is now Eritrea, leaders in Tigrai were unable to support and strengthen the Christian population, either militarily or in matters of religion.

---

91   Littmann 1907, 6, Rodén, *Mensa. Något om dess land...*1907, 17–34 and Volker-Saad 2007, 735.

92   Anthony D'Avray's *Lords of the Red Sea* reads, "Hamed and his rivals [...] were descendants of Kantibai Hadad I. Under Hadad's brothers, the Kantibais Ghirgis, Ezaz and Giang, the slide to Islam among the ruling class had begun, culminating in the defection of Hadad I, the last Christian Kantibai. He led the Bet Asgedè and the Shumagallè over to Islam in the nineteenth century, when Christian Ethiopia seemed to represent a lost cause, and Turkey and Egypt the future." D'Avray 1996, 96. See also Littmann Preliminary Report ... 1906, 6. (Ed.)

Most hard-hit were the Christian groups that lived in areas controlled by the Egyptians, such as the Bilén and the Mensa. At the same time Islam was undergoing a spiritual re-awakening. As of this period one notices many cases of persons with Muslim forenames, like Ali, and Christian surnames like Waldés, giving the combination Ali Waldés.[93] Plowden, who was the British Consul in Ethiopia 1844–1860, maintains that these changes were due to the "anarchic conditions of the country and the influence of Muslim traders and missionaries." [94]

Another voice, Fr. Giuseppe Sapeto, speaking about his experiences in this respect when he first entered the country in 1838, says that he found the process of islamization in full swing among the Ad Taklés.[95] In the early 19th century two Islamic movements came to exert a strong influence on the people of northern part of what is now Eritrea. One was led by a Sheikh al-Amin (also known as Lamin) ibn Hamad who joined the Ad Sheikh group of Tigré-speaking people living north of the Mensa at the beginning of the nineteenth century. He claimed to be of Quraishile origin from Arabia and "gathered around himself lone Muslims and Tigré vassals fleeing from their masters".[96] He gained a reputation through miracles performed amongst the Tigré vassals of the Christian Biet Asgedé. Sheikh Al-Amin became the focus of a special cult but was later displaced as the leading religious figure by the Mirghaniyya family.

The founder of this latter movement was Muhammad Uthman al-Mirghani (1793–1852). He was sent by his master Ahmed ibn Idris to Egypt and Sudan and preached among the Bani Amir in 1817. He sent out his sons to win proselytes in other regions.[97]

---

93   For similar exampels see Trimingham 1952, 160.
94   Quoted in Trimingham, 160. See also Longrigg 1945, 85–87, Rubenson 1976, 118 ff.
95   Trimingham, 160. Volker-Saad writes, "In the middle of the 19th cent., the majority of the M. converted from Orthodox Christianity to Islam, approximately between 1820 and 1850, especially thanks to the 'Ad Shek and Nai'ib families." Volker-Saad, 2007, 736. In line with Trimingham, Arén and D'Avray, Qeshi Asfaha maintains that plundering and killing by Ethiopian warlords from the south had alienated the Mensa from Christianity. Trimingham 1952, 162, Arén 1978, 204–205, D'Avray 1996, 62ff. On the history of Islam in Eritrea, see Miran 2005. (Ed.)
96   Trimingham 1952, 141. Longrigg 1945, 86–87. See also Miran 2005, 186–187. (Ed.)
97   Most local claims to kinship with "holy families" from Arabia have been challenged. (Kolmodin's Zanta, 1914, 31; Trimingham 1952, 141). Jonathan Miran cites cases of migrations and marriages of notables from the Arabian Peninsula into families of local tribal chiefs, who then contributed to the spread of Islam in Eritrea. (Miran 2005, 181–189). On Islam in Eritrea, see Miran's study on the history of Massawa, 2009. (Ed.)

By 1865 the Mensa as well as many other groups, like the Bait Juk, were still Christian, at least nominally.[98] However, without the support of the Christian forces on the Hamasen highlands and in Tigrai, Christianity in this area was dwindling fast. No new priests were entering service. Church buildings, and in some cases the most holy object among the relics, the *tabot*, were falling into disrepair.[99] Priests used to travel with the faithful as they migrated to the coastal lowlands during the rainy season. On such occasions they carried the *tabot* along. On one occasion a priest had hidden the *tabot* away, for fear that it would fall into the hands of robbers. On recovering it, he found that termites had eaten through it.[100] Without *the ark*, the sacraments could not be administered, and this meant that children could not be baptized, neither could mass be celebrated. Christian worship could simply not be held there, as tradition would have it. The priest would not officiate at any service in the church and the congregation saw no point in maintaining the building.[101] This happened at a time when, as already mentioned, some charismatic Muslim missionaries were making a great impact on the whole region.

In spite of having abandoned their *ma'täb* (the neck-cord received at baptism) and embraced Islam, the people continued to observe many Christian customs.[102] They kept Christian festivals, such as the observance of two Sabbath days and the festival known as *Going Mariam*.[103] However, four of the practices that they embraced had

---

98   Trimingham 1952, 164, on the basis of G. Sapeto 1857, 223.
99   A replica of the Jewish Ark of the Covenant that is found in every Orthodox Church in Eritrea and Ethiopia. See article "Ark of the Covenant" by Stuart Munro-Hay in *EAE*, vol.1 (2003), pp 340–341.
100 Trimingham 1952, 162.
101 Trimingham 1952, 162–163, Arén 1978, 353 and Rodén 1907, 58–60.
102 *Ma'täb* is a neck-cord that indicates that the bearer is a baptized member of the Orthodox Tewahdo Church.
103 Littmann writes, "Two other customs practiced alike by Christians and Muhammedans, which show that the latter at one time must have professed Christianity, are the following. At every meal the Trinity is invoked; small pieces of the food – usually a sort of polenta [a kind of porridge] – are taken and thrown to the right, to the left and straight ahead, with the prayer, "*sellasê sellus* – Triune Trinity, *et ad hedûg* – At home (left as) as a protector, *et gabai mallahai* – On the road a friend!" This custom is called *sellasê* or *sêk 'iyob*." A rewording of the prayer would result, roughly, in the following rendition: "Triune Trinity! Thou who dost abide (remain) at home as Protector, and art a Companion on one's journey!" Littmann 1907, 7.

The mission station at Geleb, Mensa, according to an illustration in the Mission Periodical for 1877. The station lay in a valley between two mountains.
1. Hedenström's residence. 2. Brick kiln. Beside it, Olsson's kitchen made of mats from Palm trees. 3. Bathing hut. 4. Gable of cowshed. 5. Kitchen. 6. Hut where the blind Sagid lived. 7. House for school-children. 8. The new summertime residence. 9. The village with about 200 huts. 10. The Princess: A mountain formation with several loose rocks, about a half-hour walk from the mission station. 11. Holy trees by the riverside. Under these trees women of the village gathered to pray in times of need. The riverbed is dry for most of the year.

distinctly Muslim characteristics. These were,
- The use of Muslim names
- The prayers
- Fasting during Ramadan
- The ritual slaughtering of animals in the name of Allah

One custom that spread among the converts to Islam was the practice of *infibulation*, a type of female circumcision also known as Pharonic circumcision.[104]

104   K. G. Rodén 1913, 223.

In Closing

In his book, *Mensa. Något om Dess Land och Folk* [...] (*Mensa. Something about the Land and People* [...], 1907, pp. 62–63, K. G. Rodén writes,

> A general belief in God is regarded as something self-evident. [...] The ideas that the people have about life after death and the resurrection are rather muddled, even though they don't deny these articles of faith. Those who have gone over to Mohammedanism have neither understood the new teaching entirely nor been able to free themselves from their old, deviant versions of Christianity. [...] However, they still observe, in part, Christian festivals and days of rest, take part in Christian prayers for rain and have a great sense of awe for Mary. There is no pronounced fanaticism against Christians. Often one hears statements like, "God has created both Christians and Muhammedans. Each and every one should fear God in his own way and can be saved by his faith.

When Jesus had fed the Five Thousand, according to chapter six of the Gospel of John, He told His disciples "Gather the pieces that are left over. Let nothing be wasted." (John 6:12). This verse came to my mind after I had read K. J.'s chapter on the Mensa people and their history. Commenting on the period after the middle of the 18th century, when large sections of the Mensa population had embraced Islam, K. J. points to Muslim forenames, like Ali, and Christian surnames like Waldés, giving the combination Ali Waldés." He also writes that the Mensa people kept Christian festivals, such as the observance of the two Sabbath days, and the festival known as 'Going Mariam'.

These references remind one of pieces of bread left over from a banquet of bygone days. What story do these "pieces of bread" tell? To what extent were these "crumbs of bread" from the religious past of the Mensa people gathered and used in the missionary activities of the Swedes and their Kenisha co-workers? As we shall see in coming sections in this book, Mensa culture and history was more attuned to Evangelical Christianity than was Kunama culture and history. The speed with which the faith took root among the Mensa suggests that the pre-existing Christian vestiges served as a fertile ground for Evangelical Christianity. Has this phenomenon been studied? The subject could constitute a fertile field of research. Such a study too would surely throw light on the subject of intercultural encounters and the role of language and symbols in the meeting and interaction of different religious traditions. (Ed.)

A Church festival at the monastery of Inda Abbona, near Addi Ugri.   Photo: Mikael Holmer

Orthodox priests and the faithful on a festive occasion.

Chapter Three

Orthodox Roots of the ECE (I):

By Ezra Gebremedhin And K. J. Lundström

Introduction

He was born in Wekki Dibba, Hamasen, the only child to his parents, both of whom were descended from families of Orthodox Tewahdo priests. To the dismay of his parents, he had taken to the way of the Kenisha. Though already a priest in the Orthodox Church, he had become one of the *Readers*. As if that was not enough, he and his young wife had expressed readiness to leave home and hearth to go to a distant land as messengers of the Gospel. They and their Kenisha brothers and sisters had been overwhelmed by the good news of God's unmerited grace towards the sinner, the gift of salvation, for the sake of the redemptive death of Christ. And now, this young priest and his wife had heard an inner call, an irresistible summons to mission. In 1897 they took their daughter and went to Oromo land in Ethiopia, the original goal of the missionary venture of the SEM. Interestingly enough, among those who both inspired and encouraged this young Eritrean priest in his resolve, was the Oromo, Onesimos Nesib, who was still in Eritrea at the time.

The young man from Wekki Dibba served both as an Orthodox priest and as a Bible teacher of Evangelical conviction among his fold in Bojji, western Ethiopia. He died in April 1905 in a sudden fire, while trying to save the mule of a neighbour from a burning *tukul* (hut).

His name was Gebre-Ewostatweos Ze-Mikael (1865–1905) and his wife's name was Gumesh Wolde-Mikael (1878–1962).[105] Gebre-Ewostatewos is a classical example of Kenisha who were once nurtured in the very bosom of The Orthodox Tewahdo Church. Many were to follow in his footsteps.

When A. Kolmodin visited Eritrea in 1908–1909, a course for evangelists was in progress in Asmara. He writes,

> There are no less than five former deacons from the Abyssinian Church in this course for evangelists. These are Habtemariam (age 20) from Däk Audi; Tesfo (age 25) from Geschnashim, both of whom were from the district of Bellesa; Wolde-Kristos (age 26) from Okkedubba [Wekki Dibba], in the district of Zazega; Tedla (age 23) from Adi-Bellaj in the district of Adi-Ugri; and Gobesaj (age 24) from Tigrai. The rest were Kahsai (age 19) from Humberti in the district of Zazega, Bahta (age 21) and Jaso [Iyasu] (aged 23) both of whom were from the village of Zazega, Gebra Hätt (age 23) from Sager [Zagir]; Kidano (age 30) from Ad Tekelesan, within the district of Bellesa and Hidego (age 19) from Tigrai.[106]

What was the ethos of the Orthodox Tewahdo Church in whose bosom Gebre-Ewostatewos, his forbears and many of the Kenisha like him had been nurtured? What were its main historical, doctrinal and cultural features? And what was it in the preaching of the missionaries of the SEM that Orthodox Christians like Gebre-Ewostatewos experienced as something new, indeed as *the pearl of great price* to be shared with others, near and far, as far away as in Oromo country? This chapter and the one which follows it will seek to answer these questions. But first some background material to the history of the Orthodox Tewahdo Church.

---

105 Arén 1978, 386–393; Emmanuel Abraham, 1995, 12. See also Nordlander, "The Missiological Strategy of Niguse Tashu, Gebre Ewostatewos Ze-Mikael and Onesimos Nesib" in *Missiology and Linguistics. Papers Presented at the First Institute of the Centennial of the Bible Translation into Oromo,* Addis Ababa 1999, 29–34.

106 A. Kolmodin 1909, 64. (Ed.)

It should be pointed out at the outset that, until it became autocephalous, i.e. an autonomous church with its own Patriarch, the Orthodox Tewahdo Church of Eritrea was a province of the Ethiopian Orthodox Tewahdo Church. Its history is therefore intimately connected with that of its Ethiopian counterpart.[107]

Initiatives to link the Church in Eritrea with the Coptic Church in Egypt were taken after Eritrea's independence in 1991. The same year Pope Shenuda III consecrated two Eritrean bishops for service in the United States and the United Kingdom. The first moves to form a Holy Synod came, however, on September 28, 1993. Five Eritrean bishops were consecrated on Pentecost Day (June 9) 1994. One can say that the Holy Synod of an Eritrean Orthodox Tewhado Church came into being on this day. On May 7, 1998, Pope Shenuda consecrated Abune Fillipos as Patriarch of the Eritrean Orthodox Church, thus establishing the autocephaly (autonomy) of the new church.[108]

Orthodox Tewahdo Church of Ethiopia and Eritrea
Early Contacts

Jewish practices in the Aksumite kingdom have been associated with the coming of the Ark of the Covenant to Axum, the influx of Diaspora Jews from the island of Elephantine (Egypt) on the Nile to the same region, the immigration of Yemeni converts to Judaism, or to Yemeni Jews who intermarried with the Agew of Semien. The first bishop of Aksum, *Abune* Selama, Kesaté Berhan (The Revealer of Light), was consecrated by the Patriarch of Alexandria around 350 AD.[109] According

---

107 An excellent source of up to date information on the political, cultural histories of Ethiopia and Eritrea is the new series known as *Encyclopaedia Aethiopica*, (*EAE*) so far available in four volumes. The article entitled "Christianity" by Stuart Munro-Hay provides a compact but rich introduction on the Orthodox Tewahdo Church. (*EAE*, Vol. 1, 2003, 717–727). There is no single, exhaustive book on the Orthodox Tewahdo Church. There are however a number of sources which provide adequate material on its history and teachings. See Littmann in the larger work *Geschichte der Christlichen Orients*, edited by C. Brockelmann. (Littmann 1907, 187–246). See also Doresse 1967, especially pp 62–89, Atiya 1968, Hastings 1994, Isichei 1995 and Meinardus 2000. The bibliography contains a more comprehensive list of books on the Orthodox Tewahdo Church. (Ed.)

108 See Meinardus 2000, 28. The present Patriarch of the Orthodox Tewahdo Church of Eritrea, the fourth in office following the removal of his predecessor, Abune Antonios, under strained circumstances, is Abune Diyosqoros. (Ed.)

109 Trimingham 1952, 21–22, Ullendorff 1973, 96–97.

to several sources, the Holy Scriptures were translated from Greek into Ge'ez, the local language of the Axumite kingdom, at the time of *Abune Selama*. Other sources maintain that this was done by the Nine Saints in the 5th and 6th centuries from a Syriac original. [110]

Burning Theological Issues – Shared with other Churches of Christendom

There was a tradition of controversial questions which the Orthodox Tewahdo Church shared with the Christian Churches at large, and a tradition of controversial questions which were more or less home-grown, though these too were not free from external influence. The first category of questions has to do with Christology and Trinitarian Theology. Issues like the divinity of Christ, the question of how many natures there are in Him, reconciling the idea of God's absolute unity and the idea of Persons within the godhead, the issue of the Holy Spirit and of whether He proceeds (comes out) from the Father only or also from the Son, belong to the first category of questions. The controversial questions which are home-grown have to do with different views of the Incarnation, i.e. the assumption of manhood by the divine Son of God.

Issues that Engaged the Church at Large

The Christian Church needed to grapple with a number of burning theological issues in the early centuries of its life. As we have already indicated, Orthodox Christianity in Eritrea was, in matters of teaching and church life, part and parcel of the Ethiopian Orthodox Church, with its close historical connections with the Coptic Church of Egypt. This meant that Orthodox Christianity in Eritrea too accepted the decisions of the first three councils of the Universal Church. The first of

---

110 See article "Bible Vorlage: Syriac, Hebrew, Coptic Arabic" in EAE, Vol. 1. 2003, p. 565 by Michael A. Knibb; and article "Bible Canon" by Peter Brandt in EAE, Vol. 1 (2003), A-C, 571–573. For a concise presentation of the historical background of the Orthodox Tewahdo Church see Edward Ullendorff's book The Ethiopians. An Introduction to Country and People (1973), especially the chapter entitled "Religion and the Church". See also Jones-Monroe's book A History of Ethiopia (1935), especially pages 26–43 (Ed.). Qeshi Asfaha, President of the Evangelical Church of Eritrea, maintains that the impact made by James Baradaeus (with whom the name 'Jacobites' is associated), a prominent preacher of the Monophysite faith in the north of Eritrea (Sudan) during the middle of the sixth century', should be studied. He refers to Trimingham 1952, 40, 60. (Ed.)

these was the Council of Nicaea (325) that condemned the teaching of Arius (d. 336), who denied the divinity of Christ. The second was the first Council of Constantinople (381) that affirmed the divinity of the Holy Spirit and condemned such theologians as Eunomius (d. 394) who had questioned the divinity of the Holy Spirit. The third was the Council of Ephesus (431), summoned at the urgings of Cyril of Alexandria (d. 444). At this council, the Antiochene theologian Nestorius was condemned for questioning the propriety of the designation of *Theotókos'* (Mother of God) for the Virgin Mary. Two leading theologians from the schools of Alexandria and Antioch, Cyril of Alexandria and John of Antioch (d. 441), came to a written agreement (The Formula of Union of 433), on a number of theological issues. However, the tension between the two sees continued after the death of these two theologians. The Ethiopian Orthodox Church and, by extension, the Orthodox Tewahdo Church in Eritrea, still regard Cyril of Alexandria as their main teacher. Their most important doctrinal manual bears the name *Qerlos*.[111]

The Term 'Bahriy' (Nature)

There is one word that comes up again and again in the theological and polemical writings of the Orthodox Tewahdo Church. It is the word *bahriy* (nature, with its background in the Greek: *physis*).

By the beginning of the fifth century, all the Christian Churches taught that there were two components in the person of Christ: a divine and a human one, united fully but without confusion (mixture) or change. The question was: should one speak of *two* natures in Christ (thus underlining the distinction between the two components in his person) or should one speak of only *one* nature (thus underlining the complete unity of the two components in his person)?

In either case, the concern of the theologians was the maintenance of both the integrity (unreduced composition) and unity of the person of Christ. Here it should be pointed out that two pedagogical pictures were used to underline this unity. The first was that of the unity of body and soul, in which the body represents the human nature and the soul the divine nature. The other picture is that of a red-hot piece

---

111   See article on "Christology" by Bandrés and Zanetti in *EAE*. Vol.1 (2003), A-C, 728–732, and Ezra Gebremedhin 1977, 25. On Cyril's life and works in general see pp. 13–33. (Ed.)

The Church of Qiddus Giorgis (St. George) in Tse'azzega, the centre of the Orthodox Tewahdo priests who were known as Bible Readers, and who became the pioneers of the Evangelical Church of Eritrea. Picture from the book "Twoldo Medhen" by Rosa Holmer, 1938.

of metal, in which the metal represents the human nature and the glowing heat represents the divine nature. In both examples there was, it was believed, complete unity but not a mixture. The rule was: "Distinguish but do not separate!"

Patriarch Dioscorus (d. 454) of the Coptic Church of Egypt, and Eutyches (d. 454), the archimandrite (abbot) of a large monastery at Constantinople, taught that there was only *one* nature in Christ after the Incarnation, i.e. the becoming or assuming of flesh by the Son of God. This teaching has been traditionally known as *Monophysitism* (One Nature Teaching), although the Tewahdo and their comrades in the faith (e.g. those in the Coptic, Syrian Orthodox, Armenian churches) object to being labeled Monophysites. Both Dioscorus and Eutyches and their teaching of "one nature" were condemned at the Council of Chalcedon in 451. This council upheld the teaching that there are two natures (i.e. the divine and human) in Christ, after the Incarnation.[112]

112   Kelly 1980, 310ff; Latourette 1975, 170–172. The teaching of two natures in Christ is the official teaching of the Lutheran Church to which the missionaries of the SEM belonged. See Tappert (Ed), *The Book of Concord* 1959, 594, 600. (Ed.)

The Coptic Orthodox Church and the churches related to it (The Orthodox Tewahdo churches of both Ethiopia and Eritrea belong to this category) have dissociated themselves from the teaching of Eutyches. However, they have continued to adhere to the teaching of *one nature*, propagated by Dioscorus of Alexandria. Discussions between the Oriental Orthodox Churches (adherents of the "One nature" teaching) and the Eastern Orthodox Churches (which include the Orthodox Churches of Russia, Greece, Rumania and which are adherents of the "Two nature" teaching) have led to a very high level of mutual understanding and agreement on the issue of *nature* in Christology. In short, the different views around the term *bahriy* are no longer regarded as divisive.[113]

The Procession of the Holy Spirit (The 'Filioque' Issue)

Another subject that was sometimes taken up by theologians of the Orthodox Tewahdo Church in their encounters with Swedish missionaries and the Kenisha was the question of the *procession* of the Holy Spirit. A basic Trinitarian formula of the Early Church maintains that The Father begets (i.e., gives birth), the Son is begotten (is born) and that the Holy Spirit proceeds (or comes out of). The question is: From whom does the Holy Spirit proceed? Only from the Father or from both the Father *and the Son*, (Latin: *filioque*)? The Orthodox (i.e. broadly speaking, the entire Eastern block of Christianity) teach that the Holy Spirit proceeds only from the Father. They base this teaching on John 15:26. Churches in the West (and these include the Lutheran Church, to which the missionaries of the SEM belonged), teach that the Holy Spirit proceeds from both the Father and the Son, since there is complete unity of being and *movement* in the Trinity. However, the issue of the procession of the Holy Spirit didn't seem to have engaged

---

113   On conversations on this issue between the Eastern Orthodox Church and the Oriental Orthodox Churches see the report entitled Towards Unity. The Theological Dialogue Between the Orthodox Church and The Oriental Orthodox Churches. (eds. Christine Chaillot and Alexander Belopopsky) 1998, Geneva. The report covers discussions held on different levels from 1970 to 1997. Of particular importance is "The Second Agreed Statement and Recommendations to Churches, Chambésy, Switzerland, 23–28 September 1990" (Chaillot and Belopopsky, 63–64). The latest discussions are from 2005, in Sigtuna, Sweden. Discussions continue, though at a slower pace. A delegation from four Orthodox churches of both traditions, here in Sweden, visited Patriarch Kirill of the Moscow Patriarchate in April 2010. (Ed.)

the Orthodox and the Kenisha in frequent and intense discussions.[114]

The home-grown controversies revolved around the question, "How and when did the union of Christ's humanity with his divinity take place?" Some scholars maintain that divergent views on the answers to this question came to the fore at a synod of the Orthodox Tewahdo Church around the year 1621.[115]

The Council of Boru Meda
  - Place: Boru Meda, Wällo, Ethiopia. Date: May 29, 1878
  - Conveners: *Atsé* Yohannes and *Nigus* Minilik
  - Subject: Severe Dissension around the question: How many births can one attribute to Christ?
  - Contending Parties:
  1. Proponents of Two Births (*Hulät Lidät*) – Tigrai and Gojjam
  2. Proponents of Three Births (*Sost Lidät*) – Shewa
  - Verdict: In favour of Two Births

The Council of Boru Meda – State Intervention in a Doctrinal Conflict

The controversy around this latter issue came to a head at the Council of Boru Meda in Wällo, Ethiopia on Ginbot [May] 22, 1870, according to the Julian calendar, in the presence of Emperor Yohannes and *Nigus* (King) Minilik.[116] The two potentates felt that the controversies around the different understandings of the person of Christ, which were tearing the country apart, should be settled once for all. But what was

---

114 On this question see Ezra Gebremedhin 1998, 113. On dialogue on this and other central theological issues between Lutheran theologians at the University of Tübingen in Germany and the Patriarchate of Constantinople in the years between 1573 and 1581, see Mastrantonis 1982. This is indeed a work which should be available in Tigrinya, even though the issues taken up in it reflect the views of the Eastern Orthodox and not those of the Oriental Orthodox, to which family the Orthodox Tewahdo Church in Eritrea belongs. (Ed.).

115 O'Mahoney 1982, 134. The Ethiopian historian Bahru Zewde writes, "The controversy was ignited by Jesuit theology, more specifically the doctrine of the nature of Christ. It was the absence of a unanimous response to the Jesuit doctrinal challenge that gave birth to the diverse doctrines that have continued to baffle students of Ethiopian history." Bahru Zewde 2002, 14. (Ed.)

116 See Eloi Ficquet's article "Boru Meda" in *EAE*, Vol. 1, 2003, A–C, 609.

the substance of the controversy? Many have written on this question, which is often difficult to pin down. We shall let a Kenisha, writing in Sweden and in the Swedish language in 1890, give us his views on the subject. Here are the words of *Qeshi* (Pastor) Marqos Girmai, rendered into English,

> Another teaching which has engaged the theological world in Ethiopia intensely is that of a threefold birth of Christ. At the beginning of our century [meaning the beginning of 1800], a spiritual authority from Gondar, the capital of Abyssinia, taught that Christ was born three times. The first birth was from the Father, in eternity, the second was from the Virgin Mary in time, and the third was a birth through baptism. This theologian maintained, namely, that baptism was a means of regeneration and that even Christ must be born anew. In other words Christ, who had emptied himself of His divine glory by becoming man, must be exalted again to divine majesty and honour through baptism.

> One calls the followers of this teaching kibet [*qibat*] – meaning *anointing*, since they teach that the Saviour became anointed through the pouring out of the Holy Spirit to become the King of Peace and to be restored to the possession of honour and power which He had before being born in time. Their teaching approaches that of the Nestorians since they have in fact rejected the significance of the teaching that Mary is Mother of God. [...] Those who defend this heresy passionately are, primarily, the Shewans. [...] The Abun (Marqos Girmai calls him *the bishop of the Abyssinian Church*) hurled the one excommunication after the other at this heresy, but in vain. Finally, in 1856 Teodorus (sic) forced the Shewans and their king (Sahle Sellassie), by dint of battle, to submit to the pope (sic) of our church. The supporters of the new heresy called the teaching that had forced them into submission *karahajmanot* (Sword-faith). The struggle still continues with undiminished strength, but the new teaching has not been recognized as yet anywhere, as the official confession of the State Church. The teaching of the Church on this subject is: Jesus Christ, God's Son, Mary's Son, has been glorified through a twofold birth.[117]

Was *Qeshi* Marqos Girmai not aware of the measures taken at Boru Meda? We don't know. In any case, he does not mention the council and its decisions. We shall therefore complement the passage quoted above with the words of a contemporary Ethiopian scholar, Professor

---

117   Marqos Girmai 1890, 204–205. (Ed.)

Getatchew Haile,

> The origin of the controversy was the faith in either two births or
> three births. "The Son was born of the Father before the (creation of
> the) World – one birth. Then He was born of Holy Mary through the
> Holy Spirit: second birth. Therefore Christ became God by nature, in His
> body, through the Union (of godhead and manhood). The faith which
> the Tewahdo adhere to (especially in Tigrai) is this. The other party
> (especially those from Shewa) affirms the two births but adds that the
> body of Christ underwent a further birth by Grace and thus became the
> Son of God either at the Annunciation by the Angel Gabriel or at His
> baptism by John's hand at the River Jordan: third birth. These people
> say, "Son of Mary in the flesh, Son of God by Grace". This is why those
> who believe in three births are called *Children of Grace* [Yetsegga Lijjotch].
> The judges (Emperor Yohannes and *Nigus* Minilik) judged in favour of
> those who believed in two births.[118]

Was there a biblical basis for these controversies or were the
controversies of a purely theoretical nature? Professor Getatchew Haile
has pointed out that the term *qibat* (unction) in the controversy goes
back to the words in the book of Acts 10:38 and that the reference to
several births goes back to Romans 8:29, where the term *bekwr* (firstborn) is used.[119]

Since the Orthodox Tewahdo Church, particularly on the highlands
of Midri Bahri (today's Eritrea), and the Monastery of Debre Bizen, had
close relations to the ecclesiastical authorities at such religious centres
as Axum, the Christological teaching that was favoured in Midri Bahri
was that of Two Births.

Though motivated by the search for truth, a number of the
controversies presented in this chapter are indeed highly theoretical
and at times confusing, not least for the average reader. Nevertheless,
they are a part of the heritage of the people who now inhabit Northern
Ethiopia and large parts of Eritrea. And a heritage cries out to be known
and recorded, whether it is subsequently embraced or rejected.

---

118 Getatchew Haile 2000, 266. Bahru writes: "the party which still claimed to espouse the
orthodox doctrine preferred to call itself Tewahdo (Union), although its opponents
gave it the more pejorative appellation of Karra (Knife)." Bahru Zewde 2002, 14. (Ed.)

119 Getatchew Haile 1991, 986. Acts 10:38 reads, "… how God anointed Jesus of Nazareth
with the Holy Spirit and power, and how he went around doing good and healing all
who were under the power of the devil, because God was with him." RSV. Romans
8:29 reads, "For those God foreknew he also predestined to be conformed to the
likeness of his Son, that he might be the firstborn *bekwr* among many brothers." (Ed.)

Important Dates in the History of the Church (Gregorian Calendar)

30–33 Pentecost (The Birthday of the Church). Acts 2.

Ca. 50 The Council of Jerusalem (The First Council of the Church). Acts 15.

325   The Council of Nicaea. Assertion of the divinity of Christ.

Ca. 350–370. An officially established Christian Church in the Axumite Kingdom.

451   The Council of Chalcedon. Split around the question of the number of "natures" in Christ.

622   Birth of Islam and the Prophet's hijra (emigration from Mecca to Medina).

1054 The Final Split between the Church in the West (Rome) and East (Constantinople).

1176 Peter Valdes or Waldes, Father of the Waldensian movement in Italy, embarks upon his mission.

1517 Birth of the Reformation. Posting of Martin Luther's 95 theses.

1532 The Waldensian movement becomes a church in the spirit of the Reformation.

1593 The Uppsala Convocation which confirmed the adherence of the Church of Sweden to Lutheranism.

1856 The Swedish Evangelical Mission (SEM) founded.

1866 The first three missionaries of the SEM arrive in Massawa.

1926 The Evangelical Church of Eritrea founded.

1998 Abune Filippos consecrated as the first Patriarch of an autocephalous (autonomous) Orthodox Tewahdo Church in Eritrea.

2006 The ECE and The Lutheran Church of Eritrea are united to constitute the Evangelical Lutheran Church of Eritrea.

The Lutheran Missionaries and the Controversial Issues

As far as Orthodox Tewahdo theology was concerned, what we have described above was the lay of the land that awaited the Swedish missionaries. Having received a thorough theological education in Sweden, many of the missionaries were well acquainted with the Christological and Trinitarian issues that engaged the Orthodox Tewahdo, although their knowledge of the finer Tewahdo distinctions in this theology may very well have been limited.

Lutheran Christology has always been regarded as well attuned to the Christology of Cyril of Alexandria, the main teacher of the Orthodox Tewahdo Church. It is true that on the question of the *nature* or *natures* in the person of Christ, the Lutherans, who were after all heirs of a western, Catholic church tradition, followed the decisions of the Council of Chalcedon (451). This council taught that there are two natures in Christ after the Incarnation, a divine and a human nature which subsist in his person in complete unity without confusion, without change, without division, without separation.[120] And Chalcedon was not, as we have mentioned above, popular among the Orthodox Tewahdo. The Swedes were surely aware of this fact and therefore kept a low profile on this and other controversial issues. Luckily, on the issue of the *births* of the Son of God, the Lutherans held, in conformity with the official line in the Orthodox Tewahdo Church, that one could only speak of two, and not three, births of the Son of God: a birth in Eternity from the Father and a birth in time form the Virgin Mary.

One thing was clear: For the Swedish missionaries, the primary target of missionary outreach were the Oromo, not the Orthodox Tewahdo community. Hence, they, who now found themselves delayed on the highlands of Eritrea, preferred the simple proclamation of the Gospel of grace among the Tewahdo to polemics on the intricacies of high theology. It is symptomatic that the signature melody at the commissioning of missionaries in Sweden had the recurring words,

> Go, go, sower man, go!
>
> Go, go, sower man, go!
>
> (Hasten) the noble seed to sow
>
> Go, go, sower man go![121]

---

120 Kelly 1980, 339–340. See also article on *Council of Chalcedon* by Witold Witakowski in *EAE*, Vol. 1, 2003, 709–711. (Ed.)

121 This is a free translation of the refrain of the Swedish hymn which begins with the words, "Tänk, vilken underbar nåd av Gud, att du får vara hans sändebud…" (Imagine! How wondrous God's grace is, that you are allowed to be His messenger …) See hymn nr. 524 in the Swedish hymnal, Sionstoner, Edition of 1972, Evangeliska Fosterlands-Stiftelsens Förlag. Stockholm. The words are inspired by the Parable of the Sower in Matthew chapter 13:1–23.

In Closing

The purpose of this chapter has been to portray the general theological landscape that met the missionaries of the SEM and their Kenisha colleagues when they came in touch with Orthodox Tewahdo theologians. Orthodox priests and theologians must have engaged Swedish missionaries and their Kenisha co-religionists in the discussions of the finer distinctions of high Christology and Trinitarian Theology. It is interesting to read that the missionaries of the SEM were first suspected, by the monks of Debre Bizen, of being adherents of Nestorius. Per Eric Lager writes,

> They [the monks] were particularly interested in discussions about the two natures of Christ and were happy to learn that we did not adhere to the Nestorian doctrine as they had believed.[122]

However, there is a glaring lack of deeper studies into Patristic or Orthodox Tewahdo theology in the written material that has come down to us from the missionaries of the SEM and their Kenisha co-religionists.[123] In connection with his visit to Asmara in 1905, as leader of the Princeton University Expedition to Abyssinia, Enno Littmann writes,

> From the merely scholarly standpoint the work of the missionaries in studying these languages (i.e. Tigriña, Tigrë, Kunama, Galla and Suaheli) and creating written literatures where formerly there were none, is of the greatest value and importance.[124]

Some of the Swedish missionaries to Eritrea were indeed excellent Linguists, Anthropologists and Ethnographers. However, research in Theology was not given comparable attention.[125] The central point, the

---

122 Arén 1978, 174. On Lager and the Orthodox see Beskow 1884, 206–208, 234–235. (Ed.)
123 An exception was *Aleqa* Tayye Gebre-Mariam, who has left several scholarly works behind him. See Arén 1999, 19–58. and Gebremedhin 1998, 101–120.
124 Littmann 1907, 4.
125 Some Eritrean Catholics have, on the other hand, left an impressive tradition of scholarship behind them. Examples are *Abba* Jerome (ca. 1881–1983), a linguist and theologian, *Abba* Tecle Mariam Semharai Selim, a scholar in the field of the Sacraments and the Liturgy, with several works to his name (see Teklehaymanot 1998, 144–145) and *Abba* Paulos Tzadua (translator of the *Fitha Nägäst* into English, 1968), a graduate in both Canon Law and Jurisprudence from the University of Milan. *Abba* Jerome, who took part in a number of diplomatic missions on behalf of Ethiopia, and who rubbed shoulders with illustrious European Semitists and Orientalists, wrote a number of books, the majority of which are still unpublished. See article on "Jerome, *Abba* ", by Alain Rouaud, in *EAE* 3, p. 272.

focus of the theology of these Evangelical Lutheran missionaries from Sweden, was the Atonement, the Substitutionary (or Vicarious) Death of Christ as the basis of salvation. A recurring theme in their theology and hymns was the Blood of Christ and its power to cleanse from sin. Though not enemies of scholarship and theological inquiry, they held forth the paramount importance of the simple, personal faith which relied solely on the Crucified. The Kenisha are heirs of this tradition.

The long range effect of such an attitude seems to have been a gradual, almost imperceptible, relinquishing of the demands of prolonged theological studies at a high level of abstraction.

As we shall see in our continuing narrative, the first batch of candidates for the priesthood among the Kenisha in Eritrea were trained at Johannelund's Mission Institute in Stockholm, a centre of learning in its own right. The practice of sending students to Sweden for theological studies was, however, interrupted after the storm caused by the marriage of *Qeshi* Marqos Girmai to a Swedish missionary, Regina Johansson, a storm exasperated by Italian racial sanctions. The ruling against sending students to Sweden led to a gradual eclipse in the tradition of a high-level theological education within the ECE, a trend which has still not been reversed. There are indeed some exceptions to this statement, especially in view of developments during the period between the early nineteen-sixties and the nineteen-eighties, when pastors of the ECE did in fact undertake post-graduate work. In 1987, after ten years as General Secretary in the ECE, Pastor Yacob Tesfay left for the Institute for Ecumenical Research in Strasbourg. He was Research Professor for five years and director for four. While there, he edited *The Scandal of a Crucified World* (1994) and authored *Liberation and Orthodoxy: The Promises and Failures of Inter Confessional Dialogue* (1997) and *Holy Warriors, Infidels and Peacemakers in Africa* (2010). However that was a later development. We must first go back to the issue of dialogue and polemics between the first Kenisha and representatives of the Orthodox Tewahdo Church. (Ed.)

A close-up of a part of the highland region in Eritrea with some of the places mentioned in the following chapter: Nefasit, Debre-Bizen (Debra-Bizen), Asmara, Addi Qontsi (Addi Qunzi) and River Anseba.

Chapter Four

Orthodox Roots of the ECE (II)

Dialogue and Polemics

By Ezra Gebremedhin And K. J. Lundström

Introduction

Perched on top of one of Eritrea's highest peaks about 25 kilometres from the capital city, Asmara, on the road to Massawa, not far from Nefasit, stands the monastery of Debre-Bizen (DB), also known as Inda Abune Filippos. From its elevated position, the monastery offers an awe-inspiring view. On a beautiful day, one can let one's eyes wonder over the plains which start at the foot of the monastery and stretch out to the dim shores of the Red Sea. The winding road from Asmara to Massawa is part of this wonderful scenery. On a visit to the monastery in 1997, the editor of this work was told that on a clear night one could see the lights of Massawa!

Abune Filippos, a monk who had come from Adiabo in the neighbouring Ethiopian region of Tigrai, is believed to have founded the monastery around 1132 A.D, according to the *Mashafa Heregreg* or *Hassaba Berhan*, the book used traditionally for the reckoning of dates at Debre Bizen, or in 1360 (ca 1368) according to the Julian and Gregorian methods of reckoning respectively.[126]

The establishment and development of the monastic movement in what is now northern Ethiopia and Eritrea goes back to the period stretching from 400–700 AD. The founders of the movement are believed to have come from Syria and Egypt. Orthodox Tewahdo tradition maintains that most of the pioneer monks were originally attached to the monastery of St. Pachomius in Egypt. Debre Sina and Debre Libanos, two monasteries in today's Eritrea, were established by Yohannes Kama and are perhaps the oldest. The monks of DB and the faithful revere the memory of the monk, Abune Ewostatewos (ca 1273–1352). He and another monk (a relative) by the name of Daniel

---

126 See the articles "Appunti in margine a una nuova ricerca sui conventi eritrei" (Marginal Notes on a New Research on Eritrean Monasteries), by Alessandro Bausi and Gianfrancesco Lusini in *RSE* Volume XXXVI, 1992. Roma-Napoli 1994, 5–36; "Su Alcuni Manoscritti Presso Comunita Monastiche Dell'Eritrea" by Alessandro Bausi in *RSE* Volume XXXVIII, 1994. Roma-Napoli 1996, 13–69; and "Su Alcuni Manoscritti Presso Comunita Monastiche Dell'Eritrea. Parte Seconda." by Alessandro Bausi in *RSE* Volume XXXIX, 1995. Roma-Napoli 1997, 25–48. The studies were part of a wider project led by Professor Irma Taddia, attached to the Department of Historical Disciplines of the University of Bologna. The articles provide geographical locations, glimpses into history, topography, human environment, buildings, personalities and literary history as well as passing comments on the contents of specific MSS. Rich footnotes provide further facts on sources and literary studies.
 Among the monasteries in Eritrea mentioned in the first article are: Dabra Abuna Abranyos, Enda Abuna Buruk Amlak, Dabra Sige, Dabra Duhuhan, Enda *Abba* Enderyas, Dabra Abuna Busus (Bitsu'i?) Amlak, Dabra Qusquam, Dabra Marqorewos, Dabra Maryam, Dabra Bizan, Enda Abuna Takla, Dabra Libanos. For more recent articles on Tewahdo monasteries, see Gianfrancesco Lusini's entries in *EAE*, vol.2, (2005, 39–40, 41–42, 45–46, 50–51.) It has been pointed out to the editor that *Tsa'ida'imba* (lit. "White Mountain" in Anseba) should be numbered among the famous monasteries of Eritrea. (Ed.)

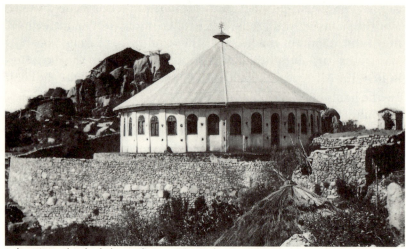

Debre Bizen, Church of Abune Filippos. Picture taken in 1930.

of Gere'alta in Tigrai belonged to a movement that struggled for the right to celebrate Saturday as a Sabbath-day, alongside Sunday. Abune Filippos, the founder of DB, belonged to the same circle.

This movement was to suffer much persecution before its teachings on the subject of Saturday as Sabbath was fully accepted.

Professor Getatchew Haile writes,

> One of the leaders of the opposition was Abba Ewostatewos (ca. 1273–1352). [...] Ewostatewos left his monastery in Sara'e (Eritrea) and went to Egypt, accompanied by a few of his disciples, to seek the support of the patriarch himself. To his disappointment, the view of the patriarch Benjamin (1327–1399) was not different from that of his opponents. Ewostatewos died in Armenia. In Ethiopia his followers left the church and established their own fully independent monastic communities. Ewostatewos' most important and immediate descendants founded important monasteries, including Absadi [founder] of Dabra Maryam (Qohayyen), Marqorios of Dabra Sarabi, Gabra Iyyasus of Dabsan (or Dabra San), Matewos of Barbarre, Gabra Masqal of May Qwerqwer, Buruk Amlak of Maraquz (Märaguz?) and Sewa (Tsiwwa?) Dengel of Bur. All these disciples became monastic leaders with many followers, including the celebrated Fileppos, the founder of Dabra Bizen (in Eritrea), which is one of the leading religious centres of Ethiopia even today. Since the council of Dabra Mitmaq (1450), at which the church

accepted their position, the Ewostatewosites have again become part of the established church.[127]

In 1938, when Abune Marqos (1877–1953), a monk of DB, was elected as Eritrea's first Eritrean bishop, another monk by the name of Merigéta Fesseha Bahta composed a passionate eulogy in honour of both the monastery and the new bishop.[128] On my visit to DB in 1997, I was told that an ecumenical committee had started collecting funds for the repair and extension of the monastery, with the support and encouragement of the government.[129]

Why Begin with an Orthodox Monastery?

Why begin a chapter on the history of the ECE by writing about Debre Bizen? Two answers can be given to this question.

In the first place, DB has been the flagship of Orthodox Tewahdo Christianity in both Ethiopia and Eritrea, the main defender of the Faith among the Orthodox Tewahdo against both Catholic and Protestant missionary efforts.[130] Furthermore, no institution of the Orthodox Tewahdo Church in Eritrea has been engaged in dialogue and debate with the Swedish Evangelical Mission and the Kenisha as actively as has DB. To be acquainted with DB, its history and its theological tradition is, for the Kenisha, to acquire knowledge of the main challenger and dialogue-partner of their forefathers in the faith.

There is a second answer to our question. DB happens to be in the same geographical region in Eritrea where the earliest highland centres of Evangelical Christianity are located. Asmara, Beleza and Tseʻazzega are

---

127 Getatchew Haile 1991, 992–993. On *Gädlä Ewostatewos*, see Lusini 1993, 35–67.
128 Fesseha Bahta 1985–1986, 159–165.
129 According to the resident monks at DB, there were, in 1997, a total of eighty monks who belonged to brotherhood. They lived and worked among the local inhabitants at different places, almost all over Eritrea. In 2007, the number of monks attached to the monastery was reported to be about 200. The monastery has a rich history. Once it was indeed rich in terms of property and money, since it owned land and was able to engage in Agriculture and cattle breeding. At the same time I was highly impressed by the limited number of manuscripts (MSS) that I had occasion to see. The handwriting in most of the MSS is of very high quality. For a more up to date description of the monastery see the article on "Däbrä Bizän" by Gianfrancesco Lusini in *EAE*, Vol 2, 2005, 15–17, and the work *Proceedings of a Workshop on Aspects of Eritrean History*, sponsored by the Cultural Assets Rehabilitation Project (CARP) and published by Hidri Publishers, Asmara, in 2007. (Ed.)
130 See Arén 1978, 174ff. *Birhan Yikun* 1912, 184ff; T. Negash 1987, 129. (Ed.)

all within this area. Having given a survey of the history, culture and religious traditions of Kunama and Mensa, we feel that it is proper that we provide a similar survey for the highland, Christian areas in Eritrea, the third area of origin of the ECE. There is, furthermore, Evangelical literature that reflects contacts and exchanges of theological views with DB.

Written Records on Highland Eritrea and the Centres of Evangelical Christianity

The fact that we have chosen to focus on DB doesn't mean that Swedish missionaries and their Kenisha co-religionists didn't possess knowledge of other centres of Orthodox learning and piety in Eritrea. In 1910, the scholarly Swedish Missionary, Richard Sundström (1869–1919), translated the story known as *The Martyrs of Nagran,* in what is present day Yemen, from Ge'ez to Swedish. This work narrates the story of Arab Christians and their sufferings (due to a persecution encouraged by a Jewish king) during the period 523–524, the fifth year of the reign of Emperor Justinian I (483–565). The version translated by Sundström was unique in the sense that it was, according to Sundström, previously unknown to the churches of the West, even though philologists knew of its existence. Its publication in a European language can be said to be a contribution from Eritrea and, more specifically, the monastery of Debre Sina where Sundström first heard about the work. The work was bound into one volume with the Swedish version of *Aleqa* Tayye's *A Theological Debate before Ras Mengesha.*[131]

In 1916, K-G Rodén, published an article entitled *"Ett besök i munk- och nunneklostret å Debra Sina"* (A Visit to the Monastery and Convent at Debre Sina) in the Swedish mission periodical known as *Varde Ljus* (Let There be Light.) Nils Nilsson, whom we have already mentioned, and his Kenisha co-workers were acquainted with the monastery of *Inda Abbona* near Addi Ugri. Jonas Iwarson and Olle Eriksson visited the monastery of *Debre Menqorios* (Merqorios) in 1911.[132] The editor has in his possession an undated parchment in Amharic, containing an

---

131 Sundström 1910, 1–32. See also article "Nagran" by Alessandro Bausi in *EAE*, vol. 3, 2007, 1114–1116. (Ed.)
132 See Iwarson 1936, 66–71.

The rock of Tsaʻda Imba, in the region of Anseba, with the monastery at the very top.

Orthodox catechetical work entitled *Haymanotä Abäw hawaryat, wäliqanä pappasat wäepiskqoposat* (Book of the Fathers, Apostles, Archbishops and Bishops). The book was copied at the monastery of Debre Sina in Eritrea. A copy of this same book is available at the University of Lund, Sweden, under the designation *Codex Odeberg 3.*

But now back to three documents which deserve special attention. Two of these have a direct link with DB. The first is a narrative from the year 1912 contained in *Birhan Yikun,* under the title, *Nai Wängel Birhan ab Hamasen kämäy ilu käm zi'aton käm itägältsen* (How the Light of the Gospel Entered and was Revealed in Hamasen), written by *Qeshi* Selomon and *Qeshi* Zer'a-Tsion.[133] The second is Rev. Nils Nilsson's

---

133 The narrative by pastors Selomon and Zer'a-Tsion has been published in *Birhan Yikhun,* O. Eriksson 1912, 184–196.

translation into Swedish of *Mäzgäbä Haymanot* – A Treasury of Faith (Swedish: *Trons Skattkammare*).[134] This work originates from Debre Bizen. The third source is Johannes Kolmodin's *Zanta Tsazeggan Hazzegan* from 1912. This work is a collection of oral tradition on the political and cultural history of Hamasen.[135]

Claim of Jewish Connections

There has always been a strong sense of the religious, of God's calling and guidance in the consciousness of the people of the highlands of Eritrea, an awareness of a participation in the calling of the people of Israel. The narrator in *Zanta Tsazeggan Hazzegan*, who stands in this tradition, embellishes his stories with the niceties of the Tigrinya language. His main intention is however, to tell a story.

The material in *Zanta* is an example of a tradition in which history is remoulded in the minds and mouths of storytellers, and woven in minds fertile with imagination, on the basis of a great variety of sources, among which are the Bible and the history of Israel. And in the telling of a story, one must start at the beginning. A question of primary concern in this regard is genealogy. Thus the first chapter of *Zanta*, entitled *The Genealogy of Hamasen* begins with the words,

> This is the genealogy of Hamasen at which we have arrived by inquiring from the great and the knowledgeable.

The chapter continues with the title: *The Queen of Sheba Goes to King Selomon*. Then follows the text itself,

> After Abba Jigo [a colloquial Tigrinya designation for God], had destroyed his entire creation by the flood, he let one called Noah, a chosen one, survive with his three children, Shem, Ham and Japheth, in order that there wouldn't be a gap in mankind's genealogy. Afterwards, Noah gave Egypt and all countries to the East to Shem as an inheritance. He gave Japheth all the country to the West as an inheritance. And to Ham he gave the place where we are, as an inheritance. But about Jerusalim (sic) he said, "Let him who is chosen among you inherit it!"

There is something artless and brisk about the way history is retold in this narrative. These traits come forth in the way the story of the

---

134 Nilsson 1921, 48–77. The work includes brief notes and comments on theology and Church practice. See also E. Gebremedhin pp. 127–143 in *Amidst Crosses and Minarets*, Uppsala University, 1997.

135 For *Zanta* see J. Kolmodin 1912 and Kiros Fre Woldu, 1989.

A series of Orthodox paintings: The two texts in Ge'ez read, "How priests and pure virgins praised our Lady at the monastery of Debre Mitmaq [a monastery in Ethiopia]" and "How the angels bowed for you".

Preparing parchment for the inscription of texts in Ge'ez, Tigrinja or Amharic.

visit of Minilik to his father Selomon is narrated,

> King Selomon received him and honoured him. He appointed him saying,' Go and reign over your mother's home region.' In his company Selomon sent some members of Ruben's, Mosef's [Joseph's[, Minab's

[Binyam's, i.e. Benjamin's], and Judah's tribes. He also sent some of Levi's children so that they would take care of priestly functions. He gave them the Ark of the Covenant named after Minki'el [Michael] to show them the way home. However, the sons of Levi, who knew the ins and outs of the Temple, exchanged the ark named after Minki'el for an ark named after Mariam. After bidding the king farewell, they started on their way. Soon after, the king discovered that they had taken Zion with them and followed them in hot pursuit. Minilik and his family crossed the Red Sea at the place where the children of Israel had done so before. Upon arriving at the crossing, Selomon remembered the fate of Pharaoh and didn't dare to follow them![136]

The fact that the Ark of the Covenant belonged to the period of the Old Testament and that Mary the Mother of Jesus belonged to the period of the New Testament does not seem to bother the narrator. He is not concerned about following the demands of chronology or logic. The story must be retold with all the force and constancy with which tradition has imbued it. This is the kind of oral tradition and understanding of history in which a great number of the members of the Orthodox Tewahdo Church in Eritrea were moulded, around the time when Swedish missionaries arrived in Eritrea. There was a residue of biblical knowledge among these Tewahdo faithful, even though this residue was often embellished with legends.[137] There were, however, also highly qualified theologians in the Orthodox Church. These were well versed in the history and teachings of their church and in the use of polemical tools developed over the centuries.

Examples of Literature from Debre Bizen

There are several works which reflect the erudition of the monks of DB. Some of these are catechetical and polemical in nature. Others are of a hagiographical character. The latter narrate the dramatic stories of persons considered to be saints (Greek: *hágioi*, meaning holy men). An

---

136 J. Kolmodin *Zanta* 1912, 5.
137 In connection with this section of the book, the editor was asked why the *Felasha* (the so-called Ethiopian Jews) were not given more attention. This religious group is not a significant part of the religious map of Eritrea. For facts on the Felasha as such, see the second edition of Henry A. Stern's well-known book from 1862, *Wanderings Among the Felashas in Abyssinia* (1968), Ullendorff 1973, 105–107 and S. Kaplan's *Fils d'Abraham. Les Felashas.* 1998. (Ed.)

example of this category of literature is the *Gädlä Ewostatewos* (EMML Pr.N. 1636). Examples of the first category of catechetical writings are some older works from Debre Bizen now available in print, basically in Amharic, with shorter sections in Ge'ez. Two of these are *Mäshafä Tebäb* (The Book of Wisdom, available in EMML. Pr.N.1064), and *Mäzgäbä Haymanot* (The Treasury of Faith). Their contents take up subjects discussed and debated between Orthodox monks and Protestant missionaries – more specifically Swedish Lutherans missionaries who came to Massawa in 1866.

Mäzgäbä Haymanot (The Treasury of Faith– *Trons Skattkammare* in Swedish) is basically a catechetical work. In his study of this work on the basis of a Swedish translation made by him, with the assistance of an Eritrean called Burru [Birru?], the Swedish missionary Nils Nilsson (1881–1954) writes that the work "[...] was composed by the monks at the monastery of Debre Bizen within our mission area for the benefit [service] of the faithful."[138]

The Narrative of Qeshi Selomon and Qeshi Zer'a-Tsion in Birhan Yikun

It should be pointed out that though the narrators of this story are *Qeshi* Selomon and *Qeshi* Zer'a-Tsion, the main figure and spokesman for those with Evangelical conviction, was *Qeshi* Haile-Ab Tesfai.[139] The two fathers of Evangelical Christianity in Eritrea narrate their story with a quiet sense of conviction, and with hardly any trace of self-pity or bitterness. As the title of the narrative indicates, the first encounter with monks from DB took place in Hamasen.

The point of departure of those who were of Evangelical persuasion was that the Bible and only the Bible [*Tsiruy qal Igziabher* – the pure Word of God] should be the guide and norm for teaching and practice in the Christian Church.[140] Of course these Evangelical fathers were thinking of the Bible with the sixty-six books which they regarded

---

138 Nilsson 1920, 47. Catechism: book of questions and answers on Christian teaching.
139 *Birhan Yikun* 1912, 187. *Qeshi* Haile-Ab and Per Eric Lager were killed by one of the soldiers of *Ra'si* Woldenki'el outside of the church of Qiddus Mikael in Addi Qontsi in July 1876. *Birhan Yikun* 1912, 193. Arén 1978, 199–200.
140 *Birhan Yikun* 1912, 185.

as canonical, not the eighty-one books of the Orthodox Tewahdo Church.[141] These fathers of the ECE, a number of whom were still priests of the Orthodox Church, were brought up in the classical theological literature of their mother church. Their understanding of the Trinity was based on the teachings of *Haymanotä Abäw* (Faith of the Fathers). Their standards for life and behaviour were set and guided by works like *Fetha Negest* (Law of the Kings) and *Sinodos*, even though the narrators add that they found the rules of *Sinodos* "harder than the rules of *Orit*" i.e. the Old Testament.[142] They had respect for *ser'at abbotat* [The rule of the fathers].[143]

When the time came for them to enter holy orders, Selomon and Zer'a-Tsion had traveled to Adwa with a certain *Haleqa* Afeworq, the archpriest of Hamasen, to be ordained by *Abune* Atnatewos. After their ordination, they were received in a private audience by the bishop, who is reported to have told them, "If you can preach the Gospel in another country do so; if not preach it in your own country"[144] *Haleqa* Afeworq then took them and introduced them to a certain Johannes Maier, a messenger of the Gospel from Switzerland who lived in Adwa at the time. Maier encouraged them, gave them portions of Scripture and other writings in Amharic. He also promised to supply them with further copies of Scripture from a bookstore in Massawa.[145]

---

141   For books recognized by the Orthodox Tewahdo Church, see Peter Brandt's article "Bible Canon" in *EAE*, 1, 2003, 571–573, and Ullendorff 1973, 197–198.

142   Two works which have permeated the religious life of the Orthodox Tewahdo are believed to have originated, at least in translation, in the reign of Emperor Amde Tsion (1314–1344). These are the Sinodos, and Didisqiliya. Coptic monks are believed to have assisted in their translation. The Sinodos (Synodicon) is a collection of canonical regulations, taken from the different church councils recognized by the Coptic Church. The canons from the council of Chalcedon (451) are not included. Abba Selama, an Egyptian Metropolitan who arrived from Cairo in 1350 and stayed in office for forty years made a highly significant contribution to Ethiopian ecclesiastical literature. Under him Ethiopian monks translated the Sinodos and Didisqilia from the Arabic. On Didisqiliya (Also known as The Ethiopic Didascalia), a work on canon law, see A. Bausi's article in EAE 2, 2005, 154–155. (Ed.)

143   *Birhan Yikun* 1912, 184.

144   *Birhan Yikun* 1912, 184.

145   *Birhan Yikun* 1912, 185.

To the left:
Qeshi (Pastor)
Selomon Atsqu
(1848–1926), one
of the fathers of
the Evangelical
Church of Eritrea.
Picture from 1909.

To the right:
Qeshi Zer'a-Tsion
Musé (1850–1940),
one of the fathers
of the Evangelical
Church of Eritrea.
Picture from 1909.

Monks from Debre Bizen Accuse Fellow Orthodox in Tse'azzega

According to the narrative in *Birhan Yikun*, monks from DB, intent on challenging the early fathers of the Kenisha, first appeared in Tse'azzega in May 1873, according to the Gregorian calendar. The narrative states,

> It happened that in May 1873 some monks of Debre Bizen [...] were on their way to bring charges against us. *Qeshi* Gebremedhin, who was on a journey, happened to meet them at Addi Qontsi. Believing that they were still on friendly terms, he alighted from his mule in all sincerity and greeted them with a "Good morning!" However none of them responded to his greeting. He therefore interrupted his journey, returned at a gallop to his comrades and told them about what had transpired. Convinced that they [i.e. those of Evangelical persuasion] would be interrogated in proper order, for good or for bad, they laid out welcome carpets in church and waited for them. The others

however, about thirty monks altogether, came in procession, carrying the seat (stool) and cross of Abune Filippos, which were covered with embroidered cloth, and walked straight towards the residence of Blatta Gebre Kidan. Blatta Gebre Kidan sent his servants and had us brought into his presence.[146]

Subjects Discussed

The subjects taken up at this session were the role of the saints as mediators, the significance of the *Tabot* (The Ark of the Covenant) in the worship of the Orthodox Tewahdo Church and the piety of the faithful.[147] The main spokesmen for the Evangelical group were *Qeshi* Haile-Ab and *Qeshi* Gebremedhin. The first encounter seems to have ended in a deadlock. In any case, another appointment was made for a meeting at a place known as *Miku'at Meret.*

The same issues were discussed in greater detail at the session in *Miku'at Meret*. The Orthodox Tewahdo priests argued energetically in favour of the thesis that angels, saints and the righteous had been given promises by God that they would be able to mediate on behalf of the faithful. The Kenisha maintained that such a teaching was based, in the last analysis, on secondary sources of dubious quality and not on the Bible.[148] Since the views of the two parties were found to be irreconcilable, the matter was referred to a judge in Tse'azzega. Once before the judge, the spokesman of the Orthodox Tewahdo monks, *Abbat* Haile-Yesus, argued,

> Don't give these people their *rim* [i.e. rations or rightful dues].[149] Let them not enter the church. I excommunicate all those who associate with them. Let him who has the power to excommunicate do like wise!'

146 *Birhan Yikun* 1912, 186.
147 The Kenisha never questioned the propriety of mutual intercessions (i.e. "praying for each other") here on earth, i.e. in *atsädä siga* (the realm of the body). What they questioned was the propriety and "biblical legitimacy" of communicating with the departed in *atsäda näfs* (the realm of the soul or spirit), by seeking their intercessions. Furthermore, the Kenisha felt that the unique and utterly sufficient role of Christ as the Mediator of Mankind before the Father should be underlined. (Ed.)
148 *Birhan Yikun* 1912, 187.
149 *Rim* could in fact imply gifts in kind, e.g. food items like *ingera* (thin, soft bread) and *ssewa*, a local beer, often with the consistency of ground and fermented grain of different kinds. The term *ingera* can also mean food in general. The use of the term *rim* in BY implies, very likely, gifts or rations of a similar kind, though we cannot be sure. See Bausi, Dori, Taddia 2001, 18. (Ed.)

At this, all the monks present said, "We have excommunicated!"

Then *Qeshi* Gebremedhin replied, "Behold, my master! How can they excommunicate us while we stand here before the law? Isn't this like deciding that a person be made to forfeit his cattle before he is convicted or that he be made to lose his wife before he is divorced?"

At this stage, some elders like Ayte Barya'ou from Shiketi and Kentiba Zemui from Tse'azzega stood up and pleaded with those who had uttered the excommunications: "Restrain yourselves! Take back your excommunications!' However, the former said, "We shall not!"

We then replied, "Well then, we too have authority, just as you do. We would have excommunicated you. However, since you are rulers of the land and the bestowers of worldly appointments, let a thousand carpets full of gold and a thousand slaves bearing guns, protect you."[150] We then pronounced, "Don't give them their *rim* and "Don't associate with them."[151] The judges told us, "Go home. Let your mutual excommunications remain in force." We spent the night at our homes and they spent the night locked in church. On the morrow, mediators came to us and told us: 'Keep to the Bible, which is lofty enough. Don't refer to *questions*.[152]

We answered, "As long as we have the Bible we have everything we need in it. Indeed, that is why we preach on the basis of the Bible". Having said this, we considered the matter, approved of their request and agreed to become reconciled. The mediators then took us to the church where they were. After the reconciliation we greeted and embraced each other. We then spent two days discussing books. At last we agreed that we would rectify wrong practices in the church. Having agreed that we would meet at Miku'at Meret on the feast of Be'alizgi in Meskerem, we parted company.[153]

---

150 They were saying, in effect, "We know that our excommunications can't hurt you, since you have such rich resources anyway, by virtue of your positions." (Ed.)

151 *Birhan Yikun 1912,* 188.

152 The word *question* is clearly a reference to a catechism. Se *BY*, p. 185, where the word catechism is used. Arén refers to a translation of a catechism of the Church of Würtemberg in Germany, a Lutheran church. See Arén 1978, 176. (Ed.)

153 *Birhan Yikun 1912,* 188. *Be'alzgi* is the twenty-ninth day of the Ge'ez (Julian) month. The day of the appointment would coincide roughly with October 7, even though the greater part of Meskerem corresponds to the month of September. (Ed.)

A Good Will Visit to Debre Bizen

Qeshi Haile-Ab and Habte-Giorgis of the Evangelical group paid a goodwill visit to DB before the date of the coming meeting at *Miku'at Meret*, hoping to facilitate the dialogue that had been started. They were given the cold shoulder. The proposed October meeting was postponed to *Be'alzgi* in Tiqimti, i.e. the 29th of Tiqimti (ca. the 7th of November). On the day of the meeting, the Evangelicals felt that the mood between the two parties had deteriorated. A spirit of confrontation had replaced that of dialogue. According to the narrative in BY, the friendly and conciliatory Blatta Gebre-Kidan had been left out of the negotiations, intentionally. Soldiers under the command of *Ra'si* Barya'ou were sent to arrest and take *Qeshi* Haile-Ab, *Qeshi* Selomon, *Qeshi* Gebre-Medhin and Habte-Giorgis to Areza, where they were made to stand before *Ra'si* Barya'ou.

The priests of Evangelical conviction were openly ridiculed and stripped of their priestly head-covers and attires. Issues which the Evangelicals had questioned, like the mediatory roles of the Virgin Mary, saints, the righteous, the martyrs, angels, the *Tabot* (Ark of the Covenant), the cross, sacred images, and certain regulations on fasting, were taken up and discussed. No agreement could be reached on the debated questions. At last the monks of DB pleaded with *Ra'si* Barya'ou that the accused be forgiven "for today". They continued,

> If they sin in like manner in the future, we elders who live in our monastery shall keep an eye on them. If we send them back to you, do what you want with them. We would then be free from any responsibility for them.

> Then the *Ra'si* replied, "Since they are priests from the jurisdiction of my friend Hailu I shall have mercy on them for today."[154] He then asked the accused, "Do you prefer religion or punishment?" And our brothers answered, "When did we ever abandon the faith of the prophets and the apostles?" At this reply, the *Ra'si* answered, "In that case, swear that you will not abandon the faith of the prophets and apostles and the Three Hundred!" They agreed to do so. Then, Matthew 25:41–46 was read, after which they gave their oath to abide by the promise they had

---

154　*Degiat* Hailu, a close friend of the Swedish missionary Lager, was the prince or chief of Tse'azzega. Johannes Kolmodin, *Zanta* 1912, 136 ff.

Part of the highland village of Tse'azzega

given.[155]

The *Ra'si* added, "If I hear, from now on, such an accusation against you, woe to you! You will be responsible for the consequences." He then released them and sent them away on bail, for a small sum of money. On their way to their home region they reasoned, "As far as faith is concerned, what else did the prophets and apostles have, except faith in God? And as far as the Three Hundred are concerned, what else did they have except the faith in the Trinity which they had formulated at Nicaea? What was the point of binding us by oath on such obvious matters", they said, laughing as they moved homeward. And those of us who had stayed at home received them with joy.[156]

155 Matthew 25:41–46 deals with the Final Judgement and underlines the importance of feeding the hungry, giving drink to the thirsty, receiving the stranger etc. The reason for the Tewahdo insistence that this section of Matthew be read must have been the mention of good deeds in connection with the Final judgment, in the face of the Kenisha insistence that salvation is a gift based on the grace of God alone.

156 *Birhan Yikun* 1912, 191. The 'Three Hundred' is a reference to the presumed number of bishops and other leading theologians who were believed to have been present at the Council of Nicaea in 325, where the Alexandrian theologian Arius was condemned for denying the divinity of Christ. For more details on this council see Kelly 1980, 223–251, and the article on "The Council of Nicaea" by Witold Witakowski in *EAE*, vol. 3, 175–177.

Feudal chieftain, from the Orthodox highlands, in ceremonial trappings and flanked by his body guards.

Alas, their joy and laughter were not to last long. Soon persecution, flight, hunger and thirst, fear, exile to the burning heat and humidity of the Red Sea coast, were to become their lot.

Birhan Yikun – A Mirror of the Historical, Cultural, and Religious Features of Highland Eritrea

As already indicated, the narrative in *BY* is, in many ways, a mirror of the historical, cultural, social and religious features of life among the Orthodox Tewahdo. It reflects the tenor of the times when Swedish missionaries and the Kenisha were slowly starting to gain a foothold on the Orthodox highlands of Hamasen.

The narrative reflects quite a homogeneous Orthodox society in which local chiefs and leaders of the church worked in concert, listening to complaints and litigation. These leaders also meted out punishment or took measures to reconcile parties in conflict. The

Barambaras Golja, one of the chiefs who supported the Evangelical movement in Seraye. 1909.

power to excommunicate that the Orthodox priest possessed was held in high respect. In the course of the conflict, priests representing the Orthodox Tewahdo Church and those Orthodox priests who had arrived at Evangelical conviction excommunicated each other. Others, both civic and church authorities, pleaded with the parties in conflict to lift their excommunications.[157]

157   *Birhan Yikun 1912*, 188.

Links with the Church Hierarchy in Abyssinia

The links with the Church hierarchy in neighbouring Abyssinia are clear. The narrative in *BY* states that ordinations and admissions to sacred office took place in Gondar or Axum. It is interesting to read a rhymed saying in Amharic, quoted by the accused in defense of their case.[158] The use of Amharic among the early Kenisha on the highlands of Eritrea, in latter years, was, partly, a result of their stay as fugitives in Imkullu, where Amharic was the language of communication among the Swedish missionaries and the Evangelical Christians.

The *BY* account reflects a rural, communal tradition in which efforts were made to iron out conflicts, through the offices of elders and men of authority. However, danger was always around the corner. Many who had espoused the Evangelical cause eventually withdrew from their new venture of faith.[159] They felt that the risks involved in leaving the faith of their forebears were too big. Others fled to the coast at Imkullu, unwilling to allow the noose to be slipped around their necks, as it were. In near by Abyssinia both ecclesiastical and political authorities thundered away at the heretics. In short, the highland society where the Kenisha found themselves was a society in which religious, social, political and cultural issues were intimately tied to each other. To abandon the Orthodox Tewahdo faith was to forfeit one's right to live in peace in the village of one's forefathers.

The Word 'Rim' and the Privileges that it Reflects

It is to be remembered that the mutual excommunications in *BY* made reference to something called *rim*, which we have translated as "rations or rightful dues". "Don't give them their *rim!*" was one of the concrete injunctions in connection with the excommunications. The term *Rim* needs to be spelled out in greater detail, since it too reflects a culture

---

158 The saying used reads, in a somewhat defective rendition of the original, "*Sayireta kebtu! Sayifata mishtu!*". The saying should read,"*Sayireta kebtun! Sayifata mistun!*" and means: *How can one lose one's cattle before losing a court case! How can one lose one's wife before being divorced?*" *BY* 1912, 188. (Ed.)

159 The account in *BY* hints at this fact with the simple words, " […] and others became weary and returned to their home regions" *BY* 1912, 193.

of ownership and use of land on the highlands of Hamasen.[160]

The word *Rim* belongs to a family of designations connected with ownership and use of land, both in Ethiopia and Eritrea. The main designations in Amharic, for varieties of ownership of land were *rist, gult, madärya* and *Rim*.[161] The terms represent a chain of related concepts, roughly in a descending order of importance and permanence, as far as the use of land is concerned. *Rist* in Amharic, and *risti* in Tigrinya, is "the right to claim to a share of land based on kinship to a historical ancestor held in common with other *rist holders*."[162] According to Professor Bairu Tafla "*Gult* and *madärya* represent systems devised by the rulers to procure revenues by exploiting the *rist-system. Gult* or *gwelt* [...] refers to a royal grant of a piece of land, a village or a district to a full-fledged church, monastery, a nobleman or noble lady of merit in order to enable them to derive an income from it for a living."[163] Irma Taddia quotes T. L. Kane's definition of *Rim,* which could serve as a general orientation on the meaning of the term. The definition runs: "land around a church deeded to it by the founder and assigned by the church (to those who serve it) for their upkeep (in lieu of pay). Such land did not pass out of the possession of the church."[164]

Some Privileges Connected with Rim

As far as traditional practice in highland Eritrea was concerned, the first religious privilege connected with *Rim* was the naming of Rim-holders first in the intercessions at the end of the Qiddase, the Tewahdo Mass. It has been stated that the second privilege implied that the households of Rim-holders were the first ones to receive their Easter Palms from the priests of the village on Palm Sunday.[165]

However, there are also other views on this subject. Grazmatch Mesghenna Almedom, an elderly Kenisha who was kind enough

160 The subject of *Rim* was studied at an intentional conference in Bologna, Italy in 1999. See Taddia, 2001. (Ed.) See also the two articles by G. H. Tesfagiorgis (Customary Laws in Eritrea) and T. G. Gebremedhin (Traditional Agricultural Sustenance in Eritrea) respectively, in *Traditions of Eritrea*, 2008, 1–36 and 131–154, a collection of essays edited by the two. (Ed.)
161 Tafla, 50, in Bausi, Dore and Taddia 2001 (Ed.).
162 Bairu Tafla, 50, in Bausi, Dore and Taddia 2001.
163 Bairu Tafla, 52, in Bausi, Dore and Taddia 2001.
164 Taddia 15, in Bausi, Dore and Taddia 2001.
165 Tekeste Negash and Kjetil Tronvoll in Bausi, Dore and Taddia 2001, 108.

to comment on this issue, among several other topics in the book, maintains that what was distributed was a variety of grass known as *setti* (in all probability *setti ruba* – Latin : *Cyperus Dichroästachyus*) a plant that grows on the banks of rivers, not Easter Palms. Furthermore the distribution took place, according to him, on *Qedam Si'ur* (The Saturday before Easter Sunday) and not on Palm Sunday. According to him, the practice was discarded already before the independence of Eritrea. It was *Abune* (Bishop) Marqos, Grazmatch Mesghenna maintains, who took the lead in finalizing the change by teaching that no discrimination should be practised around religious functions. Those who wanted to secure their *setti* could do so at their parish churches on the day before Easter.

Traditionally, the *Rim*-holder had to be a descendant of the original inhabitants of the village, one of the *däqqäbbat* (lit. *children of fathers*, meaning *native born*). A descendant to late comers to the area, a so-called *ma'ikälay 'alet* (a member of a *middle* tribe or clan) could not participate in the periodical administration of land. Both categories had however equal rights to usufruct in land.[166]

The reference to *Rim* in the narrative in *BY* opens a window into a whole tradition of rules and regulations pertaining to the ownership and use of land, not least among clergy in the church and to privileges connected to such land. To lose one's right to *Rim* was, in other words, to lose one's livelihood and, in a sense, one's history. The Kenisha ran this risk.

In Closing

Was the Orthodox Tewahdo Church Devoid of Light?

It will be remembered that the narrative by *Qeshi* Selomon and *Qeshi* Zer'a -Tsion in *Birhan Yikun* is entitled *How the Light of the Gospel Entered and was Revealed in Hamasen*. And yet, the Orthodox Tewahdo Church, in which these two fathers of the Kenisha were once ordained, called its apostle, St. Frumentius, *Kesaté Birhan* (The Revealer of Light).[167] Wasn't there Light' in

---

166 *Usufruct* is the legal right to use and derive a profit or benefit from property that belongs to another person, as long as the property is not damaged. For highland traditions on land ownership and use, see Kidane Mengisteab's article "Traditional Institution of Democratic Government in Eritrea" in Tesfa G. Gebremedhin and Gebre H. Tesfagiorgis (Editors.), 2008, 41–45.

167 For Rufinus' version of the story of the conversion of the Kingdom of Abyssinia see Jones and Monroe 1971 26 ff; and Ullendorff 1973, 96–97.

the Orthodox Tewahdo Church (OTC) when the missionaries of the SEM arrived on the highlands of Eritrea in the second half of the nineteenth century? Don't the roots of the OTC go back to the fourth century and even earlier? And hadn't this church fought for and preserved its faith over the centuries, through thick and thin?

There were admittedly Swedish missionaries who could be critical of the Orthodox Tewahdo Church which they encountered in what is now Eritrea. Per Eric Lager, who was on very good terms with Orthodox Christians, high and low, and who had great respect for them, could nevertheless write words like the following, albeit to Swedish readers,

> It seems to me that the only way to revive Abyssinia's crumbling church, indeed a matter of absolute necessity, is to begin quietly through [the introduction of] Bible reading, the spreading of Scripture and teaching people to read.[168]

K.G. Rodén once wrote an article about a gasping (puffing) Orthodox Christianity in Mensa! And surely there were Kenisha who were even more critical on this point. Having said so, we must add that neither the missionaries of the SEM nor the Kenisha in leading places, ever taught, as a matter of principle, that the Light of the Gospel was absent from the Orthodox Tewahdo Church. Many would have described this Light as *dim* or *flickering*.[169] All would have said that the light, the candle, needed trimming. Adolf Kolmodin writes about the "yeast of the Gospel" in the Orthodox Tewahdo Church in Eritrea, suggesting a power which had the potential to cause fermentation in the dough of the church body, (understood: if it was allowed to ferment).[170] Both missionaries and the Kenisha believed that the OTC could use its potentials in a better manner, not least in the matter of paying greater attention to the Bible as the norm for teaching and practice. However, neither the leading Swedish missionaries nor the leading Kenisha ever taught that the Orthodox Tewhado Church was devoid of the Light of the Gospel.

---

168 R. Holmer 1937, 133. See also Beskow I 1884, 206.
169 See K. G. Roden's article *Ett besök i munk- och nunneklostret å Debra Sina* (A Visit to the Monastery And Convent at Debre Sina) in *Varde Ljus* 24 (1916) 65–84, in which this attitude is quite pronounced. Rodén writes, "Indeed, the Abyssinian Church and its teachings are, all told, as petrified as the stone church of Debre Sina." Rodén 1916, 68.
170 A. Kolmodin 1909, 62.

What was Good about the Good News?

What the fathers of the ECE felt that they lacked at the time when the missionaries of the SEM came to Eritrea, was a clear, Bible-centered emphasis on one aspect of the Gospel, the Good News, as the word *Gospel* (Greek *evanggélion*), understood literally, implies. They asked, "What was '*good*' about the Good News? What did terms like *Medhané Alem* (The Saviour of the World), and *Mäsqäl bezanä* (The Cross, our ransom), terms used commonly in the Orthodox Tewahdo Church, really mean? Why wasn't the absolutely unique role of Christ as the Mediator between God and man underlined (First John 2:1)? Why wasn't it taught clearly and unequivocally that salvation is a gift of God, a fruit of God's undeserved grace towards fallen and helpless man?"

Indicators of the Good News in the Orthodox Tewahdo Church

In spite of the foregoing questions, some Kenisha saw clear indicators of the Gospel as Good News in the piety of the Orthodox Tewahdo Church. A part of the daily devotions of the Tewahdo faithful reads: *Mäsqäl haylinä, mäsqäl tsin'inä, mäsqäl bezanä, mäsqäl medhanitä näfsinä [...] nihnäsä amännä, wä'ilä amännä bähaylä Mäsqälikä, dihinnä!"* (Translation: *The Cross our power, the Cross our stability, the Cross our ransom, the Cross – medicine for our souls [...] as for us, we have believed and we who have believed in the power of your Cross, are saved.*) On reading these words, many a Kenisha may break out in surprise: "But isn't this what we too believe? Was this comforting truth spelled out for our forefathers, simply and clearly?"

Though critical of the Orthodox Tewahdo Church on some points, *Qeshi* Marqos Girmai, a Kenisha educated in Sweden from 1884–1888, writes,

> But Christianity in my fatherland has not missed its goal. No! It has spread blessings in abundance. How much spiritual refreshment, comfort and solace hasn't this church offered to the people of Abyssinia in their countless sufferings![171]

---

171   Markus Germei, 1890, 217.

Four Eritrean students at Johannelund: Haile-Mikael Kidanu (1881-1886), Tewolde-Medhin Gebre-Medhin (1883–1887), Marqos Girmai (1884–1888), Hagena Natnael (Jigo) (1884–1888).

A Village with Open Arms

I remember visiting relatives of my wife in Ad Tekelezan, Eritrea, during Lent in 1994. From Ad Tekelezan we walked and rode for a couple of hours on mule back down to a small village in the valley of River Anseba where we were received by a nephew of my wife. When it was time for us to eat, our Orthodox hosts brought in a meal of chicken, in spite of the fact that the time was the season of Lent. We regretted the fact that our hosts went out of their way to accommodate us. However, what was even more surprising and touching was that the hosts requested a relative to eat with us. Was he particularly liberal? For us, such an attitude stood in stark contrast to the intolerance that comes forth in parts of the conversations between the monks of Debre Bizen and the Kenisha recorded by *Qeshi* Selomon and *Qeshi* Zer'a-Tsion in *Birhan Yikun* in 1912. Times have indeed changed.

K. J. Lundström, who used to greet the editor of this present work with the Amharic words, "Abaté, Yiftugn!" (Father, Absolve me!), had respect for the Orthodox Tewahdo Church, among whose members he had many close friends. He would have been happy to hear the little anecdote from our visit to the village. (Ed.)

Chapter Five

Models, Means and Motivation

Introduction

A mission in East Africa is not tempting God, but rather compatible with God's good will, which embraces the most miserable and abandoned. Africa is the part of the world which has fallen into the hands of robbers and to whom Christians should show the love of the Samaritan, not least to those who stand closest to the Holy Land. [...] If the Gospel were to be established in and around Abyssinia, it would soon have a great impact not only on the inland regions of Africa but also on Arabia. [...] A mission at the Red Sea would stand on soil that has the special promise of the Scriptures.[172]

These words are taken from a letter written by the Reverend Ludwig Krapf (1810–1881), to the board of the Swedish Evangelical Mission on April 11, 1865. Krapf was born in Germany but was sent to Abyssinia as a missionary of the Church Missionary Society (CMS), an Anglican missionary organization. He was one of those who strongly urged the SEM to start mission in East Africa.

In John 4:37–38, Jesus says to his disciples, "Thus the saying 'One sows and another reaps' is true. Others have done the hard work, and you have reaped the benefits of their labour". One cannot apply these words of Jesus in an unqualified sense to the labours of the first

---

172   From a letter by Ludwig Krapf, quoted in G. E. Beskow 1888, 29–30.

Ludwig Krapf
A German citizen and once a missionary
to Ethiopia, who encouraged the SEM to
begin mission work in East Africa.

missionaries of the SEM who landed at Massawa in March 1866. Theirs was indeed a pioneer missionary venture. They had to go through bitter trials during their first years of missionary work in Kunama. However, these Swedish missionaries were in fact heirs to an East African, Protestant missionary heritage to which pioneers like Peter Heyling (1607?–1652), Samuel Gobat (1799–1879), Christian Kügler (1801–1830), Carl Wilhelm Isenberg (1806–1864), and Ludwig Krapf (1810–1881) had contributed.[173] These former missionaries, who were of German and Swiss origin, became a decisive factor in the choice of the first mission field of the SEM.

Scripture portions in Amharic, made available through the auspices of the British and Foreign Bible Society, had already found their way into what is now Eritrea when the Swedish missionaries arrived in the country. In short, the first missionaries of the SEM were heirs to models, means and motivation. Sweden's own Christian, Lutheran tradition, reinforced by a revival movement in the nineteenth century, a movement embraced by both clergy and laity, provided the catalyst for the launching of a home-grown Swedish missionary movement. K. J. Lundström has given us the broader background to this development. His text follows. (Ed.)

173 For a survey of the work of the Church Missionary Society (CMS) in Ethiopia, 1830–1843, and for Protestant missions in Ethiopia for the period between 1855 and 1868, see Crummey 1972, 29–57 and 115–144, respectively. See also Arén 1978, 45–84, the article on Church Missionary Society by Donald Crummey in *EAE*, vol. 1, 2003, 740, and Fekadu Gurmessa 2010, 67–68. (Ed.)

Revivals in Britain and the Initiatives of the Church Missionary Society (CMS) in Ethiopia

Religious revivals swept the British Islands in the eighteenth century. The *Church Missionary Society*, a society within the Church of England, was formed in 1799 to propagate the Gospel. It was particularly interested in the ancient churches of the Near East which, the society felt, could be vehicles for reaching Muslims with the Gospel. However, if this purpose was to be fulfilled, these churches would need to be re-vitalized and come to a realization of their obligation to reach out to their non-Christian neighbours. Now that the four Gospels had been published in Amharic the CMS was faced with the challenge of distributing these Gospels in Ethiopia. They chose to contact Swiss and German missionary organizations.

Early Missionary Models

The first two to be chosen for this venture were the European clergymen, the Rev. Samuel Gobat (1799–1879) and the Rev. Christian Kügler (1801–1830). They arrived in Massawa in late December 1829 and proceeded to Tigrai. After a short stay there, Gobat left for Gondar where he arrived by the end of March 1830. Here he distributed the 60 copies of the Gospels and the few copies of the Acts and the Epistle to the Romans in Amharic that he had brought along. *Ichegé* Filipos was grateful for the gifts Gobat had brought with him and distributed the books to the main churches, urging that the books be read to the people.

Gobat left in 1833 but returned to Ethiopia in August 1834. He had already become ill during his first trip to Africa and his illness persisted. He remained in bed for almost a year and had to leave the country in September 1836. He was carried to the coast on a litter. He gave up his missionary career but never lost his concern for mission. Ten years later he was appointed Anglican bishop of Jerusalem.

The activities of the remaining missionaries were not received well by the people. In March 1838 the missionaries were forced to leave Tigrai. However, during his stay there, one of the missionaries, Carl Wilhelm Isenberg (1806–1864), had initiated a translation of the Gospels into Tigrinya, in cooperation with a certain *debtera* Matewos.[174]

---

174   The Gospels were not actually published until 1866. Arén 1978, 64.

John 3:16 in Amharic and Oromiffa and Matthew 25:40 in Tigrinya. Copied from a series of photos on glass.

Means – the Bible and a Catechism in Amharic

The labours of the CMS missionaries seemed to have yielded very little fruit. The eager reception of the Amharic Bible had, however, given important results. One such result was the discovery of a consignment of several hundred Amharic Bibles and New Testaments in Massawa in 1866. These had been sent there by the British & Foreign Bible Society. Missionary Martin Flad too had sent a large supply, four mule loads in all, to the governor of Hamasen, Dejjazmatch Hailu Tewolde-Medhin (1813–1876), who had distributed the Scriptures among his people.[175]

These volumes of the Holy Scriptures kindled an unexpected interest, thus setting in motion a Bible movement among the Orthodox

---

175 Flad (1831–1915), who was Swiss by origin and who belonged to the Pilgrim Mission, first came to Debre Tabor, Ethiopia in 1855 and was received by the Metropolitan, Abune Selama, and later by Emperor Teodros. He and his colleagues made efforts to work among the Felasha, Jews of Ethiopian origin, especially by way of schools. See Arén 178, 88–91. See also the Swedish version of the autobiography of Missionary Johan Martin Flad, Ett liv i tro, kärlek och utgivande för Abessinien. Missionär Johan Martin Flads självbiografi. (*A Life in Faith, Love and Sacrifice. The Autobiography of Missionary Johan Martin Flad*) by Elsie Winqvist, 1927. Se also Fekadu Gurmessa 2010, 163–166.

of Tse'azzega and neighbouring villages. The seeds of the Evangelical Church of Eritrea can be said to have been sown at this time.[176]

Interest in the Scriptures in Ge'ez and Amharic had taken root particularly among the priests of the church of *Qiddus Giorgis* in Tse'azzega, an influential centre in Hamasen. In the early eighteen-sixties, a young deacon had discovered a copy of Abu Rumi's Bible in a niche in the wall of the church. The book must have been there for quite some time, most likely from the middle of 1843, just before the work of the CMS in Ethiopia came to an end. The study of the Bible and a catechism in Amharic caused lively discussions among the clergy, particularly on the role of angels, saints and the Virgin Mary.[177] These books pointed towards Christ as the only mediator between man and God. The clergy of Tse'azzega began to teach boldly that Scriptural truth must prevail over what they felt were man-made traditions. They stressed what they understood to be the Scriptural meaning of salvation. This insight created in them an eager longing for a spiritual revival.[178]

Their opponents maintained that the Bible-readers had embraced a foreign faith. As we have already stated, their teaching was strongly opposed, particularly by the monks of the monastery of Debre Bizen. The latter contested the views of the Tse'azzega clergy at public hearings, but this only helped to draw attention to the reform movement.[179] Among the ranks of the clergy, many wanted a reform but not a break with the Orthodox Church. The leader in this group was the chief priest, *Qeshi* Gebremedhin Tesfai (d. 1876). His younger brother, Haile-Ab, was for a more radical reform.[180]

---

176 Arén 1978, 104. On *debtera* Wolde-Sillassé Kinfu (1841–1876) and his connection with the Bible Readers, see Arén 1978, 189–191. See also Wolbert Smidt's coming article on *Wäldä Séllase Kénfu* in vol. 4 of *Encyclopaedia Aethiopica (EAE)*, 2010. (Ed.)

177 In a footnote in his book *Evangelical Pioneers in Ethiopia* (1978), Gustav Arén writes, "The Württemberg edition of Luther's Small Catechism in Johannes Maier's translation into Amharic contained an introduction to the Lord's Prayer which disavowed the mediating role of the saints and thus made this booklet the chief object of Orthodox indignation." Arén 1978, 176.

178 Arén 1978, 185. Se also BY 1912.

179 Arén 1978, 14–15.

180 Arén 1978, 182–183. Tewolde-Medhin the son of Gebremedhin became a distinguished leader among the Evangelical Christians in Eritrea. See Holmer 1938.

Motivation –
The Formation of the Swedish Evangelical Mission

Lutheranism was the official religion in Sweden and pure teaching (meaning strict adherence to Lutheran doctrine) was seen as a condition for salvation. The religious policy of the government required that there be only one people and one faith in the country.[181] While the stress on right teaching became more and more extreme, there was also a renaissance of spiritual life. As a result of impulses from the various pietistic movements in Protestant Europe, a spiritual revival swept across the country. In 1726 the Swedish government passed a law that prohibited private religious activities led by non-ordained persons.[182] As the law prohibited laymen from preaching, the non-ordained leaders and their followers often met to read from the writings of Luther and other spiritual leaders. This practice was particularly pronounced in the northern parts of the country where those who adhered to the movement became known, rather disparagingly, as *Readers*. One such Reader, Carl Olof Rosenius, became a prominent figure in the revival.[183] The ban on private religious meetings was lifted in 1858, but already two years earlier, some of the leading promoters of the revival movement had formed a society that would,

> [...] further the growth of Christ's kingdom on the basis of the Evangelical Lutheran confession [...] in a free association with the institutions of our Church ...[184]

The society was given the name *Evangeliska Fosterlands-Stiftelsen*, literally *the Evangelical Fatherland Foundation*, abbreviated as EFS, but known internationally as Swedish Evangelical Mission (SEM).[185] The society saw itself as a revival movement within the Church of Sweden.

---

181   Tergel 1973, 120, Alf Henriksson 1963 (I), 357–359. Ryman 2005, 9–11.
182   Tergel 1973, 193. Ryman 2005, 11.
183   Rosenius (1816–1868) is regarded as the father of a revival movement within the Church of Sweden. His writings, biblical, Lutheran and soundly pedagogical, have left deep marks on the spirituality of large sections of the country. The definitive biography on him is the book *C. O. Rosenius. Hans liv och gärning. (C. O. Rosenius, His Life and Work.)* by Sven Lodin (1956). (Ed.)
184   Quoted from the constitution of SEM/EFS.
185   K. J. writes, "The Italian name was *Missione Evangelica Svedese*, but in his work, *Tribú dei Mensa*, Rev. Rodén used the designation *Società Evangelica Nazionale*. I was told that the word *Nazionale* or, as it could also be rendered, *Patriottica*, had caused some consternation among the Italian authorities."

Soon after the establishment of this society, many of its members began to seek ways and means to expand its work beyond Sweden's national borders. Up to that time, individual Swedes had served as missionaries in foreign lands. Furthermore, there were a couple of Swedish missionary societies in existence in the country. These were only supporters of missionary enterprises in other countries.[186] The idea of mission to the heathen had, however, been promoted through articles in Christian publications in Sweden.

The question of Foreign Mission was presented to the annual conference of the SEM in 1861. The Board resolved to establish a foreign mission department with the purpose of

> sending out missionaries and farmers who would settle at specific places in heathen regions and train indigenous mission-workers through the Word of the Gospel.[187]

Through its international contacts, particularly with Great Britain, Germany and Switzerland, the board of the SEM sought guidance in selecting a mission field. Many areas were considered, but the one that finally won the approval of the Board was the proposal presented by Bishop Samuel Gobat. He first suggested the area which was the home of the Oromo of Ethiopia but later changed his mind when he understood the turbulent state of things in the country.[188]

The German missionary, Rev. Johann Ludwig Krapf (1810–1881), who had served in Ethiopia between 1837 and 1842 as a missionary of CMS, also recommended a mission to the Oromo.[189] He suggested that the best way to reach the area would be by way of Sudan, bypassing troubled

---

186 At an early stage, members of the SEM gave money and other forms of assistance to other mission organizations, such as the Hermannsburg Mission in Germany, the Basel Mission in Switzerland and the Waldensian Church in Italy. Furthermore, funds were used towards the support of a Swedish preacher stationed in New York. From 1861–1865, the SEM gave out a Swedish translation of the German mission paper of The Hermannsburg Mission. Tafvelin-Lundmark 1974, 29. (Ed.)

187 Arén 1978, 120, Tafvelin-Lundmark 1974, 28.

188 Arén 1978, 101 and 121. Tafvelin-Lundmark 1974, 36–39, Gurmessa 2009, 128–129.

189 He served first in Tigrai and then in Shewa where his keenest interest was reaching the Oromo. He learned the Oromo language and translated some New Testament writings. In 1842 he was expelled from the country. He then continued as a missionary in Kenya, still hoping to reach the Oromo. He did not attain this goal, but he became the founder of the mission of the Church Missionary Society (CMS) in East Africa. Arén 1978, 446–447. Crummey 1972, 43–53, F. Gurmessa 2009, 99–101.

Three pioneers of the SEM. From left to right: C. O. Rosenius (1816–1868), B. Wadström (1831–1918 och H. J. Lundborg (1825–1867).

Ethiopia.[190] A third German, Rev. Louis Harms (1808–1865), founder of the Hermannsburg Mission, was also consulted and he recommended that attempts be made to reach the Oromo via Zanzibar.[191]

In Closing

The story of the first missionary venture of the Swedish Evangelical Mission is a striking example of the significance of ecumenical contacts and the sharing of spiritual and missionary insights across national borders. In Europe there was a rich store of knowledge on missions, mediated by old, weather-beaten missionaries. Mission strategists could consult such mentors, who readily pointed out and recommended the most urgent fields for missionary outreach. Lay people too shared in a common store of mission-related information, inspiration and insights. Devotional literature, histories of missions, monthly or yearly periodicals given out by mission organizations, songs and collections of sermons were shared by the spiritually awakened and revived. In this regard, Great Britain, Northern Europe and the Scandinavian countries belonged to one large Evangelical family. Sweden too shared in this common reservoir of spiritual resources. The inspiration that led Swedish Christians to undertake mission work was partly the result

190 Arén 1978, 121, Tafvelin-Lundmark 1974, 37.
191 Arén 1978, 122. Tafvelin-Lundmark 1974, 37–38, Beskow I 1884, 23.

Bishop Samuel Gobat (1799–1879),
Swiss theologian and missionary,
sent to Ethiopia by the Anglican CMS.
Advised the SEM to work among the
Oromo. Became Anglican bishop of
Jerusalem in 1846.

Bishop Gobat.

of a participation in this common heritage.

The second significant aspect of the early years of the missionary venture of the SEM was the availability of the Scriptures and a catechism in an important vernacular in East Africa, namely, the Amharic language. The members of the revival movements in Northern Europe knew, from their own experiences, how important it was for the individual Christian to be able to read the Bible in his or her mother tongue. This, they felt, was equally applicable to life on the mission field. They believed that though preaching was the primary means of initiating mission work, reading the Bible was the most important vehicle for the spread and consolidation of the Gospel. By the time the SEM started its missionary work in Eritrea, the Scriptures were already available, in part and in whole, in the Amharic language. Some very limited copies of these Scriptures had already reached the highlands of Eritrea and were to prepare the ground for some highly significant contacts between Swedish missionaries and members of the Orthodox Tewahdo Church.

However, having pointed to the availability of this reservoir of knowledge, experience and mission tools on the eve of the first missionary venture of the SEM in Eritrea, we must underline the fact that Kunama, the first mission field of the SEM, was and almost uncharted territory. (Ed.)

The call to mission both at home and abroad was strong. Mission festival at Johannelund Theological Institute on June 13, 1870. To the left the new Mission Institute built 1867.

Sewing Circle for women in the school at Laxviken in Northern Sweden, May 27, 1916. They did their needle work to collect money for missionary outreach.

Chapter Six

Marching Orders and the Pain of Withdrawal

Introduction

At the beginning I looked a little absentmindedly at a postcard that carried seven small, oval portraits, accompanied by the words "The Seven Missionaries that have been sent out". "Wait a minute!" I said to myself. Isn't that Carlsson in the middle? And Kjellberg! And Lange! Indeed, these were missionaries of the SEM, even though this fact was not indicated on the card.[192]

He was short and chubby, a man with a big head and curly hair. The scholarly type. He resembled Carl Olof Rosenius (1816–1868), the spiritual father of the SEM. At Johannelund's Mission Institute, where he taught, he was in fact called "Little Rosenius". He was a gifted preacher and teacher, like his namesake of old. Above all, he was a bookworm. He read books, bought books and wrote books. One day he was browsing through books at a shop that sold old literature, just outside Uppsala, when his eyes fell on a postcard. Right there and then a vision was born in him. He decided to write a book on the first seven missionaries of the SEM in Eritrea. He started digging into books, articles about and, above all, letters from these missionaries.

---

192   I. Hellström, *Bland faror och nöd i Kunama* 1989, 7.

The title immediately under the picture reads: The missionaries who were sent out. Photographed by E.G. Åkerlund. The first SEM missionaries to East Africa came to Eritrea in 1866: Carl Johan Carlsson (1836–1867) died in 1867, and was buried in Ouganna. Per Eric Kjellberg (1837-1869), was murdered in 1869. Lars Johan Lange (1836-1911), returned to Sweden in 1867 because of ill health.

The next group, consisting of three missionaries, arrived in 1867: Petrus Englund (1836-1911), served in Eritrea until 1870 and thereafter as a pastor for seamen in Alexandria for one year. Olof Hedin (1839-1868) died of dysentery in 1868 and Per-Eric Lager (1837-1876) was killed in Addi Qontsi on July 17, 1876.

In spite of the fact that a number of missionaries had died, the next group of missionaries came out in 1868. A member of the group, Johan Leonard Elfblad (1839-1869), was murdered in 1869, with Per Eric Kjellberg.

The result was a book entitled *Bland faror och nöd i Kunama* (In the Midst of Dangers and Agony in Kunama). The book is an account of the fate of the first seven missionaries who were sent out to what is now Eritrea in 1865 and arrived there in 1866. It came out in 1988, with a second edition in 1996. It has been read by thousands of people in Sweden. In fact, it seems to have gained in popularity following the author's death in September 1992. The writer's vision had been fulfilled.

His name was Ivan Hellström.

Who were the missionaries whose story Ivan has narrated in such a moving manner? What was it that motivated them to leave a Nordic country, rich in cool forests and lakes, and to come to the scorching winds of the Red Sea at Massawa? What hidden power was it that drew them into the unknown hinterland of Kunama?

Karl Johan Lundström has narrated their story. His text follows. (Ed.)

Preparations and Training

The Board of SEM accepted Krapf's proposal on a pioneer mission field and decided to explore "the countries of the Nile and the Red Sea coast" with the aim of reaching the Oromo.[193] The annual conference approved this proposal and two missionary candidates, Lars Johan Lange and Per Eric Kjellberg, were commissioned for the task. A third member, Carl Johan Carlsson, was nominated later.[194]

Among the three, Lange had received the most thorough education. He had been enrolled at the Basel Mission Training Institute in Switzerland in January 1857. In the spring of 1863 he wrote to the SEM and volunteered for missionary service. By then he had had six years of theological education. However, it was a foregone conclusion that he could not travel to the mission field alone.

Another candidate, Per Eric Kjellberg, had been selected for missionary service by the annual conference of the SEM in June 1865. Sometime later Carl Johan Carlsson joined the other two.[195] A question that worried the leaders of the SEM was the ordination of the three. The matter had to be resolved by the Swedish Government, and the

---

193   Arén 1978, 121–122. Tafvelin-Lundmark 1974, 37.
194   Arén 1978, 122. Tafvelin-Lundmark 1974, 33–34, 39–40.
195   Tafvelin-Lundmark 1974, 40–41.

The port of Massawa in the Eighteen-sixties. Picture published in The Children's Paper 1885.

authorities were late in finalizing the issue.[196] An approval was finally given in April 1866, with the stipulation that an application on each individual be submitted separately to the government, and that, after ordination, each missionary candidate be accountable to a specific diocese in Sweden. Due to delay, only one of the missionaries, Lange, was ordained, not in Sweden but in Germany, by the Lutheran Church of Württemberg on July 16, 1865 in Leonberg.[197]

Lange proceeded thereafter to Egypt, where he studied Arabic. Kjellberg went on to London to study English. The third missionary candidate, Carlsson, left Sweden by the end of November 1865 and reached Egypt two months later, after a tempestuous voyage.[198] The missionaries had several alternatives. They could start their forward journey on the Nile and proceed further down the Blue Nile. They could also travel on the Red Sea to Massawa and then move overland to the Blue Nile. A third possibility was to begin work in the vicinity of Massawa and remain there.[199] The missionaries were warned that

196   Tafvelin-Lundmark 1974, 41.
197   Tafvelin-Lundmark 1974, 42, Hellström 1989, 21–22.
198   Tafvelin-Lundmark 1974, 43, Hellström 1989, 23–26, Beskow 1884, 41–53.
199   Tafvelin-Lundmark 1974, 44, Hellström 1989, 26–27.

travelling up the Nile and the Blue Nile would entail great difficulties and dangers. They therefore chose the Red Sea route and arrived in Massawa on March 15, 1866.[200]

Contacts with Werner Munzinger

In Massawa the three contacted the French consulate where they met the vice-consul, Werner Munzinger (1832–1875). The Egyptian viceroy, Muhammed Ali, had previously leased the ports of Suakin and Massawa. This lease had lapsed but was renewed in 1865 by the new Egyptian ruler, Ismail Pasha.[201] Munzinger was helpful and briefed the missionaries on the political climate in the area. He told them of the confused state of things in Ethiopia where the Empire of Teodros II was crumbling. According to him, the only way of reaching the Oromo was to take the route that Krapf had suggested as one possibility, i.e. travelling north of the Ethiopian territories into Sudan and then continuing southwards along the Blue Nile. Munzinger proposed that the missionaries begin work in an area that lay closer at hand, the one inhabited by the Tigré-speaking Mensa, just a few days' journey north-west of Massawa. However, his advice provoked a strong reaction from a Catholic mission that was working in an area adjacent to Mensa. He suggested, therefore, that the Swedes proceed westwards and work among the Kunama. By his estimate this tribe numbered 200,000. He informed the missionaries that the people lived in farming communities in an area between the Mereb and Tekezé rivers.

Munzinger suggested, further, that the missionaries could then proceed to the Oromo.[202] Lange and Carlsson were both in favour of this suggestion while Kjellberg was opposed and preferred to move directly to Abbai (the Blue Nile). However, he accepted the decision of his two comrades loyally.[203]

200   Tafvelin-Lundmark 1974, 44, F. Gurmessa 2009, 128–129, Beskow I 1884, 53. The proper pronunciation of the name Massawa is *Mitsiwa'*, meaning "to call or hail". The town was located on two small islands and transport between the islands and the mainland required that passengers hail the small boats that were to transport them. Massawa is, however, the most commonly accepted name.
201   Trimingham 1952, 120.
202   Arén 1978, 131 ref. to Lange's letter 1866-03-20, Hellström 1989, 26 –29.
203   Arén 1978, 132, Hellström 1989, 48 –50.

Werner Munzinger (1832–1875), Swiss orientalist and vice-consul in Massawa under both Britain and France. He helped the first Swedish Missionaries who arrived in Massawa in 1866.

Werner Munzinger.

Portrait published in the SEM Periodical in November 1873.

Portrait from 1864, Courtesy of EAE, vol. 3. (Schweizerische Landesbibliothek, Bern)

Onward to the Interior

On April 2 the three missionaries set out on foot from Massawa, with the camels which they had hired for the transportation of their equipment. The first stretch of some 50 kms along the sandy littoral was extremely exhausting. The dry season had already come and temperatures could exceed 60 degrees C. in the sun.

Climbing up the so-called *Bahri* taxed their energies. They worked their way up the rocky heights to an altitude of some 2,000 metres, further to the west and down to Keren at an altitude of 1,400 m. Weary and footsore they arrived in Keren after nine days.[204] At the time Keren was an Egyptian garrison and an important centre for the Bilén people. A Catholic mission had been working in the area for some fifteen years.

Once in Keren, the missionaries faced the problem of huckstering

204 The literal meaning of the term *Bahri*, is "the sea" but here the word denotes the arable areas on the slopes facing the sea. Beskow I 1884, 54–56.

with camel drivers over terms of transport. Munzinger happened to be paying a visit to Keren at the time and the missionaries took the chance of consulting him on how to proceed. This took time and when they were able to resume their journey to the southwest, the month was almost over. They arrived at Mogolo, the centre of the Baria tribe who were neighbours of the Kunama.[205] The distance that they had covered from the coast was some 350 km. They could probably have covered that distance in half the time had it not been for the bickering with the camel-men.

The missionaries were now eager to reach the Kunama. However, in order to settle there, they had to secure permission from the Ethiopian governor of Adiabo, a frontier district west of Axum. Around 1856, the Egyptians had conducted raids among the Baria, destroyed some villages and released those among the Baria who had embraced Islam.[206] Ten years later however the Ethiopians appeared to be in control of the area. The governor at the time was Wolde-Tsadiq Miratch. The missionaries decided that two of their number, Lange and Carlsson, visit the governor while Kjellberg would remain in Mogolo to guard the property of the missionaries.

On their arrival in Adiabo the governor gave the two missionaries a warm reception. They were his guests for two weeks and he gave them ample provisions. However, he also presented them with a list of items that he wanted them to acquire for him from Europe.[207] Eventually the Board of SEM agreed to supply him with some of the items.[208]

The missionaries finally arrived in Kunama, a day's journey from Mogolo, at the beginning of June 1866. They found, however, that the place, to which they had come, Tanderé, was also predominantly Baria country. Carlsson therefore decided to move to Ouganna, where he felt he could learn a purer type of Kunama.[209]

---

205 Longrigg 1945, 105, Beskow 1884, 56 ff. Today the official name of the tribe is Nara.
     Paice, *Guide to Eritrea* 1996, 148. On the Baria (Nara) see A. Pollera 1935, 246–247.
     (Ed.)
206 Trimingham 217, Longrigg 1945, 105.
207 Arén 1978, 132–133.
208 SEM Board Minutes, June 11, 1866.
209 Reported by Lange, Board Minutes, November 1, 1866. Hellström 1989, 83–86.

Camel caravan of the type that the first missionaries used on their journey into Kunama.

The Mission in Kunama 1866–1870

First Contacts

Lange and Kjellberg stayed on in Tanderé, while Carlsson settled in Ouganna, where he visited people in the village. His special contact was Kolel, a wealthy and widely traveled Kunama who spoke several languages. This contact gave him a good start in learning the language. He found that the children enjoyed his company and communicating with them gave him further exposure to the language.[210]

Carlsson was impressed by the intelligence of the people. "They have", he said, "just as good brains as people in Christian countries".[211] He was healthy and enjoyed exploring the countryside. Furthermore, he began to plan for his work. His two colleagues, Lange and Kjellberg, were hampered by sickness and depression. With his background, Lange would have been the natural leader of the group, but persistent

---

210 Hellström 1989, 84–86. Arén 1978, 133–134.
211 Arén 1978, 134. U14, 1.2/E 12: Carlsson to Board 1866-09-05.

depression forced him to leave for Egypt in early December 1866. As his health did not improve he returned to Sweden.[212]

Carlsson had become the leading figure in the Kunama mission.

More Missionaries Arrive

Kjellberg continued his work but was still weak. The Home Board decided to send more missionaries to Kunama and, by the end of 1866, four new missionaries were dedicated for service. These were Per Englund, Olof Hedin, Johan Elfblad and Per Eric Lager. Elfblad went on to England for additional studies in Medicine while the other three left for Massawa. They arrived in April 1867 and had planned to proceed directly to Kunama. However, Hedin was taken ill and they had to delay their departure until the beginning of May. With the help of Munzinger they were able to hire camels that would take them directly to Kufit, a military station that the Egyptians had established. The journey proceeded without problems until they reached Kufit. The Egyptians were trying to tax the Kunama and did not want their intentions to be known by foreigners. Thus they refused the Swedes permission to proceed. They also suspected that the missionaries might be bringing in firearms for the people.

The Egyptians had founded the town of Kassala in what is today Eastern Sudan in 1840. From there they had organised raids against the isolated Christian Bilén who lived in the fertile valleys in the region of Keren. Kufit was maintained as a frontier fort and as a base for raids against the Kunama.[213] In 1867, Ethiopia was in turmoil and the Egyptians were able to strengthen their position in the area. However, the governor of Adiabo still had control over the Kunama. The three missionaries found it very difficult to move forward from Kufit. In the midst of their predicament Englund saw something: "My scouting eyes discovered him at a distance and I shouted: "Look, Carlsson is coming!" Without any discussion we raced to see who would be the first to embrace him."[214] Soon their problems were solved, and they could continue their journey to the small and simple mission station at Tendar.

---

212 This and the following are taken from Rev. Olle Hagner's article in F. Hylander 1953, 64 ff. See also Beskow I 1884, 67 ff., 80–81 (Ed.)
213 This note and the following two sentences are taken from Trimingham 1952, 11 and 138–139.
214 Hellström 1989, 104.

Bright Prospects Turn into Darkness

The arrival of the new missionaries brought joy and encouragement to the missionary corps. It also increased their prestige in the region. They began to plan for the erection of new stations and looked for a suitable division of labour. Lager, a handy blacksmith, began to set up a workshop on a slope at some distance from the house. He built it with bricks. Englund began to study the language and, after some time, was able to send home a first sample of his findings on the Kunama language, including the beginnings of a grammar.[215] Hedin was, however, weak.

Reverend Olle Hagner writes, "Many decades later, when an old Mama in Ouganna, who had once prepared food for Carlsson, heard my accordion, she exclaimed, full of joy, 'That's just the way Hedin played. Please, play it for me at my funeral!'".

But now, a backward glance at the experiences of the first missionaries. Olle Hagner writes,

> The initial impressions that the new missionaries got about Kunama and the possibilities of mission work there were very positive. Calm prevailed around them and the land lay at their feet. However, only a couple of months after their arrival the Kunama were subjected to a terrible scourge. The prince of Adiabo launched out with his blood thirsty hordes and spread death and destruction along the breadth and length of the land. While Ethiopians were carrying out their plundering, rumours arrived that the Turks (Egyptians) were approaching from Kufit to attack the Ethiopians. Now, as often on previous occasions, the Kunama were caught between two fires. First they fled westward, from the Ethiopians, with their cattle and the little property that they could take with them. And then they fled eastwards from the Turks, landing straight in the claws of their enemies from Adiabo. Everywhere in the villages there was weeping and wailing. Their huts were burnt to the ground, many had fallen in battle, and others had been murdered bestially, while hundreds of others had been carried away as slaves.[216]

When the din of battle had quietened down, the Kunama turned to Carlsson and asked him to go to the ruler of Adiabo, pay the tribute that had been demanded, and plead for mercy and peace on their behalf.

---

215   Petrus Englund *Litet prof på kunama-språket*. (Some exampels from the Kunama language). 1873. (Ed.)

216   O Hagner in F, Hylander 1953 (editor), 75–76. Se also Beskow 1884, 137 ff, 112 ff. (Ed.)

The travel took four days. Carlsson was well received but he did not succeed in bringing about the reconciliation that he had hoped for.

Hardship and Death

After his return to Tendar, Carlsson undertook a trip to Kufit. This became the last of the many journeys in his beloved Kunama. Englund wrote,

> The trip was quite strenuous. It was long and the sun was hot. However he [i.e. Carlsson] did not mention any indisposition until the 20th of September. After a meeting regarding the release of a female slave, he had to take to bed, never to rise again. He lost his appetite and his strength and he passed away on October 2, 1867. He was buried on the site where he had planned to found a new village which he had named Frida, after the Swedish word for *frid*, meaning *Peace*.[217]

He was a pioneer of faith, vision and courage but was given only seventeen months to serve. His influence, however, lasted long. He undertook several journeys to different parts of Kunama. The old men among the Kunama have narrated how they, as young boys, had accompanied Carlsson on his walks and hunting trips. His courage inspired respect and, before long, he was able to ward off deeds of violence and vengeance not only among the Kunama but also between them and other tribes. In order to preserve peace Carlsson undertook several risky and strenuous journeys to Adiabo on the other side of the Mereb River. For him, fear and comfort seem to have been foreign concepts. In one of his letters he wrote: "I believe that the Lord has sent me here and, in faith on him, I want to offer myself to the service of this people, both materially and spiritually and, if it is possible, prepare the way for others."

After the death of Carlsson, there followed a long period of peace. A nagging problem was Hedin's precarious health. He was taken ill in May 1868 and died on the 10th of June. Half a year later, in January 1869, no less than nine new missionaries from Sweden had arrived in Tendar. Four of them, Berglund, Lundahl, Elfblad and Lundholm, were missionary pastors. Three of them, Vanberg, Johansson and A. Andersson were laymen. Two of them were women. Sofia Löfvendahl

---

217   O Hagner in F, Hylander (editor) 1953, 76–77, Beskow 1884, 153 ff. In his last letter to Sweden, Carlsson pointed out that the name "Frida" does come from the Swedish word for peace. (Hellstrom, 1987, 91) (Ed.)

Old man Faki from Kunama at 110 years of age, in conversation with Olle Hagner. Faki claimed that as a boy he had helped to carry Carlsson's rifle.

At the grave of Carl Johan Carlsson who died in Ouganna in October 1867. Standing beside the grave is Yaqob Sada. Picture published 1926.

was engaged to Englund and Maria Carlsson to Kjellberg. Soon after the arrival of the fiancés the two couples were joined in Holy Matrimony. The missionaries were assigned to three stations: Tendar, Ouganna and Kulluku. The station at Frida was abandoned. Two of the missionaries were given the task of investigating sites for new stations.

Just two months later, the mission suffered a heavy blow. In April 1869 a British hunter by the name of Thomas Powell had visited Kunama in the company of his wife, a small son and some servants. He was of great help to the Swedish missionaries and invited a couple of them to join him on a trip back to Massawa, where the missionaries intended to purchase supplies. However, before returning to the coast, he wanted to visit southern Kunama. He expressed the desire that two of the missionaries accompany him as interpreters. The brethren were hesitant, but felt that they could not refuse, especially since they themselves had previously planned to make a trip into that very area. Elfblad and Kjellberg decided to undertake the journey. The inhabitants in the area regarded the group as a company of rich foreigners and consequently attacked them. The whole party was killed with the exception of a servant who escaped and could report the tragic incident. The news was brought to the missionaries in Tendar. Lundholm wrote: "Sorrow and weeping. We had a short prayer, sang two hymns, and took some food. Lager and Englund then left for Kulluku. Worst of all was the situation for Kjellberg's young wife, married only recently."[218]

Berglund, who was stationed at Kulluku, died in July the same year. In November Kjellberg's widow and their son of five days passed away. One week later Vanberg was buried at Ouganna.

A Sad Retreat

The remaining few met at Tendar, where the small mission station was becoming more and more like a hospital. Gangs of robbers raided the country and the attitude of the Kunama was now becoming more hostile. The situation was becoming increasingly critical and at the beginning of the New Year in 1870, the missionaries made the heavy decision to withdraw to Massawa. Englund writes,

> We began the journey by placing the sick on beasts of burden for transport to Mogolo. From there camels were sent to collect our goods. We had 15 to 16 days of travel ahead of us and did not know if we would make the journey; but there was no other choice.

> We had to wait for three days before we could move, but then, by God's grace, we were able to travel and reached Imkullu village on February 26. Lundholm is to move to Egypt as soon as he has improved, and we are looking back to Kunama as doves seek their nests. But where shall we labour until a return is possible? The roads to Ethiopia and Galla are still closed by war and strife. May God show us his ways![219]

---

218   O. Hagner in F. Hylander 1953, 81–82, see also Beskow I 1884, 179 ff, 201 ff. (Ed.)
219   O. Hagner in F. Hylander 1953, 81–82. (Ed.)

Attack by robbers at Kulluku on January 23, 1870. Sketch made by a traveller who travelled through the area soon after the ambush. Published in EFS periodical "Frideborg" 1883.

In Closing

Swedish missionaries had embarked upon their missionary venture in Kunama with the hope that they would be able to secure a firm physical and spiritual foothold among the people. The beginnings were promising. Contacts were established between the missionaries and the Kunama. Carl Johan Carlsson was not only a missionary but also an unofficial emissary, a spokesman and advocate for the causes of the Kunama before Abyssinian feudal lords and Egyptian intruders into the territory. The missionaries had started out as eager students of the language and of the ways of life of the Kunama. Some had started setting up simple workshops. However, a deluge of trials followed: sickness, fatigue, and the pain of seeing how tribute and slave-hungry lords treated the Kunama. Death struck, devastating the courage of the missionaries and creating questions in the hearts of the Kunama. Within two years of their arrival, two missionaries had to return to Sweden, sick and worn out in body and spirit. Between the years of 1867 and 1869 three died of sickness and two were murdered. The wife of one of the missionaries, Mrs. Kjellberg died on November 6, 1869, only days after the murder of her husband. Their five-day-old son had died on November 1.

Friendliness started changing into hostility. It was time to leave for the hot and humid coast, the only place where the missionaries could feel safe.

Here was a small company of wounded and exhausted soldiers of the Cross. They had left their dead and a good part of their heart on Kunama soil. Would these missionaries be able to return? Would they be able to proceed in any direction? Did they have the courage and patience to wait, to persevere in the agonizing heat and humidity of the coast? In short, would their withdrawal from Kunama be irreversible or would it be strategic? The thought of giving up the whole venture and returning to Sweden must have occurred to all of them on many a sleepless night. But how did things turn out? What happened after their return to base one? The answers to these questions are to be found in the continuation of the Kunama story. (Ed.)

In Sweden, it was common to set aside cultivable land for the support of mission work. Here is a report for 1872 on the income from such land at the village of Hjorted.

Tendar, oats 2:25
Ogannna, rye -:71
Massawa, rye 10:50
Kulluko, potatoes, fruit 8:32
Emtadazweni, rye 10:50

"Mission barn" in Hålland, the province of Jämtland, used to collect grain from fields cultivated by supporters of the mission.

The front page of the first number of the Mission Periodical for 1870, issued by Evangeliska Fosterlands-Stiftelsen (The Swedish Evangelical Mission). Note the dove with a small branch in its beak, a picture of the message of the Peace offered by the Gospel. The drawing represents the coast of the Red Sea at Massawa. Below the picture we see the caption: The word 'Prison' to the left, 'Mission station' in the middle and 'the Town' to the right. Under the picture are the words of a hymn "Thy Kingdom Come", by the famous female hymn-writer Lina Sandell. ▶

The hymn was composed on the occasion of the Tika ambush (Kunama) in April 1869 which resulted in the death of a British family and two Swedish missionaries. A free translation of the first three verses of the hymn follows.

1. Thy kingdom come, O Lord, our God.
Thy kingdom come on earth!
Send out your witnesses with the message of salvation.
Send them out to the South and the North
To summon and invite the entire world.

2. Remember specially in your grace our young mission. In the midst of dangers and anguish in Kunama!
O Lord, increase, yes increase our faith.
So that unbelief may not paralyze our hands.
Which we have put to the plough.

3. In your Word you have promised spring in the wilderness.
When the desert shall stand clad in lilies.
A promise we await every unfolding year.
May that time come, O Jesus!
If that is your gracious will.

CHAPTER Seven

Serving While Waiting on the Coast (I)
1870–1890

Introduction

Today at midday the *Persia* cast anchor at Massawa Harbour. Boats filled with Italian officers and soldiers jostled around the steamship. [...] The town consists of four sections: Massawa itself, Ras Möder [Midir], Taualat and Abdel Kader, which is on the mainland. [...] Soon we continued to M'kullo on mule back. [...] We are now near our station that is located between the two Bedouin villages M'kullo and Hatumblo. The railway line passes close by and on a nearby mountain there is the newly established Italian fort, Victor Emmanuelle. The Swedish flag, waving from the roof of the building, welcomes us. So do all those who live at the station, old and young. The 500 hungry Abyssinians being fed with food sent as a gift of love by mission friends [in Sweden] raise a joyful ululation, according to the custom of the country. [...] Our mission station appears to be a veritable oasis in the desert.[220]

These are the words recorded by Nils Hylander in his diary entry for December 9, 1890. They give us a quick glimpse of the mission station at Imkullu towards the end of its active years. Hylander's words not only locate Imkullu for us, physically, but also reflect something of the character of the station as a "mother of all" to the fugitive, the hungry, the naked and the sick.

220 N. Hylander 1893, 31–33.

A quarter in the harbour of Massawa, apparently taken on the occasion of the arrival or departure of someone connected with the Swedish Mission.

It took time for the missionaries who had returned from Kunama to recuperate physically and spiritually. Soon, some of them were on their feet again. Within a relatively short period, they built up a remarkable interracial and inter tribal congregation at Imkullu. The congregation was named Betel, but was also called *Medhané Alem* (Saviour of the World). Among the members of this congregation, there were the learned and the illiterate, the sick and the recovering, people who had been sold into slavery and those who could trace their births back to distinguished families in Sweden, Germany, Austria and Italy.[221]

Prince Oscar Bernadotte (1872–1953), son of King Oscar II of Sweden (who reigned from 1872 to 1907) visited Imkullu with the rest of the crew of the frigate *Vanadis*, which was on a round–the–world journey. The frigate cast anchor at Massawa on February 21, 1885. His diary entry for February 22, 1885 reads,

221   On Rosa von Hagen, see Beskow 1887, 90 ff, Arén 1978, 289 note 39 and page 216.

What I saw in M'kullo gave me, then a young man, much to ponder. There, God gave me one of those nudges forward, through which He wants to help us, human beings, to come into the path of Life. I didn't understand it then, but before long I realized that God had met me.[222]

There was evidently also a geopolitical reason for the visit of the *Vanadis* to Massawa. This was the period of the Mahdi uprisings in the Sudan. In its wake this uprising created widespread turbulence whose effects were felt on the coast. The Frigate *Vanadis* was directed to Massawa, a measure aimed at demonstrating that Sweden too could flex its muscles for the defence of its citizens.[223]

A Living Christian Community

The congregation at Imkullu had the mark of *koinonia*, a fellowship of faith and life. It practised *diakonia*, a reciprocal fellowship of service in which all members had a responsibility not only for each other's spiritual but also bodily well being. The congregation practised *leitourgia*, a fellowship of worship in which the Eucharist, the fellowship of Holy Communion, was decisive. And as a community born of mission, it practised *martyria*, a fellowship that witnessed about Christ in its surroundings. The father and apostle of this community by the Red Sea was Pastor Bengt Peter Lundahl (1840–1885).[224]

The German traveller and scholar Gerhard Rohlf's, who undertook a journey to Abyssinia in 1880–1881 and also visited Imkullu, writes,

> At the institution that was led by Mr. Lundahl, his wife and five other married missionaries (we also came to know a highly educated woman from Nürenberg), 150 Abyssinian children are being taken care of at present. It is a joy to see how the small creatures, ranging in age from infants to 12–15 years of age, are prospering and growing. Among them there are all varieties of colours of the skin, from yellow to black. Apart from learning to read, write, count etc. each child must learn a practical skill. Here one sees girls learning to knit, do crochet and sew and, over there, one sees boys making shoes, doing carpentry etc. All are smartly dressed, in European fashion. One need hardly add that there diet is

---

222 These words are taken from Nils Dahlberg's book *Under Högre Befäl* (Under Higher Command), 1953, 28. See also Elsie Winqvist 1958, 94. (Ed.)

223 Hofgren 1956, 186.

224 The four marks of the church mentioned here are taken from Professor Sven Erik Brodd. Brodd et al., 1997, 12. (Ed.)

The frigate Vanadis, under the command of Prince Oscar Bernadotte (1872–1953), cast anchor at Massawa on February 21, 1885, with the express purpose of visiting the Swedish missionaries and the Evanglical community at Imkullu.

good and that it takes local climatic conditions into consideration. Services are held in a chapel which is located in a mission building and is supplied with a small organ.[225]

The congregation was not isolated from its surroundings. It lived and worked in the political, social, and religious melting pot that characterized a harbour community. The Red Sea coast was an arena where colonial ambitions were locked in a complicated struggle for control of territory. The Italians were already there. K. J. has given us a picture of the overall context in which the missionaries and their Evangelical colleagues planned, worked and waited. His text follows. (Ed.)

A new Beginning

The small group of Kunama missionaries had reached the coast. It will be remembered that several of them were sick and depressed. At first, they felt that the only solution left to them was to withdraw to Egypt, recuperate and await a decision on future plans from the mission board in Sweden. However, Munzinger was firm in his advice to them. If the missionaries were to withdraw, their work in East Africa would come to an end.[226] He promised that he would give them all the protection he

225 Gerhard Rohlfs 1883, 117–118, Quoted in Hofgren 1956, 170. (Ed.)
226 Arén 1978, 156, Beskow I 1884, 202 ff.

could provide and assist them in obtaining permission to move up to the highlands of what became Eritrea, for rest and recuperation.

For the Swedish Mission, the collapse of the Kunama venture was a severe blow. However, the mission could not entertain the idea of giving up. The sacrifices had been great and the *Tika* incident of 17–18 April 1869, in which two Swedish missionaries, Elfblad and Kjellberg, had been murdered, had become a renewed challenge.[227] Many young men and women volunteered for mission service. In June 1869 the mission had decided to build a ship of its own in order to improve the contacts with Massawa. Funds were forthcoming from all quarters.[228]

In the meantime, another group of four new missionaries had been sent to reinforce the remaining few. Among them was one woman, Gustava von Platen, the fiancée of Rev. Lundahl. The four missionaries had left Sweden towards the end of 1869 and reached Suakin early in April 1870. They had no information about developments among the missionaries in Kunama. They had planned to continue by ship to Massawa but on hearing that their destination would now be Kunama, a local representative in Suakin advised them to proceed directly to Kassala. The route would be considerably shorter and travelling over the plains would be easier than climbing the mountains west of Massawa. The missionaries accepted the advice given to them. However, the going was slow and the temperature exacting. It took them almost a month to reach Kassala. On arrival they were told of the tragic events in Kunama, and of the withdrawal of the remaining missionaries to the coast. There was no other choice for them than to return to Suakin. They were able to cover the return journey in a shorter period but did not, nevertheless, arrive in Massawa until mid-July 1870. Upon arrival, they were told that their missionary colleagues had left for the Hamasen highlands. Finally, on July 26, 1870, they joined their colleagues.[229] A month later Gustava and Bengt Lundahl were joined in Holy Matrimony. However, both were in poor health. Rev. Lundahl's health improved gradually. His wife however contracted fever, which developed into severe rheumatism.[230]

---

227 The Tika region is in the southernmost part of Kunama.
228 Arén 1978, 149. The ship was given the name of *Ansgarius*, The Apostle of the North (801–865). Ansgar, a Frenchman of noble birth, was a Benedictine monk.
229 Arén 1978, 157–158.
230 Arén 1978, 161, Beskow I 1884, 201 ff.

Gustava von Platen 1839–1872, married   Rev. B. P. Lundahl 1840–1885.
to Rev. B. P. Lundahl.

Meeting Spiritual and Physical Needs

From the very start of their missionary venture in Kunama, the missionaries were convinced that they would try to meet not only the spiritual but also the physical needs of the people. Carl Johan Carlsson had been engaged in peace making efforts between the Kunama and the Ethiopians as well as the Egyptian forces that laid claim to them. He had also introduced some new skills, one of these being that of the blacksmith. Rev. Elfblad, who arrived in Kunama in 1869, had received both pastoral and medical training, and was hoping to put his knowledge in these disciplines into practice.

Lundahl's School at Massawa

Lundahl's School at Massawa had started with only five students. This number was all that the mission could afford to take care of. The first student, Nesib (1856–1931), became a source of much joy for his teachers. He was born in Illubabor, western Ethiopia, where slave raiders stole him from his mother and enslaved him. Having been given the name Nesib, he had been sold four times before Munzinger managed to liberate him and entrust him to the Swedish missionary, Ahlborg, as a servant. Lager and Lundahl became his teachers. After some time he requested baptism. On Easter Day, on March 31, 1872, he was baptized by Lundahl and given the name Onesimos.[231]

The Red Sea Coast – The Scene of a Power Struggle

At the beginning of the eighteen-seventies there were three main political forces operating in the region where the work of the Swedish missionaries had started. One such outflow of colonial ambition, which had two sources, had its origin in Europe. These sources were Great Britain, which became involved in a military expedition against Emperor Teodros for a short time in 1868, and Italy, now driven by its newly awakened ambitions to acquire territory on the Red Sea coast. The second outflow of colonial ambition had its origin in Egypt, whose ruler, Ismail Pasha, saw an opportunity to use the newly opened sea-route along the Red Sea to control areas along the western coast. The third was Ethiopia whose Emperor, Yohannes IV, had finally ascended to the throne in 1872, after years of struggle against other contenders.[232]

A Centre of Different Activities and Church Life

The Swedish Mission had established itself in Massawa and could expand its activities after General Charles Gordon (1833–1885) granted land to it in 1877.[233] A centre was erected at Imkullu in 1879 and a number of different activities were initiated, particularly in the area of education. For some time the Mission had close contacts with the *Readers* (i.e. Kenisha) on the highlands of Eritrea but these contacts

---

231 Arén 1978, 165; Dahlberg, 1932. Zach 2001, 4–20. Nordlander 1999, 36–52.
232 On this whole question see Zewde Gebre-Sellassie's *Yohannes IV of Ethiopia. A Political Biography.* (1975), especially Chapter Two, "The Principal Actors and their Struggle for Power". See also Rubenson 1976, 288 ff; and Bahru Zewde 1991, 24–59. (Ed.)
233 Gordon was on a visit to Massawa at the end of the year 1877. He received the Swedish missionaries in audience, bought a plot of land in Imkullu, to avoid the bureaucratic delays that would result from going through official channels, and gave the plot to the missionaries as a gift. This fact is stated in a letter by B. P. Lundahl written in Massawa on January 2, 1878. Hofgren 1956, 166. (Ed.)

Lundahl's school in Massawa, built in 1871, drawn by Gustava Lundahl. Illustration published in the Mission Periodical in 1871.

were terminated due to opposition and severe persecution.[234] Many of the *Readers* had left their home regions and joined the mission on the coast. A mission station was erected at Geleb in the Mensa area but it too was closed after a few years.[235] Activities at Imkullu grew and a local church was established. The training of teachers and other leaders was on the increase. Written material was produced and printed. Medical services lightened the burdens of the sick.

Throughout this period, several attempts were made to reach the Oromo. Five expeditions were undertaken, with Imkullu as the point of departure. However, it was only late in the eighteen-nineties that this latter venture bore fruit. Neither were the Swedes the only ones engaged in mission in this area. There was a strong Roman Catholic Mission presence in the same region.

234 It is to be remembered that this was the name given to adherents of the revival movement in nineteenth-century Sweden. The Swedish term is *Läsare*. (Ed.)
235 The first station at Geleb was established by E. E. Hedenström in 1873.

Interplay of Political Forces and Mission Endeavours

Following the death of Emperor Teodros, three princes contended for supremacy over Ethiopia. These were Minilik of Shewa, Gobezé of Wag and Lasta, and Kasa of Tigrai. Gobezé controlled an area that included the old capital of Gondar. He proclaimed himself *Nigusä Negest* (King of Kings). However, it was the third contender, Kasa of Tigrai, who finally ascended to the throne as Emperor of Ethiopia under the name of Yohannes IV. He owed his success to two factors. In the first place, he had acquired arms from the British when they retreated after their campaign against Teodros. Furthermore, he had been able to prevail upon the Patriarch of Alexandria to send him an *abun* (a metropolitan) as a successor to *Abune* Selama, who had died in captivity in Meqdela, the capital of Teodros.[236]

The opening of the Suez Canal in 1869 ended the isolation of Ethiopia and Egypt. Ismail Pasha now saw an opportunity to use the seaway to reach Massawa and from there move inland across the country up to Keren, in order to link up with territory in the possession of Egypt. To this end he appointed Werner Munzinger, formerly French Consul in Massawa, as governor of Massawa. In 1872 Munzinger was able to occupy the Keren-Bilén region.[237] Egypt continued to subjugate areas like Zeila and Berbera along the Red Sea coast and places further inland, like Harer in Ethiopia.

Italy's Entry into the Red Sea Arena

As mentioned above, Britain undertook a military expedition to Ethiopia in 1867 and 1868, to free some British and other European subjects who had been cast into prison by Emperor Teodros. As soon as the expedition had attained its goal, it withdrew.[238] It was Italy that now saw an opportunity to get a foothold in the region. In 1869 Padre Giuseppe Sapeto, an Italian Lazarist, purchased an area on the Bay of Aseb. Munzinger's new position was to the advantage of the Swedish Missionaries. As *pasha* he renewed his offer to the SEM to facilitate the opening of a school in Bogos and one in a non-Muslim village in

---

236 Arén 1978, 149–151; Crummey 1972, 141.
237 Trimingham 1952, 120.
238 On the chain of events leading to Napier's campaign see Rubenson 1966; Crummey 1972, 134–144; see also the relevant sections in Bahru Zewde 2002, 40–42.

Many children were sold as slaves and transported to Massawa. Illustration of slave trade in the Mission Periodical for 1888. The words immediately under the picture read: Purchase of a slave.

Ett flafföp.

General Charles Gordon (1833–1885) who bought and gave land to SEM in Imkullu, in 1877.

Mensa. He encouraged the missionaries to resume work at their former stations in Kunama. However, at the time the mission suffered from a severe shortage of staff. Mrs. Lundahl had died in childbirth at the end of 1872 and Ahlborg had left for Sweden, for medical treatment. Only Lundahl, Lager and Hedenström remained.

Liberated Slaves, Poor Fugitives and Exile Reformers

Different Categories of Fugitives

In spite of the different offers of help that had been made to it on the question of new targets for a missionary outreach, and in spite of its own desires, the SEM felt that it must wait. However, its missionaries were not idle. They concentrated on educational work, since they regarded education as the primary tool of enlightenment and mission schools as instruments of evangelism. They received three main groups of students at their educational institutions: liberated slaves, poor fugitives and exiled reformers.[239] They did not find it wise to extend their mission to Muslims, as such a move could jeopardize their right to remain where they were. Their long-term goal was to reach the Oromo and they felt that this could be done best through converted slaves. However, this latter category remained a small minority. When the first student in this group, Onesimos, departed for further studies in Sweden in the middle of 1876, only five students of Oromo or Sidama descent remained.[240]

The group of fugitives was larger. The reason was that *Rai'si* Woldenki'el, a former governor of Hamasen, who had changed sides and now pleaded allegiance to the Egyptians, had raided his former province. Many villages were laid waste and defenceless women and children were seized and carried away, many of them as slaves to Yemen. In a letter written in January 1878 Lundahl stated that the people of Hamasen were fighting enemies, hunger and wild beasts and trying to survive in the mountains. Others came starving and in rags to the coast, begging for bread. People arrived at the mission stations at Massawa and Geleb with their children and many died of exhaustion, illness and malnutrition.[241]

A third category of people consisted of the reformers in Hamasen. They had been ostracised and persecuted, and their number had decreased, probably due to a lack of strong leaders. However, those who remained steadfast continued to study their Bibles in secret. There were also those that had fled from the highlands and sought refuge on the coast. They came to play an important role in the development of the mission as they provided the elite among indigenous leaders, not least as teachers and translators.

Leaders and Teachers among the Fugitives

Among those who stood out as leaders and teachers already in 1877 mention should be made of *Qeshi* Zer'a-Tsion Musé (1850–1940), who was

---

239   Joseph Gabrawold names four categories: ransomed slaves, companies of traders coming from the interior, those who came to the hot springs at Ailet and pilgrims on their way to Jerusalem. Joseph Gabrawold 1972, 12. (Ed.)

240   Arén 1978, 212.

241   Arén 1978, 213. See also Chapter VIII of the Tigrinya version of Johannes Kolmodin's *Zanta Tsazzegan Hazzegan* (edited by Kiros Fre Woldu) and the Tigrinya biography of *Imbi Yale Woldu ... Gomida. A History of Ras Wolde Mikael* (1999), by Yishaq Yosef. (Ed.)

a teacher at the school for girls at Massawa. Mrs. Emelie Lundahl had trained him for the task. He moved to Addi Qontsi as a district evangelist in 1890. Another native of Tse'azzega was *Qeshi* Tirfé. He was employed in 1877 to teach boys. He died in 1880 and was succeeded by his son Habte-Giorgis who had been a close friend of the late *Qeshi* Haile-Ab. *Qeshi* Selomon Atsqu (1848–1926) had been subjected to imprisonment at Areza. He served in Geleb as of the Christmas of 1874. Segid, also from Tse'azzega, had joined the staff at the coast as a teacher for beginners. As the years went by the people at these places became known as *Evangelicals* and formed the nucleus of an Evangelical Christian community.[242]

Neglect of Evangelism among the Tigré-speaking Population

The missionaries were fully occupied with work among these three categories of people. However, very little effort was made to carry out evangelism among the Muslims in their midst. No attempt was made to learn Tigré, which was the language used by these people. Instead, the missionaries concentrated on learning Amharic. There were, however, some students whose language was Tigré. The first one was Dawit Amanuel (1862–1944). He was baptized by Lundahl at Geleb in 1877 and became a pillar among the faithful. He worked with the translation of the New Testament into Tigré up to 1902, and was later ordained.[243]

Concern for the Education of Women

One of the female missionaries, Gustava Lundahl, was particularly concerned about the education of women. However, she died already in 1872 and could not actualize her dreams in this regard. In 1874, Lager underlined the pressing need for at least four female teachers. The question of educating Christian women was urgent, not least in view of the need of Christian spouses for young Evangelical Christians.

In 1875 Miss Rosa von Hagen arrived in Massawa. She was of German origin and had been educated both in Switzerland and England. She had taken up work in Sweden and there undergone a profound spiritual experience, which led her to accept the call to missionary service abroad. She married the Rev. Olof Månsson and was in service up to her

---

242 Arén 1978, 214–215.
243 Arén 1978, 215.

death in 1885. Rosa was to become a pioneer for the cause of women. In January 1876, the couple opened a school for girls. The first to come was an Oromo girl, followed by some refugees. Due to the persecution in Hamasen, the school was soon filled with girls most of whom had an Orthodox background. The school had 20 girls in 1877, 31 the following year, and 35 in 1879. By then the school was short of space. Munzinger Pasha had promised the missionaries land for additional facilities. However, after his death during a military campaign in Ethiopia in 1875, the missionaries saw no way of acquiring land.[244]

The school could move to a new site at Imkullu at Christmas time in 1879. The girls received basic training in the domestic skills, basketwork and the like. Rosa was there to help them develop into attractive and capable women: alert, open-minded, well mannered.[245]

Church Planting

The Beginnings of a Congregation

In 1878 a spiritual awakening was in evidence among the girls of the boarding school in Massawa. The other students were also affected. The membership in the small congregation called Betel, doubled in one year and it numbered 43 in 1879. One of the members was Indrias, *Qeshi* Haile-Ab's widow. At first she had opposed her late husband's ideas on reform but had now become a devoted Bible reader. The leaders were faced with the problem of how to register this congregation. Was it to be regarded as a Swedish Lutheran congregation? If so, the move required an act by the Swedish Government. However, the leaders in Stockholm took no action on this issue.

In 1872 when Lundahl celebrated Communion with the assistance of Onesimos, he had no intention of forming a dissenting church. In 1876, however, the situation was different. The Mission was now restricted to Muslim surroundings and was thus unable to reach the non-Christian territories in South West Ethiopia. The reformers in Hamasen were scattered or exiled in Muslim-held areas. Giving spiritual care as well as education and social assistance to these believers had become a matter of necessity.

---

244 Arén 1978, 217–218.
245 Arén 1978, 218.

Devotions and Worship

At the mission station in Massawa, every weekday began with Morning Prayer. A text was read from the Amharic Bible, after which followed a short exposition and prayers. The hymns sang were composed by Lundahl, in Amharic. One of the first ones was a paraphrase of John 3:16.[246] Another hymn was based on Psalm 24:7–10.[247] Lundahl's later hymns were mostly translations and were all of western origin. The Sunday services included a shortened form of the Liturgy of the Church of Sweden, translated into Amharic. The liturgy was apparently of minor importance. The most important part of the service was the sermon. This emphasis meant that the Hamasen reformers now had to do without their rich liturgical heritage from their Orthodox past. Holy Communion was celebrated only 4–8 times a year. At Christmas time in 1874 Lager officiated at a Communion service and invited *Qeshi* Selomon to participate. Lundahl was on home-leave at the time and was displeased when he heard about Lager's move. On his return he conducted a Confirmation course for Selomon and five young men, who were thereafter regarded as rightly prepared to partake in the sacrament.[248]

Congregations Called Mahber

The members of the Evangelical congregation called themselves *mahber*, a word which has the connotation of an association or union. At the missionary conference in 1879 it was decided that people who showed a genuine desire "to belong to the Lord" be granted membership after instruction. If they were of pagan or Muslim background, the conditions for membership would include baptism and Confirmation. If, however, their background was Orthodox, Confirmation would suffice. The minimum requirement for Confirmation was knowledge of Luther's catechism. As most of the members came from the Orthodox Church,

---

246   John 3:16 reads, "For God so loved the world that he gave his one and only Son, that whosoever believes in him shall not perish but have eternal life." (NIV). (Ed.)

247   Psalm 24:7–10 reads, "Lift up your heads, O you gates; be lifted up, you ancient doors that the King of glory may come in. Who is the king of glory? The Lord strong and mighty, the Lord mighty in battle. Lift up your heads, O ye gates; lift them up you ancient doors that the King of glory may come in. Who is the king of glory? The Lord Almighty – he is the king of glory." (NIV). (Ed.)

248   Arén 1978, 222–224.

1. Confirmation rather than baptism became the gateway to church membership.

2. The significance of baptism in relation to everyday life received little attention.

3. The strong emphasis on understanding the Christian faith resulted in a literacy rate unparalleled in the history of the region, but this fact tempted people to overlook the paramount importance of a genuine faith. People were tempted to seek Confirmation in order to contract desirable marriages. This became increasingly apparent the more the church won members from schools. The Orthodox practise of baptizing boys on the 40th day and girls on the 80th day after birth was, however, not observed among the Evangelical congregations.

By and by, the Betel congregation began displaying many features and practises that identified it as *Evangelical*.[249]

In Closing

We started this chapter with a quotation from a Swedish missionary's description of the environs of Imkullu. We shall end it with another personal description of some of the activities that were carried out on the station around the period 1889–1892. Here it is, in the words of Elsie Winqvist,

> [In my recollections], these last years at Monkullo shine and are resplendent with a wonderful glow. The Lord had restored my health to me. I prayed that I would be able to devote myself more fully to His service, and he heard my prayer. At eight o'clock in the morning we used to ring the big bell, and people assembled for Morning Prayer in "The House of the Saviour of the World" [...]. We then took care of the children. The evangelist Alazar, a former Muslim youth from Mensa, baptized only recently, was a teacher and my right hand at the school. We let him teach in the Tigrinja language, which all children understood, without exception. It was interesting to hear him narrate biblical stories in Tigrinja and to notice that the children listened to him attentively and answered his questions promptly.
>
> In the afternoon, the women came for a period of sewing and knitting. We took up the same subjects in their class. Those who understood Amharic helped me to interpret into Tigrinja. They loved to sing the

---

249 Arén 1978, 223–225.

The Ansgarius, the Mission ship of the SEM, built in 1872 for service on the route to Massawa and Kunama. The ship was built by means of funds collected for mission work. Eight missionaries traveled on the ship on its maiden voyage in 1873. On the ship's stern there was a cross, a victory palm and a Bible opened at Matthew 28:18-20.

Amharic songs and memorized them, so that they too could sing at the Sunday services. [...] The patients at the polyclinic were mostly Tigré-speaking, while those who stayed in the sick-cottages spoke mostly Tigrinja. Since crops had failed on the highlands, grain and other necessary items were brought from Massawa. Monkullo became something of a guest house for both white and native wayfarers. We had to be ever ready to receive an unpredictable number of guests. [Luckily] we had a spacious kitchen in which we prepared food for the hospital, the guests and the workers, of whom we needed many. Our faithful Tokelo [Teklu Hakim], Karl's [i.e. Winqvist's] helper, was never at a loss to acquire what was needed, be the needs material or related to manpower.

Onesimus and Tayelinj [Aleqa Tayye], both of whom were earnest Christians and richly imbued evangelists, lived in Monkullo for long periods in order to be able to help with the proof-reading of material for print. They preached at the regular Sunday services in chapel. On Sunday afternoons we gathered for discussions around the Bible. These discussions were often lively. Someone called these sessions "forums for the free word", a place where the native Christians could vent their feelings and opinions."[250]

There are times when unexpected interruptions on life's journey can become opportunities for new ventures. The Parable of the Good Samaritan in Luke 10:30–37 is a reminder of this truth. A man travelling from Jerusalem to Jericho had been attacked by robbers, stripped of his clothes, beaten, and left half dead on the way. The Good Samaritan, who happened to be travelling on the same road, saw the miserable person, and stopped, (interrupted his journey) to help the victim of robbery. He interrupted his journey long enough to bandage his wounds, pour oil and wine on them, put him on his own donkey, and take him to an inn where he could be taken care of. He then continued his journey.

The mission of the Swedish missionaries in Massawa and Imkullu is, in a sense, an echo of the story of the Parable of the Good Samaritan. The missionaries had not planned to stay on the coast. The home of the Oromo in Abyssinia was their original goal, their destination, their "Jericho", to use the language of our parable. However, circumstances forced them to interrupt their journey. Massawa and Imkullu became their unexpected schools for service. Many a fugitive, many a victim of violence from conflicts on the highlands of Eritrea, many a former slave from inland Abyssinia, many a victim of hunger, thirst and sickness, and many a plagued conscience found their way to these places of mercy and healing on the shores of the Red Sea. For the missionaries and their Kenisha colleagues, the first years on the coast constituted a period of waiting, a time of learning. These "Samaritans" produced and moulded pedagogical, catechetical, medical, and social instruments for work among the needy. Surely some of them were tempted to grow impatient in their desire to move on. However, the agenda for the day was still: "Wait and serve!" They never ran short of concern and work. (Ed.)

---

250   Elsie Winqvist (Winqvist-Janér), 1958, 116–117.

Imkullu mission station, established in 1879 on land given as a gift to the SEM by General Charles G. Gordon (1833–1885).

Imkullu in 1885. Seen from the outer court.

Chapter Eight

Serving While Waiting on the Coast (II)

Introduction

1887 was a difficult year in Monkullo. Many deaths, much sickness
in the small Evangelical congregation. At such times, faith is put to
the test. The Italians were after the slave traders. The Turks, who had
previously operated in collusion with the slave traders, or had at least
turned a blind eye to the sight of Arab sail boats crossing the Red Sea
for Arabia, had now left Massawa. Larger or smaller shipments of slaves
were now intercepted. Their owners were put in prison, the slaves
liberated, and as many freed women and children as possible handed
over to the Catholic and Evangelical missions.[251]

A large number of the slaves had been snatched from Galla. These were
taken care of by our dear Onesimos, who had himself been snatched
away from his mother's bosom when he was only eight years old and
had been sold several times, until the Swiss Consul Munzinger freed
him and gave him to Lundahl with the words, "Make a good man out
of this boy!"[252]

251 Many Kenisha tend to associate Imkullu exclusively with the work of the Swedish
     Evangelical Mission. On the engagement of both Protestants and Catholics on this
     issue, see Miran 2009, 154-155. (Ed.)
252 Winqvist, 1953, 82. These are the words of Elsie Winqvist, taken from her daughter's
     Elisabet Janér's book, *Under Heligt Tvång* (Under a Sacred Constraint). The words give
     us a glimpse into the circumstances under which Swedish missionaries continued
     to take care of the needy while they waited on the coast. There are apparently two
     versions to the story of the person in whose care Munzinger left Onesimos. Arén
     maintains that Onesimos was handed over to Ahlborg. Arén 1978, 16. (Ed.)

Onesimos Nesib (1850–1931), his wife Mihret (died 1888) and their children. Picture taken in Eritrea.

Aster Ganno Salbana (1859–1964), rescued from slavetraders, became a co-worker with Onesimos in the translation of the Bible to Oromiffa. Picture taken in Eritrea.

And a man he became, this former slave boy! A man of letters and a teacher of men and women at Imkullu on the Red Sea Coast, on the highlands of Eritrea and among the Oromo deep in central and western Ethiopia. In 2004, when I attended the 100th anniversary of the Addis Ababa Mekane Yesus congregation (whose origins go back to the work of the former Eritrea missionary, Karl Cederqvist), I met Woizero Tsion Andom, a daughter of the Eritrean Kenisha, Ato Miki'el Andom. She is, incidentally, a sister of the late General Aman Andom, an officer of fame in Ethiopia and Head of State for a short, ill-fated period during the early years of the Military Regime known as *Derg*. When I told Woizero Tsion that I was editing a history of the Evangelical Church of Eritrea, she began reminiscing about her Kenisha parents and their connections with Swedish missionaries in Eritrea. She gave me an old postcard with a photo of Onesimos Nesib, evidently printed in Sweden. On the card her father had written some words of greetings to a friend, in Amharic. The simple words read,

> A short story of the teacher and doer of good deeds, Anosimos (sic). [...] Memhir (Teacher) Anosimos came form Wollega to Hamasen as a child having been captured (into slavery).[253] He was then admitted into the school of the Swedish Mission. After having learnt to read and write in Amharic, he was admitted to a school in Stockholm, Sweden, where he was trained as a teacher, in Swedish, and then returned to Asmara. In Asmara he taught us Amharic as a teacher of Amharic. He and Aster translated the Bible into Galligna [Oromo].[254]

Imkullu was a place of refuge, a human workshop by the Red Sea and a point of convergence for the hungry, the sick, the fugitive and the spiritually forlorn. In time, the simple services rendered to the needy by the missionaries of the SEM and their Kenisha colleagues resulted in far reaching consequences in the lives of many. In the course of my work on this book, Professor Asmarom Legesse wrote the following striking lines to me,

> Yet another heritage of Qeshi Zer'a-Tsion [Asmarom's great grandfather], is the fact that he was a close colleague of Onesimos Nesib. I heard about Onesimos and about his Oromo colleagues from my great grandfather in 1940, a year I spent with him in Geremi, because Asmara was being bombarded by the British Air Force, and my two brothers and I were sent to Geremi for safety. The year I spent with Qeshi Zer'a-Tsion has had a lasting effect on my thinking about Eritrea's traditional culture and led me ultimately to the study of Anthropology and customary laws. It also inspired me to go into a life long research into the culture and institutions of the Oromo, a people he held in high regard.

Munzinger, who had served under several powers in the Red Sea area, and finally become "the architect of Egyptian expansionism", perished in the sands of Awsa, during a military adventure in Ethiopia in 1875.[255] The boy Nesib, whom he had entrusted into the hands of the Swedish missionary Lundahl, went on to study theology in Sweden,

---

253 The fact is that Onesimos was born in Illubabor, not Wollega. (Ed.)
254 Aster Ganno, one of the girls who had been entrusted to the mission at Imkullu in 1886, helped Onesimos to translate the Bible into the Oromo language. See Arén 1978, 383–384. Read also article "Aster Ganno" by Kebede Hordofa-Janko and Peter Unseth in *EAE*, vol.1, (2003), pp.387–388" (Ed.)
255 The expression in quotation marks is taken from Bahru Zewde 2002, 51. (Ed.)

devoted himself to literary work in Oromo and Amharic, and was to become a source of intellectual and spiritual enlightenment to many in Eritrea and to generations of Oromo in Ethiopia.

Just over a decade after Munzinger's death, Italy succeeded in securing a firm foothold on the Red Sea coast. It had its own plans for the subjugation of the people of what was to become Eritrea. Its assumption of control on the scene was, however, something of a godsend for the Swedish missionaries and their Kenisha colleagues. In the Italian colonial authorities, these Swedish missionaries found an unexpected ally in the fight against the slave trade, and a sense of security against the occasional but often devastating swoops by Abyssinian troops from the hinterland. Karl Johan's account of this period lifts forth the complex political and religious context in which the missionaries and their Kenisha colleagues continued to wait and serve on the coast. His text follows. (Ed)

Changing Power Constellations on the Coast

The early period between 1881 and 1885 was characterized by growing insecurity on the coast. The reason was the course of events in Egypt. In 1882 the British had assumed control of that country. The Egyptian troops in Massawa were outraged by this development and demonstrated their disdain for the *Christian dogs* as they called the European residents.

There were renewed threats to the highlands from Alula (1845–1897), the governor of Mereb Millash, as present day Eritrea was then known. He took advantage of the weakness of the Egyptians and moved towards the lowlands at Christmas time in 1882. His troops advanced almost as far as Imkullu. However, Suleiman Pasha, the Governor General, came with reinforcements towards the end of 1883 and restored relative security in the area. This was the state of things when Lundahl returned from his vacation in Sweden.[256]

The British authorities in Egypt had advised the Egyptian garrison in Sudan to withdraw to Egypt, but this was not done. In 1884 the British wanted to enlist Emperor Yohannes' help in rescuing this garrison. In exchange for this favour the Bogos area would be handed over to him.

---

256 Arén 1978, 280–281. On the broader ramifications see Anthony d'Avray 1996, 104ff.

The Betel community in Massawa viewed this possible development with apprehension, as it would deprive them of the chance to withdraw from the heat of the coast to the highlands of Eritrea during the hot season. Since Geleb station had been closed earlier on, Keren was the only place to which they could withdraw for rest.[257]

Italy Steps In

Tension increased in the latter part of 1884. Lundahl, however, maintained his composure and was confident that the people of Imkullu wouldn't suffer any harm.

People had reasons to be worried. The coast had been turbulent for several decades. Violence had flared up already in the late eighteen forties. The Egyptians had,

> [...] from their island fortress of Massawa [...] made repeated raids on the neighbouring mainland. Hirgigo had been burned to the ground and its Christian population had sought refuge in the hills. There was an ever increasing danger that such incursions might only be the prelude of the establishment of permanent footholds on the mainland, and Dejach Wubie could not leave such a threat to go unchallenged. He sent a stern demand to the Egyptians that they should withdraw immediately from the mainland [...] When the Egyptian governor refused the demand a Tigrean army of about 3,000 horsemen, led by Kokebie of Addigrat, descended on Hirgigo and Emkullu in early January 1849. As the army went on the rampage Muslims on the mainland were massacred and in the general melee Mgr. de Jacobis only just managed to escape to the island of Massawa before his church at Emkullu was burned.[258]

But now back to 1884. Lundahl thought the British would come to their aid. In this he was mistaken. It was in fact the Italians who stepped in.

By the time that Italy had attained unity in 1870, the Great Powers in Europe had already begun dividing the African coastlands among themselves. As mentioned earlier, an Italian Lazarist, Padre Giuseppe Sapeto, had acquired a site at Aseb for an Italian trading company by

---

257 Arén 1978, 282.
258 O'Mahoney 1982, 77–78. The rout of the Egyptians at Gundet (1875) and Gura (1876) "exposed the missionaries and their few Evangelical Christian followers to the direct rule of Yohannes." The very idea frightened them. Joseph Gabrawold 1972, 20 ff. (Ed.).

Abba Gebre-Egziabher Kokebe-Worq, (d.1941), a former Ethiopian soldier who became a monk to atone for his sins. He found a radical peace of conscience at Imkullu when he heard a sermon on the Atoning Death of Christ.

Aleqa Taye Gebre-Mariam (1860–1924), a highly gifted Ethiopian who embraced Evangelical faith at Imkullu and who developed into a scholar of international fame.

the name of Rubattino in 1869. The Italian Government obtained a larger area in 1882. In 1885 the Italians secured an even more important foothold on the coast, the port of Massawa. After they had consolidated their hold on the harbour, they continued to move inland and fortified two water wells at Sehati and Wiʻa. This led to a conflict with *Ra'si* Alula who routed the Italians at Dogali early in 1887, but then withdrew.[259]

259 O'Mahoney 1982, 282–283; See also Haggai Erlich's book *Ras Alula and the Scramble for Africa. A Political Biography: Ethiopia and Eritrea 1875–1897,* (1996), especially chapters 10 and 11. (Ed.)

Italy Declares a Colony

As a reward for assisting the British in rescuing the Egyptian garrison in the Sudan, Emperor Yohannes had been given control of the Bogos region. However the British now preferred Italian control of the area, for fear that France might occupy it. Emperor Yohannes was of course deeply offended by this act of deceit on the part of Britain and transferred his forces from the Sudan boarder to the North. This weakened the defence of his now exposed boarder and Sudanese forces were able to invade Ethiopia. In one of these encounters (The Battle of Metemma on March 9, 1889) Yohannes was fatally wounded.[260] The Italians took advantage of this situation and occupied Keren and Asmara in mid 1889. The following year they declared the area a crown colony and named it Eritrea.[261]

The community in Imkullu experienced the Italian annexation as a change for the better. The first half of the eighteen-eighties had taxed their strength severely. Physically, the missionaries and their co-workers were worn out, since Geleb was no longer available to them as a refuge for rest. Sickness had sapped their powers. Their hopes for openings to the Oromo regions were dashed. In 1881, newcomers like Arrhenius had expressed grave concern over the spirit of resignation that characterized the attitudes of missionary colleagues.

Three Ethiopians: Nigusé, Aleqa Tayye and Abba Gebre-Egziabher

In 1872 two brothers, merchants from Gondar, had come to Lundahl and asked for Scriptures in Amharic. They received a New Testament and departed. Five years later one of them, Nigusé Tashu, returned and asked for admission to Lundahl's school. Lundahl was hesitant. Nigusé was a mature man of forty and a successful merchant. But Lundahl finally gave in and Nigusé was admitted.[262]

Lundahl was on the lookout for people with an enterprising spirit, "people of faith", as he put it. Amanuel, Nigusé's assistant, was the type

---

260　Bahru Zewde 2002, 59. Rubenson 1976, 384. Emperor Yohannes' death was a serious blow to the stability of Ethiopia and a prelude to a series of woes. Hunger and cattle diseases hit not only Tigrai but also surrounding areas. Thousands of refugees from the region left their homes and hundreds came to the Swedish Mission station at Imkullu in search of food and medical treatment.

261　Arén 1978, 285–286, Bahru Zewde 2002, 71, 84.

262　Arén 1978, 233.

Elsie och Karl Winqvist. Elsie took the leading role in the translation of the Bible into Tigrinja. Her husband was both a medical doctor and a translator of the Bible.

Yishaq Hemmed, the first patient at the mission clinic in Imkullu, was baptized at the age of about 20 and became a noted proclaimer of the Gospel. Here with his family.

Abba Gebre-Egziabher Kokebe-Worq,
a former monk from Ethiopia and later
an Evangelical Christian who distributed
Christian literature and witnessed
about his faith on his many journeys.
Picture taken in Addis Ababa, ca 1925.

of evangelist he was looking for. But there were others as well. One was *Aleqa* Tayye Gebre-Mariam (1860–1924) from Yifag, east of Lake Tana in Ethiopia. He had joined the school for boys at Imkullu at the age of about 20. He was already well versed in the teachings of the Orthodox Tewahdo Church and spent hours, often late into the night, comparing these teachings with the Scriptures in Ge'ez. In 1881 he became a communicant member of the Betel congregation. The following year he returned to Begemder with the intention of studying *qiné* (religious poetry) and sharing his insights into the Bible with his countrymen. He earned the title of *Aleqa*. In December 1885 he was back in Imkullu and joined the staff as teacher, translator and preacher.[263]

263   Ezra Gebremedhin 1998, 105 ff. Arén 1999, 19–58. (Ed.)

We have, furthermore, the person of *Abba* Gebre-Egziabher Kokebe-Worq (d. 1941). He too was to discover the liberating power of the Gospel of grace and become a fervent witness to his faith both at the Ethiopian monastery in Jerusalem and later in different parts of Ethiopia. We shall say more about him presently.[264]

The Winqvists Arrive at Imkullu – Medical Care and Evangelism

Towards the end of 1883 the arrival of Rev. Dr. Karl Winqvist (1847–1909) and his wife Elsie, nee Hefter (1863–1957), reinforced the Imkullu staff. Dr. Winqvist had left his ministry in a parish in western Sweden and taken up medical studies in Edinburgh. On his way to the mission field he married Miss Elsie, who was from Frankfurt-am-Main, in Germany, and a graduate from a new and modern institute for the training of teachers for girls attending secondary schools. Her active missionary service turned out to be both distinguished and long, covering a total of seventy-four years. Her husband Dr. K. Winqvist was the first qualified missionary doctor to practise in this part of East Africa. Healing body and soul remained his lodestar. He had been instructed by the home board to integrate three tasks: evangelism, counselling and medical care. The first to benefit from the doctor's instruction was Teklu Uqbai, one of Lager's students from Embaderho. Teklu was to serve for three decades as a medical assistant.[265]

The Death of Lundahl – The End of an Epoch

In December 1885, Lundahl died of small pox. He was 45, and the last of the pioneers to Kunama. He may not have been the greatest of leaders, but he held firmly to his aim of reaching non-Christians with the Gospel. Unable to reach the area where he wanted to serve the Oromo of Ethiopia, he had faithfully prepared many of the tools that were needed for the ministry of the Gospel. Among these were a hymnbook, an order of worship and other church rites for the congregation, some textbooks and, above all, material for the training of men and women who would enter the preaching ministry. The following year, Anders Svensson was appointed as the new leader of the SEM in Eritrea. The shift in leadership entailed some changes in policy and practice.

264 Arén 1978, 288.
265 Arén 1978, 290–291. SEM/MT 1928, 452.

Svensson had a close understanding of the Orthodox Church. However he too retained, throughout his life, a concern for a ministry among the Oromo.[266]

1885 was an exceptionally hot year, and there was no possibility for the people to seek relief in the Bogos area, which was once again in Ethiopian hands. Many of the students contracted typhus and died. So did Rosa Månsson, the head of the school for girls and the teacher, Habte-Giorgis Tirfé. Emelie Lundahl took over the leadership of the girls' school with Zer'a-Tsion as a colleague. Onesimos joined them as a staff member after his return from Sweden in 1886. Two new teachers, Gebre-Giorgis Baryaw and Daniel Dabala (1866–1904), were employed. The former was a refugee from the highlands and the latter, an Oromo entrusted to Lundahl in 1873. Svensson and Påhlman completed the staff.[267]

Wages and Salaries

The labour market in Massawa had changed considerably with the arrival of the Italians. Skilled workmen were in great demand and could also demand a higher salary. The mission had provided not only theoretical but also practical training and many of the members of the Betel congregation were employed for comparatively high salaries. This created dissatisfaction among mission employees who continued to receive much lower pay.

Lundahl had followed the principle that a messenger of Christ should be satisfied if his (her) earnings were sufficient to cover the bare necessities of life. He was of the conviction that others too should set a personal example by living in utter simplicity.[268]

Complicating Factors

There were, however, several complicating factors. Onesimos and Påhlman had been given the same level of training at the Theological Institute at Johannelund in Stockholm. As we shall see presently, on

---

266 Every year, the Evangelical congregation at Tse'azzega, of which Svensson was the pastor, collected gifts for the work among the Oromo, Svensson also assisted Oromo students in his schools.

267 Arén 1978, 293–294.

268 Arén 1978, 297.

the expedition to Famaka in 1881, in connection with the second Oromo Expedition, the members would share their resources equally. However, on their return to Imkullu other considerations came into play. Should Onesimos be entitled to a salary that corresponded to his training? Or should he be remunerated according to the salary scale that applied to local employees? A single missionary, such as Arrhenius, received an annual allowance of £ stg 55, while the most prominent of his Eritrean colleagues, Zer'a-Tsion, Selomon and Habte-Giorgis Tirfé, were given only £ 18/each. The leaders in Stockholm seem to have adopted a principle laid down for the salaries of evangelists in Sweden, and awarded Onesimos £ 30, a sum which reflected a status somewhere between that of the foreign missionary and his non-Swedish colleagues. In the budget of 1884, Onesimos was granted £ 30. The others continued to receive the same amount, i.e. £ 18 a year each.

The wages of ordinary workers rose to a rate that gave them an annual wage of £ 38. In 1886, this led to a rise in the salaries of mission employees. When Tewolde-Medhin returned to Eritrea in 1887, after his studies in Sweden, he made it clear that he could not manage on less than half of the salary of his missionary colleagues. Stockholm ruled that he should get only 24, as he was still single. When he married a year later, however, he was granted the same salary as Onesimos. However, the question of determining the salaries of those trained abroad remained controversial.[269]

Language

Amharic Given Priority

In the early eighteen hundreds, Protestant missionaries had used mainly Amharic as a language for evangelization and teaching, since a Bible was readily available in the language. Furthermore, Amharic was the common working language round Lake Tana and the medium of communication with Ethiopian authorities. Lundahl undertook an ambitious programme of publishing literature in this language. He tried early to compose hymns for devotion and for services of worship. The first collection of 412 hymns was published in 1881 and a second

---

269   Arén 1978, 299–300.

edition of 93 hymns came out before his death. With the help of *Aleqa* Tayye, Lundahl gave out commentaries on the Gospels of Matthew and John. These were based on the works of a German theologian, Otto von Gerlach.[270] He also wrote two Bible commentaries with the help of *Aleqa* Tayye. Furthermore Lundahl acquired a small printing plant and recruited a printer. The first book to come off the press was in the language of the Oromo, a hymnbook containing one hundred hymns.

Need of Literature in Tigré

While Lundahl himself continued to use Amharic as a medium for preaching and teaching, he had felt a keen need for books and other literature in the Tigré language, which was spoken in the environs of Massawa. At an early stage, he assigned Dawit Amanuel to the task of translating the Gospel of St. Mark into Tigré. Tewolde-Medhin assisted him, although his own tongue was Tigrinya.[271] With the aid of the Bible versions in Ge'ez, Amharic and Swedish, they had translated material as far as the middle of the fourth Gospel, before Tewolde-Medhin went abroad for studies. Doctor Winqvist helped in explaining different passages with reference to the original text in Greek. In May 1890, Dawit completed his translation of the New Testament. This translation required a systematic study of the Tigré language itself, its vocabulary and grammatical structure. Winqvist advised Dawit to collect material for a grammar as well as a dictionary. The collection grew to several thousand words. In addition, Dawit collected Tigré ballads, dirges, epigrams and proverbs. The production of vernacular literature turned out to be one of the most important activities in the Evangelical community.[272]

New Opportunities for Evangelism, Particularly around Hirgigo

Under Egyptian rule, evangelizing among the tribes of the lowlands was prohibited, as these were Muslim. Winqvist's medical mission gradually changed the attitudes of these tribes. His skill and personality broke down their enmity and opened a door for the Gospel. Devotions were held in Tigré, the language spoken in the lowlands. Dawit

270　Arén 1999, note 10.
271　Arén 1978, 303.
272　Arén 1978, 303–304.

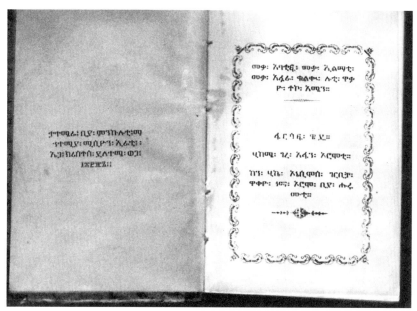

An Oromo hymnbook, the fruit of the joint efforts of Lundahl and Onesimos. Printed 1886 according to the Julian Calendar (ca. 1894–1895).

Amanuel served as an evangelist together with the more experienced *Qeshi* Selomon.

Winqvist had planned to build a hospital at Imkullu, but Lundahl was opposed to the idea. He wanted to save the money for the time when a hospital could be erected at another place, inland. However, this opportunity was slow in coming. At Imkullu the number of people seeking medical help grew steadily.

In 1886, the mission saw new opportunities for the expansion of its work. While the Egyptians had forbidden any Christian outreach, the arrival of the Italians made it possible to proclaim the Gospel at Massawa and the surrounding villages. A new station was established at Hirgigo (the Italians called it Arkiko), some 10 kms south of Imkullu. *Qeshi* Selomon and the Rev. K. G. Rodén (1860–1943), a recent arrival, led the new venture. Winqvist and Teklu helped to pave the way for the Gospel through weekly medical visits. Selomon was, however, released for evangelistic work at the port of Massawa and his place was filled by Tewolde-Medhin (1860–1930), son of Gebre-Medhin Tesfai, the former chief priest of Tse'azzega.

The Betel Congregation

It is to be recalled that Lundahl regarded the communion service of December 1, 1872 as the first step towards the formation of an Evangelical congregation. A second step was taken in 1877 when he instituted an Evangelical ministry.[273] Five years later he gave the congregation a democratic structure by arranging for an election of leaders. He did so following models that he knew from his own background and his approach served its purpose. However, the local church members were not used to the model. In their traditional society, issues were discussed until a consensus was reached, not voted on.

In 1889 the number of communicant members, including the missionaries, was 84.

In Closing

The waiting period on the coast was a time of education for the Swedish missionaries and their Kenisha colleagues. They were obliged to look into the theological implications of church planting and membership in an Evangelical Lutheran congregation outside Sweden. The question of ordination and of the status of former Orthodox priests were matters that required study. Pondering these theological questions became a preparation for the future ministry of the SEM and the ECE in the hinterland of what became Eritrea.

The waiting period on the coast provided the Swedes and their Kenisha colleagues opportunities for a first hand observation of the evolution of political and colonial history. Imkullu was next door to Big Power Politics in the making on the Red Sea Coast. Some of the missionaries were friends to prominent contemporary figures like the Swiss Orientalist and Ethnographer, Werner Munzinger, and Britons like Charles Gordon and J. C. Kirkham, who was a general in the service of Emperor Yohannes and who died in Massawa, a prisoner of the Egyptians. The fact is that Kirkham died under the care of missionaries of the SEM and the Kenisha.[274]

This period provided, furthermore, opportunities for exposure to the implications of the encounters among different tribal and

---

273 K. J. doesn't say in what way an Evangelical Ministry was instituted. (Ed.)
274 Arén 1978, 197, note 64. On cosmopolitan Massawa see Miran 2009, 118 ff.

religions groups. Massawa was a melting pot of cultures and religions. It was a place to which traders, adventurers, slaves and fugitives came. There was something strikingly cosmopolitan about Imkullu. The convergence of different nationalities and tribes on Imkullu provided the SEM and the Betel congregation insights into the distinguishing features of different cultural and linguistic groups and into factors that led to both harmony and conflict among them.

The waiting period was a time of education in diaconic work, a period of training in the art of assistance to people in need. After all, the SEM was engaged in medical, educational and social work. On more than one occasion, Imkullu was engaged in famine relief, with thousands of people coming down to the coast from the highlands of what is now Eritrea and from Tigrai. Through its medical services, the mission accumulated valuable knowledge on tropical diseases and their treatment.

Seaports are meeting places for people from different parts of the world. Imkullu, with the banner of the Cross as its tacit emblem, became a special meeting place, a school for people from north and south, from east and west. K. J. Lundström's account offers us a wealth of details on this melting pot on the shores of the Red Sea. (Ed.)

The house where Onesimos lived in Asmara, now on Street 137-4. (Picture from 2008, by Prof. Mehari Gebre-Medhin.)

Chapter Nine

Probing While Waiting on the Coast
1870–1890

Introduction

I hope that you have received my former letter in which I wrote about
the impending departure of our brothers to Abyssinia and about our
calling to go to Galla. They, namely Hedenström, A. Svensson and P.
Carlsson, as well as the others who have been assigned to go to Galla,
Negousie, Emanuel and Johannes, are already on their way. They struck
out on November 3.[275]

These words are taken from a letter written on November 8, 1877 by
B. P. Lundahl, the grand old man among Swedish missionaries on the
coast at the time. The passage provides a brief glimpse into the subject
of this chapter, i.e. the resolve of the missionaries to keep probing in
the direction of the hinterland of Eritrea in pursuit of their original
missionary vision.

For a while, Massawa, and eventually Imkullu, were the only places
where the missionaries felt safe and where they could work more or less
freely. However, they never forgot Kunama and the highlands of present
day Eritrea. Places like Geleb and Keren were always in their minds.
Werner Munzinger had been kind enough to allow the missionaries to

---

275 SEM/MT, January 1878, 3.

spend the summer of 1870 on the highlands of Hamasen. The SEM had started work in Geleb already in 1873. Occasionally the missionaries and their Kenisha colleagues did come back to some of these places, up country.

What were the factors that made them start out, again and again, from the coast and move in the direction of the Eritrean hinterland? An obvious reason was the oppressive heat and humidity of the coast, especially in summer time. The missionaries and their Kenisha colleagues longed for relief from their endless battle with sweat, sleeplessness and fatigue. However, on a more ideological level, the main reason for their probing into the hinterland of Eritrea was the pull of their original vision of mission to *Galla* i.e. the Oromo. They wanted to find ways of penetrating into the land called Abyssinia.[276]

K. J.'s account in this chapter lifts forth some of the highlights on the hidden and overt factors that were at work in this period of probing while waiting on the coast. His text follows. (Ed.)

A new Beginning

The Board of the SEM had to reconsider its mission strategy in view of the collapse of the Kunama venture. It resolved to write to Dr. Krapf who had resigned from his work, due to poor health, and returned to Germany. In his reply, Krapf described the situation in Ethiopia, which he thought gave reasons for some hope of openings, and urged the Swedes to pursue their original plan for mission to the Oromo.[277] Two Christian craftsmen had been sent by Bishop Gobat (and CMS) to Ethiopia in 1856 and had laboured for Emperor Teodros up to his death in 1868, when they withdrew to Jerusalem. They were both married to Ethiopian women and had now returned and settled in Adwa. They were, however, eager to move to Shewa in the south in order to begin work among the Oromo in that province. They advised the Swedish

---

276 Most of the missionaries were quite consistent in their use of the term Abyssinia for present day Ethiopia. To take only one example, A. Kolmodin describes the Addi-Ugri district of the Evangelical Church as the "border-district to the Independent Abyssinia". A. Kolmodin 1909, 223. He refers, furthermore, to the Abyssinian Church. Native Eritreans among the Kenisha too referred to themselves as "Habesha". However there were both missionaries and Kenisha who also used the term Ethiopia. See the dedicatory page to *Birhan Yikun* 1912. (Ed.)

277 Arén 1978, 156–157.

missionaries against moving into Tigrai, something that Lager had planned, hoping to reach the Kunama from there. The Swedes felt that they had to await instructions from their home board.

On June 28, 1870 the Board in Stockholm resolved to send Englund and Lager to Tigrai, where they would translate books and educate Kunama youth. The other missionaries were to attempt to reach Oromo territory by way of Shewa. They were, however, authorized to adapt their moves to prevailing circumstances.[278]

Stay on the Highlands

Upon the recommendation of Munzinger, a local chief by the name of Kentiba Bekhit Tewolde-Medhin took care of the missionaries on the highlands of Hamasen. Bekhit was in charge of seven villages. At first the missionaries stayed in the village of Kwazen but the Kentiba moved them to his own village, Embaderho, where he could give them more spacious accommodations.[279] The missionaries felt refreshed in the cool climate and decided to devote their time to the study of languages. As their final aim was to reach the interior of Ethiopia they took up the study of Amharic. It was difficult to find good instructors in the language, but a Felasha by the name of Teklu was able to give them some lessons.[280]

By the middle of September 1870 two of the newcomers, Mr. W. Ahlborg and his assistant, decided to move to Massawa. They had been sent out to set up a commercial agency for the mission. Massawa was the site chosen for this enterprise. The other missionaries stayed in Hamasen, awaiting information on what their next move should be. They were expecting to hear from Johannes Maier from whom a reply arrived only in the beginning of October.[281] Maier informed them that his travel to Shewa had had to be postponed. He suggested, however, that the Swedes proceed to Shewa via Tajura, (in present day Djibouti). Rev. Englund rejected the proposal as being too fanciful and suggested

---

278 Arén 1978, 156–157.
279 Arén 1978, 158–159.
280 According to Arén, Teklu was about twenty years old, had been in the service of J. Martin Flad (1831–1915, Missionary to the Felasha) for three years, and knew some German and Arabic, in addition to his vernacular, Amharic. Arén 1978, 159. See also pp. 88–91. (Ed.)
281 On Johannes Maier, see Arén 1978, 151–152 and Crummey 1972, 122–125.

The hot water springs at Ailet, located 50 kilometres from Massawa. A place where the SEM established a clinic and a school already in the eighteen-seventies. Picture from ca 1913.

the taking up of a temporary mission among Ethiopians working in Massawa. Soon thereafter, the Englunds decided to leave for Egypt for medical care. They remained there for some time, in charge of the Seamen's mission in Alexandria, and later returned to Sweden.[282] Lager too was sick and had planned to join the Englunds in Egypt. However, on his way to the coast he changed his mind because he found the mineral springs at Ailet wholesome.[283]

By this time the political situation in Hamasen was taking a turn for the worse. The governor of the area *Dejjazmatch* Hailu Tewolde-Medhin, was the head of a family in Tse'azzega, the chief market in the area. Kasa, the ruler of Tigrai, had brought Hailu into subjection and taken

282 Arén 1978, 161, Hellström 1989, 114–115.
283 Hellström 1989, 151–153. Ailet is located some 50 kms inland from Massawa on the river Makat Salim and has a number of hot mineral springs. *Guida dell' Africa Orientale Italiana* 1938, 185. There are reasons to believe that Lager felt that proceeding to Egypt for medical help would intensify his longing to return to Sweden and thus tempt him to abandon his calling as a missionary. Holmer 1937, 88–89, 94–95. (Ed.)

him as prisoner to Adwa in April 1868, probably suspicious of Hailu's contacts with Egypt.[284] Hailu was replaced by *Dejjazmatch* Woldenki'el Selomon from Hazzega, another branch of the house of Deqé Teshim. After some time, Woldenki'el himself was placed under custody and the governorship was transferred to the *Niburä'id* of Aksum, Gebru Wubet, Kasa's trusted general.[285]

Early in September 1870 the *Niburä'id* left for Tigrai. One of Woldenki'el's sons, Mekonnen by name, took up arms, causing the people to flee. Kentiba Bekhit too tried to escape but was killed in November of the same year. However, Mekonnen assured the missionaries that they could stay and that they would be protected. He requested, however, that he be given a revolver as a gift.

Towards the end of the year the Lundahls moved from the highlands to the coast to celebrate Christmas there. However, on the suggestion of Ahlborg, they decided to stay in Massawa, to initiate an urban mission and to establish a school at Imkullu.

It was impossible to implement the proposals on new enterprises that had come from the home board in Sweden and from German mission-leaders and their colleagues. The only tangible result after five years of missionary labour was a class of five students. And yet, out of these meagre circumstances, something remarkable emerged. Lager and Hedenström, a new-comer, remained for a few months on the highlands continuing their language studies and giving medical care to the victims of the many skirmishes.[286] On March 25, 1871 the two settled at Ailet, a place they thought would be suitable for evangelistic outreach.

Lager's and Hedenström's Ministry at Ailet

In June 1871 a certain Hemmed (1845–1891), a Muslim of Oromo origin, had appeared at Lager's place, destitute, hungry and sick. After three years of study at a Sheikh school he had been sent to Mecca where he had

---

284 S. Rubenson 1976, 290, Arén 1978, 159.

285 Arén 1978, 160–161, Hellström 1889, 151–152. On the life and times of Dejjazmatch Hailu, see the Tigrinya version of Johannes Kolmodin's Traditions de Tsazzega et Hazzega 1912, Archives d'Etudes Orientales Vol. 5:2 or the Tigrinya text entitled Zanta Tsazzegan Hazzegan, Vol.5:1, sections V–VIII, or the French version, Vol. 5:2. See also Yishaq Yosief's book in Tigrinya *Nigsinet Hagärä Midri Bahri (Eritrea). The Story of Degiat Hailu <Abba Galla>* 2000. (Ed.)

286 Arén 1978, 162, Hellström 1989, 151–152.

studied for another six years. He was on his way home, as a *hadji*, when his fellow travellers deserted him. The care he received at Ailet opened his heart for the Gospel. He decided to stay on and became a Christian.[287]

In 1872 Lager initiated a small agricultural project with the aim of augmenting his resources towards assisting more needy people. He leased some land up country from Ailet, and entrusted the project to a young man by the name of Teklu Uqbai (1852–1935), from Embaderho. Unfortunately the project did not succeed. A locust invasion destroyed the first crops and the project had to be abandoned. In 1877 Tewolde-Medhin Gebre-Medhin became an evangelist at Ailet. Six years later, he was sent to Sweden for further training. It is to be remembered that on his return from Sweden, he was stationed at Hirgigo.[288]

In 1874 Lager learned of the arrival in Hamasen of a legate from *Abune* Matewos. He hurried to Tse'azzega and was thus present when a letter allegedly written by the *abun* was presented, ordering that, as "apostates and propagators of heresy", Haile-Ab and Wolde-Sillassé [Kinfu] be put in irons and brought to him. The letter was found to be a fabrication. The *abun* had in fact given orders that no harm should befall the *Readers*. They were however to be prevented from officiating in Church. If they refused to obey, they were to be excommunicated.[289]

J. C. Kirkham, a British adventurer who was in the service of Emperor Yohannes, had taken the persecuted reformers under his protection and offered them land at Ghinda.[290] The refugees found it difficult to stay in the hot lowlands and went into hiding in the Tsilalé Desert but later returned to Ailet.[291]

In the spring of 1875 new missionaries arrived from Sweden. Among them were two deaconesses, Beata Karlsson (nee Andersson, b. 1843) and Bengta Nilsson (1842–1913). Bengta, Lager's future wife, opened a clinic at Bet Mekha in August 1875. This was one of the very first medical institutions in this part of East Africa.[292] In 1875, Bengta sent the first diagnostic report on 325 patients who suffered from 52 different ailments, mainly sicknesses of the eyes.

287   Arén 1978, 163, Hellström 1989, 153–154. On Ailet see also Miran 2009, 98–99.
288   Arén 1978, 297, Hofgren 1956, 200.
289   Arén 1978, 178. On "Wälde Selase Kinfu", see Smidt *EAE* Vol 4, 2010.
290   Arén 1978, 178, 181, Beskow I 1884, 222–223.
291   Arén 1978, 191.
292   Arén 1978, 192–193.

Lager and Lundahl: Divergent Views on Relations to Different Power Constellations

The two leaders, Lager and Lundahl, held different views on the policy to be adopted towards the different political constellations.[293] Lager had established good contacts with the emissary of the *abun*, who was present at his and Bengta's wedding on November 22, 1875. This contact and the open atmosphere it had created made it possible for Haile-Ab to conduct a series of spiritual meetings at Tse'azzega late in 1875.[294]

Lundahl was worried that this contact would lead to strained relations with the Egyptians, whose Khedive, Ismael, had already made plans to attack Ethiopia on three fronts. However, his attacks on Adwa and Tajura were complete failures and Munzinger Pasha was killed at the latter engagement on November 14, 1875. The only attack that succeeded was the one on Harer. Another attack in the north, in early 1876, also failed.[295] One consequence of Munzinger's death was that the Swedish missionaries could not return to Kunama just then.

Another result of the failure of the military adventures of the Egyptians was the resurgence among Ethiopia's rulers of a protective attitude towards the Orthodox Church. This led to increased pressure on and persecution of the *Readers*. The missionaries decided that they would approach the Emperor with an appeal for toleration. Kirkham, who had hitherto been their best contact person, had been taken prisoner by the Egyptians, as already mentioned, and later died in Massawa. It was therefore decided that Lager should take over the task of approaching the Emperor. However, Lager was delayed due to a short but very severe bout of sickness that almost cost him his life. After his recovery, he left for the highlands. It was now the month of June and the rains would soon come. When Lager finally arrived, Emperor Yohannes had already left Hamasen and Lager had to postpone his travel. He stayed for a while in Tse'azzega with his friend Haile-Ab.

---

293 On this subject, see especially chapter V, "Trials of strength with Egypt and Italy" in S. Rubenson 1976, Bahru Zewde 2002, 25–26. (Ed.)

294 Arén 1978, 194–195, Beskow I 1884, 232–234.

295 Arén 1978, 195–197, Beskow I 1884, 230–232.

Per Eric Lager, who died on July 17, 1876, was buried here in Addi Qontsi. The gravestone was erected on the occasion of the visit of Professor Kolomodin in 1909.

The Death of Lager and a new Period of Hiding

At this point of time, a former prince of Tse'azzega, *Degiat* Hailu, was set free after eight years of detention by order of Emperor Yohannes. His attitude towards the *Readers* was positive and these were now making themselves ready to return to their highland homes. Hailu's old rival, Rai'si Woldenki'el lived in the neighbouring region of Hazzega. He had been dismissed from his position when Hailu was reinstated. Woldenki'el decided to give battle. Lager and Hailé-Ab, who had decided to watch the impending conflict, took up a position near the Church of St. Michael, in the nearby village of Addi Qontsi. When they saw that the battle was going in favour of Woldenki'el, they decided to take refuge in the church. However, an enraged warrior from the region of Tsaida Kishtan brought them out, and put them to the sword. This was on the 17th of July 1876. Many of the other *Readers* withdrew again from Hamasen and sought refuge at the different stations of the SEM.[296]

296   Arén 1978, 197–201. See also Ezra Gebremedhin 2006, 92.

Mensa 1879–1880

In 1879, after the Council of Boru Meda, Emperor Yohannes sent his favourite general *Ra'si* Alula to restore Orthodoxy in the North. Upon his arrival in what is now Eritrea in July 1879, Alula issued a decree that made the possession of Evangelical scriptures a criminal offence. Individuals who obtained and read such books or sent their children to the mission school at Geleb would be held guilty of harbouring erroneous beliefs, sentenced to 40 lashes of the whip, chained and placed in solitary confinement at Debre Bizen for correction.

At the beginning of October in the same year, Hedenström received an order to appear before *Ra'si* Alula. He found the prince surrounded by some 200 priests and monks who complained that the whole of Hamasen believed that man was justified by faith alone and that people denied the mediating role of the Virgin Mary.[297] Alula let Hedenström choose either to deliver four of the Evangelical leaders whom he mentioned by name (Selomon, Zer'a-Tsion, Tirfé and Wolde-Gebriel), or to leave Mensa within six days. Hedenström protested against this order but to no avail. The station had to be vacated, after which it was looted.[298] The students had to leave for the coast together with Hedenström. The eighteen-seventies thus ended in uncertainty. [299]

Since there was lack of space in the premises of the mission on the coast, a missionary conference resolved to explore the possibilities of a return to Geleb. The local assembly of the village in Geleb gave their approval and in February 1880, the station was manned once again. The two schools there were repaired and 36 boys and 12 girls were soon enrolled. Only 9 students were from Mensa, all the others being from Hamasen. The low number of students from Mensa was probably due to several factors. The routines of the school interfered with the seasonal migration of the Mensa to the coastal plains. Education had probably little immediate relevance for the people and the language used at the school was Amharic rather than Tigré, their native language. However, a few students did come, probably attracted by the

---

297 *Birhan Yikun* 1912, 195. According to *Birhan Yikun* Alula held court at a place called *Addi Teklai* at the time. (Ed.)

298 Joseph Gabrawold writes, "Finally at the end of 1881, the Ras sent an army under Dejazmach Gebru which looted and plundered Galab. Two of the teachers at Galab were killed and the rest were dispersed." Joseph Gabrawold 1972, 41. (Ed.)

299 Arén 1978, 225–226.

food and clothing that was provided at this time of dearth. Around midsummer in 1880 Alula again ordered the missionaries to abstain from all teaching in matters of religion, if they wanted to remain in Geleb for the hot season. They had no other choice but to return to the coast. As a consequence of the Emperor's religious policy the mission was now cut off from the highlands.

New Challenges: Pondering the Next Move

Lundahl never abandoned the vision of reaching non-Christian tribes with the Gospel. Current developments were, however, a matter of grave concern. In the areas to the north and west the Egyptians were bringing the tribes to submission to Islam and there seemed to be no way to reach the Oromo. The school at Massawa did not develop into the educational centre Lundahl had expected it to become. The premises were poor and offered limited possibilities for expansion. The composition of the student body was the greatest problem. It proved impossible to recruit freed slaves for training as evangelists. The great majority of students were Orthodox refugees. The leaders of the SEM in Stockholm began to look for other alternatives, and in 1877 they decided to open a mission in the Betul district of Central India.[300]

In March 1877, when General Charles Gordon (Gordon of Khartoum) paid his first visit to Massawa, he had sent for the Swedish missionaries and told them of his plans for Sudan. He was a devout Christian and advised them to close the mission at Massawa and take up a field along the White Nile, in the province of Fatiko (near today's Juba) among the big pagan tribe called Beri. Lundahl however did not feel that it was reasonable that they should abandon their East African fields for one in Equatorial Africa, before they had done their utmost to reach the Oromo. The general respected this standpoint and assisted the missionaries in different ways.[301]

300 Hofgren 1956, 156, Arén 1978, 231.
301 Arén 1978, 232.

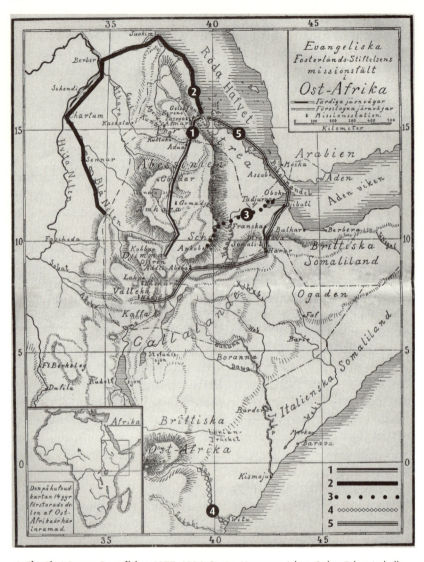

1. The First Oromo Expedition 1877–1884: Route: Massawa, Adwa, Debre-Tabor, Imkullu.
2. The Second Oromo Expedition 1881–1882: Route: Imkullu, Suakin, across the Nubian Desert to Berber on the Nile, Khartoum, Sinnar, Karkog, Famaka, Imkullu.
3. The Third Oromo Expedition 1884–1886: Route: Imkullu, Tajura (Djibouti), Shewa (Ethiopia) hoping to proceed to Jimma. Forced to return to Imkullu.
4. The Fourth Oromo Expedition 1893–1895: Route: Lamu, Zeila, Harer, back to Imkullu.
5. The Fifth Oromo Expedition 1897–1898: Route: Asmara, Derita, Yejubé, Zegé (all three places in Gojjam), Jiren (in Kaffa), Gudru, Naqamté, Boji Karkarro (Wollega).

The Oromo Expeditions

The First Oromo Expedition 1877–1884

Point of departure: Massawa. Leader: the Rev. Erik Hedenström. Other members of the expedition: Haile Mikael Kidanu (1856–1919), the Rev. Peter Carlsson (1849–1905), the Rev. Anders Svensson (1849–1928), Nigusé Tashu, Amanuel Hemmed and Yohannes Faraja. Route: Massawa, Adwa, Debre-Tabor and back to Imkullu. Nigusé and his colleagues advanced to Gojjam, and to Jimma and Jiren, in the province of Kaffa.

The Second Oromo Expedition 1881–1882

Point of departure: Imkullu. Leader: the Rev. Gustav Arrhenius (1850–1882). Other members of the expedition: Onesimos (1851–1931), A.W Påhlman (1852–1931), Hailu, Filippos. Route: Imkullu, Suakin, across the Nubian Desert to Berber on the Nile, Khartoum, Sinnar, Karkog and Famaka. Forced to return to Khartoum where Arrhenius died. Back to Imkullu.

The Third Oromo Expedition 1884–1886

Point of departure: Imkullu. Leader: A. Påhlman. Other members of the expedition: A. Bergman, Onesimos and his wife Mihret, and an eighteen-year old Oromo by the name of Petros Chibsa. Route: Imkullu, Tajura (in present day Djibouti), Shewa (Ethiopia) hoping to proceed to Jimma. Forced to return to Imkullu where they arrived in May 1886.

The Fourth Oromo Expedition 1893–1895

Point of departure: Imkullu and Lamu on the Somali coast. Leader: the Rev. Karl Cederqvist (1854–1919) Other members of the expedition: the Rev. and Mrs. Nils Hylander, the Rev. Heinrich Riggers (who dropped out early in the expedition), Mr. Karl Nyström and a boy from Lamu, by the name of Stefanos Bonaya. Route: Lamu, Zeila, Harer, back to Imkullu (Cederqvist), back to Sweden (Hylander).

The Fifth Oromo Expedition 1897–1898

Point of departure: Asmara. Members: Phase 1, Abba Gebre-Egziabher Kokebe-Worq, departed alone in September 1896 for his hometown of Zegé, in Gojjam, Ethiopia. Phase 2. Leaders: Meshesha Lulu and Mekonnen Nigusé. Other members of the expedition: Qeshi Gebre-Ewostatewos and Woizero Gumesh, Daniel and Woizero Tiru. Caravan departed in 1897. Route: Asmara, Derita, Yejubé, Zegé (all three places in Gojjam), Jiren (in Kaffa), Gudru, Naqamté, Boji Karkarro (all three places in Wollega).

The Beginning of the Oromo Expeditions

The First Oromo Expedition

Not a few visitors came to Lundahl. Among these, there were some Oromo traders from the Sultanate of Jimma, southwest of Shewa. When they were ready to return home they requested that some evangelists accompany them, to teach them about God and baptize their children. Lundahl saw this as a call from God and resolved to send Nigusé Tashu and Amanuel Hemmed. A young Sidama, named Yohannes, joined the team as an interpreter and personal aide to Nigusé. At the Sunday service on October 29, 1877 Nigusé and Amanuel were commissioned as evangelists. Lundahl put them under an obligation to teach in accordance with the Word of God, to use Luther's Small Catechism in their teaching, and to follow the order of the Church of Sweden in their worship services and in the administration of the sacraments.

This became the first Oromo Expedition, which lasted from 1877 to 1884. The big caravan that now started out for the south included also four people from the Mission: Haile-Mikael Kidanu (1856–1919), a 21 year old student from Hamasen, as interpreter, and two recent arrivals from Sweden, the Rev. Per Carlsson (1849–1909) and the Rev. Anders Svensson (1849–1928). The head of the expedition was Erik Hedenström. Having arrived in Adwa, the group approached the governor of Tigrai, *Ra'si* Baryaw Gebre-Tsadiq. An imperial order had been issued to the effect that no Europeans would be allowed to enter Ethiopia. The Swedes were therefore given a very cool reception. Hedenström, who was worried about his wife and small child, wanted to return to Geleb, and was given permission to do so. The others were kept as hostages. They remained there for a year and a half.[302]

Per Carlsson and Anders Svensson took the opportunity to study Amharic with Haile Mikael as their tutor. They also had the opportunity of attending Orthodox services and acquainting themselves with the culture of the Christian highlanders.[303]

They were well received at the Sillassé Church in Adwa and could even take part in theological discussions with its clergy. Five months later, in May 1878, the threat of war loomed on the horizon. Woldenki'el had revolted against Yohannes and started marching towards Adwa. The missionaries decided to seek refuge in Aksum. In July, Svensson fell seriously ill. Carlsson ventured back to Adwa to seek help from a certain German botanist by the name Wilhelm Schimper, who had lived in Tigrai since 1836 and was to stay in the country for over forty years.[304] On arrival Carlsson found out that *Ra'si* Alula Ingida, the Emperor's trusted general, was reorganising the army to bring the rebellious Woldenki'el into subjection. Schimper informed them that

---

302 Arén 1978, 238–240.
303 Arén 1978, 238–239. Svensson continued to use Amharic throughout his life although he lived in Tse'azzega where the population spoke Tigrinya.
304 Arén 1978, 237–238, 141. On Schimper see Rubenson 1976, 106–118.

the long expected "mission postman" had brought some mail and funds. He had, however, been arrested and the mail and funds had been seized and taken to the *Ras*. Per Carlsson and Schimper asked for an audience with the *Ras* and requested that the mail bee released. Alula promised to fulfil their wish, provided that they were *Lager's brothers*, indeed a remarkable statement, which implied that Lager's name was well known even at court.[305]

The delegates also sought ways to approach the Emperor with a request for permission to reach the pagan Qimant of Dembia. They had hoped that they would be able to proceed to the Oromo from that point. However, it was not until April 1879 that the team could leave Adwa and move on to the imperial camp at Debre Tabor. Their appeal to the Emperor did not meet with any positive response. "Return to your country, and teach the Felasha and pagans who are there. Goodbye!" was his reply. The delegates had to return to Imkullu.[306]

Nigusé Advances to Gojjam

Nigusé and his team had reached Gojjam early in 1878. Elsie Winqvist has the following story to tell about their experiences at this point of time,

> Indeed they were on the way. However in this country, riddled as it is by internal conflicts, there is no straight path to one's destination. Sometimes, they had to go forward and backwards from the one province to the other. Nevertheless they did not lose hope. They taught people, especially children, wherever they came. At one stage they stayed at a certain place long enough for their students to learn to read and write. That was in Godjam, from where the missionaries received, to their great joy, letters from their former students and children in the faith, who in fact addressed them as fathers and mothers and thanked them for sending teachers to them. From another place, the missionaries received letters from fifteen disciples. However, it took eight years for the missionaries to get a letter informing them that the party had finally reached Jimma. [...] [307] (Ed.)

Here it should be noted, by way of a digression, that Nigusé eventually proceeded to Shewa since he had heard that Minilik had

305   Arén 1978, 240–241.
306   Arén 1978, 242.
307   E. Winqvist 1953, 123–124, 153. (Ed.)

granted some Pilgrim Missionaries permission to work there. He and his companions stayed with the Pilgrim Missionaries up to 1882 when they moved on to Jimma.[308]

Let us continue with E. Winqvist's account, which gives us glimpses into the trials through which the members of the first expedition went,

> The letters, which were sent by way of caravans of merchants at long intervals, had a touch of the Acts of the Apostles about them. Alone, abandoned by wild heathens and fanatical Muslims, these simple messengers of the Gospel carried on with their calling. On several occasions they were forced to leave everything and flee. On one occasion an infuriated mob dragged them to the market place to kill them. However, Yohannes moved calmly to the centre of the market place, with his Bible in his hand. The prince [Abba Jifar II) and his soldiers came at the last minute and saved them.[309]

Eventually, the development of Nigusé's enterprise took a very interesting turn. E. Winqvist writes,

> In 1895, Missionary Nils Hylander, who happened to be in Harar, met a caravan which had been sent by Nigusé from Jimma. Its leader was Wolde-Mariam, a brother of Nigusé. He told Hylander that Negusie had become a well to do and respected person who owned large tracts of land, which he had either bought or received as gifts from the prince, by whom he had been employed. Though a Muhammedan, the prince loved the Gospel. Negusie had, in time, succeeded in buying thirty Galla children who were slaves. They worked on the farm and were given instruction by Yohannes. A number of Christian families from Godjam had joined the party. It appeared that a small mission settlement had been established in Jimma, where it had succeeded in sustaining itself. However, they had apparently not succeeded in winning a single Muslim over to the Gospel.[310] (Ed.)

The Second Oromo Expedition

In 1881 Lundahl launched a second expedition to the Oromo. This

---

308 Arén 1978, 247. These Pilgrim missionaries were Maier and Greiner, from the Pilgrim Mission of St. Chrischona in Switzerland. Whereas Greiner was a newcomer, Maier had been in Ethiopia since 1856, sent by Bishop Gobat. In 1870 Maier moved on to Shewa, where Minilik welcomed him. Greiner had joined Maier in 1874.

309 E. Winqvist 1953, 123–125. (Ed.)

310 E. Winqvist 1953, 123–125. (Ed.)

time he planned an outreach to the regions south of the Abbai [the Blue Nile]. His plan was to send an expedition by way of Sudan. The expedition would then cross the border and proceed into Wollega, Ethiopia. The Rev. Gustav Arrhenius (1850–1882) was appointed leader of the enterprise. Onesimos, who had returned from his studies in Sweden in the autumn of 1881, was with him on the expedition. In his company Onesimos had Mr. A. W. Påhlman (1852–1931) and a young highlander by the name of Hailu, a commissioned evangelist. A recently baptized Oromo youth by the name of Filippos was the fifth member. Two women, Onesimos' wife Mihret and Hailu's wife Sema'itu, were also among those who participated.

The expedition took the sea route to Suakin, and then proceeded up the Nubian Desert to Berber on the Nile, a journey that took only twelve days. From there, the company travelled by dhow to Khartoum. The party sailed up the Blue Nile for another two weeks past Sinnar as far as Karkog, from where they continued by camel and reached Famaka, the Egyptian border-post on the Abbai, on January 4, 1882. However, the officer in charge [E. Marno Bey] told them that it would be impossible for them to proceed. They moved on, trying to reach the Beni-Shangul area. The odds were however, against them. The local authorities advised them not to move into the area as tribal war was in progress. Tropical diseases posed a threat and finally Arrhenius saw no other alternative to an interruption of the journey and a return to Khartoum. On reaching the city, Onesimos was taken seriously ill and the team had to stay on to nurse him. As Onesimos grew stronger, plans were made for him and Arrhenius to make a quick trip to Imkullu and then return for a second attempt to reach the Oromo. However, on the day when they were expected to depart Arrhenius fell ill suddenly and died after only a couple of days. The rest of the expedition had to return to their base.[311]

The Third Oromo Expedition

In 1884 it seemed as if Minilik was ready to grant permission to the missionaries for a passage to Jimma. It was now time for a third expedition. Two Swedes, Axel Påhlman and August Bergman, Onesimos and his wife Mihret and Petros Ibsa, an eighteen-year-old Oromo, were

311 Arén 1978, 258–259, Beskow 1884, 266–278.

chosen for this expedition. The group sailed south to Tajura where they arrived in early December 1884. They had, however, to wait there for three months, before they could proceed inland.

After a dangerous journey, which lasted for a month, they arrived at the border of Shewa, and made plans to proceed to Jimma. However, when their intention was reported to Minilik, he forbade them from entering his kingdom. Nevertheless, since several members of the team were sick they were allowed to remain in Shewa until they could recover. They stayed there up to February 1886, when a caravan finally started out for Tajura. They reached Imkullu early in May.[312]

The Fourth Oromo Expedition 1893–1895

In 1893, a fourth expedition was sent out with the aim of reaching the Oromo, this time from the south. The plan was to reach the Borana, an Oromo group west of Lake Turkana (then called Lake Rudolf). The expedition was led by the Rev. Karl Cederqvist (1854–1919).[313] Other members of the expedition were Rev. and Mrs. Nils Hylander, Rev. Heinrich Riggers, Karl Nyström and a 14-year old boy from Lamu, by the name of Stefanos Bonaya, who had attended school at Imkullu and Geleb and spoke several languages.[314] Riggers, who was an American of German origin, resigned after a few months.

The expedition arrived in Lamu, an island on the south Somali coast, today part of Kenya. Its members believed that they would gain access to the Borana, as these would hardly have been exposed to influences from Ethiopia. The missionaries were also confident that the British would step in and protect their interests on the coast as far north as the home of the Borana. Cederqvist found out that these presuppositions were all wrong. The group decided to wait at Lamu. Cederqvist recommended that the Hylanders leave for Ethiopia and proceed via Harer to Jimma. They did so together with Stefanos, and settled in Harer in May 1895. Nyström returned to Europe for medical training.[315]

The Hylanders had planned to move on to Jimma, but Minilik did not permit them to proceed any further. They remained in Harer up

---

312   Arén 1978, 274–278, Beskow II 1887, 11, 23–32.
313   On Cederqvist and his work see Arén 1999, 105–174, Hofgren 1956, 212–213.
314   Arén 1978, 378–379, Hofgren 1956, 212–213.
315   Arén 1978, 379–380, Hofgren 1956, 217.

The teacher Debbas Negasi (sitting) with some of the young men, fruits of the Gospel, who had come from Wollega, Ethiopia, and who were to stay in Eritrea for a year, for purposes of instruction and visits to the various congregations. Picture taken at the school in Asmara 1911. The entire group consisted of Abraham Tato, Yishaq Boji, Samuel Danki, Yaqob Gimbi, Sukessa Abbayé, Beko Suya and Dinsa Tulam.

to June 1896, when they were ordered to leave. They had to return to Sweden due to sickness. Cederqvist had returned to Imkullu late in 1895.[316] All attempts to reach the Oromo to date had failed.

The Fifth Oromo Expedition –A Breakthrough (1897–1898)

Having parted from his colleague [Daniel], Gebre-Ewostatewos proceeded directly to Neqemte, where he approached a priest, who belonged to the governor's retinue, and inquired of him whether there was an opportunity for employment as a secretary or teacher. The priest introduced him to Fitawrari Dibaba, who happened to be at Neqemte and was looking for more priests for his church at Bojji Kärkärro in Central Wollega. Gebre-Ewostatewos now produced his books in Oromo, read some portions from the New Testament and sang some hymns, for he had a beautiful voice. Dibaba marvelled. He had never imagined that it would be possible to use his own native language for sacred scriptures

316　Arén 1978, 381–383.

and Christian poetry. Excited, he offered the priest from Hamasen employment instantly.[317]

It was December 1898. The old dream had come true after almost forty years. Swedish Christians in their remote Nordic home had sensed the inner movings of a missionary calling to preach the Gospel among the Oromo. And now an Eritrean from Hamasen and his wife were the first to come to the finishing line, torch in hand, after a long relay race which had started in Massawa already in 1877. A motley team of runners, (Swedes, an American of German background, and "Abyssinians", as the Swedish missionaries called their African partners in the faith) had taken part in this long and dramatic advance to the home of the Oromo in Wollega.

If the first four expeditions were amply manned by Swedes, the fifth expedition was an altogether "Abyssinian" venture. In a way there were two phases to this expedition. The monk *Abba* Gebre-Egziabher Kokebe-Worq (d. 1941), who couldn't wait until the larger part of the expedition were ready for departure, left Massawa in 1896 to join a caravan leaving Asmara in September. Where did his longing to preach the Gospel of grace originate? Gustav Arén writes,

> [He] had become a monk to make up for crimes he had committed as a raiding soldier. No mortification could relieve his feelings of remorse and he finally left his home at Zegé on the south side of Lake Tana in Ethiopia and set out for Jerusalem to obtain the merits of a visit to the Holy Sepulchre. While waiting for a ship at Massawa in 1881, he listened to a sermon on the atoning sacrifice of Christ, took to studying the Amharic New Testament, believed and found peace. His relief was profound. Postponing his pilgrimage to Jerusalem, he gave his purse for travel to the mission, joined the Bethel congregation and became its zealous colporteur at Massawa to begin with and later on in the interior. Whether preaching or engaging in conversation, he didn't miss any opportunity of drawing attention to the New Testament teaching on justification [i.e. being declared righteous before God by grace through faith], which in time earned him the nickname of Paulos [Pauli]. [318]

A year after the departure of *Abba* Gebre-Egziabher, others were to follow. In the words of Gustav Arén,

> On 11 February 1897 another caravan left Asmara for the interior. In

317   Arén 1978, 395–396, Hofgren 1956, 220, 239–242.
318   Arén 1978, 288.

Some members of the Fourth Oromo Expedition. From left to right: Rev. Heinrich Riggers, Rev. Karl Cederqvist, a boy from Lamu, by the name of Stefanos Bonaya, Mr. Karl Nyström, Mrs Edla Hylander and the Rev. Nils Hylander. Picture from 1893.

their company were Gebre-Ewostatewos and Gumesh, Daniel and Tiru. Each couple had a child. The caravan was headed by two of *Aleqa* Tayye's relatives, Meshesha Lulu and Mekonnen Nigusé, who had promised to guide the two families to the house of a big merchant in Gojjam, Adgo Haile-Mariam by name. [...] After six weeks the caravan reached Derita, a market town between Debre Tabor and the southern end of Lake Tana, where the merchants had their home. In a brief report of 7 April 1897 Gebre-Ewostatewos and Daniel praised Mehesha, the leader of the caravan, for his thoughtful care throughout the journey. [319]

At a place called Yejubé, they finally met the monk Gebre-Egziabher

319   Arén 1978, 388–389.

who had struck out from Massawa the year before. The company spent the rainy season at his home in Zegé.

It is to be remembered that both Munzinger and General Charles Gordon had offered the early Swedish missionaries on the coast different alternatives for missionary endeavours while they waited for an appropriate occasion to advance towards the Oromo. However, the missionaries never lost sight of their primary goal and resisted undertaking enterprises which would divert them from their original goal. The members of the Fifth Expedition too were offered opportunities to conduct evangelistic work along their route to Oromo country. When Gebre-Ewostatewos, his wife Gumesh and Gebre-Egziabher arrived at Jiren (the mission settlement established near Jimma, by Nigusé and his colleagues of the Fourth Expedition), Nigusé invited them to settle on his farm. They did so temporarily. However, Gebre-Ewostatewos was, "mentally not at ease", as Arén puts it. He and Daniel, who had their share of disagreements along the way, finally agreed to proceed to Neqemte together. Since Daniel had to proceed to Gudru to wind up his business, Gebre-Ewostatewos made it first to Neqemte where he met the generous and farsighted Fitawrari Dibaba, under whom he was to serve as secretary and as a priest with Evangelical convictions.

In Closing

While waiting and serving on the coast, the missionaries of the SEM and their Kenisha colleagues kept longing, knocking, and reaching out in the direction of the highlands of Eritrea. After all, Imkullu was only a station on the way. And yet there was something richly symbolic in the fact that Imkullu wanted to share something of its motherly bounty with the cool highlands. Like a small army of restless soldiers, like adventurers with distant goals, the Swedish missionaries and their Kenisha colleagues made forward thrusts, trying to find points of entry into areas where they had established contacts earlier and initiated evangelistic work. Furthermore, five Oromo Expeditions were planned and launched from Eritrean soil.

The present chapter is a record of stubborn faith, of starting out again and again, in spite of failures, disappointments and setbacks. Attempts to reach the Oromo were made by land and by sea, by way of rugged hills and hot deserts, through Abyssinia and around it. Here is a tale of repeated cases of coming in hope and retreating with a sense of having failed. In spite of the severe setbacks that they had experienced, the missionaries and their native born Evangelical colleagues didn't give up. It is a wonder that the Oromo venture didn't end up in total despair.

It is worth noting that one of the persons who took an active part in these tempts to reach the Oromo was neither from Sweden nor from Eritrea. He was a successful merchant of over forty, from deep inside Ethiopia, a person who had the money he needed but lacked peace of conscience. He too had been overwhelmed, like many before him, by the Gospel, the good news of the Sovereign grace of God that he had heard at Imkullu. His being commissioned to preach this Gospel at a special ceremony in Imkullu, his advance into Gojjam in connection with the First Oromo Expedition, the ministry of teaching and preaching which he and his team conducted on their journey towards Jimma is a story of courage, ingenuity and dedication. That Nigusé Tashu was employed as secretary by a Muslim prince (Abba Jifar II, 1861–1932) in Jimma and that his entire Evangelical community enjoyed the protection of this prince is also a source of wonder. The Evangelical community or colony at Jiren, near Jimma, is one concrete example of the initial fruits of the mission efforts of Ethiopians within the overall, Oromo-inspired missionary programme of the SEM.[320] Neither can we underestimate the roles played by Ethiopians like *Aleqa* Tayye, *Abba* Gebre-Egziabher Kokebe-Worq, Meshesha Lulu and Adgo Haile-Mariam in the evolution of the Fifth Oromo Expedition, and the evangelistic work carried out in Gojjam and its environs.

The point of departure for the various instances of mission outreach was, nevertheless, Imkullu on the coast. Finally the time of knocking and probing was over. The invisible walls gave way, the highlands and hills opened their passes and the horizons said, *Welcome!* The SEM was finally ready to come to the highlands to stay. Another chapter had begun in the missionary venture of the SEM and the life of the Kenisha. (Ed.)

---

320 Arén 1978, 266–268. See also Fekadu Gurmessa 2009, 160. (Ed.)

Chapter Ten

Mission under a Colonial Master – A Blessing in Disguise?

Introduction

On Monday the 17th [July 1876] we started hearing heavy shooting from the battlefield. Soon, fleeing soldiers returned, with the news that the governor [i.e. *Degiat* Hailu of Tse'azzega] and a big part of his troops had fallen in battle. Women, old men and children started shouting and screaming, pulling out their hair, scratching their faces bloody. Those who could, ran to the battlefield to bury their dead, since all men were away fighting. Soon one could see smoke rising from Zassega [Tse'azzega]. The victors hastened to plunder and destroy the people and burn the village. It is impossible to describe with words the sorrow of my heart, at the thought that my friend was there. I wanted to run to the battlefield but people held me back, because, as they put it, "the soldiers can kill you on the way." [321]

These are the words of Bengta Lager (nee Nilsson), the widow of Per Erik Lager, writing on the Battle of Bet Mekha between *Degiat* Hailu and *Ra'si* Woldenki'el. Joseph Gabrawold gives the following summary

---

321 Beskow I 1884, 242. On the conflict between the leaders of the houses of Tse'azzega and Hazzega, and the deaths of Lager and Haile-Ab, see the Tigrinya text of Johannes Kolmodin's *Traditions de Tse'azzega et Hazzega*, in Archivs d'Études Orientales. Vol. 5:1, 1912, pp. 221–230 and Joseph Gabrawold 1972, 30–31 (Ed.).

Swedish messengers of the Gospel: The Lundahls, Rosa von Hagen, Bengta Lager (nee Nilsson) as well as Beata Andersson (later Karlsson), who arrived in Eritrea 1875.

of the background to the conflict,

> After the war of 1876 at Gura [i.e. between Egyptian and Ethiopian troops] the two Ethiopian (sic) political rivals for control of Hamasen were Dejazmach Hailu and Ras Wolda-Mikael. Both of them had been important people since the time of Wubé and Teodros. In the latter days of Wubé, Hailu became Dejjazmatch and was appointed governor of Hamasen by Wubé. He successfully defeated Ato Selomon of Hazaga. Sometime in the 1850s, Wolda-Mikael was then a young man and lived in the court of Dejjazmatch Hailu after his father's death. [...] Hailu gave Wolda-Mikael some districts to rule over. When Kasa [the future Emperor Yohannes] came to power, both Hailu and Wolda-Mikael were imprisoned and the governorship was given to Wagshum Gebru who later became *Dejjazmatch* Gebru, Ruler of Hamasen from about 1870–1875. Wolda-Mikael got Bogos from the Turks in 1876 and a lot of arms

and ammunitions too. He rose against Hailu and intended to become the Sole ruler of Hamasen.[322]

The passage quoted at the beginning of the chapter is not a description of a battle with an external enemy. It is the anguished cry of a young Swedish widow over the devastation resulting from a conflict between two houses of the same bigger family, in Eritrea, in July 1876. The account is only one example of the cruel conflict that went on between the houses of Tse'azzega (with *Degiat* Hailu as its prince) and Hazzega (with *Ra'si* Woldenki'el as its prince). The writer is Bengta Lager, whose husband, Per-Erik Lager, was killed on July 17, 1876 outside of the Church of Qiddus Miki'el at Addi Qontsi by one of the soldiers of *Ra'si* Woldenki'el.

Bengta was born on March 14, 1842 in Sniberup in the county of Hörby, in Southern Sweden. After being trained as a nurse at the Diaconal Institute in Ersta, Stockholm, she was sent to Massawa in 1875. On November 22, 1875 she married Per-Erik Lager. Following her husband's death she returned to Sweden in November 1876, where she gave birth to a daughter, named Erika on March 4, 1877, who died the same year. In 1880 Bengta migrated to America and settled in Chicago, where she qualified as a medical doctor in 1885, the first Swedish woman who did so. She died in Chicago in 1913.[323]

Italian colonial rule was not exactly an enterprise of charity for the people of Eritrea. There is much that can be said about its darker sides.[324]

---

322 Joseph Gabrawold 1972, 30–31. The specific reason for Woldenki'el's attack on Hailu was the fact that Emperor Yohannes had, upon his return from Gura and Woldenki'el's defection to the Turks [Egyptians], reappointed Hailu governor of Mereb Millash, a move which was bound to awaken the jealousy of Woldenki'el. See the Tigrinya version of Johannes Kolmodin's *Zanta Hazzegan and Tse'azzegan* on the broader background to the conflict (Kiros Fre Woldu 1989, pp. 222–229). See also Sven Rubenson 1976, 333 and Redie Bereketab 2000, 80–81. (Ed.)

323 SEM/MTBB nr. 23, 2003, 20–21. (Ed.)

324 See Michela Wrong's book *I Didn't Do It for You. How the World Betrayed a Small Country.* 2005, especially pp. 35–51. See also T. Negash 1987, 55. In her *Images of Poverty in Colonial Eritrea*, Ulrica Russo Engblom writes, "There exists substantial documentation in the colonial archives in Rome that describe how little girls or teen-age girls – especially orphaned girls who had no family to support them – who were working as servants in European households, were forced to become concubines." Engblom 2003, 29. Yebio Wolde-Mariam's article *Italy: The Unpaid Debt,* (September 17, 2008, published on September 18 on *Awate.com*) is a passionate account of the high cost paid by Eritreans in terms of man power and human lives in Italy's colonial wars. (Ed.)

However, it did bring about some benefits to the people. It stopped a senseless conflict between the two ruling lineages of Deqeteshim in Hamasen. The conflict between the two houses of Tse'azzega and Hazzega was not easily forgotten. Eritreans themselves seem to have understood that the presence of Italy had helped to cool down sentiments. A. Kolmodin, who was on an inspection tour of the Swedish Mission in Eritrea in 1908–1909 visited the homes of adherents to the two warring princes. He writes,

> On my visit to Mebrahtu's house, one of the most prominent members of the house of Hazega, Kentiba Dasda [Desta?], a man around 50 years of age, came to meet me. In my conversation with him, in which Gebre Li'ul, Pastor Svensson's main co-worker served as an interpreter, I had occasion to acquaint myself with the age-old enmity between the houses of Zazega and Hazega, and of how this enmity could be plucked out with the roots, if the Gospel of Jesus Christ were to have free access. For Jesus Christ is the Prince of Peace. The old man appeared to listen attentively to what I said. And indeed, he expressed his wish that it would be so. Now, under Italian rule, the enmity between the two houses doesn't erupt into violent acts, but unfortunately, it is a fact that this enmity is still there in the depth of the heart.[325] (Ed.)

Already in 1892, Elsie Winqvist had written,

> Emperor Yohannes had already fallen in the war with the Dervishes and Italy had used the occasion to establish contacts with the princes and chiefs in the neighbouring highland and persuaded these, by means of bribes, to remain passive as the small Italian colonial army marched up country and took possession of the one region after the other. They occupied the entire country, up to the Mereb. And the friendly Italian colonial government restored the old mission stations at Geleb in Mensa and Beleza in Hamasen to the Swedish Mission.

> The schools and the families which belonged to the congregation moved [from Imkullu] to the highland, indeed to the wonderful climate and the better economic prospects of the region. Soon, new stations were established in Tse'azzega and Asmara and houses were built everywhere.[326]

The fact is that both the SEM and the Kenisha did benefit from some of the positive side effects of Italian colonial rule, although for them too Italy's presence remained a mixed blessing, to the very end.

325   A. Kolmodin 1909, 104–106. (Ed.)
326   Elsie Winqvist 1958, 115.

The colonial authorities allowed fugitive Kenisha, who had fled for their lives, to return from the unbearably hot and humid coast around Massawa to their ancestral homes on the highlands or to other parts of Eritrea. For long stretches of time, the Kenisha were allowed to practice their faith, though grudgingly.[327] The re-entry of the Kenisha into their ancestral villages was, however, not entirely smooth. Their claims to land, though justified, irritated the colonial authorities. Nevertheless, once they were able to settle and operate in their home regions, both Swedish missionaries and the Kenisha started to plan more systematically for the pedagogical and literary work that evangelism and the nurture of the faithful required. The Tigrinya and Tigré languages began to receive the attention that they had lacked thus far as mediums of worship and vehicles for literary production.

K. J. Lundström has given us a closer look at these political, social and religious developments at a crucial time of transition in the history of both Italy and the territory that was henceforth to be known as Eritrea. His text follows. (Ed.)

SEM in the Midst of a Struggle for Control of Territory

We have now followed the development of the Swedish Evangelical Mission in East Africa and the beginnings of an Evangelical church, over a period of almost a quarter of a century. The political situation was rather chaotic due to the power struggle in which a number of nations were locked in the area. The missionaries had had to leave most of the places where they had initiated and carried out different activities. At the beginning of 1890 they concentrated their activities on the centre at Imkullu. During the period from 1866 to 1890, twenty-one missionaries had died on the field, seventeen had returned to Sweden mainly for reasons of health, two (The Hedenströms) had taken up work in Zanzibar and British East Africa, and sixteen were in active service.

European powers were busy, securing control of African territories. The area in which the Swedish Mission was working was no exception. We shall follow the establishment of the new Italian State, its ambition

---

327 Pastors Zer'a-Tsion and Selomon, two fathers of the Kenisha, have recorded this fact succinctly. They write, "Now in 1889, the government of Italy is ruling over Habesha. Consequently, a time of freedom has dawned for those who had once been driven away by the government of Habesha." *Birhan Yikun* 1912, 196. (Ed.)

Mendefera (Addi Ugri), the location of one of the main stations of the SEM on the highlands of Eritrea. The residences of Rev. M Holmer ,the teacher and Addey Bitchir. Picture from 1909.

to expand, its acquisition of the colony of Eritrea, and what this meant for the work of the SEM and its Kenisha colleagues.[328]

We also intend to look into the relations of the SEM to other religious bodies operating in the area. We must, however, begin with some historical background on the land that eventually colonized the territory which came to be known as Eritrea.

A Divided Italy Rallies under Giuseppe Garibaldi

For several hundred years, Italy had been divided into small units, many of which were ruled by neighboring states. In the early nineteenth century, a number of attempts were made to unify the country. However, only in 1860 did democratic forces under the leadership of Giuseppe Garibaldi succeed in forming a united country.[329] Some Italian regions remained

328 Among the sources of history for this period we have the two Italian books *La missione dei minori cappuccini in Eritrea, 1894–1916* by Metodio Da Nembro, 1953, *Politica e religioni nel colonialismo italiano, 1882–1941*, by C.M. Buonaiuti 1982, and Tekeste Negash's book in English, *Italian Colonialism in Eritrea, 1882–1941,* which came out in 1987. T. Negash brings out the interesting fact that among the three ambitions that the colonial government had vis-à-vis Eritrea (i.e. "A Colony of Settlement", "A Source of Raw Material" and "A Source of Colonial Soldiers"), it was the last ambition that was fulfilled in full measure. See T. Negash 1987, 32–65. (Ed.)

329 On Garibaldi and his role in the unification of Italy see Trevelyan 1911 and Smith 1969. (1982). The present Bdho Avenue in Asmara was once called Viale Garibaldi. (Ed.)

outside the country's borders. One of these was Venice, which Garibaldi annexed from Austria in 1866. The Church States, which Pope Pius IX refused to give up, were the only areas that were out of Garibaldi's reach. In 1870, however, Italian troops entered Rome. The Pope responded to this event by withdrawing into the Vatican. He was given a guarantee that he would enjoy full freedom in ecclesiastical matters.

The Acceleration of Italy's Ambitions at Home and Abroad

Italy had, like so many other European countries, been looking for possibilities of acquiring colonies in Africa. Padre Giuseppe Sapeto, an Italian Lazarist, had, as stated earlier, acquired the Bay of Aseb for the Rubattino Navigation Society in 1869. Three years later Italy took possession of Aseb and occupied Massawa in 1885. By 1887, its leaders, especially Francesco Crispi and Giovanni Giolitti, were fully committed to intensifying the effort at acquiring colonies. Italy moved on to create a protectorate over the Somali sultanates of Obbia and Mijjarten.[330]

Eritrea: What kind of Colony?

The Italians had hoped to find riches in Eritrea, either in the form of land on which they could settle their poor peasants or in the form of minerals that could be exploited. However, land was already being used by the local population, which was determined to protect its property. Not much mineral wealth seems to have been discovered. However, on this issue, Dr. Tesfayesus Mehari has a somewhat different view. In a letter to the editor he writes,

> Italy had at least three ambitions in colonizing Eritrea, and it accomplished them all. If it did not succeed like the other colonial powers, it was because of its internal economic, political and administrative weaknesses.
>
> The first ambition was to settle its surplus population along the same lines as the British were doing in their colonies of Australia, New Zealand, South Africa and Rhodesia. All colonies had indigenous populations and Eritrea cannot be an exception! In fact, initially, in 1909 and then in 1926, Italy declared all fertile lands in the most hospitable areas of the

---

330   Already in 1923, a year after his coming to power, Mussolini approved of the occupation of these two sultanates. Del Boca 1965, 9. (Ed.)

The office of the military governor (The Commissariat) at Keren. Picture taken on
A. Kolmodin's visit in 1909.

country as a state domain.[331] The second ambition was the acquisition
of cheap sources of raw materials for the expanding industrial sector
of Italy. Eritrea contained a number of natural resources useful for its
manufacturing enterprises.[332]

The third ambition was to use Eritrea as a spring board for further
colonization of lands adjacent to it, primarily Ethiopia, Somalia and
Yemen across the Sea. Its attempts in this area are well documented.

It has been maintained that Eritrea was more developed than
Ethiopia at the beginning of the twentieth century. It had indeed a
number of urban centres, and a considerable wage earning population

---

331 See for example: *Government of Ethiopia, Ministry of Land Reform Administration (1969).
Report on the Land Survey of Eritrea Province*, especially p. 42, for an exhaustive list of fertile
lands and locations that were annexed by the Italian government of the day. (Ed.)

332 Among others see: U. R. Engblom (2003). *Images of Poverty in Colonial Eritrea as Portrayed
by Swedish Missionary Sources*, NAI, Uppsala. See also Wrong 2005, 60–70. (Ed.)

with a growing purchasing power.[333]

Though this statement may be true of certain sections of the population within the urban centres, the population did suffer from shortage of food and several epidemics during the period stretching from 1915 to 1930. There was drought in many areas, both in the Tigrinya-speaking highlands and in the northern parts of Eritrea. Prices had risen considerably and imports from Italy had become more expensive. Farmers suffered from shortage of rain and crop failures. Several epidemics, such as the Spanish flu, ravaged particularly the highland areas.

Growing Vitality in the Catholic Church

In the period between 1815 and 1914, the Catholic Church in Europe displayed remarkable vitality. Several new movements were created within the church. The Society of Jesus was revived, and there was a general renewal of monastic life. Orders and congregations for both men and women multiplied in Europe and other continents.[334]

There was a revival of studies. Many institutions of learning were founded and scholarships made available.[335] One could also notice an increase of devotion to the Virgin Mary and to the Sacred Heart of Jesus.

A Council held at the Vatican in 1869–1870, under Pope Pius IX (1846–1878) gave strong support to the doctrine of the supreme authority of the Pope as the administrative head of the Church and Custodian of the Christian Faith. This claim widened the gulf that already separated other Christian churches from Rome. It also aggravated the conflict between Church and State. Pius IX promoted the reception of several teachings, among which were the dogmas of the supremacy of the Pope over the Church Universal and of Papal Infallibility. He issued a Syllabus of Errors among which he listed Socialism and Communism, and several other movements, including the Bible Societies. He rejected the views that civil power should have full control of the public schools, and that Church and State should be separated. He maintained that it was expedient that the Catholic religion be regarded as the recognized religion of the state, to the exclusion of others.[336]

---

333 Tekeste Negash 1987, 155. Reference is made to A. Pollera 1935, 76, 84.
334 Latourette II 1975, 1083–1085.
335 Latourette II 1975, 1088–1089.
336 Latourette II 1975, 1099–1101.

A view of Asmara mission station and the church, which was dedicated in 1902.
1. The Church. 2. Residence of Signe Berg. 3. The school for boys. 4. The bedroom for boys. 5. The residence of the head of the station. 6. The printing press. 7. Teachers' residence.
8. Preparatory school on first floor and residence for teachers on second floor.

The Waldensian Church
– A Protestant Minority in Catholic Italy

It is only appropriate that members of the ECE become acquainted with the Waldensian Church, some of whose members have played an important role as missionaries within the ECE. There has always been a tendency to regard Italy as an exclusively Roman Catholic country. The vast majority of its population was and is indeed Catholic. However, there have been, over the centuries, movements, inspired by the Bible, that took exception to the overwhelmingly dominant religion in the country. One such movement goes under the name of *Waldensians*. The leader of this movement was Peter Valdes or Waldes (ca 1141 to 1217), a rich, young merchant from Lyons in southern France. He was deeply moved by the words of Jesus in Matthew 19:21, "[...] Go, sell your possessions, and give to the poor, and you will have treasure in heaven. Then come, follow me."[337]

In 1176 he decided to provide for his family and his home district, and to give the remainder of his property to the poor. Many were attracted by his actions and decided to follow him. However, the Archbishop of Lyons forbade the group to preach. The Pope was more ready to accommodate the movement, but with certain restrictions. The group persisted in what they believed to be their calling and Pope

337 Matthew 19:21, quoted from the New English Bible.

Siricius excommunicated them at the Council of Verona in 1184.

On September 12, 1532, at the Synod of Chanforan, in Northern Italy, Waldensians from both sides of the Alps decided, at a duly called assembly, to identify themselves with the Reformation. At that point, the movement became a church within the so-called Reformed branch of Protestantism.

The Waldensians refused to recognize the Pope's claims and taught that the bishop of Rome was not the head of the Church Universal. They also held that women and laymen could preach and teach, that masses and prayers for the dead were without biblical warrant. They criticized prayers in Latin, as most of the faithful did not understand the language. They constituted their own ministry, with bishops, priests and deacons, and appointed a head for their fellowship. The movement spread to many countries, but met with severe persecution and military measures at the hands of the Catholic Church. The Waldensians who survived the persecutions sought refuge in the valleys of the western Alps in Italy.[338]

In 1884 the Waldensians were finally recognized and their churches could move from the alpine villages into the towns of the Italian peninsula. In their evangelistic efforts, friends from European Protestant countries gave them assistance. So did Sweden in 1860. This relationship developed into cooperation with the SEM in Eritrea.[339]

The Waldensian Church to the Aid of the SEM

With Italy established on the Red Sea Coast, the Swedish Mission at Imkullu was faced with a new set of circumstances. Italian, a language in which the missionaries and teachers were not versed, now became one of the working languages of the area. The mission was in great need of Italian teachers and decided to request their friends in the Waldensian Church to help them acquire teachers. The Board of the Waldensian Church decided to send a young pastoral candidate, Filippo Grill, to Eritrea in 1889. He was stationed at Imkullu and was the first of a number of Italian teachers who worked with the SEM over

338 Latourette I 1975, 451–453.
339 Giorgio Tourn, *You are My Witnesses. The Waldensians Across 800 Years*. Torino 1989. 171 ff. Most of the facts in this section were given to me by Pastor Bruno Tron of the Waldensian Church, and a former missionary to Eritrea. (Ed.)

a period that extended up to 1954.

Filippo Grill worked at Imkullu for two years. In 1909, Benedetto Giudici joined the SEM as teacher and stayed until 1913. The third teacher, Alessandro Tron, arrived in 1913 and came to serve up to 1954.[340] In 1919 two teachers arrived. One of these, Armand-Hugon, left after a year while Emilio Ganz came to serve for a whole decade. In 1921 Enrico Coïsson arrived. He served the ECE over a period of 20 years at the stations of Shimanigus, Geleb and Keren. Decisions on the employment of Italian staff were made by the SEM Field Conference and approved by the board of the SEM in Sweden.

In 1924 three new Italian missionary teachers (two women and one man) arrived. Germana Olivetti was placed at the Girls' School in Beleza to help Britta Edlund, and Nora Rostan was placed in Asmara. The service of these two teachers lasted for a short period of time. Eraldo Lageard arrived at the end of 1924, was placed initially in Geleb and then moved to Asmara. He served the SEM for six years. In the Nineteen-twenties, the Waldensian teachers on the payroll of the SEM were six; in the thirties only two were left: A. Tron and E. Coïsson.[341]

The First Decade of the SEM in Italian Eritrea, 1890–1900

The Scourge of Drought, Locusts and Cattle Diseases

From the end of the 19th century up to the second decade of the 20th, the African Savannah, which had enjoyed a long period of good precipitation, was hit by drought. Locusts and caterpillars destroyed crops, cattle deceases were rampant and oxen perished in great numbers. This chain of events lead to starvation in which about one third of the population died. This was evident also in Eritrea. Crowds of people moved down to Massawa to purchase grain, which the Italians had imported from India. Many lost their lives on the way, due to hunger, assault or robbery. Some died of cholera, typhus and smallpox. In the autumn of 1889 Imkullu clinic received a great number of sick people and, while many were helped, 30–40 people died per day. In November, Dr Winqvist reported that 100 people were dying every week

---

340 Alessandro Tron was ordained Pastor by the Waldensian Church in 1924, upon the request of the SEM.

341 Coîsson R. *I valdesi e l'opera missionaria.* Torre Pellice 1979, 42 ff.

of smallpox. At Imkullu the famine relief programme of the mission assisted some 500 families with a daily ration of two meals.

In her little booklet *Livsbilder från Eritrea* (Life Portraits from Eritrea), the first of two books with the same title, which came out in 1921, Elsie Winqvist has a chapter entitled "Hunger". She writes,

> During the winter of 1890–1891 a terrible famine ravaged not only the whole of Hamasen but also the provinces to the far south. People streamed to the lowlands. The entire plain outside Munkullo Station became a massive camp with famished, sick and dying people: an overwhelming concentration of human misery. They all lay on the hot desert sands.[342]

Sometimes the number of the needy would go up to 800. As the sick and impoverished began to recuperate, they would ask for work, which could not be provided by the mission.

Imkullu mission had, as we have mentioned, been given the name Betel. The people began, however, to call it *Medhané Alem*, (the Saviour of the World). The name had the connotation of healer. Pilgrims and others who passed by the centre, stopped to kiss the wall, an Orthodox manner of venerating churches.[343]

Medical Care, Evangelism and Diaconal Activities

In 1891 Dr. K. Winqvist reported that his schedule included daily morning devotions. The doctor and his co-workers met for Bible study on Monday and Tuesday, after lunch. On Tuesday and Friday afternoons they went to the market to engage people in conversation. On Sunday at 2 p.m. the doctor had "open house" for co-workers and members of the congregation. Later on, some of those present would go out, two by two, to nearby villages. Most of the people in these villages were Muslims. Evangelists like Dawit Amanuel and Alazar Hemmed helped the faithful to establish contacts with the inhabitants of the surrounding villages.

Winqvist realised the importance of studying the Qur'an and urged his colleagues to read it and equip themselves for fruitful dialogue with the Muslims. He reported, however, about discouraging experiences, a

---

342   E. Winqvist 1921, 33.
343   Arén 1978, 319–323.

The church at the village of Kwandebba and some of the faithful. Picture taken on a visit by Professor Kolmodin in 1909.

result of Muslim aversion to the Christian faith.[344]

When Alazar was transferred to Geleb in 1890, a former highwayman known as Yishaq Hemmed took his place. The latter, who was born in 1866 in Habab, north of Mensa, was left homeless and joined a robber band, but quarrelled with its leader and moved to Massawa where he worked as a longshoreman. He happened to hurt his leg seriously and went to Imkullu to seek help. He was now eighteen. It took one year for the wound to heal and Yishaq ended up joining Lundahl's school. Some two years later he had a dream in which he saw a bright figure calling him to load his camels and proceed to the north. Yishaq saw this as a call from God to return to Habab as a messenger of Christ. However, the mission needed him at Imkullu and a long period elapsed before he could be released. When he was finally ready to move, the colonial authorities refused to give him permission. It was against their policy to allow a Christian evangelist to settle in a Muslim area.[345]

The Evangelical revival in Europe at this time also led to widespread charitable undertakings. In Sweden too, the SEM set up an organization for aid to the poor. When this organization learned of the crying needs in East Africa, it donated the amount of 24,000 SEK. Sweden was not

344   Arén 1978, 324–325. Alazar (1871–1964), was David's cousin.
345   Arén 1978, 325–326. General reference to Yishaq in SEM/MT1889, 83.

a rich country at the time, and the mission could hardly afford this amount, had it not been for the dedication of its supporters.[346]

Land Rights and Land Policies in Colonial Eritrea

Many of the Bible readers of the eighteen-sixties and seventies had taken refuge at Imkullu and spent years there studying, teaching, working on the production of literature and translating. They now saw an opportunity to return to their ancestral homes on the highlands.[347] There were, however, factors that complicated the circumstances under which the Kenisha refugees tried to return.

Land ownership had traditionally been defined as *risti*, i.e. ownership by inheritance.[348] As the population had grown and as there had been an increase of social and physical mobility, certain changes had occurred in the system of land ownership. A "Forty Years" right had been confirmed during the time of Emperor Yohannes and Ra'si Alula, whereby people who had lived for forty years in a certain area would not only be given the right to own land, but also be allowed to partake in making decisions on communal issues, even though they were not natives to the area. Previously, noblemen and ecclesiastics had special privileges. The Italians curtailed these rights and only a limited number of monasteries had the right to receive tribute and help from the population and the rulers. The Italian government also expropriated significant areas for urban land.[349]

Returning Kenisha in Conflict with their Traditional Home Regions

In 1893, the Swedish Mission had adopted a policy that had a twofold aim: the promotion of revival in the Orthodox Church and the formation of an Evangelical church community. The first of these aims

---

346 On the whole issue of poverty, and humanitarian assistance by Swedish missionaries in Eritrea, see Engblom 2003. (Ed.)

347 Arén 1978, 313–314.

348 Professor Asmarom has pointed out that, "The dominant land tenure system in Hamasien was not *risti* but *diesa*, a rotating system of ownership in which land was redistributed periodically, every few years. Risti was dominant in Seraye. In all areas however the *gulti* system was present, as a feudal superstructure on top of the actual peasant landholding system." *Gulti* is land given to a subject, a subordinate, by his overlord or superior. (Ed.)

349 Pankhurst 1968, 73ff. The 40-year rule actually predates Emperor Yohannes and Alula.

was in the process of being realized, with many village teachers and evangelists operating in the field. The realization of the second aim was, however, very slow in coming. *Qeshi* Selomon and *Qeshi* Zer'a-Tsion had been ordained in the Orthodox Church, an ordination that the mission regarded as valid. *Qeshi* Marqos had been ordained in Sweden. In 1888, the first two were authorized by the mission to perform ministerial acts. Marqos Girmai received the same authorization a year later. For the next twenty years, these three were the only national pastors. No wonder that this lack of trained shepherds resulted in weaknesses in the spiritual lives of the congregations.[350] There was, apparently, a third clergyman of Orthodox background, *Qeshi* Wolde-Giorgis of Shimanigus La´ilai, who also performed baptisms.[351]

Those who returned to their highland homes had experienced a new dimension of faith and worship and had adopted different patterns of social behaviour. Their insistence on individual conversion and a new mode of life underlined the differences between them and other villagers. Conflicts were to be expected and were not long in coming.[352]

The primary reason for the conflicts was not the question of land, a fact that would come to the fore later on, but rather the Evangelical conviction of the returnees. These were seen by many as traitors to the established values of their communities. For this reason, they were denied the right of cultivating their inherited land and owning the buildings on it, even though their legal right was confirmed, and the local community was forced to grant them residence. This issue came to a head in May 1891 when Kentiba Medhin, chief of Kwandebba and a person of Evangelical persuasion, died but couldn't be given a traditional Orthodox funeral, on the ground that he had neglected his father confessor. Kenisha in Beleza took the responsibility for his funeral.

The convent of Debre Bizen was, as stated earlier, by tradition the bulwark of Orthodoxy in the north. In May 1891, the abbot tried to have *Qeshi* Selomon banished from Addi Kolom as an intruder and a disturber of the public peace. The colonial tribunal in Asmara rejected the charges and upheld the principle of religious liberty. In the spring of 1891, the Orthodox Church excommunicated a number of distinguished priests for associating with the returning exiles. The

350 Arén 1978, 348–349.
351 Arén 1978, 348 note 184.
352 Arén 1978, 326–327.

excommunicated were the venerable *Abba* Wolde-Yohannes, chief priest of Beleza, *Qeshi* Gebre-Ewostatewos Ze-Mikael (1865–1905) of Wekki Dibba, and debtera Tekle-Haimanot Mihirka (1869–1932) of Hatsebo, near Aksum in Tigrai, who lived in Wekki at the time. These persons lost their livelihood and the mission granted them emergency aid.[353]

Ambivalence and Irritation of Colonial Authorities
Towards the Kenisha

The opposition of the Eritrean peasants to the returnees as well as the memory of the debacle at The Battle of Adwa in 1896 made the Italian colonial authorities sensitive to any development that could disturb the peace and order in the colony. *Haleqa* Tewolde-Medhin Gebru from *Mai Misham* in Tigrai, had moved to Addi Deqqu Tochula in Serayé during the great famine in the early eighteen-nineties. In March 1899 he came to Beleza to seek a cure for suppurating ulcers. He was bitterly opposed to every *Tsärä Maryam* (Enemy of Mary), a derogatory designation for Evangelical Christians. One day he heard a sermon at the hospital. The text was the *Magnificat* (Luke 1:46–55, Mary's song of praise). The preacher spoke with reverence about the Virgin Mary.

What Tewolde-Medhin saw in Beleza as his health improved led him to become a diligent reader of the Scriptures. After returning to Addi Deqqi Tochula, he made it a point to emphasize the Scriptures in his teaching. This provoked strong opposition in the village and charges were brought against him and his wife. However, a provincial court sentenced the village to pay a fine for having brought false charges against him. This led to more unrest and the governor-general of Eritrea, Ferdinando Martini, ordered Tewolde-Medhin to leave the village. The latter did so and took refuge in Beleza. Many priests and monks now felt encouraged to oppose the Evangelicals openly and bring charges against them. The monks at Debre Bizen took to the war path when they became aware of the great impact that another monk with Evangelical convictions, *Abba* Gebre-Sillassé Mengistu or *Abba* Mä'asho, was making through his teachings at the monastery of Inda-Sillassé.

Orthodox complaints about the growing influence of Evangelical Christians irritated the Italian authorities. This led Martini to use diplomatic channels to ask the Swedish government to exert its

353   Arén 1978, 328.

influence to moderate the zeal of the Swedish Mission.[354]

He also claimed that the mission had violated the colonial code of conduct by allowing *Qeshi* Marqos Girmai to marry Miss Regina Johansson (1857–1943), a Swedish schoolteacher engaged in work among women. The Swedish Government responded to the allegations by stating that it was unable to exercise control over the Mission as the latter was an independent organization, but that the government was prepared to put pressure on the Home Board of the Mission to observe the requirements of the Italian Government in this regard.

The Mission stated that it hoped that the colonial government would uphold the principle of religious liberty that it had proclaimed, and that Evangelical Christians too would be granted the same rights that were enjoyed by others. The issue of interracial marriage was more controversial. The Mission Board stated that it had advised against the marriage, for practical reasons, but that it had no objections, in principle. It declared, however, that the problem would not arise again, as the Mission had ceased to send students to Sweden for further studies. The Italian authorities were satisfied with this declaration and *Qeshi* Marqos and his wife were permitted to continue their services as husband and wife.[355]

Amharic or Tigrinya? The Language Issue

At Imkullu, the multi-ethnic composition of the Evangelical community made the use of a common language necessary. Lundahl felt that this had to be Amharic, the most widely used Ethiopian language within the Evangelical community on the coast. However, portions of Scripture and hymns were eventually made available in the language of the Oromo. The fact that portions of Scripture were already available in Amharic was an added impetus for the use of the Bible in Amharic. Amharic was the easiest medium for contacts with the "political, commercial and scholarly elite" on the highlands. The language of the ordinary man and woman on the Eritrean highlands was however Tigrinya. When the Winqvists began promoting Tigrinya as a medium for Bible teaching, even Tigrinya speakers objected. Some of them regarded Tigrinya as a "language of nomads, which hardly has the words and expressions for

354 Arén 1978, 344.
355 Arén 1978, 345.

anything but the undeveloped life of the nomads."[356]

The Winqvists delegated a *debtera* (a scribe) to collect proverbs, riddles and legends that would provide a basis for the Tigrinya vocabulary needed for a translation of the Holy Scriptures. In spite of opposition, even from missionaries, the Winqvists began to produce some written material with the help of the reluctant Marqos Girmai, who found the task very exacting. However, the undertaking gathered momentum when a young man by the name of Gebre-Ewostatewos came to Winqvist's aid as his assistant. In 1897 a Tigrinya Reader was completed and two years later a Catechism was ready.[357]

In Closing

The declaration of Eritrea as an Italian colony opened a new chapter in the lives of the SEM and the Kenisha. If fear and flight were the marks of the descent of the Kenisha to the coast around Imkullu, return and reintegration became the marks of their ascent to the highlands. They returned not only to the cool highlands of the hinterland but also to their ancestral homes. The returning Kenisha needed to be reintegrated, not only because they had been away for a long time but also because they came with a more or less modified identity. They now spoke not only of *deqqi Addi* (children of one's home area) or *deqqi godebo* (children of a neighbouring village) but also of *deqqi mahber* (children of the same religious community or association).

The reintegration of the Kenisha into their home communities was not free from friction. In fact, in many cases, it was marked by conflicts, by court-cases before Italian authorities and attempts at mediation by community elders. The situation was no doubt painful for both the Kenisha and their mainly Orthodox relatives and compatriots. These conflicts were part of the price that the Kenisha had to pay for their stand in matters of faith.

Having left the church of their forefathers, the Kenisha were naturally not made to feel welcome to it. There were now a number of practices about which they didn't feel comfortable. They didn't kiss the cross that Orthodox priests offered them. They didn't bow down as

---

356 Words are attributed to *Qeshi* Marqos Girmai. See Alazar Menghestu 2003, 32. (Ed.)
357 Arén 1978, 333–334.

they passed by an Orthodox church. They had become people of new meetings and new songs. They were no longer bound by the rulings of fasting or by many of the religious holidays of the Orthodox Church.

They had ceased taking part in *gwaila*, the traditional dances, at weddings and other festivals.

It is to the credit of many traditional, rural Eritrean societies, that the Kenisha could eventually be reintegrated into the social fabric moulded through generations by their common ancestors. Most of these traditional highland societies were big-hearted enough to embrace their rebellious kith and kin who had become adherents of another Christian tradition. However, it is also to the credit of the Kenisha that they maintained a basic respect for their forefathers and the traditions that they had inherited from them.

Professor Asmarom Legesse has shared with me some very interesting glimpses into this remarkable phenomenon of adjustment to tradition among the Kenisha. On the role played by his great grandfather in this regard, he writes,

> Equally significant is the fact that Qeshi Zer'a-Tsion was also one of the authors of the customary laws of Karneshim, as well as the keeper of the book (*tehaz debter*) throughout his life. That meant that whenever conflict broke out in Karneshim he was called upon to mediate, open the book and interpret the relevant articles. The role of *Tehaz Debter* was passed on to his son and grandson and it is in the possession of the family to this day and has been entrusted to me to bind and preserve.[358]

Loyalty to a common ancestral tradition as well as the magnanimity of kith and kin did play an important role in the return and re-integration of fugitive Kenisha into their home villages. Nevertheless a speedy and more or less smooth re-integration would have been well nigh impossible without the staying hand of the Italian colonial administration. (Ed.)

---

358 On a somewhat similar note, Professor Bereket Habte-Silassie writes, "I always thought it remarkable that the people of our village [Addi Nifas] had such high regard for my father despite his conversion to the Lutheran Protestant faith from Orthodox Christianity, the faith of his forefathers. The overwhelming majority of Christians in our country subscribe to the Orthodox faith, and my father had been an ordained priest. His conversion had convulsed the village; yet his standing in the community was not adversely affected by it, although a few stalwarts distanced themselves from him." Bereket Habte Selassie 2007, 11. (Ed.)

Chapter Eleven

Return to Mensa 1889

Introduction

In 1889 the supporters of the SEM in Sweden could read,

> We would like to make known [to you] that the old houses have now been
> repaired and that Twoldo Medhin [Tewolde-Medhin], a disciple who had
> to flee to save his life about ten years ago, has now returned with his
> family as a messenger of the Gospel, to serve His Lord and the mission
> which once became the means of his salvation and which contributed
> to the nurture of his Christian life. So be it! May the Lord grant our
> brothers and sisters a solid refuge, when times of severe testing come!
> Glory and praise be to the Lord for everything.[359]

Tewolde-Medhin had started training for church orders in the
Orthodox Tewahdo Church, at an early age and was ordained deacon
by Abune Atnateos in 1872. Two years later he had joined the school
run by Hedenström at Geleb and became a communicant member of
the Betel congregation in 1876. In 1877 he had become an evangelist at
Ailet. In 1883 he was sent to Sweden for further training. On his return
from Sweden he was stationed at Hirgigo.[360]

In 1879, the station at Geleb had been evacuated in a hurry, by order
of *Ra'si* Alula. Villagers took to looting almost instantly.[361] Indeed, only

359   SEM/MT No 3, 1890, page 19.
360   Arén 1978, 297.
361   Arén 1978, 225–226. (Ed.)

ruins were left of the Swedish mission. However, the faithful returned to the site of the ruins of their church in 1889, ten years after the abandonment of the station.

Following the withdrawal of the first Swedish missionaries to Kunama, there was almost a total lack of contact between this mission field and SEM. This was not the case with Mensa. Contacts were maintained with Geleb and some other areas. This element of relative continuity in the missionary venture in Mensa was vital for the slow but steady consolidation and growth of an Evangelical community in the area. The flame of Evangelical Christianity continued to burn, though its strength fluctuated from time to time. Eventually, Geleb became a success story in the history of the ECE.

Several factors must have contributed to this state of things. One possible factor was the receptivity of the people of Mensa who carried memories of the Christian Gospel and Christian practice from their past. As a mission field, Mensa was evidently far easier to plough and cultivate than was Kunama. Another possible factor was the presence of some highly gifted and motivated missionaries as well as Mensa pastors and evangelists in the area.

Having said so, we must add that some of these gifted missionaries were also sources of problems. Mensa appears to have been the one field of the SEM where the disagreements of strong-minded and stubborn missionaries led to internal conflicts also among the Kenisha of the area, who took sides in the state of disharmony caused by missionaries. The work in Mensa flourished in spite of these weaknesses. One is reminded of the words of St. Paul in 2 Corinthians 4:7, "But we have this treasure in jars of clay to show that this all-surpassing power is from God and not from us." Let K. J. Lundström develop the Mensa story for us. His text follows. (Ed.)

A Station Reopened

Evangelical mission in the Tigré-speaking areas dates from December 1873 when Hedenström started work at Geleb. The local population, which was semi-nomadic to a large extent, showed little or no interest in literacy and formal education. Instead, the station became a refuge for young Bible Readers from Hamasen. Their teacher was *Qeshi* Selomon. Mission activities in this area continued up to 1879 when *Ra'si*

Alula ordered the mission to hand over Selomon or leave the area. The mission could of course not agree to this demand and the station was therefore vacated. Some time later a new attempt was made to resume activities, but Alula was adamant and Geleb was again abandoned in 1881.[362] After Italy's occupation of what is now highland Eritrea, the station at Geleb was reopened in December 1889.

Tewolde-Medhin Gebre-Medhin moved with his family from Hirgigo on the coast to Geleb in the hills. In the spring of 1890 Dawit and Alazar returned as well, now in the company of the Rev. Karl Gustaf and Mrs. Emelie Rodén. Hirgigo was now reduced to a substation under Imkullu and Geleb became the centre for mission activities among the Mensa and people in the surrounding areas.[363] In the eighteen-seventies, the majority of the people in Geleb had been Orthodox Christians and those who turned to Islam ran the risk of being ostracised. In 1890 the situation was reversed. The Christians were now a minority and Orthodox Christianity was fighting a losing battle. All churches in Mensa were in ruins. One exception was the Mariam Tsion in Geleb, but it was very simple and lacked even a tabot.[364] When the old priest who served at the said church died, a Protestant missionary, Pastor K.G. Rodén, performed the funeral.[365]

Serving the Community

The reopening of the station at Geleb coincided with a great famine that hit the whole of East Africa. The Mensa area was no exception and people were clamouring for help. The mission distributed food free of charge to the famished and enfeebled, but also sought ways by which the people would be able to earn a living. A limited number of people could be employed as labourers at the mission compound, but other forms of help had to be found. One of the routes from the coast to the interior

362 Arén 1978, 352.
363 Arén 1978, 353.
364 A replica of the Ark of the Covenant. There is a lot of secrecy around the contents and substance of the *tabot*, a sense of awe which is an echo of the attitude of reverence which was attached to the original Ark of the Covenant in Israel. It is generally believed that the tabot is made of choice wood or marble on which the Ten Commandments and other engravings or texts have been inscribed are made. No Tewahdo Orthodox Church building is regarded as rightly dedicated if the altar doesn't contain a *tabot*. (Ed.)
365 Arén 1978, 354.

Pastor Tewolde-Medhin Gebre-Medhin (1860-1930), a leading light in the history of the ECE. Here with his family.

passed through Geleb. However, even camels negotiated the rocky and mountainous terrain with difficulty. Road building became Rodén's answer. This took much time, but the project resulted in an improved road connection with Keren. The limited resources at Rodén's disposal were soon supplemented by larger grants from the colonial government that had witnessed his initiatives with great pleasure. Governor Ferdinando Martini, who had initially been quite critical of the Swedish Evangelical Mission in Eritrea, changed his attitude completely when he saw the way the missionaries operated.[366] In 1905 Martini paid a visit to Geleb. He expressed his pleasure at seeing that the station at Geleb had expanded and added: "I have heard that you even wish to build a house in Keren. You have my permission to do so".

According to Rodén, Martini also urged him to extend his mission work there by establishing a day school. The commissioner of Keren who stood nearby approved, but added that it ought to be *una bella casa* (a beautiful house). The Governor also gave a gift of 1,000 Lira towards

366 Arén 1978, 355–356.

the printing of *Fetih Mehary*, Rodén's study on the laws of the people of Mensa, and told Rodén that he, when he first came to Eritrea in 1891 as a commission member, had his fears that the mission would act in ways that were detrimental to the colonial government.[367] He was wary of movements that Abyssinians could use against the colony. However, after having seen the mission in function, he added, he had found out that it was indeed making efforts to "imbue the people with civilization". He went on to say, "I have changed my policy towards your mission and I wish to support it." In closing, he advised Rodén to do even more to direct the activities of the mission towards Muslims.[368] This attitude changed when his successor, Salvago Raggi, took over. Rev. J. M Nilsson, who was in charge of Geleb station temporarily in 1912, wrote,

> The Tigré mission is experiencing a period of weakness, not least due to the rapid expansion of the Catholic mission which has the strong support of the government.[369]

Evangelism

Rodén's main interest was in the area of production of written material for evangelism. The first book in Tigré had appeared in 1889, a spelling book and reader composed by Tewolde-Medhin Gebre-Medhin. The Gospel of Mark was translated by Dawit Amanuel and published by the mission press at Imkullu. Dawit had translated the New Testament and it was resolved that he, Tewolde-Medhin, Rodén and Winqvist would review the work, paying attention to the Greek original as well as to the Ge'ez and English versions. Yishaq Hemmed served as secretary. It took the group twelve years to complete the work that was published in 1902. In spite of the fact that the entire staff had contributed to the translation, the final version was attributed to Rodén.[370]

In many respects, the approach to mission work in this region was different from that used on the Eritrean Highlands. As mentioned earlier, the people of Mensa were semi-nomadic and the system of working through village schools was not applicable among them. It

367   EFS Annual Report 1905, 64.
368   SEM/MT, 1906, 42–45.
369   SEM/MT 1914, 12. In spite of the reception S. Raggi gave Kolmodin in 1909!
370   Arén 1978, 357.

The church in Geleb, Mensa. A painting based on a picture taken by Holmer in March 1900.

Baptism of former Muhammedans at the church in Geleb. The text above the altar is taken from John 1:17 and reads, "Grace and truth came through Jesus Christ".

was felt, therefore, that Christian boarding schools would be the most effective way of carrying out mission in the area. A considerable number of young people had been converted while attending school at Geleb. It is noteworthy that the entire group of fifteen students admitted to the boarding school for boys in 1892, joined the Evangelical congregation. After some years of further training some were commissioned as teachers: Timoteos Faid (Yohannes) (1879–1956/7) was sent to Mihlab, Yosef Hemmed (1881–1966) and Natnael Negasi (1882–1939) to Imkullu, Samuel Etman (1881–1940) and Abraham Etel Jeme (1881–1926) to Geleb. [371] Most of them came from Muslim homes.[372]

Arén writes,

> All of them seem to have come from Muslim homes, though Natnael's earlier name Takles (Tekle-Yesus) might point to an Orthodox background.[373]

One of the very first converts was a remarkable young Muslim woman from Ad-Takles, by the name of Medhin Hemmed (1878–1931) or Amna, as she was originally called. She came to work with the Rodéns and became a Christian. She was instrumental in leading five of her relatives to Christ. She was married to Petros Resiq (1875–1926), who later became printer at the Mission Press in Asmara. He was a member of the holy Mirghani family, whose religious leadership extended over much of Eastern Sudan and Eritrea. It will be remembered that the founder of the Mirghani movement was Muhammad Uthman al-Mirghani (1793–1852). He was sent by his master Ahmed ibn Idris to Egypt and Sudan and preached among the Bani Amir in 1817. Medhin was, in many ways, an example of a new category of women in this area, instrumental in contributing to the emancipation of Muslim women and the promotion of Christian witness.[374]

Disagreement on Choice of Tigré Language Forms

A question which caused discord with Richard Sundström and other co-workers who transliterated Tigré words, was Rodén's unyielding preference for the first vowel of the Ge'ez alphabet (the so-called *Ge'ez*)

---

371 Arén 1978, 357. Abraham Etel Jeme was likewise called Jeme before his baptism and his father's name was Etel.
372 Arén 1978, 360–361.
373 Arén 1978, 361.
374 Arén 1978, 360–363.

The Children's Home and school in Geleb, 1908.

to the fourth, (the so-called *rabi'*). Rodén was not prone to yield on
this matter and the printing of the NT was delayed for two years, when
his views finally prevailed. At the missionary conference in Beleza in
October 1900, Rodén requested that the rules that the local staff had
proposed be changed. The minutes of § 42 read,

> As brother Rodén did not want to yield in any way, the conference
> cannot take the responsibility for opposing his wishes. The conference
> feels that he be allowed to follow his opinion, even if this is in conflict

with the rules laid down by the Board [...], as the indigenous teachers have asked for a definite answer in order not to delay the printing of the NT unduly.

Professor Enno Littmann decided to use the fourth vowel of the Ethiopic alphabet whenever the vowel *a* came at the end of a word.[375]

This was also the conviction of Richard Sundström, who came to Geleb with his wife in 1898. Besides undertaking studies in Theology, he had taken courses in Medicine at Livingstone College in London. While serving as a doctor, he studied language, culture and traditional beliefs among the Tigré-speaking people. With his keen sense for languages, he composed hymns and started on the translation of some books of the Old Testament. A young convert from Islam named Naffa wod Etman (1882–1909) introduced Sundström and Littmann to Mensa folklore and culture. Naffa's father was a minstrel and knew a number of Tigré songs and ballads about his Mensa ancestors. Naffa used to ask his father to recite these poems and explain every simile and metaphor. He thus acquired exceptional insights into his own language, history and beliefs. Against the will of his Muslim family, he went to the mission school where he became a follower of Christ and was baptized. In 1901 he was employed as a teacher. He was very close to Sundström who owed much of his Tigré production to him. In April 1907, Naffa was invited to go to Germany to assist Littmann in his work. He contributed much to the work that was published under the title: *Publications of the Princeton Expedition to Abyssinia.*[376] Naffa had a desire to continue his education in Sweden. The SEM Board, however, stood firm in its resolution not to educate any more Eritreans in Sweden. He therefore had to return home. On his way home he disappeared from the ship on which he was sailing, under mysterious circumstances. His death was a great loss to Tigré evangelism and scholarship.[377]

---

375   Arén 1978, 356–357. Littmann, *Publications of the Princeton...*Vol I, 1910, XIV.
376   In his *Preliminary Report of the Princeton University to* Abyssinia (which was published in 1907) Enno Littmann lists "Various folk-songs, collected by R. Sundström, numbering 549, some of which consist of as many as 100 lines." Littmann 1907, 12. The publications, which covered four volumes, were published by E. Littmann in Leiden between 1910 and 1915. For details see Arén 1978, 468. (Ed.)
377   Arén 1978, 357–359.

Itinerant Mission to Marea and Bogos
– Sundström and Alazar

Sundström concentrated on medical work and on evangelism in the outlying areas around Keren. In the latter part of 1903, he and Alazar paid a visit to an area in the vicinity of Marea. He reached the Malabso plain that lay at an altitude of 1850 metres. The Barka lowlands lay to the west of this area, the Barka River to the north, and the Anseba River to the east. From Keren the place could be reached in some five hours. The people there used to be Christians but were now Muslims. Sundström was moved by the situation and writes,

> We have already been confined to Geleb far too long, and allowed our dim lights to burn almost exclusively for its people. We now want to expand. Our question is: "In which direction first? To Marea!" He writes that he burst out with joy over the beautiful place he had come to: "Wonderful! Just like a glorious day in July in Scandinavia, with the fragrance of flowers and the songs of birds. And I began singing, at the top of my voice, "Great, forsooth, it is to be here! O, how sweet life tastes just now!"[378] And here a group of black-skinned children are seated together with me! Oh, that we could unfurl the cross-marked banner which speaks of peace and rest, just on this hill ahead of me, where I have marked out land for a new station![379]

Early in 1904, Sundström paid another visit to the high plateau of Marea in order to secure the place he had already selected for a new centre. The people of the area were, however, not ready to allow a Christian to settle in their midst, and he had to look for other sites.[380]

Alazar reported that the reasons given by the local leaders were,

> 1. If you come here many of our people will join you. Who will then watch our cattle?

> 2. There are many fever-related diseases here.

> 3. The Catholics have built a church at Halhal. Since then the river has

---

378 From a letter which was published in SEM/MT, no 23 of December 1, 1903, 178–179 but was written on September 24, 1903 at the end of the rainy season. The words are the beginning of a verse in a famous Swedish ballad by the poet Gunnar Wennerberg (1817–1901). The song begins with the words "Här är gudagott att vara ..." (Literally: It is divinely good to be here ...") (Ed.)
379 SEM/MT 1903, 178–179.
380 Letter of February 2 published in SEM/MT, 1904, 81–83.

dried up. If you come we will face the same problem here.

4. This land is of no use for you.

5. We are Muslims while you are Christians.[381]

Sundström now began to consider Agordat as a possible location for medical missionary work, and a way of reaching out to the Marea with the Gospel. He stated that he would have gladly settled there himself had it not been for the fact that his wife and children were sick.[382] In 1905 he still entertained a fervent wish for a missionary trained in Medicine to be recruited urgently and placed in the area. However, no such person was forthcoming.[383] In the meantime he continued with his itinerant work, particularly in the Bogos area, and with the production of literature.

Mediation on Issues of Language

Rodén complained that his eyesight was failing and felt that he had to delegate certain duties to Sundström. However, he continued to follow his routine with unabated rigour. On Wednesdays he visited nomads; on Thursday afternoons he had prayer meetings; on Sundays he held church services.[384] In 1906 the Rodén family left for Sweden and the following year the Sundströms did likewise. Rev. A. Renlund and his wife, who had remained in charge of Imkullu station, were then transferred to Geleb. However, Renlund died in April 1908, of a severe abdominal disease.[385] During his home-leave, Rodén had spent some time in Berlin where he had undertaken an assignment, on behalf of the British and Foreign Bible Society (BFBS). The task involved a revision of the Amharic New Testament together with *Aleqa* Tayye.[386] Rodén returned to Eritrea in 1908 to resume his work in Geleb, while Sundström remained in Sweden to proceed with further studies, research and writing. He did not return to Eritrea until 1910, when he was made superintendent of the station at Geleb, since the Rodéns

---

381 SEM/MT 1904, 154 –156.
382 Agordat is located in a hot lowland area to the west, some 600 m above sea level, while the salubrious Geleb is located in a highland area.
383 SEM/MT, 1905, 106–108.
384 SEM/EFS Annual Report 1904, 37–39.
385 N. Rodén, 1938, 152.
386 SEM/EFS Annual Report 1906, 64–65.

had left for Sweden again.[387] The following year Sundström requested a leave of absence, as he wanted to work full-time on his research. The Rev. J. M. Nilsson from Kunama took his place. Sundström's research took him to different areas of Eritrea, including the old Red Sea port of Adulis where he made a number of archeological discoveries.[388] His research was acknowledged internationally. He returned to full time missionary service again in 1913, and was placed in Keren.

Already in 1903 serious disagreements had arisen between Rodén and Sundström on linguistic issues. Their conflict was no longer only a question of different views on linguistic questions. Both were people of strong convictions but they were also men of different temperaments. Rodén was older and had served for a considerably longer period. He was a man of strict discipline and an indomitable will. Sundström, on the other hand, was a man with an artistic and imaginative turn of mind.[389] The conflict between the two giants was so serious that in October 1903 a missionary conference was called to settle the dispute between them. A summary of the long statement of the measures taken by the conference reads,

> By nature both of them have difficulty in subordinating themselves to each other. Rodén appears to have too strong a tendency to wish to dominate. Sundström is closed in and tends to go his own way, without giving enough consideration to his co-workers. And as both of them have independent characters, it is rather understandable that discord has arisen between them. We therefore feel that, in the future, they should be assigned to different places in order that their capabilities may be used to the full and their good qualities allowed to come to the fore.

Both were urged to confess their shortcomings and ask one another for forgiveness.[390] They did so. For various reasons, the question of their

---

387 SEM/EFS Annual Report 1910, 85.
388 A written account of R. Sundström's findings in Adulis was published in E. Littmann's *Preliminary Report of the Princeton University Expedition to Abyssinia* under the title "Report on an Expedition to Adulis". See Littmann 1907, 22–32. On pp. 20–21 in the same book, there is a brief report on "The Greek Inscription of Däqqi Mahari, discovered by R. Sundström". There are some short words on Sundström's role in the excavations at Adulis and Kohaito in the first volume of Littmann's *Deutsche Aksum-Expedition*, 1931, 154, 165–166. (Ed.)
389 Mr. Yohannes Naffie of Keren, who had spent some time as a student at Geleb, confirmed this fact for me (author).
390 The full text is available in the SEM archives in Uppsala.

placement could not be resolved until 1913, when the Sundströms moved from Geleb to Keren. Rodén resumed his work at Geleb the same year, after having completed the publication of his Italian edition of *The Tribes of Mensa*. He had handed over a copy of the book personally to the Italian monarch, Vittorio Emmanuelle III, on the 6th of June 1913 (Sweden's National Day) at a ceremony in Stockholm, in connection with a visit by the Italian king and queen to the Swedish Royal House. The chairman of the board of the SEM, Baron A. E. Rappe, held a speech before the Italian royalty, expressing his gratitude for the king's and his governors' magnanimity towards the missionaries and their work. The king responded: "The Italian government has found the Swedish missionary enterprise well worth all support."[391]

The Dilemma of Placing Two Missionaries

Prior to the annual conference of missionaries in Eritrea in 1913, a meeting was held on August 27 and 28 of the same year to discuss the placement of Rodén and Sundström. Two alternatives were suggested: The first was to place Rodén in Geleb, where he would be in charge of the station and where he would have some of his material published. Sundström would take up work in Keren and be in charge of the production of literature. The other proposal called for the placement of Rodén in Keren, where he would be in charge of the production and publication of literature, while Sundström would be in charge of the Geleb station, where he would be engaged in medical services and the production of literature. It was resolved that the final decision on this matter be left to the Mission Board in Sweden. At the annual conference held in November the same year it was disclosed that the Board had decided that Rodén would be stationed in Geleb and Sundström in Keren. However no love was lost between the two. Sundström was not prepared to print any material that followed Rodén's system of spelling and Rodén, for his part, was opposed to having even some of Sundström's equipment stored in Geleb. Literature work in Tigré seemed to have suffered from a complete breakdown. However, at the annual conference in Addi Ugri on October 1–6, 1914, Rodén and Sundström reported that they had come to an agreement

391   Reported in SEM/MT, 1913, 136.

The mission house in Keren, built in 1919.

R. Sundström (1862-1919) and K. Rodén (1860–1943), missionaries to Mensa, scholars of international renown and men of strong wills!

A Copy of K. Rodén's book 'Le Tribu dei Mensa' (The Tribes of Mensa) , was presented to the Italian Monarch Vittorio Emmanuelle III on June 6, 1913, (Sweden's National Day), in Stockholm, in connection with a visit by the Italian royal couple to Sweden. In Eritrea, an Italian by the name of Ilario Capomazza had helped Rodén in the translation of his work into Italian.

on the spelling of Tigré words.[392] The disagreement between Rodén and Sundström had, however, a negative impact also on the Geleb congregation, with divisions resulting among its members.[393]

Both Rodén and Sundström were engaged in anthropological and cultural studies. Rodén completed his work on the Mensa Tribes (published in Tigré and Italian in 1913) while Sundström's work on the *History of the Mensa People* was published in Tigré and English, in

392   Field Conference 1914, § 6.
393   Statement by *Qeshi* Asfaha Mehari, December 2001. (Ed.)

1913 and 1923 respectively. Sundström had also published a number of articles on diseases and their remedies in *Le Monde Oriental*, in 1909. Other works were still at the manuscript stage. However, most of the literature produced by them was focussed on furnishing the Tigré speaking people with material for the nurture of the Christian life. This material included books of the Bible, readers, hymns and a liturgy.[394]

The death of Dr. Richard Sundström of cancer on June 16, 1919 was a major loss. Before his death, however, he had completed both a Tigré grammar, which was to be printed in Italy, and a translation of the books of Isaiah, Genesis and Exodus into Tigré.

Other Labourers in the Vineyard

Besides Rodén and Sundström, there were a number of other labourers who worked faithfully and diligently in Tigré-speaking areas. There was a group of mature teachers and evangelists who had had their early schooling in Imkullu or under Rev. Hedenström during the first Geleb-period. The group included Dawit Amanuel, Alazar Timoteos, Yishaq Be'imnet, Naffa wod Etman, Abraham Etel Jeme, Yosef Hemmed, Natnael Negasi and Timoteos Faid. The work expanded and there was a steady growth of membership in the Evangelical Church at Geleb. From a membership of 67 in 1902, the congregation had grown to 309 ten years later. The number of confirmed members was 26 in 1902, thus constituting 40% of the total membership. This indicates that a large number of members were youngsters, not yet confirmed. Geleb was a congregation of the young, probably as a result of the educational work conducted among boys and girls who lived in their own quarters. In 1902 Geleb reported 45 students, 36 of whom were boys and 9 girls. Later on, when a separate home for girls was built, the proportion of girls increased sharply and in 1906 there were 56 boys and 22 girls. In 1909 the number had grown up to 114 male and 65 female students.

The number of baptized was also much higher than the number of confirmed. In 1902, 13 were baptized, and 1 confirmed, whereas in 1908, 12 were baptized and 2 confirmed.[395] Louise Lindfors was in charge of the work among women. She later married Iwarson. She

---

394   Rodén, N 1938, 136 and 153.
395   SEM/EFS New Annual reports, 1902–1912.

The teacher Timoteos Faid (Yohannes) with his family outside his hut in Mihlab. To the left, Louise Lindfors (later married to J. Iwarson). Picture from ca 1903.

had an assistant by the name of Marta, whom she valued highly and praised wholeheartedly. Louise writes,

> I can not fully describe how much Marta has meant for me. First and foremost she has been my invaluable help in the work and my good and faithful friend. She has been a warm sunbeam who has gladdened me in many bitter moments.[396]

Marta was married to Timoteos Faid (Yohannes), the teacher at Mihlab, Louise describes a visit to Marta on a Sunday towards the end of May in 1903,

> We started riding early in the morning. The road was difficult, but I love riding and I fell in full gallop rather soon. It was as nice as skiing! I arrived before the others, and soon the coffee pot was on and hmbasha (a round, thick cake made of wheat) was served. Then Timoteos led the Sunday service under a tree. Rather few attended, as most of the people were in the lowlands at the time. But his sermon was very good: short and rich in content. And then Marta and I sat down in the shade and chatted about happy old days.[397]

396 SEM/MT 1903, page 4.
397 Louise Lindfors in letter in SEM/MT, 1903, 115–116. Miss Lindfors was from the interior of Northern Sweden. Hence the reference to skiing.

In Closing

This chapter has dealt primarily with the history of the missionary efforts of the SEM and their Eritrean colleagues in Mensa. However, there were also other important actors on the scene. Here, mention should be made of W. Munzinger, E. Littmann and Carlo Conti Rossini. The combined efforts of men of the cloth and professional scholars made the period under consideration something of a golden era in the study and recording of Mensa history and culture. Though missionaries were not the only actors on the scene, the heritage which was acquired through their contributions is a striking example of the academic and cultural by-products of missionary work, understood as an enterprise which included "native" actors. In the list of sources and literature that appears at the end of her article on *Mänsa*, (*Encyclopaedia Aethiopica*, Vol 3, 2007, 737), Kerstin Volker-Saad has included works from the latter half of the twentieth century, like Maria Höefner's *Das Feteh Mahari: Sitten und Reicht der Mänsa'* (1951), G. Spencer Trimingham's *Islam in Ethiopia* (1952), Mikael Hassama Raka's *Future Life and Occult Beings*, (1984), the same author's *Zanta Eretra* (History of Eritrea), 1992, and William Shack's *The Central Ethiopians. Amhara, Tigrina and Related Peoples* (1974). What is striking is the extent to which some of these latter works are dependent, directly or indirectly, on earlier works by missionaries and other scholars.

Although we don't know what proportion of their time went into the study of non-theological subjects, both Rodén and Sundström did devote time to the translation of works needed for evangelization, teaching, devotions and worship. However, they were not alone in these activities. They had Eritrean co-workers. We have already mentioned Naffa wod Etman. We have, furthermore, made the acquaintance of the highly gifted and motivated *Qeshi* Tewolde-Medhin Gebremedhin. Mensa was also blessed with a number of dedicated foot soldiers of the Gospel, pastors and evangelists who worked among the faithful. Among these were Dawit Amanuel, Alazar Timoteos, Yishaq Be'imnet, Abraham Etel Jeme, Yosef Hemmed, Natnael Negasi and Timoteos Faid. Swedish missionaries and their Kenisha co-workers, like the highly gifted bearer of knowledge on Mensa culture, Naffa wod Etman, put Mensa on the map of the world. Missionary centres in Mensa became workshops for fruitful research and the production of literature

The teacher Natnael Negasi and his family who laboured in the Geleb area for many years.

intended for Christian nurture. It is partly this fact that made Edward Ullendorff write,

> No praise can be too high for the scholarly work accomplished by Swedish missionaries in Eritrea.[398]

And that in spite of the tension and lack of co-operation that marked the relationship between two highly gifted Swedish missionaries. (Ed.)

398   Ullendorff 1973, 19.

Chapter Twelve

Return to Kunama (I):
Reunion and Resumption of Activities
1897–1915

Introduction

The first one whom we met in Ouganna was Chief Adim Billa. He greeted us welcome. He recalled the names of all missionaries from memory. As a young boy, he had been Carlsson's errand boy, and his mother, the daughter of Chief Kolel, used to cook food for our brothers.[399] Adim Billa's father and mother were still alive, and they came to greet us, along with other dwellers in the village. Adim brought a goat, firewood and water. The women said, "You come in the middle of the night. We have therefore not cooked food for you." Being reminded of bygone days made the sisters of old Kolel very happy. Even though it was dark, they wanted to look at my face and see if I looked like my brothers. They asked, "Are you like Carlsson, Hedin or Lager?" Soon the tent was put up and the coffee pot was puttering away. When the coffee was ready, we drank it to the dregs. From the very beginning we felt that we were old acquaintances and good friends, thanks to my predecessors.[400]

The time was December 1897, and these are the words of J. M. Nilsson, the first missionary to return to Kunama. Martin Buber once wrote: "All real life is encounter". And some of these meetings leave

---

399 Note that Adim was a *maternal* grandson to Kolel, hence his position as chief. (Ed.) Kolel was a wealthy and widely travelled Kunama who spoke several languages. He and Carlsson had established a close friendship in the early days of the Kunama mission.
400 Quoted in A. Andersson 1947, 142.

The family of Isaias Bekhit in Ouganna.

indelible marks in our memories. Among the Kunama who had met the first missionaries during the period between 1866 and 1869, there were those who hadn't forgotten. They gave proof of this fact when they met J. M. Nilsson. Something of the same spirit is reflected in a much later visit by a missionary among the Kunama. About his visit to Kunama in May 1940, Olle Hagner writes,

> Meeting our people made me glad and, for them, (my coming) was a source of surprise. They came running, from different directions to greet me and wish me welcome. Most of them were from the village. Abel [Fagi] and Joel [Fafi] were with the cattle at Zona. After I had greeted them the (Italian) Major, who now has Febe Fafi as his cook, invited me in. He couldn't find words good enough to praise her talents as a cook [...] I went to town to greet Mati, among others, still alive [...] and still in good spiritual condition. "He was so happy that we sat for a good while and talked about old friends and current questions. I talked about Christ, as I used to previously. [...] He agreed with me entirely. [...]"[401]

How did the reunion initiated by J. M. Nilsson in 1897 develope?

401   Book 3, 9–10 in the diary itself and p. 40 in OHD/K.J.S.) (Ed.)

How much did the spiritual children of the SEM among the Kunama remember of the early years with their Swedish parents, i.e. the first missionaries? How welcome were the successors of these parents when they finally returned? And how did the life of the family evolve? K. J.'s account on the return to and continuation of the work of the SEM in Kunama is an inspiring bit of history. His text follows. (Ed.)

Re-Establishing a Mission

For twenty years after their withdrawal from the scene of their first engagement, the missionaries had nursed the hope of returning to Kunama. With the arrival of the Italians, they saw a possibility that their hope might be fulfilled. Rev. Rodén made two attempts to reach Kunama, first in 1893 and then two years later. However, the Italians did not have full control of the area yet. In 1897 Rev. J. M. Nilsson, a missionary who had been stationed at Geleb since his arrival in 1894, obtained permission to move from Geleb to Agordat. In December the same year he undertook an exploratory trip to the former missionary stations in Kunama. The headman of Ouganna village, Adim Billa, who was Kolel's grandson, and who knew many of the older missionaries, gave him a warm welcome. He told Nilsson that they had experienced many difficulties, and that while some Kunama had become Muslims, most of them still practised their old religion. On receiving Nilsson's report, the Mission Board of the SEM resolved to resume its mission in Kunama.[402]

At the end of February 1897, Nilsson applied to the Italian Government for permission to erect a small building in Agordat. When permission was granted he proceeded immediately with the implementation of his plans. Towards the end of the year, his fiancée, Lina Hallendorff, arrived from Sweden and they were married at Beleza, together with another couple, the Rev. Jonas Iwarson and Anna Sahlström.[403] The situation on the western front had now stabilized and Nilsson was able to pay a second visit to Kunama. Early in 1898 Nilsson undertook a journey to Kunama once again to choose the most suitable place for a mission station. He sought a place that would be both salubrious

---

402   Arén 1978, 364–365.
403   A. Andersson 1947, 139–140.

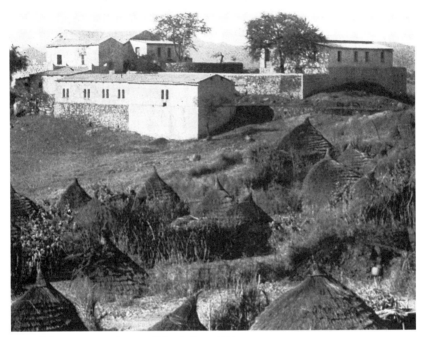

View of the mission station at Kulluku, built ca 1899.

and appropriate for evangelistic outreach. In consultation with his colleagues he chose Kulluku as the most suitable location, a choice that also pleased the grand chief of the area, Mako Abinakora. The local chiefs agreed to welcome Nilsson and promised to make available all the land that the mission would need for a station.[404]

Rev. J. M. Nilsson became soon convinced that the work in Kunama was far too demanding to be handled by only one missionary couple. He therefore requested that a new missionary be sent to assist him.[405] The board of the SEM, which was in favour of the request, acted quickly and Rev. August Andersson arrived in Eritrea already by the end of October 1898.[406]

404   Arén 1978, 365–366.
405   Applied at the spring conference 1898. SEM/MT 1899, 279. A. Andersson 1947, 152.
406   In the company of Rev. Mikael Holmer, E. P. Eriksson and Miss Hanna Broberg, Rev. Richard Sundström's fiancée. A. Andersson 1947, 152.

In May 1898 Nilsson could report that he had experienced his first "Pentecost" in Kunama, in company with his wife who had joined him on what was his third visit to Kunama. Mako, the chief of the area, offered to build huts for them in return for "a small reward". A great number of men and women joined hands in putting up the building, and the first hut was completed in one day. Three thalers were paid to the chief as agreed. "On Sunday we rested in peace, praying for the salvation of the Kunama," Nilsson wrote.

Two more huts were erected, and on June 10 the Nilssons returned to Agordat, as they felt that the risk of contracting sickness would increase with the onset of the rains. However, by the middle of August the Nilssons had to return to Geleb in order to assist Mrs. Rodén who had become ill.[407]

August Andersson

His Call, Preparation and Start as a Missionary

August Andersson was to play a prominent role in the development of the Kunama mission. He had grown up in a Christian home and experienced a radical conversion at the age of 18. He felt the call to become a missionary, but decided to stay in Sweden to assume the running of his father's farm. A severe illness brought him to the brink of death, and when he recovered he was fully convinced that he should accept God's call to become a missionary.[408] After two years of teacher training followed by five years of theological studies at Johannelund's Mission Institute in Stockholm, he was ordained and commissioned for missionary service.[409]

He went into his calling in Kunama with vigour. On his arrival in Kulluku he immediately began to study the language and became an ardent collector of words and expressions.[410]

On his arrival in Kunama, the local chief had taken him around to show him the place where Lager once had his smithy and where Hedin, Mrs. Kjellberg and her son were buried. August Andersson found the

407 A. Andersson 1947, 150–151.
408 A. Andersson 1947, 155–156.
409 N. Rodén 1938, 148.
410 His Swedish-Kunama and Kunama-Swedish dictionary (in manuscript, not found yet) included some 20,000 words. Rodén 1938, 149 and A. Andersson 1947, 175.

people very open, affectionate and honest. As he travelled around in the area, he was surprised at how much people remembered from the days of the early missionaries. They recalled not only names but also words and expressions in Swedish.[411]

In January 1899 a caravan for the transportation of food provisions, furniture and building material as well as medicine and medical equipment intended for Kunama was made ready at Massawa.[412] On arrival in Kunama, A. Andersson took the lead in erecting the mission station at Kulluku. He was a born leader and took immediate steps to prepare a site for the construction of houses on a small hill above the plane. He reported,

> I acquired a spit and a sledge-hammer and had begun breaking the largest pile of stones, when the local chief came running, grasped my arm and said: "Don't touch those stones! This is God's place." Since I could not answer him with words but only through signs, I put my hand on my heart, looked heavenwards and continued working. The chief left saying: "He has no ears". We learned later that the place was an old site for sacrifices. We kept this fact in mind. It was truly *God's Place*. After that I heard no more of the bewitched stones. We built the main station house in a short time and half an hour after its completion, we were on our saddles, on our way to Asmara for a meeting.[413]

This was on March 30 1899. Andersson was a person of action, not one prone to listen to others or to seek advice.[414]

Jack-of-All-Trades: Builder, Scholar and Healer

August Andersson was a jack of all trades. He had begun his work not only as a builder but also as a student of the Kunama language, its culture and history. He was regarded as a doctor and a person to call upon in cases of conflict and quarrels. He felt that it was his duty to defend the Kunama against neighbouring peoples who tried to exploit them. As a leader he took the initiative to establish rules for the work of the mission and the life of the Kunama. People began to turn to August for arbitration in cases of conflict. Sometimes, the local Italian

411   A. Andersson 1947, 177.
412   A. Andersson 1947, 178–179.
413   A. Andersson 1947, 180–181. A summary by K. J., not a direct quotation.
414   The stones were evidently *furda talla*, 'an altar'. See Dore 2007 78 and Dore *EAE* 2007, 453.

administration became alarmed when people who felt wronged by the commissioner's court appealed to A. Andersson.[415]

August used to narrate about the many adventures that he had experienced. He had encountered poisonous snakes, leopards, lions and Abyssinian robbers.[416]

Marriage and Short-lived Bliss

On October 17, 1901 August married Lydia Thorsell, a teacher who had been serving as a missionary in Beleza since 1896. They had known each other before starting their missionary careers but had, in accordance with the rules of the SEM, waited until the would-be husband had completed some three years of service on the field. After the wedding the couple settled in Kunama. Lydia had brought a student, a girl named Gidey, nicknamed *Ni'ishtoy* (the small one) from the school at Beleza to assist her at home and the two set out to learn the language with August as their teacher.[417] They were full of confidence and faith in what they were doing. However, the bliss was short-lived. On February 21, 1902, four months after their wedding, Lydia passed away of what was diagnosed as brain fever. The climate in Kunama was still taking its toll. The death of his wife was indeed a severe blow to August. He and the Nilssons had enjoyed sturdy health, even if they had occasionally suffered from attacks of Malaria.

By 1903 August had prepared a primer and a reader for the students of his school and, in 1905, when he was the only missionary in Kunama for a period of seven months, he translated the Gospel of St. Mark, which was published in 1906.

In November 1903 still another missionary arrived in Kunama. He was the Rev. Olle Eriksson. However, like so many others before him, he had to leave, due to illness, after only a short period of service. He came to be a leading figure in the production of literature on the highlands, first in Eritrea and later in Ethiopia. Another missionary had come to Kunama with Eriksson. He was Peter Andersson and he remained in Kunama together with his wife Emma up to 1929.[418]

---

415   From Olle Hagner to author.
416   A. Andersson 1947, 189–194.
417   Reported in a letter from Agnes and Karl Nyström April 22, 1902, in SEM/MT 1902, 99.
418   A. Andersson 1947, 217.

Peter Andersson (1868–1947) with a travelling companion on a visit to Asmara in October 1908, in connection with the visit of Professor A. Kolmodin. The man from Kunama is reported to have refused to be photographed unless Peter would be photographed with him.

Peter and Emma Andersson in Kunama

Peter – A Meticulous Missionary

At Awsa Konoma, a Swedish missionary watched as the spring rains poured down and turned into a turbulent stream. The missionary, usually called *Bietro*, was not only concerned but also highly upset. During the dry season, he had dug a deep well. And now the well was being filled with all kinds of rubbish. He complains to his Lord,

> God, why did you allow this flood to come to day? In my working plans I had fixed a date next week to fill the well with clean sand. And now this well has been destroyed!

Bietro, or Peter as he was officially known, was a very orderly man, a special character in the history of the Swedish mission and the Evangelical Church of Eritrea.[419] Peter Andersson was born in 1868 in the southernmost part of Sweden. Already in his childhood he was convinced that the Lord had called him to become a missionary to the Kunama. He went through a short elementary school education, as was

---

419   Olle Hagner to author.

the practice at the time, and then took up work on the family farm.[420] At the same time, he served as a lay preacher in local associations established to promote the cause of mission. In 1902 he decided to apply for studies at Johannelund. He was then 34 years of age and therefore considered too old to undergo the regular programme of studies. He was, however, given a one-year course of theological studies and departed for Eritrea late in 1903.[421]

The Systematic Recorder

Peter arrived in Kulluku on December 28, 1903. There was already one missionary by the name of Andersson there. Thus the team decided that he be addressed by his Christian name, Peter. However, since the Kunama do not have the sound "p" in their language his name was pronounced Beter, Betero or Betros.[422] He was given various duties to perform and carried them out faithfully. Peter recorded whatever he had observed in detail: names, time, quantities, distances, work assignments, finances, Kunama customs, climatic conditions etc. In order to teach the Kunama the meaning of the concept of *week,* Peter began hanging up ebony of different shapes on a tree: one for Monday, another one for Tuesday, and so on. On Sundays he hanged a cross.[423]

Husband to an Obedient Wife

After a few years in Kunama Peter felt a keen need for a life partner. He sought among the single female missionaries, but he found what he was looking for, not in Eritrea, but in Sweden on his furlough in 1909. His choice fell on a teacher by the name of Emma. She was 41 and Peter was 42. Emma's students in Sweden collected funds for her and she used this gift to purchase a mule.[424] Emma was a good and sturdy worker, but also let her husband rule. It has been said that whenever she was faced by a decision she would add, "God and Peter willing".[425]

The work in Kunama progressed fairly well and by the end of 1915 there were 59 registered church members. At the beginning of the

420   Joëlson 1994, 9ff.
421   Joëlson 1994, 12ff.
422   Joëlson 1994, 32.
423   Joëlson 1994, 40.
424   Joëlson 1994, 96.
425   From Olle and Greta Hagner to author.

following year, however, things took a turn for the worse.[426] One by one the members began to withdraw and go back to their old religion. Only three boys, seventeen years of age remained. These were Yaqob, Yosef and "the wavering" Daniel Luli. Peter had to open a new register. There were only five members left, "three boys, a rather ignorant man, and old Mama, Adim Billa's mother, in Ouganna."[427]

Ordination of a Hesitant Candidate

From the end of 1915 to 1919, Peter and Emma Andersson and one nurse were the only missionary staff in Kunama. However, in 1917 they could rejoice over the fact that the first Kunama girls had come to study. Furthermore the school now had 20 male students.

Peter had come out to the field as a lay missionary, but during his stay in Sweden in connection with a furlough, the question of his ordination was raised. The Secretary of the Mission had suggested that Peter stay in Sweden for an extra year to supplement his theological studies after which he would be ordained. This, however, did not tally with Peter's opinion. Basically, he wanted to be ordained in Eritrea, not in Sweden. The reason he gave was,

> Although there are a great number of living and diligent servants of the Lord in the Church of Sweden, I have noticed a terrible amount of the new rationalism and of the anti-Christian views that have been brought into the Church.

The Director of the Mission was rather upset with Peter's views and felt that ordination was out of the question. On his return to Eritrea in 1921, however, Peter found out that Rev. Svensson had received a cable from the Chairman of the Board in Sweden authorizing Svensson to "ordain Peter Andersson before he leaves for Kunama!" This was done on October 2, 1921 in the church of Tse'azzega.[428]

---

426 Ref. to SEM/MT 1915, no 22, where Johannes Eriksson had expressed, already in 1914, his worries over the young Christian men who were participating in pagan rites. SEM Annual Report 1914, 98.

427 Joëlson 1994, 64–65. According to *Qeshi* Hezqiel Gulai, the reason for this grave loss of members had to do with the understanding of the word: *Eternal Life*. When the first Kunama Christian died, the faith in *no death* faded and many relapsed into their old ways. Another alleged reason for backsliding was that several men had been recruited for military service in the colonial army. (Author)

428 Joëlson 1994, 153 ff.

On their return to Kunama, the Anderssons found that the number of missionaries had increased and that the work had grown. J. M. Nilsson and his wife were among those who had returned. The period that followed was, however, full of problems due to severe financial constraints in the SEM in Sweden. Peter, who checked every *lira* that came into his hands, was shocked by the way finances had been handled. He wrote,

> Had SEM had the world's most stupid hag as its director of finances, the state of the economy of the society would probably have been in a better shape. A hag couldn't have led them into such disastrous affairs.[429]

Further Glimpses from Developments in Kunama

The Visit of a Colonial Governor and Other Sundry Matters

On June 15, 1902 an agreement was reached among the British authorities in the Sudan, those of Ethiopia and those of Italy on the demarcation of the borders in the Setit region.[430] In 1903, Kunama was formally joined to the colony of Eritrea, and the office of the *residente* was set up at Barentu.[431] In 1923 Jacopo Gasparini, Governor of Eritrea, came to visit Kunama. An order was sent out that all head chiefs come to a place near the River Gash. The Swedish missionaries were not required to be present, but attended out of courtesy. A large tent was raised and furnished with mats and chairs. The Governor made a major speech that included some praise and some criticism of the SEM. As the speech rambled on Peter suddenly rose, went up to the Governor, interrupted his speech, said "Good bye!" and left.

His companion, Olle Eriksson, was rather upset, but went along with him. He asked Peter why he left so abruptly. Peter's answer was: "I could not stand there waiting. At six, I have to move the chairs from the Church to the School."[432] He was a stickler for details, as the saying goes.

Women too were now joining the church, but there were a lot of

---

429 Joëlson 1994, 133 ff.
430 Giuseppe Puglisi: *Chi è dell Eritrea 1952* xv. See Bahru Zewde 2002, 96, 113.
431 A. Andersson 1947, 217. The *Commissario* (Commissioner) had his seat in Agordat.
432 Joëlson 1994, 70–71. Peter had to follow his time plan, regardless. Olle Hagner to author.

The ordination of Peter Andersson in Tse'azzega on October 2, 1921. From left to right: Nils Nilsson, Axel Jonsson, Peter Andersson (ordained), Anders Svensson, Daniel Berg and Mikael Holmer.

practical problems connected with their status. Emma reports about two baptized girls who had consented to marry Christians. Their parents were, however, against the marriages and had planned to take the girls back by force.

In Awsa Konoma a husband and wife had requested baptism. However, as they were now Christians, no one wanted to help the would-be bride plait her hair for the occasion. She had to go to Kulluku to get help with her hair. [433]

Both Emma and Peter suffered from Malaria. Peter's illness was particularly severe. His weight went down from 68 kilos to 51. In the autumn of 1929 the couple had to return to Sweden.[434]

433 Anders Joëlson 1994, 130–131.
434 Anders Joëlson 1994, 166–167.

Daniel: An Assistant Bible Translator, "Backslider" and Pastor

Daniel Luli, who had been described as "a restless spirit" by Peter, was of help to Magnus Nilsson in his work in the translation of the New Testament. The task had been started some twenty years earlier by August Andersson and J. M. Nilsson, and it was high time that it be completed. However Magnus was not very willing to take advice from a Kunama. Instead he kept telling Daniel: "You don't understand this!" Peter was evidently upset by these comments.[435] Following the return of the Nilssons to Sweden in 1925 August Andersson and Magnus Nilsson completed the translation of the New Testament.[436]

In 1925 Daniel was making plans to marry according to traditional Kunama custom, and was therefore excommunicated. However in 1928, when Olle (Andersson) returned, Daniel turned up clean, proper and changed.[437] Three years later he was ordained.[438]

August Andersson Marries again

In 1906 August Andersson was granted home-leave. During his stay in Sweden he found a spouse. He wrote: "In the person of the teacher, Octavia Lindström, God gave me, once again, a precious spouse".[439] The couple were married in September 1907 and by the end of the year they landed in Massawa. During the voyage, August had thought out, in detail, about what he would need to buy in Massawa, for the completion of the building programme in Awsa Konoma. He found that he would need 33 camels as well as a caravan for the transport of food provisions and the customary Christmas consignment.[440]

SEM used to send Christmas gifts not only to the missionaries but also to the children at the boarding schools, to church workers etc. The gifts were highly appreciated and if the consignments were

---

435 Anders Joëlson 1994, 139. A small team of translators was later set up by Olle Hagner. He found that the Kunama staff thought that much of the translation made no sense. (Hagner to author.)
436 Anders Joëlson 1994, 145–146.
437 He was accused of living with a woman before marrying (Ed.)
438 A. Joëlson 1994, 139 ff.
439 A. Andersson 1948, 8.
440 A. Andersson 1948, 11 "By doing my purchases at Massawa rather than in Asmara, I saved 2,000 Lira", he stated, rather satisfied with himself. By the end of January 1908 the couple had arrived at their home in Awsa Konoma.

August Andersson (1868–1952), Kunama, and his wife Octavia (1874–1909). Picture from ca 1907.

delayed or failed to appear, as was the case during the First World War, the disappointment would be great. A. Kolmodin, who celebrated Christmas in Asmara in 1908, writes,

> And then the lofty occasion of Christmas came, with all the joys connected with it. [...] At 4 o'clock all the children at the children's home were gathered at his [Iwarson's] home. After singing and prayer, coffee was served. Then followed the distribution of gifts to the children from their friends in the homeland [meaning Sweden] and from others here [in the country]. A short letter from my youngest child, a message received shortly before, was read to the young, who were delighted to hear it. Finally I said some words about the meaning of Christmas gifts, which are reminders of the Great Christmas Gift [meaning the birth of Jesus].[441]

Christmas was the great event of the year for the Swedish missionaries, as it is indeed for the majority of Swedes. No wonder that the Kenisha have inherited this preference for Christmas. In contrast, the Orthodox Tewahdo regard Easter as the Great Church Feast of the year.[442]

The happy Andersson couple settled in Kunama. Some time passed and August rejoiced: "God gave us a fine son, Augustin Natanael". Kunama got yet another missionary, a nurse by the name of Erika Larsson, and a close friend of August's wife. The following month Professor Adolf Kolmodin, Director of SEM, paid a visit to Eritrea, an event that resulted in much encouragement to both national and expatriate mission staff.[443]

441 A. Kolmodin 1909, 191.
442 See entry in Book 2, January 6, 1940, 11–15 in OHD and p. 18b in OHD/K.J.S on the celebration of Christmas in the church in Asmara. (Ed.)
443 A. Andersson 1948, 20.

Mission in Kunama Praised by Colonial Administration

At an audience in Asmara with the Governor of the Colony, Marquis Salvago Raggi in 1908, Kolmodin was told that the government acknowledged the work of the mission. Salvago Raggi hoped to be able to pay a visit to Geleb and Kunama. He even promised to give instructions that the Governor's house be placed at the professor's disposal.[444] The local commissioner in Kunama was also well disposed towards the mission. He told the missionaries that he had observed the positive influence they had had on the people and expressed the wish that they would increase in number.[445]

In Closing

The reception given to returning Swedes by the Kunama was not a new plant come alive. It was old, simmering fire, love kindled again. This fire was there already in February 1870, when the Swedes were forced to leave. At the time, Chief Kolel of Ouganna dictated the following letter for delivery to the Chairman of Johannelund's Mission Institute in Stockholm,

> Kolel sends you peaceful greetings. I am an old man. If that hadn't been the case I would have learnt to read and write. Just as Kjellberg died [murdered in the Tika region 1869] so shall I. Send letters quickly and tell me about yourself, while I am still alive. The dwellers (residents) of the village where Kjellberg lived haven't committed any wrong. That I know. Neither have those from Englund's village, where I too live. Those who speak evil or well about him don't understand anything. But I do. Those who live in the village where Lager lives haven't committed evil. None of these villages have committed evil. The whole country, i.e. those who knew him, are grieving for Kjellberg. If you come here again don't turn to the right or to the left, but come straight to my village. If I am still alive I shall guide you. When the Kunama become outraged they take vengeance but Europeans don't. Shall we take vengeance or shall we let things pass? If you don't want to take vengeance, God shall do so. Fear not, God lives! I know both Turks and Abyssinians. They have regard for Europeans. The whites from the country of the missionaries do not commit any evil, [...], the Kunama are like children and lack

---

444   A. Andersson 1948, 27–28. A number of entries in *OHD* reflect the same attitude.
445   A. Andersson 1948, 32–33.

knowledge and understanding. But I shall teach them. Now I am old and I shall soon die and be buried.

Live in peace. Your friend Kolel [446]

Two of August Andersson's books on Kunama have the telling title: *På gamla återställda stigar* (On Old, Restored Paths).[447] The title reflects continuity between past and new efforts. When Swedish missionaries finally returned to Kunama, twenty years after their withdrawal to the coast, they did so with vengeance, to speak figuratively. Some of these missionaries were people with enormous energy and strong wills. August Andersson came to Kulluku in 1898 and worked in Kunama with great energy for a total of seventeen years, at a great cost to his family. He and Rev J. M. Nilsson laboured with muscle, heart and mind. Surely assisted and encouraged by many a Kunama, they worked with the language, with questions of health, building and agriculture. The two completed the translation of the New Testament into Marda Kunama, even though the quality of their translation has been subjected to criticism. Another missionary, Peter Andersson, was known for his highly independent nature, his enormous engagement in his work and his correctness in doing things. Among them, these missionaries built up small Christian communities among the Kunama.

Sweden and the Swedes eventually became the first love of the Kunama. No wonder that Olle Hagner (1895–1978), an old missionary to Kunama, was bequeathed the honorary title *Samina*,[448] ("source of wisdom or counsel") by the Kunama while he lived and worked among them, and was later given a grave in Kunama, even though he died and was buried in Sweden!

It is true that the Christian faith didn't win converts at a gallop among the Kunama. At times it seemed as if the Kunama were impervious to the Gospel. However, there was an enormous amount of dedication among the labourers in this Vineyard. They simply wouldn't give up once more. And, surely enough, a break through was not far away. Time was evidently a crucial element in work among the Kunama. (Ed.)

446   A. Andersson. 1947, 127–128.
447   A. Andersson 1947 and 1948.
448   Gianni Dore maintains that he had been told that the title "Samina" was used only for Jesus Christ among the Christian Kunama. (Ed.)

Chapter Thirteen

Return to Kunama (II)

Signs of a Breakthrough

Introduction

It seemed to me that I was out on a potato field and that I was picking potatoes. I pulled out the one potato plant after the other, but found only one potato at the bottom of each plant. However, the potato was large, approximately the size of two big fists. As I stood there wondering about this strange experience, I thought I saw my wife coming towards me. But I felt as if my feet were almost nailed to the ground. I had to use all the energy at my disposal to move forward. And so I woke up. That was the dream.

In the morning I narrated my dream at the breakfast table and asked if someone could interpret it. Missionary Nilsson began right away. He was of the opinion that the dream was simple and easy to understand. I had come to Kunama to see if the work that had been carried out by the congregation of the faithful had produced fruit. The fact that I found only one potato under each plant indicated that there was only one big chief at every [mission] station – Adimbilla, for example. My wife, whom I saw coming, was "the woman" in the book of Revelation, i.e.

the congregation, to which I was eager to tell what I had discovered.[449]

– So far Nilsson.

> The first part of the interpretation is probably right. With the respect
> for authority which is obvious among the Kunama, it is very possible
> that the movement towards Christianity is going to develop in that
> direction, i.e. that those who have the greatest authority among the
> people, i.e. the chiefs, are going to show the way and embrace the Gospel
> first. Then the others will follow. The latter part of the interpretation
> seemed, however, hardly probable to me. The interpretation didn't
> explain the part of the dream that I found most puzzling and that
> had caused me such fruitless efforts to pull my feet out of the locked
> position in which I found myself. After all, I woke up before I could
> reach the dearest person I have in this life [meaning his wife]. The dream
> has, probably, another interpretation, in my opinion. I was in Kunama
> as a representative of the faithful [i.e. the members and supporters of
> the Swedish Evangelical Mission]. The fact that the many efforts, not
> least the enormous amount of work which has been put into this place,
> hasn't given any obvious results, can tempt the faithful to abandon
> such a mission field. However nothing, not even this [i.e. the fact of
> lack of results] can lead her [the congregation of the faithful] to give
> up. She is in Kunama, and she will wait here until victory is won. The
> interpretation of the dream may move in many possible directions. The
> dream itself gave me much encouragement.[450]

This is admittedly a long passage to quote at the beginning of a
chapter. However, I have chosen to use it because what it describes
is something of a parable of the mission efforts in Kunama at the
time when the subject of the dream, Professor A. Kolmodin, visited
the region, and more specifically, Awsa Konoma, in December 1908.
The story actualizes both limitations and possibilities, both setbacks
and progress, both frustrations and hope. The element of hope in this
instance is tied, in no small measure, to the role of traditional chiefs in
Kunama and their attitudes to the Gospel. K. J. has narrated for us the
overall story in the context of which these different factors came into
play. His text follows. (Ed.)

---

449   The reference must be to the woman in the Book of Revelations, chapter 12. (Ed.)
450   A. Kolmodin 1909, 185–186.

Chief Adim Billa Declares Interest in the Gospel

During his visit to Kunama, Professor Kolmodin preached a sermon at the mission station in Awsa Konoma. Among those who attended was the head chief Adim Billa from Ouganna. After the service Kolmodin had a long talk with Adim and his sub-chiefs. The question that was taken up was the education of the children, a matter that had been taken up in Kulluku previously. The Kunama found it difficult to solve this issue, as the boys functioned as shepherds. Kolmodin suggested the possibility of evening school sessions. Adim was happy and stated that he himself and his people were ready to receive instruction. Kolmodin was convinced that the chief "was not far from the Kingdom of God."

Education for Boys and Young Men

It was almost impossible to get teachers from the highlands to come down to Kunama, "due to hatred between the races".[451] The Tigrinya speaking Christian highlanders and the Muslims from Sudan had hemmed in the Kunama. Both groups claimed taxes from the Kunama and intruded in other ways into what the Kunama felt was their territory. The mission, however, saw one possible way of solving the concrete problem of securing a teacher: Isayas Bekhit, a Christian Sudanese who spoke Tigré, was serving at the Agordat mission centre. He could function as a teacher in Kunama, as many people there also mastered Tigré. Isayas and his wife accepted the idea of a transfer and moved to Kunama. However, many more teachers would be needed.

By the end of the year, an increasing number of boys and young men came to attend school. The programme included morning prayers, practical work in the forenoon and school in the afternoon. The students brought their own food and spent the nights at home. Thus, they were able to disseminate what they had learned. Those who came from afar were helped to erect small huts on the slopes of nearby hills where they could also prepare their own food and spend the night. On Sunday mornings the students participated in worship services. In the afternoon they attended Sunday school and practised singing.[452]

---

451 Kolmodin 1909, 186. On the historical background to this sentiment, see Longrigg 1945, 68ff, 83ff, Trimingham 1952, 216–217 and Tronvoll 2009, 178–181.
452 A. Andersson 1948, 47.

Chief Adim Billa, the first Kunama to be baptized on the mission field, in February 1910. As a boy, he had met the first missionaries and his mother used to cook for them.

Andersson and Nilsson: In the midst of Tribulations, Opportunities, and small Joys

August Andersson was to face more tribulation. On March 30, 1909, he wrote a letter to his friends and supporters in Sweden: "Dear friends! God is our help! This time I am writing to you with a crushed heart and a depressed body." He goes on to describe how his dear wife Octavia had been struck by dysentery. On the 23rd she was confined to bed. Her condition deteriorated and she "died in the Lord" on the 29th of March. August Andersson was left with their baby son.[453]

The Rev. J. M. Nilsson too reported about the many obstacles that stood in the way of the work of the mission. He writes,

> The Kunama do not show any willingness to receive the Gospel [...] the women come in large numbers, but pass by the station and do not want to enter our place. Nilsson writes about how he had permitted Eta, the tax chief, to shove in cattle on to the mission yard and perform offerings there. The oxen, calves and donkeys were shoved into the yard.

453   A. Andersson 1948, 48.

One of the men took a white sheep in his arms and went around the animals twice. Thereafter he pushed out the cattle, and the sheep was offered on a flat slab of stone in front of our doors. The meat was then boiled and eaten. By then it was time for the Morning Prayer. I rang the bell and some thirty Kunama joined us. The text I chose had to do with the meaning of the blood that Jesus had offered. It was a joy for me to share this message with so many, even if their number was limited.[454]

Mission work moved forward. Nilsson reports that he had met the governor and discussed the matter of opening more schools in Kunama.[455] In November 1909, another missionary, Rev. Johannes Eriksson, arrived in Eritrea. Over and above his theological studies he had undergone medical training in England before proceeding to Kunama. He writes the following about his first impression of the countryside,

> On a high hill we saw something white, almost like snow. Someone told us that that was Awsa Konoma. We also discovered the beloved blue and yellow [Swedish] flag which was hoisted to welcome us.[456]

Adim Billa Declares his Faith in Jesus Christ

At the beginning of 1910, a sheikh from a Sufi brotherhood (*Khatmiyya*) came to Ouganna for the collection of alms (*zakat*). He spent the night with Chief Adim and August was afraid that the chief would be tempted to become a Muslim. But Adim professed that his faith was in Jesus Christ and not on the teaching of Muhammad. Adim had already asked for more instruction and in February 1910 he was baptized in Awsa Konoma, the first Kunama convert in his own homeland.[457] August

454 A. Andersson 1948, 17–18. A summary by K.J., not a direct quotation.
455 A. Andersson 1948, 52.
456 A. Andersson 1948, 56. In spite of the fact that they lived and worked in an Italian colony the missionaries maintained a high Swedish profile. For example, when the servants went to the administrative centre at Barentu both they and their donkeys wore blue and yellow ribbons, the colours of the Swedish flag. Reported by Olle Hagner and Gunnar Svensson.
457 A. Andersson 1948, 58–59. A Kunama, Natnael Hagena Djigo, from Tika in Kunama had been freed from slavery and taken to Lundahl's school at Massawa in 1873. He studied at Johannelund Mission Institute, Sweden from 1884–1888. However, he died in 1888 of pulmonary tuberculosis and was buried at Bromma Cemetery, Stockholm. N. Rodén 1938, 144.

had asked J. M. Nilsson, who was the oldest missionary on the Kunama field, to perform the baptismal rite.[458]

Although very few Kunama were Muslims, six *khalifa* toured the area and demanded that people pay taxes. August reacted very strongly to this intrusion and persuaded the commissioner in Barentu to prohibit the system. Adim Billa was a fearless defender of the Kunama and the Christian cause. He had openly declared that he

> [...] believed in Jesus Christ, the Son of God, born of the Virgin Mary, who had died for the sins of the world, been resurrected, returned to heaven and would come again to awaken the dead and pronounce judgement.[459]

More Missionaries Enter the Field

Reinforcement of Pastoral Outreach

In 1910, the Rev. J. M. and Mrs. Lina Nilsson went to Sweden for furlough, taking August's young son with them.[460] They were not back in Kunama until 1913, as they had had to serve in Geleb for a year, upon their return to Eritrea in 1912.[461] The missionary team was, however, reinforced by the return of Peter Andersson and his wife Emma. The couple settled at Kulluku where, on Easter day in 1911, three elderly men were baptized. Adim Billa was present on the occasion and spoke to the assembly on Creation, the Fall and the Salvation wrought by Jesus Christ. There were many who listened, but time was needed for the Kunama to relate their new faith to their own culture. One morning, August was working at the cemetery planting trees together with his pupils. He writes,

> My close friend and neighbour Mati passed by and we sat down under the tree that overshadowed Octavia's grave. He began talking to my boys and said: "The whole of this plantation will be full of tombs. Here we shall dig tombs after tombs".
>
> Did he mean tombs for European missionaries? No, I understood that he was talking about the Kunama. I had not thought of the possibility

458 A. Andersson 1948, 59.
459 A. Andersson 1948, 62–62.
460 A. Andersson 1948, 63.
461 N. Rodén 1938, 147.

that a Kunama would be buried anywhere else but at the traditional pagan sepulchre. Now the idea of a Christian burial was voiced by one of their sons.[462]

Since Johannes Eriksson was now there to assist him, August could pay regular visits to more than twenty villages. In Kulluku district he used the kind of projector known as a *magic lantern*, a modern devise that attracted much attention. On May 5, another baptism took place at Kulluku.[463]

Still another missionary was on his way to Kunama. His name was Johan Andersson and he arrived in Kunama in time for Christmas 1912. He began work at Kulluku but was soon taken ill and had to return to Sweden after a period of hardly a year.[464]

Reinforcement of Medical Staff

The arrival of Sister Maria Nilsson in 1913 reinforced medical staff in the area. Joseph, a friendly and faithful pupil, became her assistant. Here is Joseph's story in his own words,

> I was a small boy when the missionaries came to my village. The first to come was *baba* Andersson [August]. Later on his friends too came. I and a boy called Elisa (a name he got when he was baptized) used to water our donkeys at a well in the river bed. As a reward we sometimes received lumps of sugar that we chewed with joy. When *baba* Andersson began to build the walls, my father and others carried stones and received payment, but I carried small stones directly to him. One day, *baba* said to my father "Your son shall be my servant". My father answered: "Alright, take him. But what is a small boy good for?" Baba replied, "I shall teach him to do what I tell him to do". I was happy [...] I heard the word of God, but did not understand that it could be of any use. When, however, the truth became alive in me, that God had sent His Son to save me, then I became glad. I confessed all my sins before God and I listened happily to His word [...]. When it was time for me to be baptized, I was in great trouble, as my father wouldn't permit it. But finally he agreed and I was happy and so I was baptized. [...] When I then received Holy Communion, God strengthened my faith.[465]

462   A. Andersson 1948, 68–69.
463   A. Andersson 1948, 71.
464   He later assumed the new surname Hagner, and came to serve for many years as the Director of Foreign Missions of SEM.
465   Reported by A. Andersson 1948, 74–79.

School for girls in Kunama. Peter Andersson is seated to the far right of the girls in the front row. Middle row, far left, Emma Andersson and behind her Joseph Mati.

Maria Nilsson with one of the very first Christian couple wedded in Kunama: Yoseph Mati, a teacher, who was later ordained and his wife Sillas, who was from Geleb.

Lina Nilsson: Concern for Outreach among Women

A few students and a couple of older men came to faith and were baptized. However there were no women among them. A. Andersson does not comment on this fact, but Mrs. Lina Nilsson had evidently paid much attention to the issue. In a letter written in 1910 she comments in detail on the Kunama woman and her development from childhood to adulthood. Her letter is in fact an informative summary on the role of the feminine in Kunama society. Descent is, according to Lina Nilsson, reckoned through the female only. A Kunama woman is considered mature for marriage at 14-15 years of age. A man cannot be hard on a woman with impunity. A woman who has been wronged leaves her husband and her home and takes the children along. The husband will have to humble himself before her if he wants to get her back. At funerals the women are the most conspicuous. They are also the most superstitious, being always the guardians of tradition. This, suggests Lina, is probably the reason why it has been so difficult to bring them under the influence of the Gospel.[466]

Even if she was not aware of the concept known as *matrilineal*, Mrs. Nilsson has given us a good description of a society in which the women are the bearers of tradition and must therefore be protected from factors that would change their status.[467]

Literature in Kunama

Both August Andersson and J. M Nilsson had been working on the translation of the New Testament to Kunama. The first translation to come out in print was St. Mark's Gospel, which Andersson had translated in 1906. He had also translated *Bible Stories* which were ready in 1913. A small hymnbook had been used for some time when August Andersson published a collection of 270 hymns translated mainly from Swedish, in 1914. However, the translation of the New Testament took much longer. One reason must have been the lack of qualified local staff. The work was completed and published only in 1927, when

466   See SEM/MT 1911, 104–105.
467   According to Rev. Arén, Olle Hagner seems to have been the first to observe that the Kunama social structure was matrilineal. (Arén 1978, 369, note 282). However Munzinger had done so already in 1864. The missionaries were aware of the fact though many didn't see all its implications. See also Trimingham 1952, 14.

Pastor Olle Hagner (earlier Andersson) with his family and the congregation outside the church in Awsa Konoma.

The church bell in Awsa Konoma, a gift from school children in Borlänge, Sweden.

qualified Kunama Christians joined the translation team.[468] We have noted that August Andersson was a man of action. He tended to dictate. This attitude had some negative consequences, not least in literary work. Sections of what he had written were difficult for the Kunama to understand.[469] Furthermore, variations in the different dialects made the choice of standard expressions difficult.

The Formation of a Youth Group

A number of Kunama had been baptized, but it was only in December 1914 that the first woman asked for instruction, came to faith and was baptized. She was the mother of Chief Adim, who had been baptized four years earlier.[470] On January 24, 1915, August formed a youth organization with 20 members, recruited mainly among his students.

The following rules were adopted:
1. We love studying God's Word,
2. What we have learnt we want to pass on to others.
3. We shall pray to God morning and evening.
4. We shall say grace [table prayer] and give thanks for the food He provides.
5. We shall not participate in the nightly visits of the youth.
6. We shall not participate in the dances.
7. We shall not carry amulets.
8. We shall meet every first Sunday after the new moon for edification and joint prayers and also invite outsiders to our meetings.
9. We shall read God's Word every day.
10. We shall pray for the guidance and power of the Holy Spirit that we may keep the Word that we have read and heard in our hearts. [471]

The rules were probably influenced by August, if not dictated by him. Hardly anything is said about the bearing of such regulations on the Kunama people and their culture, except by way of warnings against certain practices.

---

468 J. M Nilsson has stated that he was assisted by Daniel Luli and by a new missionary, Olle Andersson. See also A. Andersson 1948, 185.
469 Olle Hagner gave the author examples of translations of hymns that were incomprehensible.
470 A. Andersson 1948, 95.
471 A. Andersson 1948, 100–101.

Five newly baptized boys in Kunama, in February 1914. From left: Bodda (now Yaqob) later nurse, Lokki (now Haggai), Ummadi (now Elisa) son of a Chief, Bai (now Yohannes) later pastor, and Kelej, (now Hizqi'el) later pastor.

Ups and Downs

In 1915 the missionaries and the Kunama Christians were able to rejoice on seeing that many were taking part in the instruction for baptism and being baptized. From Kulluku, Johannes Eriksson reported that five men and one student had been baptized and that a further sixteen young herdsmen were receiving instruction. The young men told the girls that they would not marry them if they did not receive instruction, learn to read and write and become Christians. Indeed, the boys uttered the threat that they would look for wives in Asmara if the girls did not meet these requirements! The need for the education of girls was great and Lina Nilsson saw to it that a school for girls was opened. The first Christian Kunama marriage was celebrated at this time. Chief Adim Billa was married to a middle-aged woman who had been received into the congregation through baptism.

The Mission had laid out regulations for marriage. These were formulated with the situation in the Tigrinya or Tigré-speaking areas in mind. In Kunama things were different. We have already noted that, among the Kunama youth who had first responded positively to the

Gospel and become Christians, there were only young men. Kunama Christian youth had earlier maintained that the question of marriage would not pose any problems, since they could certainly get Christian girls from the highlands. However the differences in mentality between the Orthodox Christian highlanders and the Kunama was so great that, at the time, marriage between representatives of the two groups was hardly thinkable. Among the students at the school in Addi Ugri there was, however, a girl of partly Oromo origin, by the name of Sillas. She and Josef Mati were united in marriage. Prior to the marriage, his Kunama parents had been very much opposed to the very idea. However, on their return to Kunama after the marriage, which took place in Tse'azzega, the couple was received well by the Evangelical community as well as by the parents of Josef. A second wedding was celebrated in 1921 when Stefano married Aster, who worked at the boarding school in Geleb.[472]

The Attraction of Traditional Practices

The many years of struggle and hardship were finally over and the fields were white for harvest. At least this was what the missionaries believed. However, already in 1914, Johannes Eriksson had started worrying about the fact that many of the young Christian men were participating in traditional rites, dances at night and the like. In the autumn of 1915, a large part of the male students left the school to participate in harvest celebrations.[473]

August Andersson and Johannes Eriksson Expelled

There were also other factors that led to a drastic change in the state of things. August Andersson describes the development thus:

> Thursday October 28, 1915 at 1 p.m., the hottest time of the day, when I was taking a nap, someone knocked at the door. I thought that the sound came from a knock on the door by a student, but when I asked the person to enter, a native soldier came in and handed me a parcel from Barentu. It contained mail, but also a message, which read: "You

472   Anders Joëlson 1994, 131–132. SEM/MT 1922, 60.
473   SEM/MT 1915, 188.

Daniel Luli, Yoel Fafi and Hezqiel Gulay, ordained under the leadership of Jonas Iwarson in Beleza on September 18, 1932. Rev. Mikael Holmer and Qeshi Girma-Tsion took part in the service of ordination.

and Eriksson will have to present yourselves in Asmara no later than Wednesday, for direct passage to your country of origin." A catastrophe was in the making.[474]

August decided to ride over to Kulluku to inform Rev. Eriksson about the message he had received. However, on the way he met his colleague and by midnight they were back in Awsa Konoma. They were quite bewildered. Already in 1914 when the First World War erupted, Eriksson had been worried that he might be called up for military service in Sweden, and thought that this might be the reason for the summons he had received.[475] In the morning, August sent a telegram to Asmara asking the Mission if the order had to do with mobilization in Sweden, as this was the second year of the First World War. An answer came but it only stated that a ship would leave [Massawa] the following Friday and that there was place for Erika, a Kunama missionary, who was due for home-leave. On their arrival in Keren, the two missionaries met Dr. Sundström who informed them that they had been expelled

474 A. Andersson 1948, 108–109. Summary by K.J., not a direct quotation.
475 A. Andersson 1948, 111.

from Eritrea. A. Andersson suspected the order might be the result of intrigue by Muslims. Both he and Rev. Johannes Eriksson had to leave Eritrea the first week of November.[476]

In Closing

It is interesting to note that when a breakthrough did occur in Kunama, the chiefs where the ones who showed the way. Nevertheless, the ground had been prepared for years through practical measures taken to ameliorate the lives of the Kunama. Literacy, education, medical care, concern for women and children: all these arenas of service had spread their quiet message among the Kunama. The Kunama now knew, beyond any doubt, that the missionaries and their colleagues who served among them were there on a mission of genuine love. They were there as friends. When Adim Billa, headman of Ouganna, was baptized in 1910, the ice began to thaw. Here too, the "Follow–the–leader–principle" began to operate. The baptism of Chief Adim Billa's mother, and later his would-be wife, made a strong impression. These events paved the way for Kunama women, who traditionally play a vital role in the decisions and ways of Kunama society. When Chief Mako Abinakora in Kulluku offered the SEM a plot of land for a mission station, he too showed the way and reinforced an attitude of openness towards the Christian faith.

Among the Kunama, there seem to have been two main reasons for hesitating to embrace the Christian faith. In the first place there was the firm grip of an all-embracing Kunama tradition. To abandon this tradition was to be left out in the cold, figuratively speaking. It was to invite the censure of a closely-knit society in which people were absolutely dependent on each other for mutual approval and help. The attraction of the old was too strong to be replaced by the ways of the

476   A. Andersson 1948, 111–113. In a letter to the editor of this work, Pastor Bruno Tron comments: "Buonaiuti adds the information that the Swedish missionaries (read Jwarsson) had had contacts with German seamen in Massawa at the eve of the war. Del Boca, in his book on the Italian colony, mentions a German explorer-adventurer who had travelled from Massawa to Sudan about the same time, crossing the Kunama-region [stopping at the Swedish Mission stations?]. This means that politics, combined with security measures, were the only real cause for the expulsion; the Muslim intrigue was probably an excuse to cover the action of the government." On Iwarson's pastoral contacts with German seamen in Massawa read Iwarson 1936, 136–141. For period after 1939, see *OHD*. (Ed.)

Christian Gospel. The harvest festivals, the sound of the distant drum accompanying many a night-time dance, marriage according to the rites of one's forefathers – these were ancestral practices that were too dear to abandon.

A. Kolmodin writes about his conversation with a traditional priest in Kulluko on the subject of the customs of the fathers. With his simple logic, the priest had maintained that what he was hesitant about in the teaching of the missionaries was not the teaching itself, but rather the consequences of accepting such a teaching. The priest was apparently not zealously attached to his religious practices but did his duty out of respect for his forefathers. He asked Kolmodin the disarming question, "Isn't what you want to teach us, something that you have learnt from your parents?"[477]

The second reason for hesitating to embrace the Christian faith had the character of frustrated expectations. The Kunama had expected the God of the missionaries and the missionaries themselves to be more powerful, more invincible than they turned out to be. The fact that the Algeden (a neighbouring tribe under Turkish rule), the Governor of Adiabo in Northern Ethiopia or the Egyptians could strike, killing the Kunama, raiding their cattle and carrying many a Kunama into slavery, with impunity, was a source of despair for them.[478] The Kunama were tempted to regard the Christian God as powerless in the face of these atrocities, a God not worth embracing.

After many years of missionary work among the Kunama, the attraction of the old, the pull of the harvest festivals, the sound of the distant drum accompanying many a night-time dance, were still there. Many Kunama youth were drawn back to them, much to the chagrin of the missionaries. However, the Christian congregation now offered an alternative community, a context of security, a new family. Individual Kunama now dared to step forward to be counted for Christ. (Ed.)

---

477 Kolmodin 1907, 176. A little earlier Kolmodin had been obliged to admit, "The authority of parents and forefathers is strong among the Kunama. That in itself is something positive and it must be preserved." A. Kolmodin 1909, 173–174. (Ed.)

478 This train of reasoning is clearly hinted at in Arén 1978, 147. See also Hellström 1989, 147–148. (Ed.)

Beleza (Bellesa) and its environs.

Chapter Fourteen

Highland Centres of Evangelical Christianity – Beleza

By K. J. Lundström And Ezra Gebremedhin

Introduction

With the declaration of the colony of Eritrea, the SEM and the Kenisha had begun to lift their eyes and hearts in earnest to the highlands of

Eritrea. The highlands of Hamasen, once ravaged by internal conflicts, were no longer inaccessible and unfriendly destinations. They had become doors of opportunity, open and inviting. It was now time to plan more seriously for work on higher ground. The leaders of the SEM in Sweden were aware of the new opportunities and outlined some principles for planning and action. The following words of K. J. reflect this readiness,

> The Director of the Swedish Evangelical Mission, K. J. Montelius, who had paid a visit to Imkullu in 1889, saw the opportunities that the new circumstances offered. He advised the missionaries to concentrate on the production and dissemination of Scriptures, on village evangelism and on the training of indigenous leaders, who, he thought, would be better fitted for service among Eritreans than would expatriate missionaries. He added, however, that the Mission should implement these programmes without neglecting the vision of reaching the Oromo.[479]

The new policy now adopted required that the mission be provided with additional resources. New buildings had to be erected. A boarding school for girls was opened at Beleza in 1890 and a similar school for boys at Tse'azzega the following year. While these institutions were a continuation of the work that had been begun at Imkullu, a new form of schools was initiated on the highlands. The goal was a spiritual revival through Bible study, a continuation of what was started some thirty years earlier in Tse'azzega. The village schools would serve as instruments for a broad outreach. In many villages the Orthodox Church had a *Degé Selam*, a place where young boys were trained in reading and reciting and singing Ge'ez texts in preparation for a career in the Church. The Evangelical schools however aimed at general literacy that would lead to the reading of the Bible. Such literacy would also constitute a preparation for Confirmation.

Imkullu – The Eclipse of a Mother Station and Congregation

During the Eighteen-nineties, the station at Imkullu was dismantled successively. Doctor K. Winqvist continued his medical work there until 1897 when he moved to Beleza. Pastor K.G. Rodén laboured in

---

479   This line of thought comes forth in Arén 1978, 316.

Hirgigo, south of Imkullu, from 1886 to 1890 when he too moved to Beleza. With the exception of some years after the turn of the century, when the work at Imkullu was directed by Anders Renlund, the work at the station and its surroundings after 1897 was taken care of by native Kenisha evangelists. In time the station became increasingly dilapidated.

After inspecting the buildings at Imkullu (then no longer in use as a mission station of the SEM) in October 1908 A. Kolmodin wrote,

> My second wish is related to the station itself. I have gone through every room thoroughly in the company of Brothers Svensson and Rodén and examined the building in general, both from the inside and the outside, and considered what should be done if this valuable station is not to be reduced to ruins. In fact this option has been discussed. It has been stated that Monkullo was no longer suitable for any proper mission activity. And at the moment this seems indeed to be true. Nevertheless, we should simply not let Munkullo fall into disuse. The station at Monkullo is the Mother of our East African Mission. Isn't it a matter of honour for those engaged in the cause of Mission in Sweden to see to it that at least the station is not reduced to ruins? [480]

Kolmodin's wish could not be fulfilled. The pause that Imkullu had taken from active service became a retirement, indeed a preparation for the twilight of life and eventual death.

The Italian colonial authorities wanted to buy Imkullu station, but the home board of the SEM was hesitant to sell the station lest the supporters of the mission would regard the move as sacrilegious. At last, in 1913, the board did decide to sell the station but the decision was never implemented.

In the nineteen-thirties, the station was repaired by the Italians for use as a hospital for soldiers wounded in the Italo-Ethiopian War. However, after the war, the station was again abandoned. It deteriorated even more under the British occupation of Eritrea during and after the Second World War. In spite of the fact that the British authorities had promised to protect the property on the station, the lawless were left to plunder the station, bit by bit. The corrugated iron sheets on the roofs of the station constituted a special source of temptation. The station which Nils Hylander had once described as "The most beautiful

---

480   A. Kolmodin 1909, 44.

Imkullu after being hit by an earth quake and storms in 1913.

on the whole Red Sea coast" was reduced to ruins.[481] Nowadays there is nothing left of the station, with the exception of the graveyard, a pale reminder of the heroic efforts made to bring the Gospel from the cool shores of a Nordic country to the steaming coast of the Red Sea and beyond.[482]

Up Country – For Good

In our narrative on the roots and development of the ECE, we have now come precisely to those geographical regions on the highlands which Montelius had in mind when he outlined his plans for the future of

481   In an article entitled "Plantskolan i Öknen" (The Plant School in the Desert), published in the first volume of *Bortom Bergen*, Elsie Winqvist writes, "It was the architect and composer Wilhelm Stenhammar [1871–1927] who made the drawings for the house at Imkullu. He used to put the initial draft of his drawings on his piano and play in order to get ideas. Lundahl was up there to see him and when he heard him play, he [Lundahl] thought to himself, "If our house becomes as beautiful as the music that he plays suggests, then it will turn out to be a beautiful house indeed!" E. Winqvist 1953, 128. (Ed.)

482   The description of Imkullu's last years is a summary of the material available in Tafvelin and Lundmark's book 1974, 73. (Ed.)

the missionary activities of the SEM in Eritrea. By 1889, the Italians had taken control of much of the highlands, and the establishment of the colony provided opportunities for the expansion of mission work. Early in 1890, General Baldassare Orero issued an order that the mission should be given a site at Beleza. Some months later the mission received permission to begin work in Asmara. The following year the mission moved its headquarters from Imkullu to Tse'azzega, some 16 kms west of Asmara, even though the station at Imkullu was not closed.[483] It is time for us to look into the stories of these three places of special significance in the history of the ECE, namely Beleza, Asmara and Tse'azzega.[484] We shall begin with Beleza.

A Mission Director's first Impression of Beleza

On the morning of October 29, the head of the home for girls in Belesa [Beleza], Missionary K. Nyström, came to get me. The plan was that I would travel on horseback. The trip was pleasant, even though a good part of our journey took us on a road which can hardly be called a road. After about three quarters of an hour, we caught sight of Beleza station at a distance, perched on a height and enveloped by the light of the sun. We arrived after about one hour. The hospital was located at the bottom of the incline of the station grounds. Since our path went precisely by the hospital, I had a chance to greet the patients and their doctor, Dr. Winqvist, who had come out. The children's home was located higher, on an elevation. We stopped when we arrived at the latter place. Here I was given a hearty welcome by all our dear co-workers within the district of Beleza and all those involved in the children's home. Even the chief of the village was there, beside others. When I greeted him, he explained that both his father and his brother, who had been chiefs before him, were friends of the mission. He too was a friend, because the mission had done so much good.[485]

---

483 Arén 1978, 315.
484 These three places constitute something of a triumvirate of mission stations, known far and wide. Enno Littmann, Leader of the Princeton University Expedition to Abyssinia in the autumn and winter of 1905–1906 , writes about Asmara,
    "... the largest and most important station", Zazega (Sa'adsega) the station of Herr Svensson, the venerable Nestor of the Swedes in Abyssinia, and Belesa (Beleza) where Dr. Winqvist, one of the foremost Tigrinya scholars, is stationed." Littmann 1907, 3–4. (Ed.)
485 A. Kolmodin 1909, 74.

Beleza mission station, with school children dotting the hill side. Picture from 1908.

On October 31, 1908, 15 girls from the Children's' Home and one widow were confirmed in Beleza. Their teacher was Qeshi Zer'a-Tsion. From left: Kibra, Mähanzäl, Lette-L'eul (not from the Children's Home), Tiblets, Qidusan, Timnit, and Desta. Seated in front: Mission Director Adolf Kolmodin, who took part in the Confirmation.

These are the words of Adolf Kolmodin, head of the SEM and Professor at the Theological Faculty of the University of Uppsala. Having arrived in Asmara on October 19, 1908, he proceeded to Beleza, the nearest mission station on October 29. His brief description of Beleza gives us glimpses into the variety of activities which were carried out at the station. Though small in size, Beleza has a high stature in the history of the SEM and the ECE. It was indeed a place where the saying "A healthy mind in a healthy body" was followed as a tacit motto, in the context of the Christian Gospel.

The SEM actually began work in Beleza already in 1872, when E. E. Hedenström came to the village.[486] Mission work was resumed in this village in 1890. Asmara came next as a regular station, in 1891. Tse'azzega came soon after, in the same year.[487] K. J. Lundström has given us a broader picture of Beleza's early beginnings and its development. Here below is his text, compiled from different, longer references to Beleza. (Ed.)

The Rev. August Bergman – A Man of Many Gifts

The Rev. August Bergman had moved from Imkullu to Beleza already in 1890. He not only took practical measures to facilitate the work of his missionary colleagues, but also made efforts to meet the spiritual needs among the faithful in the area.

Bergman was a very industrious and energetic person, a man with many gifts. He was a medical doctor, a builder, a preacher, indeed a jack-of-all-trades, in the best sense of the term. Looking back to the time when the SEM moved to Beleza permanently, Mrs. E. Lundahl writes,

> Our immediate need was to get started with the grinding of grain and with baking. In Abyssinia there was no other means of grinding grain than a hand-operated grinding stone in two parts; the longer, oblong part that rests on the ground and a smaller one which is moved back and forth on the bigger one. This latter stone is called "the baby grinding stone". [...] I don't know what we would have done if God had not given us help in the person of Missionary Bergman. He personally carved out grinding stones for us and acquired a kneading trough. He constructed an oven, made a cupboard for provisions and put things

486   Beleza district included Karneschim, Dembesan (Dimbezan) and Anseba. (Ed.)
487   Hofgren 1956, 138, 204, 205.

Haile-Mikael Kidanu (1856–1919). Took part in the First Oromo Expedition which started in 1877 and later studied Theology in Sweden from where he returned in 1886. He taught at Beleza, among other places.

August Bergman (1855–1923). Pastor, medical doctor and person of many gifts. He took part in the Third Oromo Expedition in the company of Axel Påhlman and Onesimos

in order. His big worry was getting enough millet flour for the bread. A severe famine ravaged the country, since locusts had eaten up all available seeds. Grain had to be brought from Massawa by mule.[488]

In April 1892, church leaders were invited to Beleza for a few days of spiritual renewal. Six months later another meeting was held at Tse'azzega. This convention, known as *gubaé*, filled a need and became a permanent institution. The meeting was held in a *das* (arbour). The programme included Bible studies and discussions on subjects "related to the Orthodox." Prayers and singing continued late into the night. The highlight of the convention was the Communion service on Sunday morning. In conformity with Orthodox practice, fasting was practised before communing. Tea and bread or a meal was served after Communion. Apart from sharing in worship and instruction aimed at bringing about spiritual edification, the participants discussed certain practical questions, such as how to relate to the Orthodox practice of fasting. It was agreed that there was nothing wrong in following this custom. Everyone could act according to his/her conscience in matters of secondary importance.[489]

488 A. Bergman 2006. Quoted from a letter by Mrs. E. Lundahl in 1899. (Ed.)
489 Arén 1978, 330.

Nyström – Homeopath, Administrator, and Translator of Hymns

Another missionary couple, Karl and Agnes Nyström, served at Beleza during the same period. Karl Nyström had arrived in 1893 and participated in the so-called Fourth Oromo expedition. However, as the expedition could not proceed as planned, Nyström had returned to Sweden for further medical studies. He was trained as a homeopath.[490] In 1896 he returned to Eritrea together with his wife. They were assigned to Beleza where they were given responsibility for educational activities. The first institution that had been established in Beleza was the School for Girls, which had been transferred from Imkullu in 1890. In the year 1900 the number of students was 43. Two teachers, Haile-Mikael Kidanu and Anna Svensson, assisted the Nyströms in the activities at this school. The subjects offered were Bible, Reading in Tigrinya and Amharic, Mathematics, Writing, Geography, Science and Singing. By 1903 the number of students had risen to 64.[491]

Leaders in Beleza Parish – Winqvist and Nyström

In 1897 the Winqvists left Imkullu and moved to Beleza. However, since a residence had not yet been readied for them, they spent four months together with Teklu and Girma-Tsion in Shimanigus La'ilai, at the home of Beyin Ristu who had recently been confirmed.[492] In 1898, Bergman was forced to resign and return to Sweden due to ill health.[493] Dr. Winqvist continued the medical work that his predecessor, A. Bergman, had begun when he moved up to this highland village in 1890. The Beleza parish had members in 12 villages out of a total of 36 villages in the Karneshim and Dimbezan districts. Among the indigenous staff there were two pastors, Selomon Atsqu and Zer'a-Tsion Musé. In 1902 the members of the parish numbered 183, of which 85 were communicants. An eritrean teacher, Haile Mikael Kidanu, a

---

490 Homeopathy is a system of medicine in which a disease is treated by giving extremely small amounts of a substance that has the same effect as the disease. (Longman Dictionary of Contemporary English, Third Edition, 1995.) (Ed.)
491 SEM/EFS Annual Report 1903, 68–69.
492 Arén 1978, 336.
493 Arén 1978, 335; Tore Bergman 2006, 138.

The waiting room at the hospital in Beleza. Picture taken 1908. Teklu "Hakim" sits at the table registering patients and receiving fees. Patients where expected to pay according to their means, either in money or kind. Usually, the sum of 25 centisimi (=1/4 franc) or a small measure of grain.

native of Beleza and a graduate of Johannelund's Mission Institute in Stockholm, taught at the School for Girls. Four other teachers, Teklé, Haimanot, Mihtsun and Bihil served in some of the seven rural schools. Among those engaged in medical services there were some local staff, prominent among whom were Teklu Uqbai and Birru Tirfé.[494]

Winqvist – Medical Work and Translation of the NT

Winqvist, who was an ordained pastor, became the supervisor of the Beleza Parish. However, he was also in charge of medical services. In his opinion, Beleza was not the ideal place for a hospital. He would rather have such an institution near the border with Tigrai. However, due to government restrictions following the defeat of the Italians at The Battle of Adwa in 1896, his desire could not be realized. Winqvist pushed on with his medical work. He had more patients than he

494   SEM/EFS Annual Report 1902, 74 (Ed.)

could take care of, some 50–60 outpatients a day. In addition, he had the responsibility for the supervision of the inpatients, some 24 at any given time. However, his passion was the translation of the New Testament into Tigrinya. Since his assistant, Gebre-Ewostatewos, had volunteered to go to the Oromo in 1897, Winqvist lacked qualified co-workers. However, in 1903 and 1904, two well qualified men came to his assistance, since Tewolde-Medhin Gebre-Medhin had returned from Geleb and *Haleqa* Tewolde-Medhin Gebru, a scholar from Tigrai, had come to Beleza.[495]

Which type of Tigrinya?

The translation of the Bible into Tigrinya was complicated by the fact that there was no normative, written-Tigrinya at the time. The Winqvists wanted to produce an idiomatic version of the Scriptures. Only after years of revisions did they arrive at what was regarded as an acceptable translation. They followed the Ethiopic text i.e. the Ge'ez version, whenever it corresponded to the *textus receptus,* i.e. the received text of the Greek Text of the New Testament. Winqvist argued,

> The same thought that came to the mind of the Greek reader should come to the mind of the one who reads the Tigrinya translation.

The team consulted several other Bible versions, besides Greek. Among these were the German, Swedish, English, Amharic, Danish and Italian versions. Particular attention had been paid to the English Revised Version. In order to arrive at an idiomatic Tigrinya, the translators felt that it was necessary to place the subordinate clause *before* the main clause.[496]

Over and above the task of translating the Bible, an undertaking in which Mrs. Winqvist too participated, the Winqvists were engaged in preparing other written material. Thus, they translated two *Bible Stories* and *Manual for Religious Knowledge.*[497]

---

495   Arén 1978, 337.
496   SEM/MT 1910, 26–27.
497   See Jwarsson-Tron1918, 37. Winqvist-Janér 1958, 160–161.

Tension between two Gifted Missionaries

During their years together, the Winqvists and the Nyströms had found it difficult to cooperate. Winqvist was the head of the Beleza Mission but Nyström was responsible for the administration of the station. Nyström was fluent in Tigrinya and skilful in writing. A great number of hymns from his pen found their way into the Tigrinya hymn book, *Mezmur Selam*.[498] Winqvist had first learned Amharic and then Tigrinya but was not fluent in either language.[499] As we have already noted, however, he was a very good translator, equipped with a thorough knowledge of Greek and Hebrew. Winqvist's reputation as a doctor was established and it was he who ran the hospital in Beleza. Nyström too had acquired medical training, but only as a homeopath. All these factors contributed to strained relations.

Winqvist Succumbs to Overwork

Winqvist's workload was heavy. One Sunday morning, in the middle of 1906, he collapsed in his room, due to a minor brain haemorrhage. He stayed in bed for three weeks, under the care of his faithful friend and co-worker Teklu. He then returned to his work at the hospital and to his writing table.

The leadership of the SEM were very eager to see the New Testament in Tigrinya in print as soon as possible. Winqvist appealed to the Mission Board to send a young doctor to assist him, as soon as possible. However, seven years were to pass before a doctor could be sent. Winqvist felt that he simply had to push on. He could not rest until the New Testament had been printed. His colleagues and his family urged him to rest, but he could not. He promised, however, that he would take a long rest, once the New Testament was printed. Later, his wife, Elsie, recorded what had happened by the end of 1909,

> Karl had just seen the last pages (of the New Testament) off the press when a new brain haemorrhage supervened, and in the early morning

---

498 In 1907 he gave out a new hymnal that contained a large number of hymns translated mainly from Swedish, and which was very well received. Even in the hymnal of 1961 (Mezmur Selam) no less than 92 hymns out of 306 bore his name.

499 Winqvist-Janér 1958, 154–155.

of December 6, 1909 he was called home.[500] He was laid to rest with a copy of his beloved Tigrinya New Testament.[501]

Tewolde-Medhin Gebre-Medhin

Even though Beleza constituted the center of activities in the area, the local congregation there was comparatively small, since only a relatively small number of members were from Beleza itself. Other parts of the parish were much larger. This was the case with Shimanigus La'ilai where the congregation itself undertook to build a church. Other Evangelical congregations provided help in both cash and kind.[502] The congregation in the Beleza district continued to grow, from 183 members in 1902 to 642 in 1915. Beleza district was responsible for 7 schools with 136 students in 1902. In 1910 however, the district ran 20 schools with an enrolment of 500 students.[503]

Among the Eritrean staff, Tewolde-Medhin Gebre-Medhin held a unique position. He had felt the movings of the Spirit among the Hamasen Readers, and had served as pastor and Bible translator on the coast, up in the Tigré speaking highlands and in the Tigrinya speaking areas. During his years of study in Sweden, and on later visits to the country, he had won renown among both church leaders and friends of the mission.

Frans Lindfors: A Promising Life Cut Short

In 1909, a young missionary pastor by the name of Frans Lindfors came to serve as director of Beleza mission. He was a very industrious person and established a great number of personal contacts in the nearby villages. In early 1912 he married a nurse, Gusti Steinwall. However,

---

500 A. Kolmodin, who met Winqvist only a month earlier, writes, "Dr. Winqvist, who is now 63 realizes, naturally, that his strength is no longer sufficient for this very demanding, double-undertaking [i.e. that of a medical doctor and a translator of the NT.] Since he now doesn't dare to operate on eye-cataracts, due to a deterioration of his sight, it is his sincere wish that he, as soon as possible, can devote his energy exclusively to the work of translation. We therefore need a new mission doctor." A. Kolmodin 1909, 84. (Ed.)

501 Janér E. 1953, 159–160.

502 E. Winqvist 1958, 154–155.

503 SEM/EFS Annual Report 1910, 83–84.

The funeral of Dr. Karl Winqvist in Beleza, on December 7, 1909.

The dedication of the church at Shimanigus La'ilai on February 21, 1909 in the presence of Professor Kolmodin, and the assistant pastors Tewolde-Medhin, Wolde-Giorgis, Selomon, Zer'a-Tsion, Olle Eriksson, Jonas Iwarsson, Karl Winqvist and Anders Svensson.

only a few weeks later he died as a result of a severe infection. A young boy in the nearby village of Addi Nifas had drowned in a pool. His brother rushed to his friend Frans for help. Frans, who was a good swimmer, dived into the pool and brought the boy out. Unfortunately, the boy was lifeless. Frans contracted a severe infection from the cold, dirty water, and died within a few days. Not only the Beleza mission but also the whole area came out to mourn him and to express its gratitude to the young Swedish pastor.[504]

The medical services at Beleza continued even after the death of Dr. Winqvist. Thérèse Palmqvist, who had served with Dr. Winqvist since 1903, ran the hospital. At the time, sickness ravaged the highland areas and many died. There was, furthermore, shortage of food.

A Theological Conflict in Sweden Affects Mission and Church in Eritrea

Between 1910 and 1912, Beleza became the scene of a conflict that was to cause disruption in the activities of the mission. The cause of the problem was a theological controversy within SEM in Sweden. In 1908, Professor A. Kolmodin had published a work entitled *Christianity and the Bible of the Ancient Church*. In it he had stated that there were certain texts, especially in the Old Testament, which could not make the same kind of claims to authority as texts of the New Testament. Axel B. Svensson, the preacher of the prestigious Bethlehem Church in Stockholm, where the Grand Old man of the SEM, Carl Olof Rosenius, had once preached, went to a frontal attack against the leadership of SEM for harbouring what he believed was heresy. He had taken the initiative to form the *EFS Bibeltrogna Vänner* (the Bibletrue Friends, shortened as BV) as a subgroup within SEM. This group constituted a relatively small minority and when the final votes were taken at the mission conference in 1911, there was a unanimous vote of confidence in the Holy Scriptures, but a *no* to accepting the "SEM-Bibletrue Friends" as a separate unit within SEM.[505]

A large section of the Bibletrue Friends now left SEM and formed their own society, *Bibeltrogna Vänner (The Bibletrue Friends)*. From the

---

504   SEM/MT 1912, 131–133.
505   E. Levander (Ed.) 1931, 311, Hofgren 1956, 258–263.

very start, the SEM had seen the promotion of foreign mission as its main task. There had been plans of moving into new areas. Certain Oromo areas had been mentioned, with the hope that two of the missionaries of SEM, Cederqvist and Onesimos, would assume the challenge of taking up work there. This idea was, however, dropped when a letter arrived from Marqos Girmai and his wife in late summer 1911, in which they offered their services to *The Bibletrue Friends*. Soon after a second letter arrived, in which Karl and Agnes Nyström too offered their services to BV.[506]

Qeshi Marqos Germai's Dealings with Seventh Day Adventists Questioned

Qeshi Marqos Girmai had expressed dissatisfaction with housing, and the terms of his employment, on different occasions. At the annual conference in Geleb in November 1910, he was given a serious warning for having assisted two teachers to be employed by the Adventists, after they had been suspended from their employment with the Swedish mission.

Why was the measure taken by *Qeshi* Marqos regarded with disapproval? Was there a veiled competition between the SEM and the Seventh Day Adventists in Eritrea? When did the Adventists come to Eritrea and what was the purpose of their mission? During his visit in Eritrea in 1908–1909, Adolf Kolmodin took note of the activities of the Adventists. He writes,

> There was one thing which burdened my heart. And I felt that it must come out into the open. Perhaps I may not get such an opportunity again in the Asmara congregation. Swedish Adventists arrived in our mission field in Hamasen a year ago. Upon their arrival they maintained that they were not planning to stay where our mission society had begun work but intended rather to move further inland. However, they have not done so. They have rather settled in Asmara and have started trying to win followers among the members of our congregation. Even though they have not made any tangible progress yet, it is to be feared that they are going to bring about much confusion and mislead those who are still not well grounded in their faith. Such a mode of action is regrettable. There are, after all, many who have not yet heard the Good News of the Gospel. And yet the Adventists go

506   A. Menghestu 2004, 46–50, Hofgren 1956, 206–207.

past such people. It is naturally more comfortable to move into mission fields which have already been cultivated and to reap where one has not sown. The fundamental mission principle of St. Paul, that one should not build upon foundations laid down by others, has no significance for the Adventists, in the face of their preferred teachings.[507]

This was not the last time that the SEM and the Kenisha would be challenged by new, highly motivated, Protestant groups operating in Eritrea. Especially in the decades after the Second World War, the ECE was to lose a number of its members to these denominations.

In our days Adventists do recommend respect and caution in mission. However, I want to underline that, on the basis of Kolmodin's words, one can understand why the steps allegedly taken by *Qeshi* Marqos to help members of the Evangelical Church to secure employment with the Adventists, could be interpreted as an act bordering on disloyalty (Ed.)

In this connection it should be stated that it would be unfair to give the impression that *Qeshi* Marqos was a trouble maker who devoted his time to petty issues. The story of his early years is fascinating. He was a highly educated pastor and proved to be an independent thinker.[508]

Marqos was a respected member of the Evangelical community right up to the time of the split with the SEM and did not lose the respect of the Kenisha even after the split. At the conclusion of his visit to Eritrea in 1908–1909, Kolmodin writes about the farewell service held in his honour on March 14, 1909,

> *Qeshi* Markus, who is to carry the responsibility for the care and guidance of the congregation during Iwarson's home leave now took to the floor and wished Pastor Iwarson and his dear ones a hearty godspeed on their trip and a warm welcome upon heir return. He then turned to me. He underlined especially his sincere wish that the bonds of trust and love which already joined the congregation and me and had become even

507 A. Kolmodin 1910, 60. Kolmodin had 1 Cor 10:16 in mind. According to their own records, the Adventists arrived in Eritrea in 1906. See Gudmundsen 1936, 73–79. (Ed.)

508 *Qeshi* Alazar Menghestu's book, *Bakgrunden och Framväxandet av en lutersk kyrka i Eritrea, 1912–1932.* Eritreanskt-Svenskt initiativ (The Background and Coming into being of a Lutheran Church in Eritrea, 1912–1932. An Eritrean-Swedish Initiative), which came out in 2004 (and its Tigrinya version), give us a captivating account about the life and work of *Qeshi* Marqos Girmai, a life story which could very well be the subject of a novel. See also A. Menghestu 2004, 24–36 and his Tigrinya version, from 2003, 18–42. (Ed.)

stronger during my visit would never snap. When he finally wished me God's blessings and protective grace on my homeward journey, the entire community stood up and entreated me to communicate the earnest greetings of this daughter congregation to the mother congregation in Sweden.[509]

Since there had not been any theological controversies among the missionaries and their Eritrean colleagues on the field, other factors may have contributed to the division among the Swedish missionaries in Eritrea. Some Eritreans sided with the SEM while others took sides with BV. When the Girmai and Nyström families decided to leave the SEM, three other missionaries from Beleza, Augusta Henriksson, Anna Holmberg, and the former missionary, now turned resident farmer, Nils Karlsson, joined them.[510]

Nyström – Leader of a new Mission Organization

Nyström, who became the leader of the new mission, settled at Debarwa, between Asmara and Addi-Ugri, where he built a mission station. As the station was within the Tse'azzega parish, the move was bound to lead to tension. At the annual mission conference held in October 1912, Anders Svensson reported that Nyström had tried to employ a certain man by the name of Tekle-Haimanot from Addi Sherefeto. When Svensson became aware of this fact he immediately employed the man.[511]

This division encouraged the Eritreans who had special attachments to the seceding missionaries, to join their missionary mentors. Thus, a split among the Kenisha congregations was now a fact. Almost a century later the division was still intact, although the two churches had almost all activities in common, apart from the fact that they had their loyalties to two different mission organizations in Sweden.[512]

---

509 A. Kolmodin 1909, 245. The responsibility that *Qeshi* Marqos Girmai was requested to assume for the Asmara congregation in the absence of Pastor Iwarson is a measure of the confidence placed in him. (Ed.)
510 A. Menghestu 1999, 31.
511 Annual Conference 1912, §19. Was it probably *Haleqa* Tekel-Haimanot Mihirka from Tigrai?
512 The two churches which grew out of the activities of the two respective missions, the ECE and the Lutheran Church of Eritrea, were united into the Evangelical Lutheran Church of Eritrea in 2006. (Ed.)

Thérèse (1876–1961) and Nicola De Pertis (1884–1931) and their daughter Anna (Jewfimiszyn). Picture from ca 1908.

An Italian Aristocrat as a Doctor
among Swedes and Eritreans

Following the death of Karl Winqvist, the hospital at Beleza was in great need of a new doctor.[513] However, the vacancy lasted up to 1913 when Dr. Nicola De Pertis joined the mission and took charge of the hospital. Nicola De Pertis came from an aristocratic family near Naples. His upbringing was Catholic, but during his studies he had come in contact with a group of students who used to meet for Bible studies in the home of an American lady. This led to contacts with different Protestant groups, one of them being the Waldensian Church. During his second year at the University of Naples, he attended a conference of the Student Christian Movement in Oxford, where he also met the famous Dr. John R. Mott.[514] He came in touch with many

513   SEM/EFS Annual Report 1910, 83–84.
514   John Raleigh Mott, an American born in 1865, was a prominent leader within the World Student Christian Federation. He died in 1955. The first conference of the Student Christian Movement was held in Edinburgh in 1910. (Ed.)

Christian groups from various parts of the world and felt a calling to missionary service. Of his meeting with Professor G. Luzzi, Dean of the Waldensian Theological Faculty in Florence, De Pertis writes, "He told me of the Swedish Mission in Eritrea and how they were looking for a replacement for the doctor that had died." Contact was established with the SEM and De Pertis was invited to Sweden. He was accepted and "ceremoniously consecrated for service as a missionary doctor".[515] In the autumn of 1913, he arrived in Eritrea and settled in Beleza. The hospital was functioning once again. In 1915 De Pertis was united in marriage to Thérèse Palmqvist.[516]

Educational Work –
The Contributions of two Women

As mentioned earlier, the Beleza mission was well known for its educational work. However, the extent of the teaching at the Girls' School was not regarded as adequate. Therefore, a special day school for women was opened. Haile-Ab's widow, Indrias, was put in charge of it.[517]

In 1908, Nyström reported that the number of female students was 50. He writes,

> They can be divided into three categories: 1. Children whose parents are members of the congregations. 2. Those that lack home and shelter. 3. Those whose parents have a negative attitude to the mission or are indifferent to the mission. These girls have come on their own initiative and are now in the majority.

> As a rule, we accept only those who are above 10 years of age. The reason is that most of them are likely to be married off when they are still as young as 10–11 years. If they come to us after the age of 10, they would reach a more mature age, following four years of schooling.[518]

Britta Edlund, who was a teacher at Beleza from 1912, writes,

> Tsehaytu had just finished school at Beleza when I arrived there.[519] The old teacher, Adey Biritu, was about to leave and Tsehaytu filled her

---

515   Hofgren 1956, 270. See Varde Ljus 1919.
516   E. Winqvist 1945, 121.
517   Arén 1978, 318.
518   SEM/MT 1908, no. 11, 82–83.
519   Edlund 1961, 14–15. Britta Edlund served in Eritrea 1912–1933 and 1948–1957.

position temporarily, teaching the young children. The choice turned out to be wise. She has continued teaching at the church schools in Beleza and Asmara. For some time she also served as an evangelist at Geshinashim. Tsehaitu was crippled from her childhood. Her parents had planned to send her to a convent as she couldn't be married off, but a relative who was working at the mission persuaded them to send her to the school at Beleza instead. There she became a believer and she found her task in life. Tsehaitu was firm, sometimes even harsh, but she won the respect and love of her pupils. Her classes were always orderly. In church the youngest ones sat in front on the floor, and they were often tempted to start playing if the services became long. However, if Tsehaitu was at hand a mere glance calmed them down. She served as a teacher for more than fifty years and even after retirement both children and adults were often seen around her at her home.[520]

The number of believers in Beleza district increased and, by 1915, the parish had members in some 20 villages, with a total membership of 642. The district ran 18 schools with some 400 students. The Girls' Home had 27 students.[521]

The Rev. Nils Nilsson (1881–1954)

The Rev. Nils Nilsson had arrived in 1913 for service in the Beleza parish. He remained in that service up to 1923. He was moved to Addis Ababa in 1924, since he was not allowed to return to Eritrea.[522] Even though he is not mentioned frequently in reports and discussions on the activities of the mission in Eritrea, he was a studious person who lived very close to his parishioners. Stories are told about his mule. It is said to have been acquainted with every Kenisha and to have made it a point to stop as soon it met a Kenisha on its way. It would not only stop but also see to it that Rev. Nilsson had his back to the wind.

The more specific explanation for this move on the part of the mule was that it wanted to make it possible for Rev. Nilsson to stop and chat with parishioners. Since Rev. Nilsson lit his pipe on these occasions, the mule saw to it that Rev. Nilsson had his back to the wind.[523]

520 Edlund 1961, 14–15.
521 SEM/EFS Annual Report 1915, 86–88.
522 It was he who baptized the editor of this work. (Ed.)
523 Reported by Dahlberg in SEM/MT 1925, 178. In his version, the story of the pipe does not appear, but the author learned about it from church members in Eritrea.

The Chapel and congregation at Geshinashim at the beginning of 1900.

Girls from the children's home in Beleza.

Largest Station on the Highlands

At the beginning of the nineteen-twenties, Beleza was the largest of the mission stations on the highlands with activities involving evangelism, medical and educational work as well as the production of literature. Two national pastors together with one Swedish clergyman, who was also a medical doctor, served in the area of Karneshim and Dimbezan. A number of teachers were engaged in promoting literacy and knowledge of the Bible. This led to the formation of Evangelical congregations and also to the promotion of Bible reading among the local population, as large portions of Scripture had now been translated and published in the Tigrinya language.

Medical services brought health-care and relief to a large number of sick people. A training institution for girls was also established, the first one of its kind in the area.

Since medical services were to be transferred to Asmara, it was decided that the buildings in Beleza be used for the setting up of a proper Industrial School for girls. The SEM Girls' Brigade in Sweden had collected some 6,000 Swedish Crowns for this purpose. Two female Italian teachers were recruited for the school and Britta Edlund was appointed head of the institution. In 1924 three new Italian missionary teachers (two women and one man) arrived. Germana Olivetti was placed at the Girls' School in Beleza, to help Britta Edlund, and Nora Rostan was placed in Asmara.

Late in 1922 a Field Conference held in Asmara declared that the school in Beleza was in dire need of qualified teachers. A grant of 1,200 Italian Lira was requested for the support of some young men who would continue their teacher training during the following year. Sibhatu Birru, Tsegay Hailenki'el, Paulos Teklé and Zacharias Teklé, all of whom had finished Grade 5 with the best scores, were selected for further training.[524]

In 1923 Efrem Tewolde-Medhin, the teacher who had been serving at schools in Beleza and Asmara, left for Addis Ababa to serve under Ras Teferi. "May God bless his work!" was the note of farewell.[525]

Under the leadership of Britta Edlund, the Beleza Technical School for Girls made progress. There was, however, a severe shortage of staff due to the ban on Swedish personnel by the colonial government. While some members of the Government were putting increasing pressure on the schools of SEM, other officials appreciated the performance of the schools. In 1925, Beleza Institute was awarded an honorary diploma, silver and bronze medals and a gold medal for "activities devoted to the education and nurture of the natives".[526]

---

524 Field Conference 1922 § 62.
525 SEM/MT 1923, 309.
526 SEM/Annual Report 1925, 220.

Qeshi Tesfu Bairai with confirmands, Beleza.

Medical Mission

When Italy entered World War I, De Pertis was called up for military service in Eritrea. He could, however, keep in touch with the Mission, and particularly with its medical work, whenever he was free. Upon his return to civilian life, he told an extra mission conference held in Eritrea in January 1919 that he was convinced that the medical work of the mission should have its base in Asmara, which is "the heart of the Colony". In his view, a hospital that met European standards ought to be erected there.

Teklu had worked as a faithful evangelist and medical assistant at the Beleza dispensary. After 40 years of service, he was now ready for retirement. A large group of friends met in Beleza to celebrate the occasion. The mission and the faithful were happy that his son, Yohannes, was prepared to follow in the footsteps of his father.[527]

527   Notes from Britta Edlund 1961, 134.

Bibeltrogna Vänner – Bible-True Friends

We have already noted that *the Swedish Mission Bible-True Friends* (BV) had taken up mission work in Debarwa, some 25 kms south of Asmara, in 1912. At the time the total number of missionaries working for the society was seven, consisting of the two families, the families of Karl Nyström and Marqos Girmai, two female missionaries and the resident farmer, Karlsson. Some more missionaries arrived in 1913 and 1914. In 1915 an American doctor by the name of Emanuel Edman joined the team, which now consisted of 12 missionaries in Africa.[528]

At the annual missionary conference of the SEM held in Geleb in September 1918 Dr. De Pertis had reported that he had been in touch with *Qeshi* Marqos Girmai who had hinted that he "might not be unwilling to return to us". Opinions among the participants at the conference were divided but it was resolved that a formal invitation be sent to Marqos.[529] However, no response was forthcoming from him. According to records in the Beleza Register, six families from Kwazen left SEM in 1921 and joined BV.[530] 1922 was in many ways a crucial year. Pastor Olle Eriksson had been transferred to Addis Ababa. However he came back to Asmara the same year to supervise the printing of a catechism in an indigenous language.[531] The language was Amharic.

In Closing

My mother, Woizero Aster Woldemariam (1900–2000), used to tell us about her days of youth in Beleza, Tse'azzega and Asmara. I remember her telling us how she used to pray as she cleaned the church in Tse'azzega. I have read about her work among the sick and dying in Asmara at the time when the Spanish flu ravaged the city. However, what I remember most vividly are her stories from Beleza. She spoke of a trio of female friends [she, Tsehaitu Ne`amin and Lete-Tsion Gebre-Mariam] who were very close to each other. In fact they had swallowed pebbles, as a sign of a covenant meant to cement their friendship.

One Easter morning they went to a nearby graveyard, to re-enact the

---

528 Missionssällskapet Bibeltrogna Vänner 1911–1961 (Mission Society Bible-True Friends 1911–1961) 79–82.
529 Miss. Conference at Geleb 1918 § 14.
530 Beleza Church Register Reg. C 1.
531 SEM/MT 1922, 291.

Teklu Uqbai, the faithful medical assistant of Dr. Karl Winqvist, with his family.

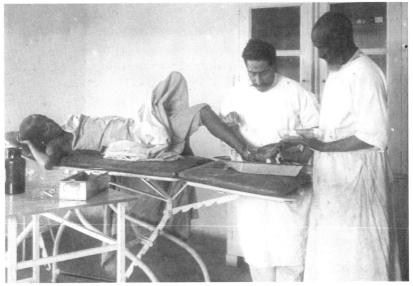

Dr De Pertis and Teklu at an operation. Published 1919 in Varde Ljus, "Let There Be Light"

scene around the Resurrection of Christ as narrated in Luke 24:1–8. One of them played the role of the angel who had asked the women, "Why do you look for the living among the dead? He is not here; he has risen" (vv. 5–6), while two of them fell on their faces to the ground.

Many a mission station or Evangelical institution in highland and lowland Eritrea symbolizes something special for members of the Evangelical Church in the country. Beleza is remembered for many things in the life of the ECE and its members. Many a future wife and mother received her education at the School for Girls there. There is, furthermore, a short but pregnant rhyme associated with Beleza. It reads: *Hakkim Beleza, sädiduläy qanza.* Paraphrased very freely, the rhyme would read: *Beleza's doctor, the good; has banished my pain and ill mood!*

The one who composed this rhyme must have found relief from pain at the hands of Dr. Karl Winqvist and his Kenisha co-workers. Around him Dr. Winqvist had a team of Eritrean medical orderlies. In fact Beleza was one of the very first bases for the training of dressers and nurses.

If the sick found relief in Beleza, there were also those who remembered Beleza for the peace of conscience, enlightenment, sound reading material and the sense of pride in one's language and culture mediated by this centre for evangelism, education, and the production of literature. The translation of the New Testament contributed to the promotion of Tigrinya as a language. Though small, the village of Beleza became a point of convergence for men of stature, knowledge and dedication from Sweden, Italy, Eritrea and Ethiopia itself.

There was one more area of activity in which Beleza excelled: the training of teachers. Those who had been trained at Beleza spearheaded not only the educational and evangelistic outreach of the SEM and the ECE, but also provided a base for the recruitment of pastors for the church. Had the ECE not had its teachers, its supply of native pastors would have been severely limited.

If the ELCE were to choose a place to build its first university, Beleza would probably win the place of honour. (Ed.)

To the left, Aster Woldemariam (mother to Ezra Gebremedhin) and Sema'itu Awalom making ready containers for grain in Asmara, 1922.

Children at a Christmas feast in Tse'azzega••Picture taken by Mikael Holmer.

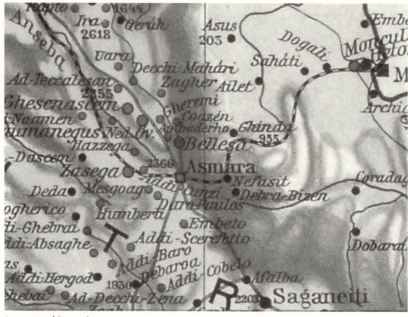

Asmara and its environs.

Chapter Fifteen

Highland Centres of Evangelical Christianity – Asmara

By K. J. Lundström and Ezra Gebremedhin

Introduction

An event which had a great significance for Anna's choice of a profession and which she still remembers, was the time when an old man in rags, carrying a big stone, asked her where the hospital was. When Anna pointed out the hospital (she was playing in the hospital garden), the man dropped his stone and walked towards the hospital with weary steps.

"When father came home in the evening", Anna continues, "I asked why the man behaved so strangely. Father told me that the man had come from the lowlands, and had promised that he would carry his burden until he came to a place where he could get help. At that point, father gave me the advice that I should never carry burdens like worry, hate and the like, which are not of any use to anyone, and reminded me that there was nothing virtuous in carrying unnecessary burdens".

These words are taken from an interview with 87-year old Anna Jewfimiszyn, daughter to Nicola and Thérèse De Pertis, missionaries to Eritrea. Her story goes back to the Asmara of the latter part of the Nineteen-twenties. It is striking that Anna speaks of a patient who had come from the lowlands of Eritrea to seek help at a mission hospital in Asmara, on the highlands of Eritrea. When this patient dropped the stone he was carrying, he did so not only physically but also symbolically. He came to a place where the words of Jesus in Matthew 11:28, "Come to me, all you who are weary and burdened, and I will give you rest", were read to patients waiting to receive medical care. Dr. De Pertis and his colleagues gave their patients not only physical treatment but also the kind of words of counsel that De Pertis gave to his little daughter. Food for body, soul and spirit.[532]

The SEM opened a station in Asmara in 1891. After 1915, a multifaceted mission venture was in full swing in the city. The venture involved evangelism, education, medical and diaconic work as well as the production of literature. Both the SEM and their Kenisha colleagues were engaged in a broad spectrum of activities that were evidently well planned and well implemented. However they also had to plan for the future. The fact that the SEM was now working in a heavily Orthodox area gave rise to questions related to mission policy.

Let us move on to K. J.'s narrative on the work of the SEM from a centre which was to became not only the capital of Eritrea but also the hub of the activities of the SEM and the ECE. His text, which is compiled from different, longer references to Asmara, follows. (Ed.)

---

532 Among the evangelists who preached and conducted devotional services at the hospital was Ato Gobezé Goshu, from Tigrai. More in Arén 1999, 265–269, 271–276, 278–280. (Ed.)

A Centre for Evangelism, Education and Literature

In 1891 the SEM established itself on a small site in Asmara. Later, more land was set aside for the development of a major centre. In time, the centre came to fulfil several tasks, besides providing a point of contact with the offices of the colonial government.

As the town grew so did the local Evangelical congregation. The missionary in charge was Rev. Jonas Iwarson. His primary task was to supervise the educational activities, with an emphasis on the training of evangelists and teachers. Iwarson did not, however, want the educational facilities of the mission to be limited to catering to the needs of the Evangelical Christians. He also welcomed students of the Orthodox faith. His main goal was to lead even the Orthodox into a deeper understanding of the Bible. This approach constituted something of a continuation of the spirit and activities of the early *Readers*. Besides offering specialized training, the mission also had a local school for boys, and some small elementary schools in the vicinity. In 1906 an industrial school was opened on condition that it be self-supporting. However, this goal could not be attained and the school was closed in 1913.

One of the most important mission projects in Asmara was the printing press. In the early years of the Eighteen-nineties, the mission was engaged in writing and printing primers for basic education. The translation and printing of Bible texts and hymn books in Tigré, Tigrinya and Kunama was a further development of this task. In 1906, Enno Littmann wrote,

> Asmara is at present the largest and most important station. Here the mission press is established in which many books are printed in several different East-African languages: Ethiopic, Amharic, Tigriña, Kunama, Galla, and even Suaheli. Herr Ivarson, the director of this station, has been of great help to me on several occasions. From the mere scholarly standpoint, the work of the missionaries in studying these languages and creating written literatures where formerly there were none, is of the greatest value and importance. On the other hand, their personal influence upon the natives must needs be a most beneficial one.[533]

In 1909, Pastor Olle Eriksson began his work of producing literature in Tigrinya. In the following five years he, *Qeshi* Zer'a-Tsion, *Qeshi*

---

533   Littmann 1907, 4. (Ed.)

The church at Asmara dedicated on April 6,1902 and its immediate surroundings.

The interior of the church of Asmara after the renovation 1932. Note the simple decorations with branches on the occasion of the dedication of the church.

Selomon and others succeeded in publishing a large number of writings. Furthermore, three bookstores were opened.

The School in Asmara was a leading educational institution. In a report written in 1921, Mrs. Signe Berg, who was to serve within the sector of education, along with her husband, had the following to report,

> The school house has been recently reconstructed and now has four rooms below and one upstairs. There are 4 or 5 classes. Lessons are held between 9–12 a.m. and 2.30–5 p.m. There is evening prayer at 8 p.m., led by a teacher. The topics taught are the following:
>
> Class 1. Bible History, Writing Tigrinya and Italian, Mathematics and the basics of Italian. Teachers: Local teacher and Mrs Tron.
>
> Class 2. The Large Bible Stories, Writing in Tigrinya and Italian, Mathematics, Introductory Amharic.
>
> Class 3. The Large Bible Stories, New Testament, Italian, Mathematics, Geography, History, Science and exercises in Amharic.
>
> Class 4. Same topics as above but on a more advanced level.
>
> Class 5. As above but with the addition of: Bible in Amharic and Ge'ez (as this class also had Old Testament.)
>
> The students were expected to assist in carrying water, bringing wood etc. Palm mats on the floor served as beds. Thursday was laundry day. On the upper floor, there were two looms where students could learn to weave.[534]

Regular Schools on a Basic Level

In 1925 it was reported that the school in Asmara had 200 students, half of whom were boarders who didn't pay. The school had now a preparatory class as well as classes ranging from classes 1 to 6. Signe Berg was in charge of the Boarding School and the Chief Accountant of the ECE. The teachers were Yishaq Tewolde-Medhin, Redda-Tsadiq, Berhe Zemmu, Yohannes and Terso. Iwarson, De Pertis and Girma-Tsion gave occasional lessons. After evaluating its activities, the Government Inspector of Schools described the institution as "Extraordinarily satisfactory."[535]

---

534   SEM/MT 1921, 307–308.
535   SEM/MT 1925, 100.

Teachers and students at the Asmara school for boys on March 24, 1914. In the middle Rev. Jonas Iwarson and Mr Emilio Ganz. Mrs Louise Iwarson is seated in the centre to the left.

Medical Work

It is to be remembered that a decision had been taken to the effect that the centre of gravity of the medial mission of the SEM be moved from Beleza to Asmara. The main promoter of this view was Dr. De Pertis. There were friends in Sweden who felt a special call to support the medical work of the Mission, almost from the very start. These were known as *Läkarmissionen* (the Medical Mission).[536] However, this large enterprise now needed a wider base of support. De Pertis decided that he would solicit funds for the establishment of the envisioned medical centre on his forthcoming travel to Europe. The proposal was approved by a field conference in Beleza in 1919.[537]

At the annual field conference in 1922, it was made clear that the estimated cost of the hospital building would rise to 55,000 Italian Lira and that another 10,000 would be required for equipment. De Pertis had advanced 50,000 Italian Lira until funds from Sweden would be forthcoming.[538]

The conference recommended further that the Medical Mission

536 Winqvist-Janér 1958, 171.
537 Extra Missionary Conference January 1919 § 2. See E. Winqvist 1944, 128.
538 Field Conference 1922 § 22, no. 4 and 5. See SEM/MT 1923, 197.

be granted its own charter and that it report directly to the Field Conference. The Medical Doctor would be in charge of the activities and his subordinates would report directly to him. Finances would be administered under a separate treasury.[539]

The following points were also agreed upon:
– The name of the Hospital shall be *Infermiera Evangelica*.
– The main local staff shall consist of:
1. Evangelist Redda-Tsadiq, who was replaced by Bahlibbi Garza when the former left for Ethiopia
2. Nurse: Samuel Habtenki'el
3. Female assistant: Nurse Ellen Kahsay
4. Students: Binega and Amanuel.[540]

The Training and Placement of Medical Personnel

There were two nurses/midwives in service, besides the doctor. One was the doctor's wife, Thérèse De Pertis (nee Palmqvist). Her fellow nurse was Isabella Stolpe. The latter had had to begin her work in the Outpatients' Department and in the hospital immediately. There was a steady stream of patients. People came from far away, many on mule back and some on camels. Others were carried on stretchers by relatives and friends. They came from all walks of life, but the poor were in the majority. There were Evangelical Christians, Catholics, Orthodox, Jews, Muslims and so-called pagans. People had great confidence in the hospital.

At dawn, the Evangelist held morning devotions and thereafter the clinic commenced its activities. When the doctor was ready with his examinations, treatment began. Medicine was distributed, patients underwent operations, after which they were either registered for treatment at the hospital or sent home with instructions. The Evangelist circulated among the patients. For those who stayed on for treatment, classes were arranged, if these wanted to learn to read. Prior to returning to their homes, the patients were given copies of the New Testament.

On a Sunday at the end of 1923, it was announced at the Church

539   Field Conference 1922 § 23.
540   Field Conference 1922 § 25.

De Pertis giving a lesson in Anatomy.

service in Asmara that a course for nurses would be started and that young women of the congregation were welcome to register interest. The course had place for six students. However, one of the places was, already reserved for Ellen Kahsay.

Two male students, Samuel Manna and Embaye Habte-Egzy, attended the course for nurses at the Evangelical Hospital in Asmara. After two years of study they were transferred to the School for Evangelists in Beleza.[541]

Isabella was given the task of running the first course for the training of nurses among the local population. The teachers were Dr. De Pertis, his wife Thérèse and the nurse Isabella. Thérèse was the matron. She was also the first one to write a textbook on midwifery in Tigrinya, a book that was published by the Mission Press in 1928.

Besides subjects directly connected with medical care, the course included Italian, Amharic, Bible, and Church and Mission History. Practical training took place at the hospital. The first public examination

541 E. Winqvist 1945, 152.

took place on January 15, 1927. Six female students graduated as nurses and midwives and were then consecrated as deaconesses. Among the deaconesses, Demmet was called to serve as nurse at the hospital in Asmara, Ellen Kahsai was employed in Geleb and Geshinashim, and Amete-Tsion in Himbirti. The remaining three moved to Addis Ababa, where they were to serve under the Swedish Doctor, Knut Hanner, at the Betä Saida Hospital.[542]

Before starting her medical studies, Lette-Tsion was a co-worker with Britta Edlund at Beleza. After her graduation as a deaconess she started serving with the Mission and was stationed at Himbirti. Later, she went into government service where she worked until she retired at 60. Britta Edlund writes, "She lives in her own small house in Asmara and gets a small pension but she still continues to give help when help is needed."[543]

The Efforts of De Pertis at Expanding Medical Work

Ivarson's Worries

In some matters, particularly regarding finances, Rev. Iwarson was critical of De Pertis' ways of doing things. In a letter written in 1925 to Rev. Dahlberg, the General Secretary of the SEM in Sweden, he states that he had had to set limits to some planned expansions, which were beyond the financial means that were available. De Pertis had planned for six large rooms for the deaconesses. Iwarson reduced these to four. Iwarson was also afraid that the nurse-trainees would get used to a large, comfortable institution, and not be able to undertake the more menial tasks that their profession would entail.[544] He stated, "They are indeed not getting used to such tasks and two of them are already engaged and will be married to important men."[545] At the beginning of 1926 the De Pertis family paid a visit to Khartoum to study the medical mission of a British missionary society, specializing in the treatment

---

542   The report on the training of deaconesses was based on E. Winqvist 1947, 156–157. See also Arén 1999, 226–228.
543   Edlund 1961, 14.
544   One of the persons who had read the preceding sentence commented, "Biased, condescending statement!" I have let the sentence stand, simply because K. J. Lundström had recorded it! The statement does reflect a rather condescending attitude! (Ed.).
545   Letter June 4, 1925. Iwarson to Dahlberg.

The first course for nursing students in Asmara, who graduated on January 15, 1927.
From left to right: Amete-Tsion Girma-Tsion placed in Himbirti; Lete-Yesus Gebre-Kidan placed in Addis Ababa ; Gabriela Tesfa-Mikael placed in AA; Mihret Mengesha placed in AA ; Demet Hailu, died; Ellen Kahsai placed in Geshinashim. Three of them moved to Betä Saida Hospital in Addis Ababa. Another nurse who moved to Addis Ababa was Askalu Tekle-Haimanot.

The family of Haleqa Kahsai, Addi Mongonti, 1912. Left to right: Minilik Kahsai, Elsabet, Medhin, Ellen Kahsai (eldest daughter), Haleqa Kahsai, Sara and Beyin.

of leprosy. They also visited the school of midwifery.[546]

De Pertis Heavily Engaged as Planner and Healer

Dr. De Pertis was heavily engaged in the activities of the hospital. Already in 1925, the hospital had received 6,300 new patients and the number of treatments had reached 25,000. There was a very heavy load of work on the staff. In 1927 the hospital in Asmara was in a position to begin a new course for indigenous nurses. Five female students and one male student were enrolled. On any given day the number of policlinic patients would average about 120, the most common types of illness being those that affected the eyes.[547]

When De Pertis and his wife were planning to depart for Khartoum to visit a mission hospital there and consult the medical staff, the colonial authorities tried to prevent the visit. However, the town physician in Asmara stepped in and took upon himself the responsibility of running the clinic during their absence. In 1928, De Pertis reports that the hospital had received 100–130 patients a day and that the training of nurses and midwives was in progress. He writes,

> It has been our goal to provide help to as many patients as possible with the small means that we have had at our disposal. That the improvement of the hospital is urgent can't be denied. 8000 crowns is the minimum amount of money needed to bring our hospital to a somewhat satisfactory state of hygiene. [...] On an average, the cost of food and medicine has risen up to ten times the sum that was current 15 years ago. [...] We wouldn't have been able to continue with the school for deaconesses if friends in Uppsala and Stockholm hadn't supported us faithfully.[548]

During the first six months of 1928, the number of patients at the clinic was 4522; treatments had been given to 13,323; there were 70 home visits, 372 cases of deliveries and other kinds of treatment of in-patients. The income amounted to 15,000 Lira. The vice Governor, Marino Mutinelli[549], had paid a visit to the hospital and the school for deaconesses and had expressed his great appreciation of the various

---

546 E. Winqvist 1945, 148–149.
547 SEM/MT 1927, 323.
548 SEM/MT 1928, 453.
549 See the Swedish version of the letter from Dr De Pertis in SEM/MT 1929, 453.

A painting describing the healing of the sick and the preaching of the Good News (Matthew 10:7–8). The post-card carries a longer text. The painter is Haleqa Yohannes from Axum. He had come to Beleza to get help for an eye-sickness and was moved by what he saw at the hospital. As an expression of gratitude for the treatment that he had received, he gave Doctor De Pertis a painting portraying the activities that he had witnessed at the hospital. It shows the missionaries of the SEM, Mrs Thérèse and Dr Nikola De Pertis (to the left bottom on the painting). A native evangelist is preaching, holding an open Bible. He is reading from Isaiah 53:4–5, the story of the Suffering Servant. Painting published as a post card in 1924.

branches of the activities of the mission. De Pertis felt rather confident that the difficult period was now over, and that the mission would enjoy the same measure of confidence with the colonial authorities that it had enjoyed before the war.[550]

In June 1929, De Pertis decided to visit Italy with his family for rest and medical treatment. Isabella Stolpe was due for furlough and left for Sweden. However, when it was time for her to return to Eritrea the Italian authorities refused to give her a permit for re-entry. Only De Pertis and his family were permitted to return.[551]

Already in February 1930, De Pertis was taken ill again and had to

550   SEM/MT 1928, 453.
551   E. Winqvist 1945, 162–163.

rest due to the heart ailment from which he was now suffering. He went down to Keren to take a break but finally had to leave for Italy for treatment. However, on June 3, 1931 he died in his room at the YMCA in Rome.[552]

Deaconesses Graduate

Thérèse De Pertis reported that the third batch of deaconesses had graduated in February 1933. Some of them attended a further course of three months at the Government hospital and graduated as the best students. They were later commissioned in the small chapel on the Mission compound.[553] One of the girls, Askalu [Tekle-Haimanot], moved to Addis Ababa where she had two brothers and where she was employed at the Betä Saida Hospital.[554] Lette-Tsion and Kibirti were assigned to districts north and south of Asmara. Lette-Hiywet was assigned to the Asmara congregation.[555]

The Training of Teachers

Since the early Nineteen-hundreds, Asmara had been a centre for the training of teachers and evangelists. During and after the First World War, when there was a shortage of missionary personnel, no further training could be given. Many had left for other services and there was now a shortage that had to be met. In 1927, Rev. Alessandro Tron reports that a small course had been initiated at Beleza. "There are only five students", he states, "but this group may be of great importance". Here are Tron's presentations of them,

> Andenkiel Wolde-Mencherios, from Addi Deku-Tsin'a in Tsilima. As a young boy he had shown a great interest in religious matters, and left home to find a place in a monastery. He was, however, sent back home, where he started learning to read. He found a copy of the New Testament

---

552   E. Winqvist 1945, 166.
553   A student boarding had been built for the deaconesses, with a chapel and classrooms.
554   These two brothers were Ato Isaias Tekle-Haymanot, married to the editor's maternal aunt Woizero Hiriti, and his younger brother, Ato Gebre-Kristos Tekle-Haymanot, who became the head of the government printing press, *Birhaninna Selam* (Light and Peace), in Addis Ababa under the regent Ras Teferi, later Emperor Haile-Silassie. See Arén 1999, 190–191. (Ed.)
555   SEM/MT 1933, 334.

Female members of the Asmara congregation who took part in a course for medical orderlies in 1928. At the top of the picture Dr and Mrs De Pertis.

in Tigrinya and "his eyes were opened". He left now for Tse'azzega and after three years of study he was confirmed. He continued his studies in Asmara and after completing these he served as assistant teacher and supervisor of the boarding students. [...] his desire is to give his life fully to the service of his Lord.

Samuel Manna was born in Himbirti, but some years ago his parents moved to Tigrai. After the death of his father, Samuel was sent by Rev. Svensson to the school in Asmara. After the completion of his studies he had some temporary employment but was then admitted to the course at the hospital run by Dr. De Pertis. He was, however, offered the chance to join the school for the training of teachers opened recently. As far as we can see, we have high hopes for his future.

The following three are younger. One is Salomon. [...] who has the special gift of reflecting and has always been kind and obedient. Tekletsen Debbas, was born in Asmara and is the son of the teacher Debbas Negasi, who has worked in Asmara for many years. He has completed fifth grade and is staying with his father in Tsada Kishtan, where he helps him in the school.

Finally we have Yaqob Gebre Le'ul, born in Tse'azzega and one of the youngest students, being only 15 years old. He has always displayed good intelligence and a mild and calm manner. Besides these students we have another very young student, only 16 years of age. He is Menghestu, the grandson of Pastor Tewolde-Medhin Gebre-Medhin, a son of Isaac. [...] His father hopes to send him to Rome for further studies, where Dr. De Pertis has been able to secure a free place for him at a Protestant school.[556]

Ato Bairu Uqbit

Two new teachers were needed for the school in Asmara, but there was a general shortage of staff. Just then a particularly gifted person, Bairu Uqbit, offered himself for service. He was regarded as a person capable of an immediate promotion.[557] In the words of a grandson,

> Mr Bairu Uqbit was born in Gheremi – an Adi commune just fifteen kilometres from the capital city, Asmara. He had a great yearning for modern education early in his life. Swedish missionaries had a school in Asmara with which the young Bairu wished to associate himself; but in those days traditional Orthodox families did not permit their children to attend schools that were run by foreign missionaries. In the end his desire for education was such that he broke away from the influence of his family and joined the Swedish Evangelical Mission.

> At the mission school he acquired a working knowledge of Italian, Amharic, and Arithmetic – that provided him with the platform to become a self-taught person. Mr Bairu built a family of nine children with Mrs. Haregeweini, the daughter of *Qeshi* Tekle – one of the founders of the Evangelical Church of Eritrea. In matters of church activities Mr. Bairu was a member of the Synod – where he advocated that Christmas and Easter should be celebrated in accordance to the Ethiopian traditions. Mr Bairu was also a driving force in the struggle to eradicate illiteracy; among the intellectual achievements of Mr. Bairu, the translation of John Bunyan's "Piligrims Progress" in 1926, and his translation of the early New Testament in collaboration with *Emebet* Elsie, in 1934, are worth noting. Mr. Bairu also translated several songs in the Tigrinya Book of Hymns.

---

556 SEM/MT 1927, 163–165. (Ed.)

557 On Bairu's qualifications see SEM/MT 1933, 529–530. The material on Bairu Uqbit was given to the editor by his grandson, Herui Tedla Bairu. (Ed.)

Ato Bairu Uqbit and his wife Woizero Haregeweyni Tekle, a daughter of Qeshi Tekle Tesfa-Kristos.

Ato Tedla Bairu

Bairu Uqbit had also wanted to send his son Tedla to a teacher training college in Florence. The Conference was in favour of the idea and decided to look for a possible donor who could help. In case Tedla would not enter the service of the Mission after his studies he himself would take the responsibility for repaying the costs of his education. Ato (later Dejjazmatch) Tedla Bairu, who was born on March 27, 1914, was to become one of the key actors on the political scene in Eritrea during the post-war years. In the words of one of his sons,

> By the time he was five years old his father taught him to read Tigrinya and Italian and to do Arithmetic. In 1926, Mr Bairu sent his son to Italy when he was only twelve years old. Mr Tedla studied to be a teacher at

the "Instituto Magistrale Statale" in Firenze, Italy. From 1934 to 1941, he worked as a principal and teacher in different parts of Eritrea. Mr. Tedla was active in the educational and musical aspects of the Evangelical Church of Eritrea. During the period of 1933–1934 he tutored Eritrean youth, and was active with the church choir as an organist and conductor. Mr. Tedla has also contributed to the compilation of the Tigrinya book of hymns.[558]

Overall Picture on Educational Activities

The Mission continued to encounter difficulties. There was however one positive development. The colonial government had abolished the order to close the Evangelical schools, although the permission to attend school applied only to children from Evangelical families.[559]
Iwarson writes,

> There is an increased request for more places in our regular schools. Had not the financial and political restrictions been so severe, our work could have increased substantially.[560]

Rev. Iwarson lamented the serious situation that had arisen in 1927, with shortage of food both in Eritrea and to the south. Many flocked into Asmara and the Mission tried to help. For a period of three months, the Mission distributed bread and grain daily to some 400 people. Help was also given to people who came to the hospital.[561]

The Production of Literature

The printing press continued operating at full capacity, with Emilio Ganz in charge. The turnover was high and a substantial part of the output of printed literature was intended for Addis Ababa. The translation of the Old Testament into Tigrinya was in progress, with Tewolde-Medhin Gebre-Medhin in Shimanigus in charge. There was also an urgent need for a revision of the Tigrinya New Testament and

---

558 The material on Ato (later 'Dejjazmatch) Tedla Bairu was provided by his son, Herui Tedla Bairu. (Ed.)
559 Field Conference 1927 § 28 and § 30.
560 SEM/Annual Report 1926, 256–257.
561 SEM/MTBB 1928, 524–525.

The Printing Press in Asmara around 1920.

Books being prepared for sale. To the right stands the head of the printing press, Emilio Ganz.

Haleqa Tewolde-Medhin Gebru had been asked to assist in this task.[562]

At the Field Conference in 1926 it was decided that the New Testament in Tigrinya was of such a high quality that no revision of it was required. However, according to the Bible Society, a reprint would be needed, with only some minor corrections. The reprint would be carried out according to the previous format.[563] At the seventh meeting of the ECE Synod in 1931, however, the congregation in Tse'azzega appealed to the Synod that the Bible should not be reprinted in the kind of Tigrinya that reflected a dialect from the Ethiopian Province of Tigrai. It was resolved that the request be studied and that nothing be included in the translation that would not be understood by the people on the Eritrean Highlands. It was stated that *Haleqa* Tewolde-Medhin Gebru should not include anything in the translation that would not meet the approval of people here.[564]

At the 9th Synod of the ECE, *Qeshi* Girma-Tsion, Pastor Holmer and Pastor Alessandro Tron reported that the New Testament had been revised. A delegation was appointed to thank Mrs. Elsie Winqvist for her share in the vital undertaking.[565] Towards the end of 1928 Rev. K. G. Rodén, then in Sweden, reported that the revision of the New Testament in Tigré that he and Rev. Axel Jonsson had carried out, was now ready. They had made use of seven European and three Semitic translations and the spelling had been made to conform to Sundström's views on the subject.[566] The new edition was published by the British and Foreign Bible Society in 1931.

Rev. Rodén had also been working on a revision of the Tigré hymnbook. One of his special concerns was the inclusion of some songs by indigenous Christians. The Mensa and Habab were very talented in composing songs and ballads. The problem was that these songs were usually composed and sung by a single person, and not by a group. This made it difficult to include the compositions in a hymnal. It was underlined that musical notes be provided and that people be trained to use the hymns that had been included.[567]

---

562   SEM/Annual Report 1926, 258.
563   Field Conference 1926, § 14.
564   Musa minutes 1931, p 9 § 9. Tewolde-Medhin had come already in 1926.
565   Musa minutes 1933, 11 § 12.
566   SEM/MTBB 1928, 624–625.
567   SEM/MTBB 1929, 372.

The new building of the Printing Press in Asmara, built by Nils Karlsson 1895.

Haleqa Tewodle-Medhin Gebru from Mai-Misham, Tigray, working on the translation of the New Testament into Tigrinya. Picture from 1926–1928.

A page from the proof of the first printing of the New Testament in Tigrinya, from December 1909. The text is part of the first chapter of the Gospel of John.

In Closing

According to BBC News for December 23, 2000, two hundred and twenty-six Eritrean prisoners of war were released in Ethiopia and repatriated by plane to Asmara under the auspices of the International Red Cross (IRC). They were received at Asmara International Airport by high and low, with relief and jubilation. Soon after this incident I talked on the phone with my older brother, Naigzy Gebremedhin, who was a resident of Asmara at the time. He told me that, at its latest Sunday service, the main congregation of the ECE in the city had sung a hymn in gratitude for the return of the prisoners of war, with only one little alteration in the hymn. The first verse of the hymn in its unchanged form reads as follows,

> When the Lord releases Zion's prisoners
> Then we are like dreamers,
> Our mouths are filled with joy
> God has done good things for us
> Lift up your voice! Praise Him mightily,
> Praise your king on high with songs
> When He releases Zion's prisoners
> Then we are indeed like dreamers.[568]

On this particular Sunday the singing congregation had replaced the name *Zion* in the hymn by the name *Eritrea*.

It is many decades since this hymn, *Nai Sion' Esurat Kifetih Goyta*, [When the Lord releases Zion's prisoners] was translated. Those who translated the hymn had a straightforward spiritual message to the faithful. Now the hymn was being used by their Kenisha heirs to express a sense of communal and national relief at the ebbing of a crisis which had hit their *Zion*: Eritrea.

By virtue of its geographical location (the highest capital city in Africa), size and its status as the capital city of Eritrea, Asmara, had become a point of convergence for the Kenisha and the biggest workshop for the moulding of their identity. It is significant that a whole quarter at one

---

568 Mezmur Selam 257, v. 1 MF 691. The biblical background to this hymn is Psalm 126:1-2, which reads," When the Lord turned again the captivity of Zion; we were like them that dream. Then our mouth was filled with laughter, and our tongue with singing. Then said they among the heathen, The Lord hath done great things for them." (Ed.)

The interior of the church of Asmara. Annual Conference held from March 4–6, 1911. Anders Svensson appears at the centre of the picture. To his left is Blatta Beraki and next to him we see two important men, one is a Bahrä Negasi (Governor of Midri Bahri) and the other is Kentiba Hagos.

A Music Presentation by an orchestra, probably in the Asmara of the late nineteen-twenties and early nineteen-thirties. Olle Andersson (Hagner) was one of the "music pioneers".

end of the city is known as *Geza Kenisha* (lit. The House of Kenisha). The institutions of the SEM and the ECE (the Central Office, the Church, the Hospital (now defunct), the School, the printing press (now defunct) etc. were, in a sense, Kenisha show pieces, a part of the Public Relations arsenal of the Evangelical community. Asmara was the place where the ECE met and sometimes rubbed shoulders with officialdom, be it Italian, British or Ethiopian. It has also been the scene of tension, conflict, splits, negotiations and reconciliation within the Kenisha community. As the seat of the Synodical Council, the highest administrative body of the church, Asmara has stood for authority in the ECE, a type of authority sometimes envied and sometimes resented by outlying districts of the church.

Where is Asmara's former glory as a centre for Kenisha identity and presence? Where is the old style school of Wängelawit Betekristian, the *Infermiera Evangelica*, the school for the training of nurses and midwives, the Printing Press, the School for deaconesses, the training of teachers etc.? And one answer would be: Times have changed. Some manners of serving the urban community, once accessible to the SEM and the ECE, are no longer within reach of a church body. And the members of the ECE are now engaged actively in the society which renders these same services which once were the privilege and opportunity of the SEM and the ECE.

And yet, would it be entirely unfair to ask: Where is Asmara's former glory as a centre for Kenisha identity and presence? In a way, Asmara can be regarded as a highland twin to Imkullu [I don't say Massawa], strange as the comparison may sound. Imkullu was a cosmopolitan centre on the Red Sea, a place of meeting, a refuge for the sharing of needs and gifts, a place of give and take in an environment where everyone needed everyone else to survive, physically and spiritually. The very idea of a busy urban centre can suggest leakage and erosion in the sense of the loss of a historical, spiritual and cultural awareness. However an urban centre can also be a cutting edge, a line of growth and development, an effective filter and mediator of sound dreams and visions.

Cities can either squander age-old memories and values or cling to them in a fanatically stiff manner. Urban centres can become innovative, imaginative cutting edges. A city can become a sound filter

Women gathered for a working session in Asmara under the leadership of Louise Iwarson. Picture published in 1934.

for new impulses coming in like high waves from different parts of our increasingly globalized world. It can also combine the latest technical skills and intellectual insights with the faith and genuine values of those who are no longer with us. As an urban face for the Kenisha, Asmara has not only a proud tradition to look back upon but also a high calling to live up to.[569] One cannot think of the Evangelical Lutheran Church of Eritrea without thinking of Asmara and the Kenisha heritage that it carries. (Ed.)

569 Professor Asmarom comments: "Granted that the Asmara evangelical centers of medical service, the hub of spiritual and secular education, and fountain of religious and secular literature in Tigrigna and Tigré are now in decline, but the impact of these institutions on Eritrea is immeasurable. As with Imkullu, the decline of the mother institutions is directly associated with the scattering of their influence. Just as the small mahber of Imkullu went on to plant it's seeds across Eritrea and Ethiopia, so too have the men and women trained in the tiny four-classroom Evangelical School gone on to do great things far beyond the small community in which they were raised and nurtured." His comment is well taken. (Ed.)

Tse'azzega (Zasega) and its environs.

Chapter Sixteen

Highland Centres of Evangelical Christianity – Tse'azzega

By K. J. Lundström and Ezra Gebremedhin

Introduction

On Saturday morning the 7th of November I left Asmara, to which I had returned from Bellesa [Beleza[the day before. Mrs. Iwarson and I travelled by a horse-drown carriage. Pastor Iwarson had sent his small horse-drawn carriage to get my son Johannes who was also invited. Our

Teacher's house in Tsa'ida Kristian. Published in 1909.

destination was Zazega [Tse'azzega]. [...] Having crossed the river-bed, now dry, we started ascending uphill when female members of the congregation, gathered outside the church, broke out in their vigorous ululations. [...]

Sunday too was a day with brilliant sunshine. At 8.30 a.m. the church bell started ringing quietly and invitingly, over the sun-drenched landscape. Soon, church people started streaming to the [mission] station from different directions. Some were coming from the village of Zazega, which lay on a hill to the west. There was a large group advancing on another path from Himbirti, where the Gospel has won some great victories in recent years. A small group from Addi Kuntsi, Zada Kristian [Tsa'ida Kishtan] etc. was advancing on a third path. To see them coming, dressed in their simple but beautiful, white clothes, moving towards the church, their common destination, was a most gratifying scene.[570]

These words are taken from A. Kolmodin's description of one of his visits to Tse'azzega in November 1908. They give us glimpses not only into the geographical location of the village that has been called the cradle of the ECE, but also into some of its satellite-villages. In the history of the ECE, Tse'azzega is not only a place but also a concept, the focus of a story with many illustrious actors. For the details of this narrative we shall now turn to a partly restructured version of some material from K. J. (Ed.)

570   A. Kolmodin, 1909, 87–88.

A Place with a Character of its Own

Even though Beleza was the earliest centre of the SEM on the Eritrean highlands and could boast a higher number of institutions, Tse'azzega had a character of its own from the beginning. It was, traditionally, the most important Evangelical centre on the highlands and had the distinction of being the home of the first *Bible Readers*, a statement which must perhaps be qualified.

Joseph Gabrawold writes,

> The elderly Orthodox priests of Sazaga have the following account: The main Evangelical leaders, whom they called Sara-Maryam ['Tsärä Mariam', i.e. Enemies of Mary], were not in fact from Sazaga. Their connection with Sazaga was solely on their mothers' side. To this statement my informants from the Evangelical Church of Sazaga also agreed. The main leaders and spokesmen of the Kanishas were Qes Selomon Asku from Adi-Akolom; Qes Zarasion Muse from Garami, Qes Gabra-Madhin and Qes Haylaab Tesfai who were brothers from Shimanigus Tahitay. All these villages are in Hamasen and are neighbours. Before they came in touch with the Amharic Bible, Qes Gabra-Madhin was the Liqa-Kahanat (Arch-Priest) and the others were the main leaders of the Orthodox Church of Qidus Gyorgis. The other Sazagan priests were jealous of the predominance of these people. This situation created a bitter conflict between them and that is why the leaders defected and followed the teaching of foreigners.[571] (Ed.)

It was natural that the chairman of the mission, Rev. Anders Svensson, chose to settle in Tse'azzega after leaving Imkullu. The year was 1891.

The number of foreign missionaries in the area was very low and the institutions were on a small scale, being mainly village schools. Rev. Svensson was the only male missionary in the congregation from the time of his arrival to his death in 1928, with the exception of a period of almost two years, which he used to renew his strength, and of a couple of short visits to his home-country in 1913 and 1927.[572] His interest was concentrated on congregational work, which implied sending out teachers and evangelists.

---

571   Joseph Gabrawold 1972, 33. On this point Professor Asmarom has commented: "Qes Zera Tsion was not from Tsazzega on his paternal or maternal sides, but from Addi *Ra'si* and Geremi."

572   N. Rodén 1938, 126.

Outside of the church at Tse'azzega. Sitting from left to right: Karl Gustaf Rodén, Karl Winqvist and Johannes Magnus Nilsson. Standing from left: Richard Sundström, Jonas Iwarson, Anders Svensson, Karl Nyström, and Nils Karlsson. Picture published in 1899.

Picnic with the school at Tse'azzega in February 1930. Sitting around the tea-kettle we see from left the teacher Bekhit, a big school-boy and the teachers Tekle-Tsion and Gubsa.

'Father' Svensson and Gebre-Le'ul

Svensson was single, but established close contact with the family of Gebre-Le'ul Tirfé of Tse'azzega. The members of the family took care of his needs, preparing his food, washing his clothes and serving him in other ways. He provided them with a livelihood and Gebre-Le'ul saw his position as that of a son of Svensson.

Svensson was thus integrated into the lives of the people in his society. He shared their food and drink, travelled like them by mule and slept on the floor, swept in his *gabi*, when he was out in the villages. At Imkullu, Amharic had been the language of communication. However, when the missionaries and their colleagues moved into the interior, most of them used the regional languages like Kunama, Tigré and Tigrinya. Rev. Svensson, however, continued to use Amharic.

He came to be regarded as a highly influential and respected elder. He even served as a mediator between the Italian government and the village of Tse'azzega. He persuaded General Gandolfi, who had succeeded Governor Orero in 1890, not to punish the community for the rebellion of Lidj Abberra.

A Eulogy to A. Kolmodin – A Credit to Svensson

A eulogy composed to welcome A. Kolmodin on his visit to Tse'azzega in November 1908 by a scholar of the Orthodox Tewahdo Church, a certain *Haleqa* Medhanä, reflects the generosity and poetic license that highland hospitality could mobilize for the purpose. Furthermore, the ease with which the cleric came to visit Kolmodin at the home of Svensson is an indirect witness to the recognition and respect that the latter enjoyed among the Orthodox. The *Haleqa* asked for permission to compose a *qiné*, a eulogy in Kolmodin's honour. Kolmodin comments,

> I couldn't turn down such an offer. He then started to sing in the kind of melody which reminds one of the music of the Abyssinian Church there. The song was in Ge'ez, (i.e. Ethiopic, the language of the church). The poetry was translated for me. Its content was as follows: It began with praise to God and then described God's apostles as "precious pearls, as they accomplished the work of preaching the Gospel", and our missionaries as their successors, who shine like "the sun and the moon". The old man then went on to praise Sweden "which had become greater than all other countries through the word of the Gospel". He

also sang about me, stating that I had come in the power of John – (that was indeed my prayer!) –and that my priestly attire was like the Abun's, the bishop of the Ethiopian Church. Finally he sang that "Sweden had filled the whole country"[573]

In his work *Traditions de Tsazzega et Hazzega*, the Swedish scholar Johannes Kolmodin, who visited the area in 1908–1910, in company with his father, Adolf Kolmodin, writes that Svensson

> was the man who united in his person all that the word *Swede* represents, in terms of influence and esteem in Hamasen and in Eritrea. He is the true chief of Tse'azzega and Deqé Teshim in an epoch that has superseded the role of the ancient chiefs of the tribe about
>
> whom our text narrates.[574]

Implications of Mission among the Orthodox

Anders Svensson served as the chairman of the Mission in Eritrea from 1886 to 1913, a period of twenty-seven years. He brought with him much of the Imkullu heritage but also had a keen appreciation of the Orthodox heritage. He had a way of fitting into the Orthodox way of life. In this sense, he lived and acted much the same way that the *Bible Readers* had done. He too was concerned about working for a spiritual reform of the Orthodox Church. The *Bible Readers* and he believed that such a reform would take place primarily through enlightenment, i.e. through the study of the Bible, a challenge directed to clergy and laity, men and women alike.

The messengers of the Gospel were also engaged in a number of social services, even though their overriding concern, while waiting to advance towards Oromo territory, was that of a reformation of the Orthodox Church. As a consequence of this vision, the formation of Evangelical congregations was seen more as an emergency measure than as a final goal of the mission. In an introductory statement in the report on the mission in 1902, the missionaries declare,

> The aim of our activities has been to prepare a reformation in this

---

573 A. Kolmodin 1909, 100. See Fre Woldu (Ed.) Zanta Hazzegan Tse'azzegan 1989, 260 and J. Kolmodin Traditions de Tsazzega et Hazzega 1915, 200. Aina Berglund 1959. On Abbera's rebellion see T. Negash 1987, 122–123. (Ed.)

574 J. Kolmodin 1912, XXIX.

ancient Church.[575] Though not our main duty, the formation of congregations is still a necessity, in view of the need to provide spiritual care for those who have been excommunicated, and have thus been left without spiritual nurture.[576]

Providing for the Spiritual Care of Evangelical Christians

The provisional church on the highlands followed more or less in the steps of the Betel congregation of Imkullu. The order of service was that of the Church of Sweden and the hymns were translations of western [mainly Swedish] hymns sung to the tunes of western origin. Apart from the clergy who had been ordained in Sweden, only two Orthodox priests, *Qeshi* Selomon and *Qeshi* Zer'a-Tsion, had been given authorization to celebrate Holy Communion.[577] Winning a large number of adherents was not the principal concern of SEM. The main goal was to influence the Orthodox community to follow the Bible strictly as its basic norm for teaching and practice.

On the basis of the experiences of the early *Readers* who had received their inspiration from studying the Scriptures, the Mission saw literature as the best way of spreading the Good News. This led to a concentration on the promotion of literacy and the publication of literature. When the question of establishing a national Evangelical Church became acute in 1925, it was not primarily the missionaries or the congregations that pushed the matter, but rather the Secretary of the SEM, Nils Dahlberg. We shall return to this question.

The need for more clergy was becoming increasingly urgent. Tewolde-Medhin Gebre-Medhin was the next one to be considered for ordination. He was ordained on January 1, 1909 by Professor Adolf Kolmodin. Two months later Teklé Tesfa-Kristos was ordained at Tse'azzega for service in the Himbirti congregation.[578]

Tse'azzega parish comprised Hamasen, and included the region of

---

575 The fact that *Aleqa* Tayye, with his rich *Orthodox* background, was employed as a teacher in Tse'azzega from 1891 to 1898 must have reinforced the vision of a mission among the Orthodox Tewahdo. See Joseph Gabrawold 1972, 59–60. (Ed.)
576 Statement given in SEM Annual Report 1902, 68–69.
577 Arén notes that this retarded the development of an independent Evangelical Church severely. Arén 1978, 348.
578 Arén 1978, 350–351.

The ordination of Tewolde-Medhin Gebre-Medhin in Asmara on New Year's Day 1909.
From left: Qeshi Zer'a Tsion, (father-in-law to Tewolde-Medhin), Jonas Iwarson, Anders
Svensson, Tewolde-Medhin Gebre-Medhin, Adolf Kolmodin (seated), Karl Winqvist, Olle
Eriksson and Marqos Girmai.

Tsilima. In 1900 the congregation consisted of 134 members, out of
whom 58 were communicant members. Besides the centre at Tse'azzega,
work had been initiated in the villages of Misgwag, Himbirti, Tjaresh,
Deqqi Mehari, Ad Tekelezan and others.[579]

There was a school run by Segid Zemui, a blind man, at the mission
station. Two evangelists, Kiflé and Gebre-Mikael (1862–1920), served in
the area, the latter at Addi Qontsi. *Abba* Gebre-Sillassé, also called *Abba*
Ma'asho, a former monk at the monastery of Inda-Sillassé, had settled
at Himbirti, after being banished from the monastery because of his
theological views. His teaching there gave rise to an indigenous Bible
movement. The monks of Debre Bizen were alarmed and persuaded
seven leading monasteries in Eritrea to anathematise Gebre-Sillassé.
He now joined the Evangelical congregation, and was forced to leave

579   SEM annual report 1901, 67. Deqqi Mehari and Ad Tekelezan were probably transferred
to Beleza parish at this time, since the 1900 Beleza report includes Dimbezan.

his work at Himbirti.[580] He moved to his home area at Addi Baro in Tsilima and settled there.[581]

According to Svensson, a certain Gebre-Tinsaé had given rise to a spiritual movement in his home village, Tsaida Kishtan, some 10 kms from Tse'azzega, in January 1901. He had, in Svensson's words, been *a Nicodemus*, but during an annual festival, when several thousand people were gathered together, he had spoken to the multitude and urged them to begin reading the Word of God.[582] This caused a division in the crowd. Some ran hither and thither shouting against him. Another group threatened to flog him. The rest defended him.[583]

Early in 1901 Rev. Svensson left for Sweden for vacation and didn't return until late in 1902. In the meantime, Rev. Iwarson and his family had moved from Asmara to Tse'azzega. Mrs. Iwarson enjoyed the more tranquil atmosphere of the latter place after her hectic days in Asmara. She was particularly relieved at the thought that she wouldn't need to entertain visiting Europeans. Many of the local people came to visit the Iwarsons, but she makes particular mention of a priest from the village of Addi Abzagé,

> An honest and quiet man who had suffered much for his faith. His wife had left him and even his children had been taken away from him. He now lives with a relative.[584]

Svensson – Patriarch of Tse'azzega and Master of his own House

A. Kolmodin was a witness to the almost feudal honour that was accorded to Svensson in Tse'azzega. In connection with his visit to the village in 1909 A. Kolmodin writes,

> Later on in the afternoon, as I sat and rested in the room of Pastor

---

580 Arén 1978, 343.
581 Arén 1978, 344.
582 The name *Nicodemus* is a reference to the Pharisee who came to Jesus by night. (John 3:1). A *Nicodemus* is a person who is a disciple in secret. (Ed.)
583 SEM/MT 1902, 96.
584 This must have been *Qeshi* Genzebu. Later on, however, his wife and children returned to him. MT 1902, no. 18, 138. His son Mebratu continued the service of his father, first as a teacher and later on as an ordained priest. During the period 1958–1959 when my family and I were stationed in Tse'azzega, *Qeshi* Mebratu and his wife came and stayed with us for a fortnight, a most enjoyable experience. (Author)

The village of Addi Qontsi. The Church of Qiddus Miki`el (St. Michael) from which Qeshi Haile-Ab Tesfai and the Swedish Missionary, Per-Erik Lager were pulled out and put to the sword by an enraged soldier of Ra`si Woldenki`el, on July 17, 1876.

Svensson, there came no less than 15 "tjekker" (meaning *chiqqa*) from the village of Zazega, i.e. chiefs for the families of the village or representatives for them. They did not belong to the Evangelical Church, but came nevertheless to welcome me to their village. Most of them were elderly people with grey hair. Their spokesman was a person by the name of Märed, who had the title of "Kentiba". At the beginning of 1890 he was among those who had opposed the introduction of mission work in Zazega. Now he stood there and expressed his sincere appreciation of the great services that the mission had rendered to the village.

He was particularly hearty in his appreciation of what Pastor Svensson had meant and still meant for them. The latter had, among other things, taken measures to save the village from being devastated by the Italians. He had saved the inhabitants from being whipped and killed when lidj Abberas [Abberra] fled in revolt with his armed men in 1892. With lively gestures, the old man enacted what could have happened if Pastor Svensson had not pleaded on their behalf before the military governor of the time, General [Antonio] Gandolfi. He also reminded me of the fact that we Swedes had mixed our blood with them when Missionary Lager was murdered at the same time that their prince *didjas Hailo* [*Degiat* Hailu] was stricken and killed by the chief of the rival house of Hazega, Woldo Mikael, in 1876. The Swedish Mission had made precious sacrifices on their behalf [i.e. the people of Tsazzega] and served them. Now, therefore, they wanted to render their hearty thanks to me, as the head of the Swedish Mission here.[585]

Svensson was a master of his own Evangelical parish, in spite of the fact that he was expected to operate under the directions of the Filed Director of the SEM in Eritrea, Iwarson. He had a number of evangelists and teachers serving in the Tse'azzega parish. In 1904 two teachers, Segid Zemui and Redda-Tsadiq, and one Bible-woman (a female evangelist), named Selela, served in the region. The former two served in Tse'azzega itself. Among the other evangelists and teachers, Gebre Mikael worked at Addi Qontsi, Teklé Tesfa-Kristos in Himbirti and Mebrahtu in Hazzega. Two evangelists, Gebre-Yesus Tesfai and Gebre-Sillassé Tesfa-Gabir had worked at Misgwag and Wekki Dibba, but had left during the year for *Galla* [Oromo,] to assist Gebre-Ewostatewos Ze-Mikael and Onesimos Nesib in their ministry.[586]

Svensson could count on support from a number of private donors in Sweden. This made it possible for him to undertake projects that other stations could not afford. The beautiful Evangelical Church of Tse'azzega was built with external help. It was inaugurated on Pentecost Day in 1904. The church was filled to capacity and many had to stand or sit outside. The dedication ceremony began with the clergy lining up at the front of the church to read portions of Scripture. Winqvist read in Tigrinya, Rodén in Amharic, Iwarson in Tigrinya, Sundström in Tigré, Renlund in Italian, Nyström and Holmer in Tigrinya, Peter Andersson in Kunama, Zer'a-Tsion and Tesfa-Gabir in Ge'ez and Tewolde-Birhan and Teklé in Tigrinya. Svensson himself read Ephesians 2:3–5, probably in Amharic. After the celebration, food was served in a large arbour, capable of accommodating more than 500 guests. An ox had been slaughtered and a thousand pieces of *Taita* (thin, pancake-like bread) had been baked.[587]

With the help of private funding, Svensson was also able to offer scholarships to a few young men from his parish. Already in 1888 he had sent Debbas Negasi and Gebre-Giorgis [Gebre-Le'ul?] Tirfé for further training at a teacher training Institute in Florence, Italy, even though

---

585   A. Kolmodin 1909, 93–94. It should be noted that Lager was killed not by Wolde-Mikael as such but by an eraged member of his troops. (Ed.)
586   SEM Annual Report 1904, 68.
587   SEM/MT 1904, 68 ff.

The family of Gebre-Sillassé Romha, at Azarna
La'lai:
Front row, left to right: Iyob Gebre-Sillassé,
Yihdegga Temelso, the wife of Gebre-Sillassé,
and Trungo Tabista.

Back row: Abeba Gebre-Sillassé, wife of Qeshi
Gebre-Sillassé Habtu, Elsabet Gebre-Sillassé,
wife of Yihdeggo Zigta, with baby Aberash
Yihdeggo, who became the wife of Woldeab
Woldemariam, Ato Gebre-Sillassé Romha, and
Me'aza Gebre-Sillassé.

Picture from 1925.

The Bible-woman Sälela, in Tse'azzega.
Picture from 1909.

they lived at the Waldensian Seminary. He had done so in opposition to the policy of the Centenary Conference of Protestant Missions in London in 1888, which had advised against sending students to Europe and America for education.[588]

Tse'azzega – The first Parish to Send Eritrean "Missionaries"

Tse'azzega parish continued to grow. Among the 183 members in 1902, 85 were communicants.[589] Ten years later the congregation numbered 502, with 225 communicants. In the same period the number of schools had risen from 6 to 12 and the number of students from 82 to 502.[590]

Besides the two teachers serving at Tse'azzega day school, Segid Zemui and Iyasu Mezengi'i, there were some who served both as evangelists and teachers. These were Kahsai Gebre in Himbirti, Mezgebe in Abarda, Gebre Teklu in Misgwag, Redda-Tsadiq in Tsada Kishtan, Gebre-Kristos in Wekki Dibba, Gebre-Mikael in Addi Qontsi and Bekhit Habelom in Addi Ni'amin. Himbirti now had an ordained pastor by the name of *Qeshi* Teklé, and *Abba* Gebre-Sillassé served in Addi Baro. Voluntary teachers filled the rest of the positions.[591]

Both Rev. Svensson and Miss Sigrid Berggren felt that they had an obligation not only to serve as missionaries but also to inspire the congregations to take responsibility for a continuing missionary outreach. It was this motivation that led Gebre-Ewostatewos and his group to leave for Wollega in Ethiopia in 1897. Upon reaching Wollega in 1904, Onesimos Nesib had met such a positive response that he and his colleagues felt an urgent need for additional help. He appealed to the mission in Eritrea and two families responded to the call. They were Gebre-Yesus Tesfai (ca 1877–1925), who had served as an evangelist in Misgwag and his wife Wuba Zaneb (ca 1879–1970) as well as Gebre-Sillassé Tesfa-Gabir (1881–1932) who had served in Wekki-Dibba and his wife Sendeq Gebre-Mariam (1887–1931).[592] Some years later, in 1911, Gebre-Yesus brought Gebre-Ewostatewos' daughter Wolete-Hiywot

588   Arén 1978, 346.
589   SEM Annual Report 1902, 73–74.
590   SEM Annual Report 1912, 87.
591   SEM Annual Report 1911, 95–96.
592   Arén 1978, 420.

Qeshi Gebre-Sellassé Gebru of Addi Hizbai and his family. He was a diligent shepherd of his widespread flock and traveled far and wide, in all kinds of weather, especially in Qolla Serayé.

The beautiful Evangelical Church of Tse'azzega was built with external help. It was inaugurated on Pentecost Day 1904.

to Beleza, where she was to be enrolled at the school for girls. In his company there were six young men from Bojji in Wollega. Three of them were confirmed in Tse'azzega. After a year they returned to Bojji.[593]

Sigrid Berggren – Champion of Work among Women and a Promoter of Missionary Outreach

In 1904, a female missionary by the name of Sigrid Berggren was placed in Tse'azzega, with special responsibility for work among women. She was well versed in Tigrinya and established good contacts with the people. Much of her time was spent on visits to the various villages in the parish. She lived at Addi Abzagé for long periods.[594]

At the beginning of 1909, Sigrid Berggren had invited some 25 women from Tse'azzega and neighbouring villages to a meeting. The purpose was to form a "working union" through which the women would contribute towards the purchase of material, such as cotton, which they could then weave into different products. The proceeds from the sale of these products would be used for mission activities in Kunama.[595]

This form of activity continued for a long period of time and was still current in the late nineteen-fifties.[596] Both in Tse'azzega and Himbirti there were women's groups that worked for "Galla" and Kunama.[597]

Svensson had not returned to Sweden after his home leave in 1902. He did take a short break for rest in Beirut in 1911. However, in 1913 he requested permission for home-leave. His request was approved and Jonas Iwarson was appointed as Field Director in his place.[598]

Svensson returned to Tse'azzega in 1914. Sigrid Berggren had carried on with her work and the Board was in favour of erecting a house for her. However, the matter was tabled pending a decision on whether she should stay at Addi Abzagé or Tse'azzega. She herself would have preferred to have the building erected at Addi Abzagé, but Tse'azzega carried the day. [598]

---

593   Emmanuel Abraham 1995, 12.
594   SEM Annual Report 1911, 97.
595   SEM/MT 1909, 163–164.
596   Aina Berglund in *Varde Ljus* 1958, 139.
597   SEM Annual Report 1911, 97.
598   SEM Board Minutes 1914–01–13, § 4.

On the way to Awsa Konoma: August Andersson, Sigrid Berggren and Jonas Iwarson with travelling companions.

Sigrid Berggren (left), who had her main duties in Addi Abzagé on the highlands, on a visit to Erika Larsson in Awsa Konoma.

Svensson, His Eritrean Family and His Protégés

As we have already indicated above, Svensson ran the Tse'azzega parish pretty much in his own way. Just as he himself was part of the Gebre-Le'ul family, he had a number of staff whom he considered, in a sense, as members of his family. Among them was a young man by the name of Gebre-Sillassé Habtu, from Addi Shimagile. After his education in mission schools he had started serving as a teacher in Asmara. At Christmas time in 1922 Svensson wrote,

> We have had an invited guest with us, the girl engaged to Gebre-Sillassé, and they were really the happiest couple [...] May she be his guide throughout his life, a support in his service as a teacher and, God willing, also as a pastor.[599]

In 1924, Svensson had planned to celebrate his 75th birthday at Vinslöv, in Sweden. He writes,

> As we came closer to the time for the start of school, and saw the large number of students, I decided not to go [...] I hope that my colleagues and the Hon. Board will give me Gebre-Sillassé Habtu as a birthday gift, in the capacity of a curate.[600]

A Leadership Crisis in Tse'azzega

It is to be recalled that when Rev. Svensson left his position as chairman of the Eritrea mission in 1913, Rev. Iwarson had been appointed as his successor. However, Svensson had, as the most senior person in the mission, a status of his own and continued to pursue his own policy rather independently, particularly in his home parish, Tse'azzega. Over a number of years, Svensson had established contacts with several persons in Sweden, people who also provided him with gifts of money. The rule was otherwise that gifts thus acquired be handed over to the mission treasury and used for budgeted items. Exceptions could be made for special, private gifts. Svensson however used the donations that he received for items that he personally considered important. For example, he used such donations to send some of his protégés for studies abroad.

---

599 SEM/MT 1923, 51. Gebre Sillassé came later to serve for a long period as the president of the Evangelical Church.
600 SEM/MT 1924, 51.

Iwarson Critical of Svensson

Rev. Iwarson was very critical of this practice and complained to the Board in Sweden. He states,

> Svensson is more interested in business. I have told Br. Svensson of my disapproval of these actions. [...]. I am considered Pentecostal and therefore unaccountable (unpredictable?). I am on the verge of despair.[601]

Another item on which Svensson and Iwarson had divergent views was the amount of money that should be a required contribution from each congregation. Svensson had succeeded in setting a lower amount, while Iwarson and Alessandro Tron called for a sum which would express a measure of self-sacrifice, an attitude that would be necessary if the church was to become self-supporting.

A Final Visit to Sweden

Svensson was growing old. He had reached the age of 77, but wanted to undertake a final trip to Sweden. Iwarson was in favour of the idea and even approved of the suggestion that "little Gebre Sillassé" act as Svensson's travelling companion. Svensson began his trip in March 1927, and traveled by way of Addis Ababa where he met many friends from Imkullu days. *Blattengeta* Hiruy Wolde-Sillassé (1878–1938), a highly placed civil servant, with Evangelical convictions (he later became Minister of Foreign Affairs), took him to the palace, where Ras Teferi received him. Svensson and *Qeshi* Gebre-Sillassé Habtu then left for Sweden together with the Stjärnes, missionaries who were due for furlough.[602]

A Patriarch Passes Away

In mid December the same year Svensson returned home to Tse'azzega together with his companion Gebre Sillassé.[603] He resumed his work in Tse'azzega but grew weaker. He had often said, "I want to die in Africa". And in Africa he died, on June 4, 1928. By then he had put in 51 years of

---

601 See his letters to Nils Dahlberg August 10, 1925 and October 27, 1925, at SEM
     Archives, E 1 1926, 256. This must be a summary, not a direct quotation.
602 Pastor Per Stjärne and his wife Valborg had served as missionaries in Ethiopia from
     1920. SEM/MT 1927, 134. See Sandström, *Per Stjärne missionären*, 1988.
603 SEM/MTBB 1928, 57.

service.[604] In a letter to Sweden, *Qeshi* Gebre Sillassé Habtu wrote,

Pastor Anders Svensson and Gebre-Sillassé Habtu, who served for many years as a president of the ECE. Picture taken in Sweden 1927.

> Our dear father Anders Svensson had, as you know, served here for 51 years. On May 23 he was to attend a minor conference in Asmara. Sister Ida (Härndahl) had come by train from Keren to Tse'azzega, from where they travelled by carriage to Asmara. I travelled by bicycle beside them. Following the meeting we returned home. The following day Father Svensson was well but felt tired and sensed some numbness in his arm. I told him that he was just tired, but he said that he had not sensed something of the like before. We called on our nurse and also on Dr. De Pertis, who came to us by car.

Father Svensson became more and more tired and several of the missionaries and friends came to join him. On May 31 a communion service was held for Rev. Svensson and he asked us to join him. His face was shining as he bade us farewell. He went to be with the Lord late in the night on June 4 and was buried the following day. The coffin was beautifully decked with flowers. Many people were gathered and Rev. Iwarson and *Qeshi* Tewoldemedhin conducted the burial service"[605]

The news of Rev. Svensson's death reached Addis Ababa, where Rev. Nils Nilsson informed *Blattengeta* Hiruy. The latter conveyed the message to H.R.H. Ras Teferi who expressed his grief and promised to send a letter of condolence.[606]

A Painful Development

Hardly had the beautiful funeral ceremony transpired, when a painful development ensued, touching on the relationship between the family of Ato Gebre Le'ul and the SEM. It will be remembered that this

604   Rev. Dahlberg in SEM/MTBB 1928, 355.
605   SEM/MTBB 1928, 396–397.
606   SEM/MTBB 1928, 412.

family was Svensson's family in Eritrea. The Mission Director Iwarson reported,

> [...] Although he (i.e. Gebre Le'ul) and his family have received greater benefits than any other of the Mission's wards up to the death of his mentor, he also received, without hindrance from the Mission, the whole property left by Pastor Svensson. But he did not find this enough. He attempted to appropriate to himself also that which belongs to the Mission, including the station-house and the land.[607]

Iwarson specifies the nature of Gebre Le'ul's claim, regarding Svensson's will, in the following words,

> He denies most of the words of his dying protector, words which I heard clearly and plainly. Rev. Anders Svensson was in full possession of his senses and Qeshi Gebre-Selassie too heard this statement word by word. [...] The Mission decided to award Gebre Leul the right to the building that Rev. Svensson had built with private sources, and to grant him a pension. However, Gebre Leul was not prepared to accept this proposal and decided to open a court case against the Mission.[608] The case was finalized in 1929 in favour of the Mission.[609]

Following the death of Rev. Svensson the Mission decided that Rev. Mikael Holmer take over his duties as head of the Tse'azzega parish. The Holmers moved up from Addi Ugri to Tse'azzega at the beginning of 1929.[610]

In Closing

The significance of Tse'azzega for the ECE lies in the fact that it became a meeting place, a point of convergence, for people with hunger and thirst for things spiritual.[611] Tse'azzega became a rallying point for people who sought righteousness before the Holy God. And they sought it where they felt that this righteousness was set forth in the most authoritative manner, i.e. in the Bible. The first fathers

---

607 SEM/Annual Report 1928, 259.
608 Letter from Dahlberg to Iwarson 1928-07-26 //NB # in letter coll..//
609 SEM/Annual Report 1929, 135.
610 SEM/MTBB 1929, 245-246.
611 We have already pointed out, in the text quoted at the beginning of this chapter, that the villages of Addi Qontsi, Himbirti Tsa'ida Kishtan (Kristian) and others belonged to the mission and church district of Tse'azzega. A. Kolmodin adds that Addi Baro and Misgwag too belonged to the same district. A. Kolmodin 1909, 92 (Ed.)

of the ECE, (Zer'a-Tsion, Selomon, Haile-Ab, and others) were intent on finding out God's will for their lives and were willing to pay the price needed to possess the Pearl of Great Price, the Gospel of Grace. Gustav Arén's account of the experiences of the priests and deacons of St.Giorgis' church in Tse'azzega is powerful in all its simplicity. [612] It says something of the ethos of Evangelical Lutheran Christianity in Eritrea. And the name of Tse'azzega will always be connected with this ethos.

Tse'azzega and the villages around it were served not only by native sons and daughters who were diligent students of the Word, but also by a messenger of the Gospel from a far away land. The Swedish missionary who was placed among them, and who was to live and die there, Anders Svensson, was a builder of bridges between two Christian traditions (The Orthodox Tewahdo and the Evangelical Lutheran), and two cultures, one Nordic and one East African. In a way, Svensson was a *monk*, married to Tse'azzega and Hamasen. He became the teacher, guide and protector of not only the Kenisha but also the entire Tse'azzega and Hamasen.

Because of a number of unusual circumstances, the environs of Tse'azzega (more precisely Addi Qontsi) became the scene of the first martyrdom among the highland Kenisha. In a richly symbolic community of blood, *Qeshi* Haile-Ab was accompanied in death, just outside the church of Qiddus Miki'el, by another Swedish missionary who had the gift of adjusting well to his surroundings: namely the mild and selfless Per Eric Lager.

The first "missionaries" to be sent out and to reach the Oromo, the original target of the missionary venture of the SEM in Ethiopia, were Kenisha (*Qeshi* Gebre-Ewostatewos, his wife Gumesh and their co-workers) sent by the congregation in Tse'azzega. Others were to follow. Thus, native Kenisha (Abyssinians as their Swedish coreligionists called them), who were not part of the original target of the missionary vision of the SEM, ended up becoming missionaries. They became partners with Swedes in the fulfilment of the original vision of preaching the Gospel to the Oromo.

However, not all was peace and joy, as the Swedes would put it, around the history of the SEM and the Kenisha in Tse'azzega. Anders Svensson's freelance style of mission activity was evidently fraught

612   Arén 1978, 13–15

with danger, especially in a simple, agricultural society in which land and property rights arouse deep sentiments. Not only did his method of going his own way create turbulence within the missionary corps, particularly in Svensson's relationship with Iwarson, the Filed Director, but also sowed the seeds of division in the parish in Tse'azzega and the ECE at large. The core of the whole problem had to do with property rights and questions of inheritance. Thus the style of work of this giant of a missionary became a warning against the dangers of a well-meant individualism in the Body of Christ.

We are not in a position to pass judgment on the conflict which followed Pastor Svensson's death. In her book *Mitt Lifs Historia* (The History of My Life), which was published in Stockholm in 1914 and which contains an account of her visit to the mission field of the SEM in Eritrea, Sophie Wallin writes,

> When Gebre-Le'ul was five, he was taken by Pastor Svensson who brought him up. When he reached the proper age, he was sent to Italy to study the language and to acquire further education. He is now in his forties and is married. He is an organist, a school teacher, a secretary, a tailor, a mason, in short a man of a thousand skills. All that he does, he does well. His wife Hilqu is a graceful woman, capable and skilful as home maker. Both are of noble birth, of the fine type, and their children are beautiful and well brought up. I was happily surprised by the fact that Gebre-Le'ul behaved like a gentleman, in matters big and small.[613]

What went wrong during the 15 years that elapsed between the recording of these glowing words about the family of Gebre-Le'ul and the period (1929) when the verdict of a colonial court in Eritrea dealt a devastating blow to the strained relationship between Gebre-Le'ul and the representatives of the Swedish Evangelical Mission in Eritrea?

There are perhaps details with which we are not acquainted in this conflict. Nevertheless the fact that the conflict led to a court case was to leave a blemish on the history of the SEM and the Kenisha. To quote St. Paul once again, "... we have this treasure in earthen vessels, that the excellency of the power may be of God and not of us." 2 Corinthians 4:7, King James Version. (Ed.)

613   Sophie Wallin 1914, 140.

Chapter Seventeen

Mission in the Context of Catholic Priorities (I)

Introduction

Visited the Governor's office where Di Croce received me with great warmth – and made my arrival known to the governor, a general [Giacomo Antonelli]. The latter was, to all appearances, a very pleasant man. [...] Here in Cheren he has always been benevolent towards our people and has supported their application for a permit to build a church wholeheartedly and has promised to donate 5,000 Lira towards the building, once they secure permission to build. He has even tried to help Coïsson [an Italian missionary of the Waldensian Church] but has apparently run into insuperable opposition from higher levels. He has shown Coïsson the circular which he has received from the authorities in Asmara [Under Giuseppe Daodiace]. The following are some of the main points,

1. *Senza precipitare niente si deve ostacolare gli evangelici in modo che siano assorbiti dalla chiesa copta o dalla chiesa cattolica.* (Without bringing about any damage one must create obstacles against the Evangelicals so that they would be absorbed by the Coptic [Orthodox Tewahdo] Church or

the Catholic Church.)

2. *Nessun bianco deve occuparsi degli indigeni evangelici (per far propaganda fra loro o interessarsi di loro).*(No white person should be involved with the native Evangelicals to pursue propaganda on their behalf or to devote any interest to them.)

3. *Non si deve più concedere nessun luogo di culto agl'evangelici.* (One should no longer make any place of worship available to the Evangelicals.)

4. *Non si deve più dare nessun luogo di culto agl'evangelici.* (One should no longer give the Evangelicals any place of worship.)

5. *Non possono più essere assunti come impiegati dell Governo.* (They can no longer be employed in the service of the Government.)

The words quoted above are taken from Olle Hagner's diary entries for the 3rd of November 1939.[614] Hagner, who first came to Eritrea in 1922, had returned to Eritrea to negotiate with the colonial authorities on the disposal of the property of the Swedish mission – an assignment which obliged him to stay in the country until 1945. He makes the following comment on the restrictive directives stated above,

> If this programme (which was presumably not to be made public knowledge) were to be implemented, the result would have simply been persecution in the guise of a policy.[615]

What was this policy and who was its promoter? A quick reading of the entry in Hagner's diary suggests that there were two different attitudes on the part of the colonial authorities towards Evangelical Christians: an open and generous policy and a highly restrictive one, aimed at bringing about their elimination as a religious entity. Which interpretation are we to accept as an expression of Italian colonial policy in this regard?

There are two further questions to be asked: Is the diary entry also an expression of the policy or wish of the Catholic Church of the specific period in Eritrea? Or was the policy solely and entirely a creation of the secular, colonial authorities? Finally, how far do these two attitudes towards the Kenisha go back in time?

According to Olle Hagner, an article in the newspaper *Corriere Eritreo* on March 17, 1940, entitled *Un convento cattolico di rito etiopico a Belesa*

614   Olle Hagners's Diaries//K.J.Summary, 6. (Ed.)
615   Olle Hagners's Diaries//K.J.Summary, 6. (Ed.)

(A Catholic Monastery of the Ethiopian Rite in Beleza) took up the inauguration of a Catholic monastery at the School in Beleza, which had been confiscated from the Swedish Mission earlier. The Apostolic Vicar of Eritrea and a representative of the government were present on the occasion, according to the newspaper clipping that is attached to the diary entry.

At the same time OH indicates that some Italian officials who were there for the occasion, had started pondering over the whole thing, seen the place and spoken appreciatively of the work of the Swedish Mission in the past. Sahle Ande-Mikael, a member of the ECE who was present, thought that they looked embarrassed and ashamed.[616]

Here again, we seem to have two conflicting sentiments within the same colonial government, towards the SEM and the Kenisha. Perhaps the following passage from Tekeste Negash throws some light on our subject, albeit indirectly,

> The colonial administration saw the Catholic mission as an institution which pursued its educational activities in an acceptable and appreciated manner. The separation between the Church and the State, which plagued the political life in Italy, was virtually nonexistent in the colony. As early as the 1890's, the colonial government was aware that Italian missionaries were useful in facilitating the spread of Italian culture and the consolidation of colonial rule.[617]

A political establishment which has come to such a conclusion on the usefulness of a church in a colonial context must see to it that such a church can operate unchallenged and unhindered. The wings of its competitors must be clipped and their freedom of movement and action limited. The SEM and the Kenisha were regarded precisely as such competitors, though the Catholics and the Orthodox Tewahdo in Eritrea were not the primary targets of Evangelical mission.[618] We are not in a position to say how much of a willing ally the Catholic Church in Eritrea was in the implementation of the policy outlined above. However, the SEM and the Kenisha felt that they were victims

---

616 Olle Hagners's Diaries, Book 2, 110–111 and Olle Hagners's Diaries//K. J. Summary, 28. (Ed.)
617 T. Negash 1987, 78.
618 In 1884, when Dr. Winqvist was in Keren to get relief from the hot season on the coast, the Lazarist missionaries asked for his help. This led to an easing of the tension that had existed between the Catholics and Protestant missions. However, such incidents appear to have been very rare indeed. (Author)

A section of old Asmara, with the Catholic cathedral in the background.

of a policy promoted by both church and state in colonial Eritrea, for decades before Olle Hagner made the diary entries which we have quoted at the beginning of our chapter.

An embittered Olle Hagner writes,

> No one asks questions if someone becomes a Muhammedan or a Catholic. "We have them among us anyway", they say. But if someone becomes an Evangelical Christian, their outcry reaches high heaven! [619]

K. J. Lundström has given us the background to the sentiments which lie behind Hagner's statement. His text follows. (Ed.)

Tug of War between the Colonial Government and the SEM after 1915

The Italian Government had left much of the running of its colonies, particularly Eritrea, in the hands of its appointed governors. While the first governors, like Ferdinando Martini and Salvago Raggi, stayed for long periods, the succeeding eight years after Salvago Raggi were characterised by quick changes in leadership. This was a reflection of the unstable political situation in Italy.

---

619   Notes on a loose piece of paper among Hagner's diary notes, Book 3, 1940. (Ed.)

As the power structure in Italy began evolving from a wavering democracy into an authoritarian Fascism simultaneously with a growing Roman Catholic mission outreach, the Swedish Mission and her followers in Eritrea came to face growing difficulties. 1915 was a turning point in their relations to the colonial government.

Signs of Colonial Hospitality

A period of mutual understanding had given the mission considerable elbowroom. To take a few examples, Kolmodin's visit in 1908–1909 was met by a generous attitude on the part of colonial authorities. From the time when he landed in Massawa to the time when he left, he was granted unfailing hospitality and assured of the support of the different colonial authorities. On October 19, 1908, a few days after his arrival in the country, Kolmodin visited the commissary for Massawa, Dante Odorizzi. Kolmodin writes,

> Since he had full mastery of French, I had the occasion to express, without the help of an interpreter, our hearty thanks for the good will he had shown our missionaries on several occasions, already when he was a governor in Cheren.[620]

In Asmara, Kolmodin was given an audience with the Governor Salvago Raggi.[621] In far away Barentu, Alberto Pollera, who was commander of the military administration in Barentu and the whole of Kunama (1903–1904), received Kolmodin and his colleagues at breakfast. His older brother, Ludovico Pollera, who was "Commissario" in Agordat, was equally friendly to the Swedish Mission.[622]

This positive attitude began giving way to increased tension and restrictions. One reason was the Government's view on SEM's alleged stand on the ongoing World War. During the early stages of the war, some missionaries of the SEM had apparently expressed sympathy towards Germany. This had created doubts among the Italian colonial authorities on the stand of the SEM as a whole on the war.

Restrictions on Swedish staff as well as delays in the transfer of funds hampered mission activities. Furthermore, after the end of World War I, bureaucracy created obstacles to the return of Swedish missionaries.

---

620   A. Kolmodin 1909, 39. (Ed.)
621   A. Kolmodin 1909, 68–73. Ezra Gebremedhin 2005, 200. (Ed.)
622   A. Kolmodin 1909, 166–168. (Ed.)

Kolmodin's photo of the office of the Military Governor in Barentu, 1908.

Inauguration of the new School for Deaconesses in Asmara on November 1, 1925.

Assistance by personnel from the Waldensian Church in Italy made it, however, possible to proceed with the work of the mission.

Educational activities continued, albeit with certain government restrictions particularly as regards the village schools. However, another sphere of activity, the one involving a centre for medical services in Asmara, grew into a significant hospital that also included a centre for the training of dressers and deaconesses.

Historical Background to the Catholic Presence in Eritrea

When the Swedish missionaries entered the region that would later be called Eritrea, and from which they planned to proceed to the Oromo, there were already Catholic missionaries working in the region. Catholic missionaries were in fact present in Ethiopia three hundred years earlier, during a crucial period in the history of the country. Towards the middle of the sixteenth century, Emperor Libné-Dingil (1508–1540) had to face the violent onslaught of Muslim forces led by a prophet-warlord of Adal origin, by the name of Ahmed bin Ibrahim, often called Ahmad Grañ. As mentioned earlier Grañ conquered vast areas of the country and destroyed many of its sacred Christian shrines and much cultural heritage. With the death of the Emperor, it seemed as if Islam had attained total victory in Ethiopia. However, a small army consisting of some four hundred Portuguese soldiers, sent as a response to a desperate request by the late king, came to the aid of the Christians of the country.

The intervention of these Portuguese troops has its Eritrean connections, even though the area to which they arrived was not called Eritrea then. Jones and Monroe write,

> In 1541, however, the Portuguese, in the course of a raid on Suez, landed a force of four hundred men at Massaua under the command of Christopher da Gama, a son of the famous Vasco. [...] Lebna Dengel had died the previous year and his son Claudius was now king. Claudius was at the moment far away in the south, in Shewa. The Portuguese were, however, received by Isaac, the Bahrnagas, and the Queen-Mother, who lived in the neighbouring fortress. The party reached Debaroa, the capital of Bahrmedr, and there stopped for the rains.[623]

When Ahmad Grañ was killed at the Battle of *Weyna Dega*, near

---

623   Jones and Monroe 1970 (1935) 83. (Ed.)

Gondar in 1543, the re-conquest of the areas that he had overrun proceeded without any effective opposition.[624]

After the death of Ahmad Grañ the Portuguese settled down in the country and intermarried with Ethiopians. A steady stream of Jesuit priests found their way into the country with the express intention of drawing Ethiopians into the Catholic fold.[625]

Renewed Catholic Contacts with Ethiopia

The first attempt to conduct Catholic mission in Ethiopia and draw the Orthodox Tewahdo Church into the Catholic fold was, however, not successful. Emperor Fasilidas (ca. 1632–1667) expelled the Jesuits in 1632. Two centuries later Catholic missionaries were back in Ethiopia.[626] This time it was the Italian Lazarist, Giustino de Jacobis (1800–1860), who took the initiative to open a mission in the northern part of the country. [627] One reason may have been that a couple of Protestant societies had sent missionaries to the area, one of these being the British and Foreign Bible Society. In March 1838, when the European, Protestant missionaries were expelled from Adwa, a Catholic missionary, Fr. Giuseppe Sapeto and a French naturalist and scholar, Arnauld d'Abbadie, were allowed to stay. The Protestants were all too ready to suspect foul play by the Catholics.[628]

---

624 Ahmed bin Ibrahim had the title of Imam and commanded the loyalty of various tribal groups of fanatic Muslims, even outside the sultanate of Adal, which saw the struggle against the Christian Empire as a holy war. On the Moslem invasions and the Portuguese expeditions see Trimingham 1952, 80–99, Doresse 1967, 124–154, Jones and Monroe 1970 (1935), 81 ff. and Bahru Zewde 2001, 9–10 (Ed.)

625 The Jesuits had met the need of a reform movement within the Catholic Church, and defended the faith against the Protestant Reformation in Europe. However, they were also engaged in vigorous mission activity in other parts of the world. (Author). An excellent treatment of Jesuit missionary activities in Ethiopia at this time is Professor Merid Wolde-Aregay's "The Legacy of Jesuit Missionary Activities in Ethiopia From 1555 to 1632" The *Missionary Factor in Ethiopia* in Haile, Lande, Rubenson 1998, 31–70, and Husein Ahmed (transl.) Futuh Al-Habasha 2003. (Ed.)

626 For a detailed treatment of this subject see Crummey's chapter "Towards an Ethiopian Catholicism?" in his *Priests and Politicians*. Crummey 1972, 59–91. See also Tekeste Negash "The Catholic Mission and the Catholic Community in Eritrea" in Haile, Lande, Rubenson (Ed.) The *Missionary Factor in Ethiopia*, 121–154. (Ed.)

627 On the work of the Lazarists in Ethiopia, 1838–1868, see Crummey 1972, 59–114. See also John Bauer's *Two Thousand Years of Christianity in Africa 62–1992* as well as O'Mahoney, 1982, especially pp. 20–21, 69–70 and 115–116. (Ed.)

628 Arén 1978, 68–69. Crummey 1972, 40ff.

Mgr. Giustino de Jacobis Arrives in Tigrai

Mgr. Giustino de Jacobis arrived in Tigrai precisely at this juncture and was very well received by the governor, Wubé. De Jacobis had refused to side with Wubé's opponents during a "contest for supremacy" and thereby earned the governor's gratitude.[629]

De Jacobis' way of approaching Ethiopian Orthodox Christianity was different from that of some of the Portuguese Jesuits two centuries earlier. He was a person with empathy, and adjusted his personal life-style to that of an Ethiopian monk. His contemporary, Bishop Guglielmo Massaia (1809–1889) of the Capuchin order, who began his work in southern Ethiopia in 1847, was impressed by the fact that De Jacobis abstained from constructing grand edifices and rich churches. He was content with huts and caves. He always wore a poor tunic, like an Abyssinian monk, and wanted his followers and pupils to dress according to the custom of the land. [630]

On to Massawa and Halai

At the end of 1844 De Jacobis constructed a small college at Gualà, east of Addi Grat in Tigrai, where he gathered his first disciples.[631] Monsignor Massaja of the Capuchin Order later ordained these.[632] De Jacobis extended his work towards Intticho, some 50 kms west of Addi Grat, and in a northerly direction to Halai, near Segeneiti, as well as to Massawa.

By 1852, his "Abyssinian Mission" counted 4 000–5,000 believers and some 15 indigenous priests.[633] Towards the end of this decade however, a ferocious persecution stirred up by *Abune* Selama (The Metropolitan of the Ethiopian Orthodox Church) with the support of various Rases and *Dejjazmatches*, and later by Emperor Teodros himself, paralyzed the work of De Jacobis and his successors.[634]

De Jacobis moved to Massawa in early 1860. He had received a piece

---

629   On De Jacobis see Crummey 1972, 65ff, and O'Mahony 1982, 46, 71–73.
       O' Mahony's book is something of a biography of De Jacobis. See Trevaskis 1960, 29
630   Da Nembro 1953, 16, note 36. On Massaia see O'Mahony 1982, 57–59, 76–80, 218.
       Trevaskis 1960, 29, Arén 1978, 128, 143, Longrigg 1945, 89. (Ed.)
631   O'Mahoney 1982, 42–48. (Ed.)
632   Da Nembro 1953, 10. O'Mahoney 1982, 57–59. (Ed.)
633   Da Nembro 1953, 10.
634   B. Zewde 2002, 37. (Ed.)

of land in the harbour town but stayed there for a short time until he moved his abode to Halai (in present day Eritrea). By then he was already sick and died the same year. He was laid to rest at Hebo in Eritrea.[635]

One of the most significant contributions made by De Jacobis was his adoption of the Ethiopian (Ge'ez) rite for the Catholic Mass.[636] This measure was in line with his general policy of adopting an Ethiopian life style and Ethiopian customs. However, the rite was carefully modified so that it would be acceptable to the Catholic Church.

Catholic Mission into new Areas in the North

In July–August 1844 De Jacobis had visited Mensa and its surroundings. In 1848 Catholic missionaries paid a short visit to the Bilén in Bogos, but returned three years later for a longer stay.[637] At the time two Lazarists, Fr. Giuseppe Sapeto and Fr. Stella were at work in the area. The latter stayed on, and his work was reported to be flourishing. He began, however, to go his own way and was finally regarded as a *defector*.[638] He attempted to create an agricultural colony in the Sciotel valley, a project that failed. Fr. Stella died in October 1869. According to Da Nembro, he left behind him a number of converts who, however, "were swept away by successive developments and passed on to the Protestants."[639]

The mission among the Bogos, and especially that among the Bilén, was more successful. After 1860, Catholic mission work faced considerable difficulties in its work in Tigrai and areas further north. Monsignor Lorenzo Biancheri, who had succeeded De Jacobis as head of the Mission, had retreated to Massawa and tried to procure more assistance during a visit to Italy and France in 1862. The only positive result of his visit was the gift of a printing press with Ethiopian

635 O'Mahoney 211–217.
636 This liturgy contains 14 Qiddasé (masses). The Catholics were, however, reluctant to use the Qiddasé of Diosqoros as it was of a later date. Da Nembro 364–365. O'Mahoney 1982, 61, 66–67.
637 O'Mahoney 247.
638 Mgr. Louis Bel, A French Lazarist, gives a very unfavourable picture of Stella's personality and missionary enterprise. He writes, "He comported himself like a Pasha, a civil governor, rather than a missionary." [...] Quoted in O'Mahoney 1982, 176. (Ed.)
639 Da Nembro 1953, 247.

characters, which he installed in Massawa, and which was later transferred to Keren, the centre of the mission to Bogos.

The first Lazarists were mainly Italian. However, the situation changed and, by 1866, the missionaries were mainly French. The leadership was in the hands of a Frenchman, Monsignor Louis Bel.[640]

Ambivalent Relations with Colonial Authorities

The general tenor of the earlier period of Italian colonial rule in Eritrea (the period leading roughly up to 1920) was secular. Even with a growing consciousness of their Catholic roots and the establishment of official links between Church and State in Italy, the colonial authorities in Eritrea maintained a mildly secular tenor in their dealings with non-Catholic groups in the colony. Relations between Swedish missionaries and Italian civil servants in the colony could be very cordial and even lead to cooperation.

An exception to this general rule was the attitude of Governor Salvago Raggi who had ordered the closure of the schools of the SEM in 1912. Otherwise, the colonial authorities flexed their administrative muscles only when they felt that Tewahdo and Kenisha displayed patterns of behaviour which spelled danger for the colony. Being overly zealous in conducting mission and betraying an obvious attraction to Abyssinia [Ethiopia], were examples of such undesirable behaviour.

In Closing

Our account of Catholic missionary work in Ethiopia and, to a lesser extent, in what is now Eritrea may help to explain the strength of the Catholic presence in the Bogos and Bilén regions and, eventually, on the Eritrean highlands.[641] Catholic missionaries had the benefit of being the first to arrive. They enjoyed the honour connected with seniority. European appointees on the coast, like Werner Munzinger, who were friendly to the Swedish missionaries, were careful not to offend the Catholics by going out of their way to accommodate the SEM.

L. J. Lange, one of the first three Swedish missionaries to arrive on

---

640 Crummey 1972, 113.
641 Up to 1895, when the Apostolic Prefecture of Eritrea was established, Eritrea belonged to the Vicariate of Abyssinia. O'Mahoney 1982, XIV. (Ed.)

the coast in 1866, writes about Munzinger's soft-gloves policy towards Catholics. Part of his diary entry for March 26, 1866, reads,

> Today I must admit, with pain, that the Consul allows himself to be influenced by Catholic priests and missionaries here. He says that if we go to Mensa, his hope of being appointed French consul would vanish. Furthermore, we would come into conflict with the Catholic priests. This is quite different from what he said when we came [...].[642]

The main reason for the preferential treatment accorded to the Catholic Church and its mission in Eritrea by the colonial administration was, however, the mere fact that the church was Italian. This fact became clearer with the consolidation of Italian colonial rule in Eritrea. Developments in the colony in this regard were reflections of developments in Italy.

The documents related to prohibitions and restrictions on missionary activity that came to the attention of the SEM were official, government documents. They were not decrees issued by the Catholic Hierarchy in Eritrea. It is therefore impossible to hold the Catholic Church in Eritrea as such responsible for some of the severe limitations placed on the SEM and the Kenisha. Nevertheless, it is also difficult to disregard the complaints of the Swedish missionaries and the Kenisha in this regard. There were far too many secondary indices of Catholic involvement in the obstacles placed before the SEM and ECE, to disqualify these complaints as unfounded.[643] The waxing strong of the Catholic Church in Italy after the nineteen-twenties, and the underlining of the claim of the Pope's right to universal jurisdiction over the Church of Christ, had its repercussions on mission and church life in the colonies. The SEM and the Kenisha were made to feel the brunt of this mobilization of resources, this growing sense of might and confidence on the part of the Catholic Church, albeit indirectly. (Ed.)

---

642 Lange 1965, 29. In 1873 Munzinger changed his attitude on the question of Mensa and asked the Swedish Mission to open a new station there. Arén 1978, 180.

643 For details see Olle Andersson's diary notes (OHD, 1939–1943 and his book *Stormen bröt lös* 1947, 46–50. (Ed.)

Chapter Eighteen

Mission in the Context of Catholic Priorities (II)

Introduction

On 11 February 1929, the Vatican and the Quirinal, in other words Pope Pius XI (1912–1939), and the Italian government, had concluded the Lateran Concordat, which made the Roman Catholic Church the state religion in Italy and in all Italian colonies. The Concordat aggravated the depressed state of the evangelical congregations in Eritrea. Catholic priests, monks and nuns blackmailed them as enemies of the Fascist regime and urged the colonial authorities to stop their work. No support of the work in Tigrai was allowed. Every communication with the evangelical community there was rendered suspicious.[644]

These words are taken from the chapter entitled "Evangelism in Wartime Ethiopia 1935–1936" in Gustav Arén's book *Envoys of the Gospel in Ethiopia* (1999). It would be hasty to accept the charges voiced above uncritically. However, they can not be dismissed summarily. Arén's words reflect two realities that affected the life and work of the SEM and the ECE in Eritrea during this period. The first is, as already

---

644 Arén 1999, 456. See also O. Andersson 1947, 46, 51, and Jonathan Miran 2002, especially pp. 125 ff.

mentioned, the impact of Church-State relations in Italy on colonial religious policy. The second is the concern and suspicion with which the spectre, i.e. Abyssinia or Ethiopia, was watched by an Italy still smarting from the humiliation of the Battle of Adwa in 1896. Both of these factors affected the way the SEM and the Kenisha were treated. The latter were watched and monitored not only because they were Lutherans, rebels from Mother Church, but also because their Swedish mentors were originally on their way to a missionary venture in Abyssinia. For the SEM, Eritrea was in fact an afterthought, a station on the way. There was a certain transit mentality among some of the Swedish missionaries operating in Eritrea. While waiting for a missionary outreach among the Oromo, the SEM had already started evangelistic work in Tigrai.

In short, the Swedish missionaries continued to cultivate and promote, albeit indirectly, an awareness of the importance of Abyssinia or Ethiopia as the big target for missionary outreach, the Promised Land of many a seeker of freedom from colonial rule. Such a state of affairs was completely unacceptable to the Italian colonial authorities. Challenging the temptation to look longingly to Ethiopia was an important factor in the tug of war that went on between the SEM and the colonial authorities. This reality is part of the background to Karl Johan's continuing narrative on the life and work of the SEM and the Kenisha. His text follows. (Ed.)

State and Church Come Closer in Italian Politics

We have already noted that the Italian Government had, from the very establishment of the colony of Eritrea, a rather anti-clerical attitude towards the Roman Catholic Church. As of 1905, however, there was a change, resulting from a more active participation by Catholics in Italian national politics. This was, partly, due to a breach between the Vatican and the French Republic. The religious institutions formerly under France were now transferred to Italy. An Italian was no longer caught in the dilemma of choosing between being a good Italian and a good Catholic.

Furthermore, Italy was succeeding in the extension of its colonial possession. It took control of the North African territories of Tripolitania and Cyrenaica and thereby reasserted her old doctrine of expansion.[645]

At the beginning of World War I, Italy had shown distrust towards France. However, this attitude changed and Italy joined the so-called "Entente" (a block which united England, Russia and France in their war efforts). The Italians had, however, not recovered from the war in Libya and the strains of World War I accentuated the extent to which the population had suffered damage and privations.

This situation caused widespread upheavals among the Italian population. The political parties were irresolute and divided. Unrest spread, and after much turbulence the King, Vittorio Emmanuelle III, (1869–1947), took counsel with the Nationalist and Fascist parties. On October 30, 1922, Benito Mussolini assumed the role of leader by approval of Parliament. In January 1925 Mussolini took on dictatorial powers. The take-over of power by the Fascist Party in Italy had its repercussions in the colony of Eritrea. It led to a strong, nationalistic trend that reacted against all that was non-Italian. The colonial government demanded that the Swedish Evangelical Mission be called the *Italian Evangelical Mission, the Waldensian Church.* By way of compromise, the name of the mission was changed to *Missione Evangelica.*[646]

Italian Colonial Policy towards Muslims and Orthodox Christians

Relations to the Muslims as well as to the Orthodox Christians were, of course, of prime importance for the colonial government, which tried to avoid any conflict with these groups. An example is its handling of the question of the land-rights of Orthodox monasteries. After the occupation of Eritrea the feudal system of *gulti* was abolished, thus leaving the Orthodox monasteries without the privileges once connected with the system.[647] Governor Martini alleviated the

---

645 In this and following conflicts, several thousand Eritrean soldiers were recruited. Tekeste Negash 1987, 48. (Ed.)

646 Bruno Tron in an oral report to the author. Bruno adds, "The change of name for the mission became a real point in question only after 1935". (Ed.)

647 An emperor or feudal lord could create *gult* (Tigrinya: *gulti*),by transferring his taxation rights on specific land to a third party or by giving the land itself to a third party, i.e. a church, a monastery etc.), so that the beneficiary in question now became a receiver of tribute or a producer of means of livelihood in his own right. See Pankhurst 1968, 135–137, and T. Negash and K. Tronvoll 2001, 96–98. (Ed.)

Dr Nicola De Pertis came to Eritrea in 1913. In 1922 a hospital was built in Asmara under the sponsorship of the SEM and De Pertis became the chief physician.

problems created by this ruling by giving back to the monasteries land allotments that were deemed sufficient for their sustenance.[648]

Salvago Raggi questioned the religious policy of all his predecessors and, in one long memorandum from 1913, explained what ought to be the new religious policy in the colony. This memorandum contained a very pointed criticism of what the governor felt were the exaggerated religious claims of Muslims in Eritrea and their tendency to exploit the magnanimity of the colonial government. Regarding the missions he wrote,

> In competing with one another, the various missions maintain that they are the ones who own the truth, not realising that Italy is liberal, and not simply "atheistic and anarchistic in matters of religion". Even if you find Christianity good or bad, more or less suitable, almost all Italians see this element as part of our civilization and thus it cannot but be seen as a privilege. Pending the change of religious policy, the Eritrean Government must break and limit the activity of the Swedish missionaries, as a first step. Catholicism is "a fundamental element" in our civilization.[649]

648　Buonaiuti 1982, 338. See also Trevaskis 1960, 53–54, 59.
649　Buonaiuti 1982, 101,Yet, Muslims enjoyed many privileges! (Miran 2005, 194–198).

Vigorous Catholic Outreach Under Mgr. Carrara

Approach to "Copts" (Orthodox Tewahdo)

For Monsignor Francesco Carrara, who was the head of Catholic mission in Eritrea during the period 1912–1925, the focal point of mission activity were the Abyssinian Copts (meaning the Orthodox Tewahdo) to which he devoted most of his resources.[650] Already in 1913 he reported that he saw "among the Copts, a small but consistent movement towards our holy religion."[651] The first significant groups of converts in Hamasen were from Embaderho and Tse'azzega, "a district which constituted a kind of fortress of the Swedish Protestants." Carrara embarked upon an intensive mission.

The Catholic Mission expanded under his leadership. He succeeded

---

650   On Colonial policy towards the Orthodox Church in Eritrea see T. Negash "The Catholic Mission and the Catholic Community in Eritrea" in *the Missionary Factor in Ethiopia*. Haile, Lande, Rubenson (Ed.) 1998, 124–127.

651   Buonaiuti 1982, 85–86. Here it should be pointed out that the term *Copts* is a reference to Orthodox Christians. The designation is properly applied to the Christians of Egypt, not to those of Ethiopia and Eritrea. (Ed.)

The Catholic Cathedral of Asmara, originally built in 1895 and reconstructed in 1923. Photo provided by Berhane Elias, Asmara, 2008.

in mobilizing a large circle of administrators and supporters who responded positively to his appeals for help.[652] He was also able to secure subsidies from the government for the work of his Church and even obtained land concessions for agricultural projects.

The Monsignor wanted every Catholic village to have a church and a school, centrally located. He paid particular attention to villages that were in a state of development and had shown signs of being progressive. More and more schools were transferred to Catholic constituencies and finally, in 1923, the only government school in Eritrea was transferred to the Catholic Mission after an intervention by the new governor of Eritrea, Jacopo Gasparini.

Mgr. Carrara had been able to secure funds from different sources and he was able to dedicate the new Cathedral in Asmara in 1923. According to Da Nembro the number of indigenous Catholics at this time was 28,000 with 34 foreign missionaries, 41 sisters of the Daughters of St. Anna and 9 Sisters of the *Pie Madre della Nigrizia*.[653] Other sources give lower figures.

652 Buonaiuti 1982, 66.
653 Da Nembro 89 ff. Pastor Bruno Tron suggests that the remark "other sources give lower figures" be added. (Ed.)

Outreach among the Kunama

Catholic outreach among the Kunama began in 1912 when Fr. Celestino and later Fr. Egidio began mission work at Barentu. However, the mission had to withdraw, after a few months.[654] In 1914 a new attempt was made and Fr. Celestino da Desio opened a station. For several years, Catholic missionary outreach among the Kunama was felt to be a "thorn in the flesh". The missionaries found that "the Kunama were thankful for humanitarian services but did not embrace conversion".[655] Attracting boys to the mission proved, however, to be a door of opportunity for an outreach among the Kunama. The boys came to serve as links between the missionaries and the people. The missionaries used "an extensive method" in order to "cut off the road for Muslim propaganda."[656] Before the death of Mgr. Carrara in 1925, 1,500 had been baptized in Kunama.[657]

Work among the Mensa

Catholic missionary work among the Mensa was officially initiated in 1922 when Mgr. Carrara had a building erected in Mihlab.[658] In his report on the Swedish Mission at this time, Da Nembro exaggerates the wealth of the Mission and the impact of its missionaries grossly. He writes,

> Equipped in modern style, with efficient schools, clinics and dispensaries and special sections for professional arts and crafts, and having at their disposal considerable financial means, they became a point of attraction for many young Mensa and even Bogos.

There was no lack of proselytes to the Evangelical faith, he states, and the influence of the school at Geleb lasted for many years, even after the establishment of the Catholic Mission among the Bogos and the initiation of a mission at Mihlab.[659]

---

654 Da Nembro, 218.

655 Da Nembro, 80.

656 Da Nembro 238. This method of mass-baptism was in strong contrast to that of the Swedish missionaries who looked for clear indications of what they felt were signs of conversion before baptism was administered. (Author)

657 Da Nembro, 81.

658 Da Nembro, 84. There had, however, already in 1915, been several attempts by a Catholic father to establish work at this place. Later on (under Fioccardi, who was a senior divisional officer in Eritrea) such a move was not permitted. Reported by Axel Jonsson in SEM/MT 1922, 302.

659 Da Nembro, 243.

Prior to this period, the number of Catholics in the Bogos area was put at 12,000, out of a total population of 20,000. In 1921 four schools with a total number of 260 students were financed by the state.

Restrictive Stance under Salvago Raggi

The governors in Eritrea were rather independent in the way they ran the colony. As already stated above, one of the few exceptions was a measure taken against an order issued by Governor Salvago Raggi. In 1912 he had ordered the closure of the schools of the SEM, an order that was reversed by Martini, who happened to be a minister in Italy at the time.[660]

The view of Salvago Raggi seems, however, to have taken the upper hand during World War I. A government decree proclaimed on October 27, 1915 (# 2434, article 11), tended to limit and control the presence of foreigners in the missions.[661]

Expulsion of Missionaries and the Challenge of other Constraints (1915–1925)

When two Swedish missionaries were expelled from Eritrea at the end of October 1915, the schools that they were running in Kunama were closed by order of the government. This marked a period of restrictions on the activities of the Swedish Mission. During World War I and up to 1919, no Swedish missionary could return to Eritrea. This stance towards the Swedish Mission seems to have been adopted by many of the successive governors. To reduce the effects of these restrictions, the SEM requested staff from the Protestant Waldensian Church of Italy. In 1909 the Waldensian Church responded by sending Benedetto Giudici and his wife Dircea, both of whom served in Asmara for a period of four years. Alessandro Tron and his wife Dina arrived in 1913 and were assigned to the school in Asmara. Tron served in Eritrea until 1954. Doctor Nicola De Pertis had arrived in 1913, a few weeks before Tron. He was not a member of the Waldensian Church but had many friends among the members of the church. On a few occasions Swedish missionaries were given entry permits, in spite of the general rules

660 Buonaiuti, 99–100.
661 Buonaiuti, 101.

against such a measure.

There was, however, also a new attitude towards the activities of the Mission in the colony after Giacomo de Martino came to serve as Governor (1916–1919). He allowed the mission schools in Kunama to re-open, was favourable to the other aspects of the work of the SEM and expressed his satisfaction in several ways.[662] Dr. De Pertis had presented a proposal for the training of Eritrean nurses and midwives to the Board of SEM. However, shortly thereafter he had been called up for military service by the Italian Government.[663] Some missionaries were worried about this move, but Iwarson maintained that it was a Christian duty to obey the law and answer the call of the colonial government in this regard.[664]

The missionaries hoped for an improvement of relations with the colonial government and in August 1916, when it was rumoured that the mother of De Martino, the new governor, was Swedish, they expected a change for the better. The same year Rodén was able to report that he and the community around him had completed the repair of a 40 km long stretch on the road from Geleb to Massawa.[665] On the local level however, there were still problems. Ottolina Holmer, stationed at Addi Ugri, received a local government order that no meetings were to be held without prior permission. Suddenly, however, new directives were given to the effect that no prior notices would be required.[666]

As many of the new leaders and the public in colonial Eritrea lacked information on the Swedish Mission, it was decided that a history of the Mission and its services be written in Italian for the benefit of the public. In 1916 Iwarson and Tron prepared a short booklet describing the history and activities of the SEM. The booklet was published in Italy in 1918 with the title *Notizie storiche e varie sulla Missione Evangelica Svedese dell' Eritrea*.[667]

Further Restrictions under Governor Gasparini

A new governor, J. Gasparini, took up duties at the end of 1923. His views on education were more liberal than that of previous governors. He was

662 Varde Ljus 1918, 43–50.
663 SEM/MT, 1916. 67, 72. He did his military service in Segeneyti, Eritrea.
664 SEM/MT, 1916, 139.
665 SEM/MT, 1916, 123.
666 SEM/MT, 1917, 3.
667 The Italian title means: *Historical and other notes on the Swedish Evangelical Mission of Eritrea*. Asmara, 1918.

The Mission Trade school in Asmara. Picture published in 1910.

A class in carpentry at the Mission Trade School in Asmara.

open to the views of the Vicar Apostolic, Mgr. Carrara. From 1923 until 1941 much of the Eritrean education system was in the hands of the Catholic Mission.[668] In 1924, relations between the SEM and colonial authorities deteriorated when Governor Gasparini complained that the Swedish Mission schools showed greater attachment to Ethiopia than to Eritrea. "Those who were highly educated and intelligent," the Governor maintained, "frequently left for Ethiopia where they were received warmly and given employment." In fact, the Mission Field Conference held from September 18 to 25, 1923, had stated,

> Some 10 boys who have finished 6th grade and who, we hope, will be qualified workers in the mission, would take another complementary course including French, particularly for use in the Southern Mission field, which would be of help also for the development of Ethiopia.[669]

As a result of this attitude, the Swedish mission was subjected to new restrictions by the government. Even senior missionaries who had gone on home-leave could not receive re-entry permits to Eritrea. In 1924 this restriction prevented the return of the Rev. Nils Nilsson, Thekla Frisk and Ingeborg Eriksson who were subsequently assigned to Ethiopia. Sigrid Berggren was likewise unable to return.[670] The alleged reason for this measure was the claim that the Swedish mission was becoming too large and powerful in an Italian colony. An annual report from the SEM on the state of the mission in Eritrea maintains,

> It is now rather obvious that those in power are purposefully trying to limit our influence in Eritrea. For a decade now, the Colonial government has assumed a negative attitude regarding any expansion of our mission work. It has refused to renew our concessions on the mission compounds and our plans for the expansion of our activities. Freedom to evangelize has been restricted. Last summer (1924) Swedish missionaries were prohibited totally from getting in touch with local chiefs and monasteries.[671]

---

668   T. Negash 1987, 72.
669   Minutes of Annual Conference 1923, § 27. The Conference had also responded positively to an application from the regent in Addis Ababa, through the consulate in Asmara, that Efrem Tewolde-Medhin be sent to Addis Ababa as a teacher at a government school. Annual Conference 1923, § 15.
670   SEM/Annual Report 1924, 203.
671   SEM/Annual Report 1924, 200–201.

A mission document: An account of the history of the Swedish Evangelical Mission in Eritrea, in Italian, recorded around 1918 by J. Iwarson and A. Tron.

J. JWARSON - A. TRON

◆ ◆ ◆ NOTIZIE STORICHE E VARIE

sulla MISSIONE EVANGELICA

SVEDESE dell'ERITREA ◆ ◆ ◆

❀ 1866-1916 ❀

ASMARA
MISSIONE EVANGELICA SVEDESE
1918

Participants in a refresher course for Eritrean teachers in Asmara, ca 1912. Picture from the book indicated above.

Increased Cost of Living

On top of the strained relations with the colonial authorities, another major problem arose. The cost of living had increased sharply, by as much as 60%. The Mission Conference in Eritrea had prepared a budget to the amount of 160,407 Italian Lira, but the Board in Sweden had cut it down to 138,928 Italian Lira.[672] The regular conference in October 1916 reported a doubling of prices. The problem was especially critical for the workers who had no land or whose crops had been devastated by a locust invasion. Now the Board accepted an increase of up to 155,000

672   Extra Field Conf. February 7, 1916.

Italian Lira, but in the meantime costs had doubled.[673]

In Closing

K. J.'s treatment of the period we have just covered in our two chapters (1915–1933) shows that, for many within the Italian colonial administration in Eritrea, the SEM and the Kenisha constituted a foreign body, a cause for concern. To the Catholics, the missionary activities of the SEM and the Kenisha were subversive. The authorities had their specifically *Italian* interests.[674]

However, such a statement should be qualified. Even though the Catholic Church in Eritrea was favoured by the colonial authorities, the lives of Eritrean Catholics were not without problems. Eritrean Catholics were not blindly loyal to the colonial authorities. In fact the most notable rebel against Italian rule, Bahta Hagos, was a Catholic. Moreover, Eritrean Catholics had to struggle long and hard in their attempts at indigenizing or "Ethiopianizing" their liturgy and rites. The issues of patriotism and resistance and the issue of indigenization within the Catholic Church in Eritrea have been treated in two scholarly essays by Dr. Tekeste Negash and Dr. *Abba* Ayele Teklehaymanot.[675]

Caution and Restrictive Measures

The colonial administration had to see to it that its potential enemies didn't use their freedom within Eritrea to undermine the stability of the colony. In short, it had to be on the look out for any activities and movements that appeared suspicious. The Swedish Mission and the Kenisha were watched through these precautionary eyeglasses. Their activities were monitored constantly. This resulted in ups and downs in the conditions under which the SEM and the Kenisha could operate within the colony.

The SEM and the Kenisha were also a challenge to the Orthodox Tewahdo, by far the largest Christian group in the colony, even though the Tewahdo were not a primary target of the missionary activities

---

673 Extra Field Conf. April 2–3, 1917.
674 Tekeste Negash's article "The Catholic Mission and the Catholic Community in Eritrea, 1894–1950" in *the Missionary Factor in Ethiopia,* gives us very useful insights into this issue. See especially the section entitled "The Italianization of Catholicism". Haile, Lande, Rubenson (Ed.) 1998, 121ff.
675 See T. Negash 1998, 121–134 and Teklehaymanot 1998, 135–154. (Ed.)

of these Protestant bodies. The colonial authorities couldn't afford to allow the Kenisha to provoke the Orthodox and the Muslims, whose size and antiquity in the country made them decisive factors in the maintenance of stability in the colony.[676] The fact that a steady trickle of Kenisha had slipped across the border into Ethiopia, where they were received well, didn't improve their reputation before the Italian authorities.

It is possible that the presence of Italian Protestant (i.e. Waldensian) missionaries working with the SEM and among the Kenisha was a blessing in disguise. Gustav Arén writes, "Co-workers from the Waldensian Church in Northern Italy were an excellent support to the Swedes and did their best to refute all calumnies."[677] Their presence may have contributed to the blunting of the edge of the restrictive measures directed at the SEM and the Kenisha.

Having said so, we must add that the position of the Kenisha and the SEM in Eritrea at this time was not enviable. They were, in a way, a besieged group. After 1919, the SEM had great difficulties getting personnel into Eritrea. The Evangelical community didn't have a sufficient number of Eritrean shepherds. The economy of the SEM was shaky. The cost of living in Eritrea was high. Missionaries were exhausted and despondent. In the earliest part of this period, some died of the flu, as did many of the Kenisha. The unpredictable nature of the attitudes of the colonial authorities towards the SEM was a source of frustration. A Jacopo Gasparini would close the door that a Giacomo De Martino had opened. This was indeed a time when both mission and church were *confined*, though one can hardly say that they had been reduced to a state of captivity. (Ed.)

---

676 One view is that the Italian colonial authorities were as unhappy about the presence of Protestants in the colony as were the Orthodox. However, the authorities tried to defend the rights of the Kenisha. See Renato Paoli's *Nella Colonia Eritrea* (1908), p. 180. Quoted in Smith-Simonsen 1997, 78. See also T. Negash 1987, 140. (Ed.)

677 Arén 1999, 183 note 20.

Chapter Nineteen

Persisting in Mission in Spite of a Gathering Storm

Introduction

> Once he had settled on the new objective for the Fascist regime's expansionist policy, the Duce found that the ground had been abundantly prepared by such flaming nationalists as Oriani, Corradini, Forges Davanzati, Coppola, Peddrazi and Scarfoglio, and by the ever-active propagandists of the Africa Society. After Adowa, Alfredo Oriani had written: "We have signed a peace but there will be no peace. We will never give up Africa – the war will be resumed."[678]

The expression "hidden agenda" has become a common term in the explanation of the motives behind the actions of states and individuals. Underlining the attitude of the colonial government to the SEM and the Kenisha there was indeed a hidden agenda, an intention, a passion, which went back to Italy's defeat at the Battle of Adwa in 1896. In his book *The Ethiopian War, 1935–1941*, Angelo Del Boca calls this agenda "The Adowa Complex."[679]

The "Adowa Complex," was not the only motive for the involvement of ordinary Italians in the war effort. In his highly readable book, *Christ Stopped at Eboli*, a diary kept during a period of exile in a poor southern Italian village for his anti-Fascist views, the medical doctor and author

678 Del Boca 1969, 9.
679 Del Boca 1969, 3–16.

Carlo Levi lifts forth the fact that individual Italians wanted to join the Abyssinian Campaign to escape from the boredom and degradation to which they were subjected in their remote villages. The invasion of Abyssinia meant money and land – soil that was so rich and fertile (according to reports) that all that one needed to do was cast the seeds on the ground and wait for them to sprout without any further effort on the part of the sower.[680]

Mussolini and Italy were evidently rearing to take vengeance on Ethiopia for their humiliation by what the Italians regarded as "the barbarous Shoan hordes." This stance coloured the attitude and actions of the colonial authorities also in Eritrea.

One would have expected that the end of the First World War in 1919 would have led to an easing of the censorious attitude of the colonial authorities towards the SEM and the Kenisha. This however was not the case. The offence of the colonial authorities at the purported sympathy of some Swedish missionaries towards Germany during the First World War was not yet forgotten, although the colonial authorities did take some steps that appeared conciliatory to the SEM. On the whole their actions remained unpredictable.

Under these circumstances, the work of the SEM and their Kenisha colleagues, in church and society, continued to be an uphill struggle. Limited resources in means and personnel were combined with the stingy and sometimes erratic attitudes of the colonial authorities, to make the day–to–day activities of mission and church something of a struggle to hold one's own. And yet, this period of shadows also had its brighter moments. There was a gradual process of consolidation and the contours of a national church were slowly emerging.

K. J. Lundström has provided us with the raw material and insights that went into this development. His text follows. (Ed.)

Changes for the Better

Already in 1917 Iwarson had written,

> Our situation has now changed, and no one has prevented us from organizing the Annual General Meeting. We even took heart enough to invite the Commissioner for Hamasen [Giacomo De Martino]. He

---

680 Levi 1945, 29, 58–59, 133–134.

responded positively and attended the first day of the conference.[681]

The Governor had expressed, both personally and through the proper government office, his wish that the missionaries, particularly those in Kunama, include education in agriculture and gardening in their activities. The response from the Mission was positive and Iwarson proposed that an experimental garden be established in Asmara.[682] In the wake of this positive atmosphere the Mission felt that it could plan for the return of old missionaries and for the coming of some new ones to Eritrea.

The first group had arrived in October 1919 when the Holmers and Erika Larsson came back to their duties in Addi Ugri, and Kunama respectively. The group included two new missionaries, the Rev. Axel Jonsson, who had been preparing himself by studying Tigré, and Elsa Gustavsson, who was to get married to Rev. Nils Nilsson.[683] These were assigned to Geleb. Four missionaries, Maria Johansson, Emma and Peter Andersson and Anna Svensson went on home leave.[684]

Anders Svensson celebrated his 70th birthday in April 1919. With his usual sense of humour, he quipped,

> The old warrior is complaining that his strength is on the ebb.

He was referring to a visit he had paid to a village where he had stayed overnight,

> As the sun was setting I felt terribly tired. My saddle is old, hard and cracked in all its seams. A new and soft one would probably fit me better – but, it is about time that I cast anchor, like an old barge. However, it would probably be easier to get hold of a new saddle than to find a new worker to take my place, wouldn't it? But who listens to this cry?
>
> Yours, a bearer of the King's armour for 42 years now! AS [Anders Svensson][685]

---

681 Varde Ljus 1918, 43–50.
682 Field Council 1918, 11–19, 1918 § 20.
683 SEM/MT 1919, 179–180. The Mission had the regulation that a male missionary should have a field experience of 2–3 years before he would be allowed to marry. Nilsson had arrived in Eritrea in 1913 but had to wait for six years, due to the war.
684 SEM/MT 1919, 156–157 and 1920, 53. Jonsson was able to undertake these studies with the help of missionaries who had lived in Geleb and Keren.
685 SEM/MT 1920, 92. The expression *the King's armour* is a reference to the spiritual equipment of a soldier of Christ. See Ephesians 6:10. (Ed.)

Farewell party held by the YMCA in Asmara 1920, for missionaries preparing to leave for furlough.

Missionaries Under Severe Pressure

Shortage of Personnel

At the annual mission conference in November 1919 a list of new and returning missionaries as well as other staff was drawn up. Those listed for Eritrea in the spring of 1920 were Daniel and Signe Berg, Olle Eriksson, August Andersson, Johan Hagner and one female worker for the Tigré-speaking area. It was stated that, upon the arrival of the new missionaries and those returning from home leave, Rodén, the Iwarsons, Vilma Nyström, Amanda Hägglund and the De Pertis family would leave for Sweden.[686]

However, as so many of the missionary staff were on home leave, the remaining few were left with even more work to do. In Kunama, Maria Nilsson lamented,

> When I heard that a female missionary would replace (August) Andersson, my courage failed me. Was this really the reinforcement we had been waiting for? So I took my assistant, Joseph, and moved to

686 Field Conference 1919 § 4.

Kulluku to continue with the school for girls.[687]

In 1919 the Trons went to Italy on home leave. As a result of the Mission's urgent appeal for more Italian teachers, two persons, Augusto Armand-Hugon and Emilio Ganz, responded to the call. Armand-Hugon stayed for only one year. A third teacher, Enrico Coïsson, joined the team in 1921. He was placed in Geleb, then in Shimanigus for a short time and then again in Geleb. He also served in Keren. His total period of service with the SEM covered twenty years.

Further Limitations Lifted

At the end of 1919 the mission was, once again, facing great difficulties. A new regent had taken over in Italy and come with the ruling that, for the time being, no missionaries of the SEM would be allowed into the country. SEM now planned to submit a petition to the authorities in Rome in the summer of 1920, for free and untrammelled rights in the pursuit of its mission activities.[688] In July 1920, the chairman of the SEM, General O. B. Malm and Dr. Karl Fries, Chairman of the YMCA in Sweden, went to Rome where they met Rev. Iwarson and Dr. De Pertis. The team approached the Italian Government with a request that it withdraw the former prohibitions and permit the society to send out missionaries without any restrictions. In February 1921 their requests were granted. The Board requested August Andersson to head a group of six missionaries travelling to Eritrea. These travelled by way of Italy and reached Massawa on April 11, from where they proceeded to Asmara and checked in with the different commissioners. August Andersson was now prepared to leave for Kunama, but, on the eve of his departure, two Italian policemen turned up requesting him to report at the police station the following morning. There he found out that he was prohibited from travelling to Kunama and that he would have to leave the colony with the first boat sailing for Italy.[689]

Sickness, Death, Separation of Missionary Families

Towards the end of 1920, Nils Nilsson, who was now in charge of the Beleza parish, grieved over the high mortality among the people. This

---

687   SEM/MT, 1920, 196–197.
688   SEM/Annual Report 1919, 113–114.
689   A. Andersson 1947, 158–159.

The board of the YMCA in Asmara, in 1920. Sitting, from left to right: Armand Hugon, Jonas Iwarson, Nicola De Pertis and Tekle-Mikael. Back row: Asfedai, Hadgu Isaias, Zekarias Mebrahtu, Emilio Ganz, Bairu Uqbit, Zeré-Gabir and Tesfa-Egzy Bidiho.

was the time when the so called Spanish Flu was taking its toll. Rev. Svensson made the same observation and noted that among about 20 candidates for Confirmation only five had turned up. "And I see sickness and death and graves along my journey to Asmara" he wrote.[690] Ida Härndahl came down with a severe sickness, accompanied by fever, but the Government doctor took very good care of her in Keren and she recovered. She was most worried over the high cost of the treatment, but no bill came. The doctor told her,

> The Government wants Miss Ida to feel well. We hope that the Government will regain its confidence in the Swedish missionaries, as was the case in "the good old times."[691]

Both Mr. A. Tron's wife, Dina, and Rev. Nils Nilsson's wife, Elsa, died towards the end of 1920. In 1922 two missionaries, Rev. Daniel Berg and a teacher, Miss Märta Andersson, passed away. Rev. Berg was one of

690   SEM/MT, 1920, 232.
691   SEM/MT 1921, 293.

the best-qualified missionaries on the field and his death was a severe blow to the work in Eritrea.[692]

Daniel Berg (1887–1922) had studied at Fjellstedtska College and Uppsala University, and been ordained in 1913. He had been selected to serve as a missionary in Eritrea, but World War I made it impossible for him to travel to the mission field just then. He taught at Johannelund Mission Institute and was made Head Teacher and Housemaster. In 1916 he married Signe Linder. This highly qualified couple arrived in Eritrea in 1921 and settled in Asmara. Daniel made an excellent start in his work but was taken ill and died in 1922.[693]

Financial Constraints in Sweden

1922 came to be a most arduous year. For a long time the SEM had struggled with its finances and, during the World War I, the fluctuations of the exchange rates had caused problems in covering expenses. Now that the situation had improved, a further problem turned up. It was discovered that the financial director of SEM in Sweden had misappropriated a large amount of funds, in all good faith.[694]

Fortunately there were, within the leadership, individuals with financial resources that could be placed at the disposal of SEM. However, for a long time, the society had to continue to repay debts. 1923 had started well. The financial situation was still very tight, and after the financial mishap of 1923, SEM was a poor organization. There was, however, a strong spiritual motivation, and the chairman of the Board, Anders Åberg, reminded the faithful: "Perhaps our greatest need is, after all, a larger measure of the Holy Spirit."[695]

Glimpses from the Post War Years

Iwarson's Visit to Ethiopia

In April 1920 Iwarson paid a visit to Ethiopia. He sailed via Djibouti and upon his arrival in Ethiopia he wrote,

> I was originally called to be a missionary to the Oromo but by God's

---

692   SEM/MT 1921, 335 and SEM/Annual Report 1921.
693   Nils Rodèn 1938, 104.
694   SEM/Annual Report 1922, 7 ff.
695   SEM/Annual Report 1923, 14–15.

guidance came to serve in northern Abyssinia. I love these people [meaning the Eritreans] in spite of their many faults. But my old love for the people of Southern Ethiopia has not died, and thus I am on my way to "spy upon the land" to some degree before I turn back to the north, to see my homeland.[696]

Upon arrival in Addis Ababa, he was met by Dr. E. Söderström, a Swedish missionary doctor who had taken charge of the mission after the death of Rev. Karl Cederqvist.[697] Iwarson was greatly moved by the many friends he met, some of whom were from Eritrea. Among them was *Aleqa* Tayyelign [Tayye], his old friend from his first years in Asmara.[698] He remained in Ethiopia for some five weeks and concluded his report by stating,

> The time has come to move forward. Addis Ababa is, at present, the most important point on our East-African field.[699]

On his return to Asmara in mid-May 1920, an extra conference was held. After the conference Iwarson was due to leave for Sweden. It was then decided that Rev. Anders Svensson serve as chairman of the conference until Iwarson's return.[700]

Svensson Authorized to Ordain Pastors

Towards the end of 1920, a very significant step was taken on the mission field in Eritrea. By empowerment of the Board of the SEM, Rev. Svensson was authorized to ordain pastors locally. An ordination ceremony was held on November 14, at the Church in Tse'azzega, where four candidates were ordained. Birru Tirfé was ordained for the Tse'azzega parish, Girma -Tsion Gebre for Asmara, Yosef Hemmed for Geleb and Gebre Sillassé Tesfa-Gabir for service in the Evangelical congregation in Addis Ababa, Ethiopia. [701]An elated Svensson adds,

---

696 SEM/MT 1920, 116. The expression "spy upon the land" is taken from the Old Testament book of Numbers 13:2. In this context it simply means "get an idea about". The expression "to the north, to see my homeland" is a reference to Sweden. (Ed.)

697 Nils Rodèn 1938, 137. Rev. Cederqvist had served in Kenya, Somalia and at Geleb, for some time, before he reached Addis Ababa in 1904. He became the leader of the Swedish mission in Ethiopia.

698 Also known as *Aleqa* Tayye Gebre-Mariam.

699 SEM/MT 1920, 149.

700 Extra Field Conference 1920, § 8.

701 SEM/MT 1921, 53–55. *Qeshi* Gebre-Sellassé Tesfa-Gabir was the father of the late Dr. Emmanuel Gebre-Sellassé, a former president of the EECMY.

The representative of the House of Tse'azzega, my former student and his ward, Lidj Abraha, son of the late Dedjatch Gubsa, and other evening school students were present. The Grand Duke of Asmara, the Knight and Blatta Berakhi, son of Kentiba Bekhit, well known from the days of Lager, Lundahl and Hedenström, had sent his youngest son Lidj Yohannes, who came with his guard of honour and squeezed himself into a seat somewhere. A large ox was slaughtered, 200 kgs of flour ... etc. were prepared.

The number of missionaries at the time was 25. The annual conference that year was unique in the sense that, for the first time in the history of the mission, female missionaries were allowed to participate.[702]

In March 1923, Rev. Iwarson returned to Eritrea and assumed his position as director of the Mission. Finances were strained and steps had to be taken to reduce expenses and sell off some of the property of the mission. Even Imkullu was put up for sale.[703] A new Governor, Jacopo Gasparini, had been installed and, once again, the Mission faced new problems. In 1923 Iwarson stated,

> Our mission has been severely hampered. Towards the end of the year, the colonial government prevented new missionaries from landing in Eritrea. No reason was given. The policy originates evidently not from the Government, which is usually very humane, but rather from the Catholic leadership.[704]

Stagnation in Spiritual Life?

At the beginning of 1924 Rev. Iwarson was pessimistic,

> If we are to be honest regarding our last few years, we must say that they have been a period of recession. We do not have the resources and our freedom is limited. We have been told that the reason for this is that we have not succeeded in fostering the natives to become faithful citizens of the colony. We have also much of internal disunity, with quarrels and legal proceedings, lack of prayer, lack of spirit-filled missionaries and co-workers and lack of funds. But by God's guidance the main centre is moving towards the South, to Addis Ababa.[705]

702 Field Conference 1922, introduction. See also Field Conference Nov. 3–17, 1924, § 1.
703 Field Conference 1923 § 9. The buildings were, however, not sold at this time.
704 SEM/Annual Report 1923, 189.
705 This is a summary by K.J., not a direct quotation, SEM/MT 1924, 135, 147–148.

Ordination of pastors in Tse'azzega on November 14, 1920.
From left to right: Birru Tirfé (for Tseazzega) Girma-Tsion Gebre (for Asmara district), Gebre-Sillasie Tesfa-Gabir (for 'Galla', i. e. Ethiopia) Yosef Hemmed (for Mensa).
Assistants at the Ordination: Mikael Holmer, Anders Svensson, Tewolde-Medhin Gebre-Medhin, Axel Jonsson and K G Rodén.

After Easter, however, Iwarson was more optimistic. The Easter festival had brought a sense of joy. A series of meetings had been held on the following topics,

  – Revival and Renewal
  – How did Jesus Meet Sinners?
  – Do you Love Me? Follow Me!
  – Prayer
  – Healing Through Faith and Prayer
  – Fishers of Men
  – What is the Position of the Mission and its Task Here Today?[706]

Alessandro Tron had been ordained by the Waldensian Church during his stay in Italy, in 1924.[707] This event was an additional source of joy. In September 1924 the first bazaar was held in Asmara and the net income from the sale of articles was 1,000 Lira.[708]

706   SEM/MT 1924, 182.
707   SEM Annual Report 1924, 204.
708   SEM/MT 1925, 5. On his ordination see SEM/Annual Report 1924, 204.

Congregational Work in Different Districts

Here is a survey of membership in the various parishes during the period extending between 1916 and 1924:

	1916	1921	1924
Asmara	460	589	679
Tse'azzega	626	677	745
Beleza	681	754	81
Addi Ugri	204	236	236
Tigré	350	397	434
Kunama	58	17	20
Total	**2,346**	**2,650**	**2,687**

These figures show a slow but regular growth.[709]

Shimanigus La'ilai

Besides the overall activities of the leadership of the Mission, work was in progress at the grass roots level. We shall cite a few examples from the period prior to 1925.

Rev. Nils Nilsson and his wife participated in a Confirmation ceremony that took place in Shimanigus La'ilai. Seven persons were confirmed, one of whom was a former Muslim. Nilsson felt that the congregation sang well and commented,

> However, we have difficulty in getting notes for all. Besides, the Swedish hymn books contain hymns taken from 13 different hymnals, and we are in urgent need of a music-edition.[710]

It is remarkable that both texts and melodies were from the West, the music being based on the diatonic and not the pentatonic scale, which was traditionally used among the Orthodox population. In the hymnals of the Evangelical Church of Eritrea there are still (in 2010) hardly any hymns set to traditional melodies.

Another report from Shimanigus La'ilai reads,

> We have among us a blind teacher in Shimanigus, a young man called

709   SEM Annual Reports for these years.
710   SEM/MT 1921, 290.

Haleqa Habtu. He is very eager to learn to sing the hymns. He and his wife never miss an opportunity to take part in the evening meetings. In spite of his handicap he is a good teacher. It was a joy to observe the confidence with which he corrected the reading mistakes of the students. He has memorized most of the New Testament and the Psalms by heart. One moment you see him teaching ABCD, the next moment, Bible History. Thereafter he corrects the reading mistakes of a priest or a deacon reading in Amharic, and explains the meaning of the text read. In spite of his handicap it is very good to have him as a teacher there.[711]

The blind teacher Haleqa Habtu, a knowledgeable and efficient co-worker from Shimanigus La'ilai

Himbirti and Amadir

Vilma Nyström, who had visited Himbirti, noted that the school had an enrolment of 75 students. Besides, the village had a large congregation.[712] Sigrid Berggren too, who lived in Tse'azzega, had some good news. She was staying at the village of Amadir at the invitation of a church member. She writes,

Many women and some ten young men are attending the reading classes. But the priests have intervened and banned all who dare to study with me. She added: My trustworthy assistant Elisabeth has been an invaluable support in the work, but is going to get married at New Year and leave me.[713]

In mid 1922 Sigrid wrote, again from Amadir, about her co-worker Tibé,

Eight years ago I took up Tibé as a small, hungry and cold mite. Since then, she has grown in understanding and efficiency. She is now my "all in all".[714]

On her return to Tse'azzega, Sigrid found out that Aster Wolde Mariam (1900–2000) had run the work there, leading the women's

711   SEM/MT 1921, 290.
712   SEM/MT 1921, 334.
713   SEM/MT 1920, 261–262.
714   SEM/MT 1922, 197–198.

meetings and teaching in the village.[715]

Prior to his travel to Sweden in 1922, *Qeshi* Tewolde-Medhin Gebre-Medhin had paid a visit to *Ra'si* Kidane-Mariam Gebre-Mesqel in Areza. The Evangelicals saw the latter as a persecutor but Tewolde-Medhin had good contact with him. At the time, Kidane-Mariam was sick in bed and Tewolde-Medhin sat down beside him and read for him. Kidane-Mariam then told Tewolde-Medhin of a dream he had had in which he had seen a crucifix. Tewolde-Medhin helped him get one.[716]

Educational Work

Below is a survey of schools and students:[717]

	1916		1921		1926	
	Schools	**Students**	**Schools**	**Students**	**Schools**	**Students**
Asmara	8	234	8	170	10	355
Tse'azzega	15	401	17	340	9	416
Beleza	18	380	18	450	10	265
Addi Ugri	13	138	13	163	6	89
Tigré	3	92	7	104		
Awsa Konoma	closed					
Kulluku	closed					
Kunama			7	30	2	36
Geleb/Keren					6	159
Total	**57**	**1,245**	**70**	**1,257**	**43**	**1,320**

At the Field Conference that was held in Geleb in September 1918, it was noted that the quality of teaching had risen and that the training of teachers was more thorough and all-sided.[718]

---

715 SEM/MT 1922, 197–198.
716 SEM/MT 1922, 58. More information regarding Kidane-Mariam is available in Puglisi 1952, 82.
717 SEM/Annual Report 1916, 1921 and 1926.
718 The Field Conferences were usually held in November, but as far as Geleb was concerned, September was regarded as a better time, with a good supply of fresh vegetables and fruit around that period. Note from introduction to conference 1918.

Church and congregation in Himbirti

Gathering in Himbirti 1908.

Since there were only limited opportunities for Swedish personnel to come to Eritrea, appeals were made to the Waldensian Church for more teachers. In 1918, the Board of the SEM had decided that three Italian teachers be called to participate in the educational programme of the mission. This was done. However, due to lack of possibilities for a regular government certificate in Education in the country, it was approved that "five intelligent male candidates from Eritrea be sent to the Waldensian Teachers' Training College at Torre Pellice to obtain a regular governmental certificate in Education".[719]

The small village schools were often run by local volunteers who received assistance in the form of school material and paraffin for their lamps. The price of the latter had increased substantially and, subsequently, the grant to the schools had to be raised.[720]

In Closing

This was a period of further ups and downs, of light and shadows in the work of the SEM and the Evangelical community. Among the *shadow* factors one can cite a lingering suspicion on the part of the colonial government towards the SEM and the Evangelical community. The expulsion of the veteran missionary to Kunama, August Andersson in 1921, only days after his arrival in Eritrea following a recent home leave in Sweden, is a telling example of this suspicion.

In 1924, the Field Director of the SEM, Pastor Iwarson, gives a pessimistic picture of the state of spiritual life within the Evangelical community. He gives the impression that stagnation had set in. Since he had visited Ethiopia in 1920, one wonders if his intense longing for the extension of the work of the SEM southwards into Ethiopia is not, partly, a reflection of his disappointment and fatigue in the face of what he believed to be the anaemic sate of the spiritual life of the Evangelical community in Eritrea.

Signs of Weakness in Spiritual Life

What were the signs of this allegedly anaemic state of spiritual life among the Kenisha? Can one speak of recurring problems in this

---

719   Extra Field Conference. held in Beleza in January 1919, § 3.
720   SEM/Annual Report 1917, 88, 90. Only a general reference to problems.

Eritrean teachers from the district of Addi Ugri 1911.
Seated left to right: Haleqa Habtu, Kifle Gila-Mikael and Haleqa Kahsai. Standing: Gebre-
Sillassé Gebru, Tedla Aflei, Yihddego Desta, Wolde-Gabriel and Fissiha Gebre-Giorgis.

regard? Just before he left Eritrea to return to Sweden, following his
five-month long visit to the colony, A. Kolmodin attended and preached
at a big conference for spiritual edification held in Beleza from March 6
to 8, 1909. Between 600 and 700 participants attended the conference.
In his teaching, he lifted forth some of the main vices with which the
congregations struggled.

The first was what he called "a sickly attitude of suspiciousness
and a tendency to spread rumours about persons towards whom one
carried a grudge."

The second was the sale of intoxicating drinks by members of
different congregations.

The third had to do with the tendency among the faithful to take
each other to court.

The fourth had to do with the relationship between pastors and
their congregations, the neglect of the poor and the sick, and the lack
of generosity in supporting evangelists. Here the challenge of generous

and sacrificial giving was taken up.[721]

Lending money with usury [interest] was evidently a practice which was condemned in the ECE. Olle Hagner writes of a certain person who had been disciplined for doing so.[722] In a fiery sermon preached in Asmara, on March 31, 1940, the preacher for the day, Bahlibbi, pointed out several shortcomings in the congregation. One such vice was the renting out of rooms or houses to prostitutes. The preacher warned that unless the Spirit of God visited the congregation, catastrophe would follow.[723]

Persistent economic problems, sickness and death among missionaries, lack of personnel and a general state of overwork seem to have added to the *shadow* aspect of the situation in the SEM and the Evangelical community.

Bright Spots

On the brighter side of things, mention can be made of a general improvement in the attitude of the Italian Government and the colonial administration in Eritrea towards the SEM, not least under Giacomo De Martino. Following an order preventing the return of Swedish missionaries to Eritrea, in 1919, the visit of a high-level delegation consisting of members of the home board of the SEM and others to Rome in 1920, played a decisive role in bringing about a more open attitude. A further factor was the stabilisation and consolidation of the Evangelical community resulting from a decision to allow the ordination of Eritrean pastors by a Swedish missionary in residence in Eritrea. The ordination of some capable and dedicated teachers was a welcome addition to the limited corps of Evangelical pastors. The educational undertakings, the medical services and the medical training programmes offered by and in the SEM and the Evangelical community maintained a high quality, considering current standards. A generous supply of Italian teachers, sent to Eritrea at different times through the auspices of the Waldensian Church, contributed to this happy state of things. These activities of The SEM won the respect and praise of the colonial government. (Ed.)

---

721   A. Kolmodin 1909, 239–240. (Ed.)
722   OHD/K.J.S. Book 2, entry for March 1940. (Ed.)
723   OHD/K.J.S. Book 2, entry for March 31, 1941, 31. (Ed.)

Gathering in Beleza from March 6–8, 1909, in connection with A. Kolmodin's visit.

Women in Addi Ugri engaged in cleaning cotton, spinning and weaving. Picture taken by Mikael Holmer 1925.

Chapter Twenty

A Church Takes Shape –
The Evangelical Church of Eritrea (ECE)
1926–1933

Introduction

Since it was in his character to strive towards freedom, self-sufficiency and growth, I would like to mention, over and above his political struggles that I have mentioned above, the exertions that he made within his own church, The Evangelical Church of Eritrea. In the years from 1921 to 1923 and in the subsequent years, he made the following appeal to the Swedish missionaries of the time, in concert with his other colleagues. "It is inevitable that the land would eventually revert to its native children and that spiritual undertakings would be transferred to the same. Therefore let responsibility be transferred progressively to the children of the country and let us be not only messengers but also co-workers." At the time, such a trend of thought was regarded as audacious. But in time, its validity was recognised even by the messengers of the Gospel.[724]

The subject of this eulogy is a Kenisha by the name of Grazmatch Zer'é Bekhit (1881–1941, Julian calendar), a dedicated son of the Evangelical Church of Eritrea and a successful entrepreneur. The text is

724 Tuquabo Aressi, 1995, 317.

quoted from an obituary by Ato Woldeab Woldemariam in the Tigrinya newspaper, *Nai Ertra Semounawi Gazetta* (The Eritrean Weekly News) on March 3, 1949 (Gregorian calendar). The words reflect the sentiment that was prevalent among leading, elderly Kenisha on the eve of the formal constituting of their church.

When the Evangelical Church of Eritrea (ECE) was officially founded in 1926, the preconditions for the presence and ministry of a church (according to Lutheran teaching) had already been in place for almost sixty years. The Word, the Sacraments of Baptism and Holy Communion, as well as ministers of the Means of Grace, called and commissioned according to the Lutheran Confessions, were on hand.[725] Different portions of the Bible, hymn books and a simple handbook for worship and other sacred acts, had been made available already at Imkullu by Pastor Bengt Peter Lundahl. The missionaries and the fugitive Kenisha, who could finally return to their ancestral homes, were soon equipped with further Tigrinya, Kunama and Tigré versions of these instruments of worship and catechetical work.

The SEM never demanded that former Orthodox priests who had become Evangelical Christians be required to undergo re-ordination, even though the placement of such priests as pastors in Evangelical congregations would be marked by a ceremony fitted for the occasion. Neither do Kenisha re-baptize those baptized in the Orthodox Tewahdo Church, or in any other church which baptizes in the name of the Trinity.

The presence of ordained Swedish missionaries had made it possible for Evangelical groups to worship and receive pastoral care in groups that, for all purposes, were Evangelical congregations. What was lacking was a legally and structurally constituted church. It was now time to enable Kenisha to take part in the leadership and care of an indigenous, nation-

---

725 Article VII of the Augsburg Confession, the main doctrinal statement of the Evangelical Lutheran Church, teaches that the church is "[...] the assembly of all believers among whom the Gospel is preached in its purity and the holy sacraments administered according to the Gospel." Tappert 1959, 32. (Ed.)

Article XIV states, "It is taught among us that nobody should publicly teach or administer the sacraments in the Church without a regular call." See the relevant articles under the Augsburg Confession in Tappert 1959, 36. (Ed.)

At the Field Conference in September 1918 a proposal was made to the Home Board that some of the best teachers be promoted to the positions of principals or assistants to the pastors. Subsequently, plans for seminary training would be worked out and candidates selected for eventual ordination. SEM Home Board Minutes December 10, 1918, § 16.

wide, Eritrean church, as partners of Swedish and Italian (Waldensian) missionaries. The impulses leading to the formation of such a church came first from the leadership of the SEM. Furthermore, discussions on church-formation on international missionary forums underlined the importance and urgency of such a measure. The Kenisha both requested and argued for such a move. In this chapter K. J. describes the process that led to the establishment of an indigenous church in Eritrea, a church that had the goal of being self-governing, self-supporting and self-propagating. His text follows. (Ed.)

Towards an Indigenous Church

Impulses from Inside

A new and radical topic was raised at the annual *gubaé* (conference) held in Geleb in 1922. One of the local leaders, Natnael [Negasi], had previously asked a question which had been tabled at a couple of previous meetings. The missionary who reported the discussions around the specific issue, writes,

> We understood, however, that he had a sly intention. Natnael's question ran, "Wouldn´t it be more pleasing to God if we were to carry out our work with our own funds and under our own leadership than if we were to do so with funds and a leadership provided by others?" After all, it has been stated that the congregation should stand on its own feet, and not under others".

Another statement ran,

> We ought not to leave the slavery under the Orthodox Church just to enter into another form of slavery.[726]

Such statements reflected an underlying tension between some of missionaries and some of the members of the Evangelical community.

Qeshi Tewolde-Medhin Gebre-Medhin acted as a mediator. He began by relating the hardship that the first *Readers* had faced and the help that the Evangelical community had received from the missionaries. He added,

> Now we ought to stand on our own feet. After all, a father rejoices when his child attempts to stand on his own feet.

---

726 SEM/MT 1922, 135. In connection with this report "a discussion followed on how the youth groups could raise funds to support their own travelling secretary."

Elders from the congregation in Asmara photographed on the occasion of Nils Dahlberg's visit in 1925. Standing to the right of Dahlberg is Qeshi Gebre-Selassie Habtu.

Impulses from Outside

During the latter part of the nineteenth century there was a growing concern in missionary circles, especially in Great Britain, about ways of conducting mission and organizing indigenous Christians into churches. The motto, "A Self-governing, Self-supporting and Self-propagating Church" had been adopted but, at the beginning, it didn't quite seem to lead to any result. In time, this motto became the corner stone of Protestant missionary policy in Africa. The organization of the Church on the basis of a democratic constitution was meant to guarantee independence under African leadership.[727]

On her mission fields, the SEM had followed a system under which ordained male missionaries were the obvious leaders of the parishes. 1919 was the first time an Indian pastor took charge of a congregation on a mission field of the SEM. In 1920 a newly appointed Mission Secretary, Nils Dahlberg, visited the SEM field in India and, together with the Rev.

727   Sundkler 1960, 45.

P. O. Fröberg, who was then the chairman of the mission conference in India, raised questions regarding the organization of a local Church.[728] Dahlberg presented a proposal for a church constitution to the India Field Conference and to the Board in Sweden. The constitution was solemnly approved at an extra conference in Chindwara, India, on February 9, 1923. The name of the new Church was to be *The Evangelical Lutheran Church of the Central Provinces*.[729]

Dahlberg Recommends Formation of an Indigenous Church

Dahlberg arrived in Eritrea just before Easter 1925, following a visit to Ethiopia in 1924. On Palm Sunday a *gubaé* was held in Asmara with some 1,200 participants. The Mission Secretary was given a warm reception and he made a deep impression by his charm and, even more, by his powerful preaching and the contributions that he made during the conversations. Many Kenisha came to remember him and to compare his visit with that of Professor Kolmodin in 1908–1909.[730]

Dahlberg underlined the view that a growing congregation must strive to become self-supporting, self-governing and self-propagating. This philosophy had been propagated by Prof. Kolmodin seventeen years earlier, but had not been realized as yet, due to many unfavourable circumstances. A committee was selected to prepare a proposal for a Church constitution "in close keeping with the pattern of our sister fields in India and South Africa".

Another important question was the upgrading of the education of indigenous co-workers. This proposal too was accepted at a mission conference in the autumn of 1925 and referred to the Board that gave its approval.[731]

Iwarson's hopes were evidently not limited to the church in Eritrea. For him Ethiopia was the ideal place for a centre for the training of teachers and pastors, not only for the Swedish Mission but also for other societies related to it. There was, he argued, a large inflow of students to the schools of the mission and there was a great need for

---

728 Dahlberg was director of overseas mission work 1919–1932 and then Mission Director up to 1959.
729 Tafvelin-Lundmark 1974, 304.
730 SEM/Annual Report 1925, 217.
731 SEM/Annual Report 1925, 217. Regarding further training SEM/MT 1925, 196.

Ordination of pastors in Asmara in connection with the visit of Pastor Nils Dahlberg, May 10,1925. From left to right: Tewolde Medhin Gebre-Medhin, Mikael Holmer, Gebre Selassie, Dawit Amanuel, Kifle Gila-Mikael, Nils Dahlberg, Gebre Selassie Habtu, Anders Svensson, Yihddego, Tewolde Medhin Gebru from Tigrai, Fissiha, Axel Jonsson, Girma-Tsion and Jonas Iwarson.

well-trained teachers and indigenous pastors.[732]

Earlier on, Iwarson had expressed interest in seeing the formation of a wider organization that would include the Church in "Southern Ethiopia", possibly also the Presbyterians. He had also discussed the matter with Karl Nyström of the Bible-True Friends, who had shown interest in participating in such an organization.[733]

A Church is Constituted

First Synodical Meeting

The First Synodical meeting, which constituted the Evangelical Church of Eritrea (ECE), was held from September 26–28, 1926 in Asmara.

Pastor Bruno Tron has pointed out to this editor that a commission of Eritreans and Europeans (Swedes and Italians) had worked for a

732 SEM Annual Report 1925, 217.
733 Letter from Iwarson to Dahlberg June 16, 1926. SSA E I, 265. SEM/MT 1926, 123–126, and 139–141.

long time, drafting a constitution for the ECE. A photo taken in Eritrea in September 1925 shows members at work on the constitution of the would-be church. The chairman was Jonas Iwarson. Among the members were Pastor A. Svensson, *Qeshi* Girma-Tsion, Dr. De Pertis, Memhir Embaye Habte-Egzy, Pastor Mikael Holmer and *Qeshi* Zer'a-Tsion. The total number of members on the picture is eighteen.[734]

Thirty-four participants were present at the assembly which constituted the church. Twelve of these were pastors, twelve were laymen from the congregations and ten were missionaries. The main item covered at the meeting was the election of a President. Rev. Iwarsson was elected to this position and *Qeshi* Tewolde-Medhin Gebre-Medhin was elected Vice-President.

The Italian colonial government had ordered that all rural schools of the Mission/Church be closed. The Synod recommended that this order should be obeyed and that there should be no obstruction of the directive issued by the authorities. It was, however, also understood that this order would not prevent members of the congregations from attending devotions and services of worship.[735]

In his annual report for 1926 Rev. Iwarson informed his hearers and readers that the larger parishes had been divided into smaller units, each under the leadership of an indigenous pastor. An attempt had also been made to make arrangements for smaller regional pastors' conferences to be held every three months. The subject of the training and dedication of elders and deacons was also introduced. Among the congregations, Iwarson had observed a tendency to take on growing responsibility for the support of their Church.[736] It was also reported that there was now a consensus that the major annual feasts of the ECE coincide with those of the Orthodox Tewahdo Church. The missionaries and church members in Kunama, however, decided to maintain the current order.[737]

Later on there was a request from the Kunama missionaries to the effect that they be permitted to hold their own conferences and not

734 A. Andersson, Normark et al. 2006, 83. (Ed.)
735 First meeting of ECE Synod Sept. 1926 § 8. Arén 1999, 537: Unpublished sources B. Ethiopian # 2. Evangelical Church of Eritrea, Synodical Council Minutes. Summary report given by *Qeshi* Musa Aron to Rev. Arén. The original documents were evidently lost during the war.
736 SEM/Annual Report 1926, 253–254.
737 Musa's Summary of Synod Minutes, p. 1.

The Committee for the drafting of the constitution of an Evangelical church, in session in September 1925, in Asmara. Pastor J. Iwarson (centre), who became the first president of The Evangelical Church of Eritrea (ECE) in 1926. Picture published in 1925.

be required to participate in the Field Council of the Missionaries. The request was voted down, but it indicates how much Kunama felt that it was "separate" from the rest of the Evangelical Christians on the highlands.[738] For a while, restrictions introduced by the colonial government caused the SEM to consider transferring the mission printing press to Addis Ababa. However, the censorship had now been eased and the leaders of the SEM were happy to keep the printing press in Eritrea. There was a great need for the printing press and the mission had more qualified personnel and access to cheaper material in Eritrea. These arguments spoke against a change of location.[739]

A Missionary Conference presented the following list of candidates for ordination: Kahsai Gebre, Mezgebe Woldu, Gebre-Yesus Medhin and Yohannes Emilios Musa.[740] The ordination would take place on

---

738 Field Conference April 9–11, 1927, § 7.
739 Field Conference 1927, § 5.
740 It has been pointed out by Bruno Tron that the arrangement known as the "Missionary Conference" lasted until 1971, when the SEM was integrated into the ECE. However, the Mission had already started transferring areas of responsibility to the Synod, gradually and over a long period of time. (Ed.)

Pentecost Day in 1929.[741] This Field Conference had also proposed rules for Church membership. The first item to be taken up under this topic had to do with the rules for the various categories of members or would-be members. Three groups were envisaged,

1. The baptized
2. Catechumens
3. Communicants

A special course in Christian knowledge would be given in each congregation. This course would be compulsory for the children of the members of the Evangelical Church but voluntary for outsiders who were seeking admission as catechumens. Those who had followed these courses might, if they so wished, be classified as Catechumens.[742]

It was stated,

> If the need arises, a shorter Confirmation course may be held leading to Communion, after the personal conviction of the candidate had been tested by the Church Council and found adequate.

The category "Catechumen" was rarely used. The most common approach was that, after having reached a mature age and having indicated a desire to become a member, the applicant would undergo a Confirmation course. Another pre-requisite was that a catechumen be able to read. Exemptions might be made for persons who were old and unable to learn to read. These would be encouraged to learn certain passages by heart.[743] Students from the Boarding Schools and other individuals may, if found mature by the Congregational Council, be accepted as communicant members directly through Confirmation, after consultation with their respective teachers. Payment of an annual fee to the congregational treasury would be compulsory even for the Catechumen.[744]

The number of Church members at the end of 1926 was 3,006.[745]

---

741   Field conference 1927 § 11. It seems strange that the decision was taken by the missionaries and not by the Church. The procedure was, however, that on the commissioning of the Board and the authorisation by the Archbishop of Sweden, the President (in this case Rev. Iwarson) would, perform the ordination with the assistance of the pastors present. See also SEM/MT 1929, 302–303. Field Conference 1928, § 21.

742   Field Conference 1927, § 1.

743   Observed by the author.

744   Field Conference 1927, § 1.

745   SEM Annual Report 1926, 297.

"Aboy" Mengesha Birru, one of the Kenisha who moved to Ethiopia. He was sent to Europe by Emperor Minilik in 1907 to buy equipment for a printing press. His son, General Iyasu Mengesha, attained to the highest ranks of the Ethiopian armed forces.

Second Synodical Meeting

The Second Meeting of the Synod was held from February 9 to 11, 1927. The main item of discussion was the problem caused by the emigration of church members from the Colony to Ethiopia. The colonial government was persistent in its criticism of the Church for these migrations. In view of the situation, it was decided that the *gubaé* (the annual convention) for spiritual edification be discontinued.[746] The Synod appealed to pastors, teachers and church members to obey the Italian Government and not revolt against it. It was also resolved that a committee be appointed to underline, for the colonial authorities, the necessity of religious liberty. Church members were encouraged to be diligent in evangelization and to increase their contributions to the work of the church and its mission.[747]

An application had arrived from Kunama, requesting that the faithful there be allowed to join the Synod. The request was granted. The mere fact that the application came seems to indicate that the Christians in Kunama had not quite grasped the fact that they were part and parcel of the Church.[748]

---

746 *Gubaé* was the type of convention which was held for the spiritual edification of the faithful.
747 Musa's Synod Summary p. 2.
748 Musa's Synod Summary. Second Synod meeting p. 2, No 6.

Third Synodical Meeting

The Third Synodical Meeting was held in Asmara from September 26 to 29, 1927. The recording secretaries for the period 1925–1930 were Miss Ida Härndahl and *Qeshi* Girma-Tsion Gebre. An item taken up at the meeting was the matter of regulations for burial services. It was decided that Muslim or Orthodox practices like *tezkar* (prayer in commemoration of the dead) should not be practised and that it was not right for Evangelical Christians to participate in such rites.

The meeting resolved to seek ways and means for a closer co-operation with Evangelical Christians in Ethiopia. Another matter that the Church underlined was that big festivals like Easter, Pentecost and Christmas be celebrated on the same dates as those observed "by the Orthodox in Abyssinia". This matter had actually been taken up at the first meeting of the Synod. Furthermore, the Synod approved a proposal by Dr. De Pertis that Evangelical Christians should not lend money against unfair interest or grain with a view to getting unfair returns or to rent houses to be used for immoral activities (brothels etc).

From Tigrai, Ato Gobezé Goshu reported that the authorities were currently more favourable to evangelistic work and urged that evangelistic outreach in Tigrinya be further strengthened.[749]

At the end of 1927, the number of Church members in the ECE was 3,098.[750]

Fourth Synodical Meeting

The Fourth Synodical Meeting was held in September 1928. The question of intermarriage between people of different confessions was raised, and it was resolved that such marriages should not be allowed. The Synod resolved that the Italian flag be raised in each congregation and that the congregations pay the expenses for the purchase of such flags. The Synod also decided that money collected that year, 2,000 Lira, be earmarked for the work in Adwa and that the sum of 3,000 Lira be allotted to the same end for the coming year.

As regards engagements, the Synod decided that the would-be bridegroom give only one ring to the would-be bride. In case more

---

749 Musa's Synod Summary. Third Synod meeting p. 3–4
750 SEM/Annual Report 1927, 257.

Ato Gobezé Goshu och Haleqa
Tewolde Medhin Gebru, Evangelical
Christians who laboured in Tigrai and
suffered for their Evangelical faith.

ornaments were involved, the couple would be disqualified for a church wedding. The giving of such ornaments after the wedding would make the couple liable to exclusion from Holy Communion.[751]

The number of Church members at the end of 1928 was 2,668.[752]

Fifth Synodical Meeting

The Fifth Synodical Meeting was held at Tse'azzega from October 12 to 15, 1929. In his report the President took up the question of the shortage of both missionaries and national workers. He encouraged the church members to assume greater responsibility and to make

751 Musa's Synod Summary. Fourth Synod meeting p. 4–5, Additional rules were evidently set in the Geleb/Keren area: At Tesenei, in the 1950s, *Qeshi* Firenkiel refused to marry a couple as the ring was made of gold and not silver which would have been proper. (Author.)
I talked briefly to *Qeshi* Musa Aron on the background to these stringent rules. His feeling is that they were an expression of the desire to maintain or preserve a specific Kenisha image. Simplicity, lack of flare and extravagance, were to be among the marks of the spiritually awakened, a witness against some of the excesses of the traditions to which the Kenisha once belonged. *Qeshi* Musa added that these strict regulations around engagements and weddings were no longer in force. (Ed.)
752 SEM/Annual Report 1928, last page.

greater efforts to improve the financial state of the church. The church had raised 11,500 Lira, half of which had been collected by the Asmara congregation. 3,000 Lira was allotted to Adwa. It was also resolved that the Ethiopian (i.e. Julian) Calendar be officially accepted and included in *our literature*.[753]

A joint meeting of members of the Synod and the missionaries was held towards the end of 1929. At this meeting, it was underlined that the task of urging the Orthodox Church to focus on the centrality of the Gospel would take a long time and that the vision required patience. The number of new members joining the Evangelical Church was low. More and more people were listening willingly to the Gospel and had begun to search the Scriptures, both on the Eritrean highlands and in Tigrai. The school work of the Mission was regarded with a growing measure of good will.[754] The number of Church members at the end of 1929 was 2,906.[755]

Sixth Synodical Meeting

The Sixth Meeting of the Synod was held in Beleza, September 27–30, 1930. The President drew the attention of the participants to the life and work of *Qeshi* Tewolde-Medhin Gebre-Medhin who had died during the year. *Qeshi* Girma-Tsion was elected as Vice Chairman. It was also decided that three of the members of The Synod attend the next Missionary Conference to be held at Geleb.[756] The number of Church members at the end of 1930 was 2,898.[757]

Seventh Synodical Meeting

The Seventh Synodical Meeting was held at Beleza from October 3 to 6, 1931. Iwarson was elected President, and Britta Edlund and *Qeshi* Gebre Sillassé Habtu, as secretaries.[758] Here again, the ever-recurring question was: How can the ECE be self-supporting? Another question

---

753 Musa's Synod Summary. Fifth Synod, pp. 5–6. This seems to have been a recurring theme at synodical meetings.
754 SEM/MTBB 1929, 547–549.
755 SEM Annual Report 1929, 194.
756 Musa's summary. Sixth Synod Page pp. 6–7. Musa Aron commented: This is the first real attempt to integrate the work of the mission into the ECE.
757 SEM Annual Report 1930, 252.
758 Musa Aron makes the remark: Very unusual for such a young pastor.

Pastoral meeting at Geremi in 1929. Front row, from left to right: Jonas Iwarson, Zer'a-Tsion Musé, Tewolde-Medhin Gebru, Mikael Holmer.
Back row: Kiflé Gila-Mikael, Alessandro Tron, Girma-Tsion Gebré, Tewolde-Medhin Gebre-Medhin, Gebre-Sillassé Habtu, Yihdeggo Desta. Picture published in 1929.

Sinodos (i.e. Church Assembly) in Beleza 1930. Picture published in 1930.

that was taken up was: "Why are the Evangelical Church of Eritrea and the Bibeltrogna Vänner [The Lutheran Church of Eritrea] two different churches? Can't they be united?" Iwarson replied that this question could only be answered in Sweden and that the answer depended on the two home-boards [i.e. those representing the SEM and BV]. A further question had to do with the church's educational activities. "What could be done in view of the limitations placed on the activities of the schools?" It was recommended that pastors in the villages give one period of religious instruction per day and that all parents be responsible for the instruction of their children.[759]

The number of Church members at the end of 1931 was 3,009.[760]

Eighth Synodical Meeting

The Eighth Synodical Meeting was held in Beleza from September 17 to 20, 1932. Three Kunama pastors, Yosef Mati, Daniel Luli and Hezqiel Gulai, were ordained in connection with the conference. In the course of the current year, 10,000 Lira had been raised towards the budget of the Church. A letter had been received from *Haleqa* Tewolde-Medhin Gebru in Adwa, in which he stated that he had rejoined the Orthodox Church. The president requested the Synod to express its opinion on the matter. It was agreed that he could be useful among the Orthodox as long as his move did not imply a break with his basic Evangelical convictions.[761] His teaching never changed. (Ed.)

The number of Church members at the end of 1932 was 3,157. [762]

Ninth Synodical Meeting

The Ninth Synodical Meeting was held at Shimanigus La'ilai from September 30 to October 2, 1933. Pastor Mikael Holmer was elected as chairman and *Qeshi* Kahsai Gebre and Signe Berg as secretaries for the duration of the conference.

Additional regulations regarding marital relations were taken up. In case of temporary separations (not divorce) the couple would not be

---

759 Musa's Summary. Seventh Synod pp. 7–9.
760 SEM/Annual Report 1931 last page.
761 Musa's Synod Summary. Eighth Synod. pp. 9–11. The resolution in fact used the words,
　　　"... if he had not rejoined them wholeheartedly." See F. Gurmessa 2009, 175–176.
762 SEM/Annual Report 1932 last page.

allowed to take part in Communion. Pastor M. Holmer was appointed President and *Qeshi* Girma-Tsion Vice-President. It was also decided that a Synodical Council be established to deal with interim business. A. Tron, Girma-Tsion Gebre, Yosef Hemmed and Gebre-Yesus Medhin were elected to serve on this council.[763] The number of Church members at the end of 1933 was 2,999.[764]

Tenth Synodical Meeting

The Tenth Meeting of the Synod was held in Geleb from September 22 to 24, 1934. Various questions regarding regulations on marital relations were discussed once again. Another item that was taken up was the need for more generous giving to the work of the Church, since offerings did not cover costs. It was resolved that each member contribute at least 12 Lira to the Central Treasury.

It was also resolved that each pastor promote the distribution of Christian literature by bringing along 10 copies of each printed book and seeing to it that they were sold.

At a later meeting in January 1935 it was decided that an application be submitted to the Government, requesting permission to run schools for 4–5 months a year for the purpose of providing religious instruction.[765]

Eleventh Synodical Meeting

The Eleventh meeting of the Synod was held in Shimanigus La'ilai from September 21 to 23, 1935. Pastor Mikael Holmer was elected as President, *Qeshi* Yosef Hemmed as Vice President, and Mrs Signe Berg and *Qeshi* Gebre-Sillassé Habtu as secretaries.

§ 14 Rev. Tron encouraged the members to make greater efforts towards evangelization.

§ 15 1,500 Lira was approved for the building of a chapel in Quolla Serayé.[766]

763   Musa's Synod Summary. Ninth Synod, pp. 11–12.
764   SEM/Annual Report 1933, last page.
765   Tenth Synod Meeting at Geleb 1934, § 1, 3, 8 and 12
766   Eleventh Synod Meeting 1935. Note by Musa Aron: The minutes seem to have been kept rather innocuous. The meeting was held less than two weeks before the Italian invasion of Abyssinia.

Educational Activities

If any specific area of concentration and persistence is to be singled out during this period of darkening clouds we would be justified in selecting the area of education in general. The following two paragraphs from K. J.'s material speak their own language. The list of figures under "Education in Evangelical Schools" indicates a losing battle, with the number of schools and the enrolment of students dwindling. Nevertheless, the enrolment of students in 1931, just before the heavy hand of the colonial authorities fell on the SEM and the ECE, reflects a fighting spirit, to the bitter end. K. J.'s text follows. (Ed.)

Education in Evangelical Schools

Year	Schools	Boys	Girls	Total
1925	47	724	294	1018
1926	43	944	376	1320
1927	26	477	235	712
1928	48	629	306	935
1929	28	614	318	932
1930	24	582	303	885
1931	16	526	251	777
1932	3	134	73	207

An order that had been issued by the Government towards the end of 1926 had caused a decrease in the number of schools and students after 1927. The proclamation ordered that all SEM village schools be closed immediately. No teaching would be permitted unless the governor granted special permission in writing. If this order was not followed, the teachers would be arrested and the missionaries held responsible for breach of law.[767] The number of students decreased, from 1320 in 1926 to 712 in 1927.

T. Negash suggests that this decline was due to the opening of *Scuola Vittorio Emanuelle* by the new Government.[768] This was, however, probably not the case. The number of students at the Asmara School remained the same but together with those in the Asmara district, the

767   SEM/MT 1926, 292.
768   T. Negash 1988, p 90, note # 87.

Teachers in Geleb. (Picture published in 1930.)
Sitting, from left to right: Qeshi Dawit Amanuel, Ida Coïsson, Ida Härndahl and Eleazar Hedad.
Standing: Eyassu Be'imnet, Tesfa-Le'ul, Timoteos, Samuel Etman, Enrico Coïsson.

students numbered 355 in 1926. When the village schools were closed again, the number declined to 281 in 1927. The following year, when some schools reopened, the number was 355 and in 1929 it numbered 275. In 1930 however, only 2 schools remained open and the number of students was 234. These facts were taken from the last page of each annual report, from the years 1926 to 1930.

Sunday Schools, Training of Teachers and Evangelists

Some of the churches had organized Sunday Schools and in 1932, the number of students attending them exceeded 500. In 1933, however, only three of them were running and the number of students was 197, half of whom were in Geleb. An improvement was reported from Kunama, with 85 children in attendance.[769] In the second half of the

---

769 SEM Annual Report 1933, last page. In May 1927 Britta Edlund gives a report on a visit she had paid to Kunama. On her way she had stopped at Agordat and met Lette Hiywet, (wife of Gustavo Mensa), who had been one of her students. She was very pleased about the fact that the home was clean and orderly. In Awsa Konoma she met Ellen Gustavsson who was devoting all for her boys and the Kunama. The Sunday service was held in the beautiful church *tukul*. Ellen served as a pastor (sic) at the morning service. SEM/MT 1927, 148–149.

nineteen-twenties, there were eight Italian teachers working with the Mission: Rev and Mrs. Alessandro Tron, Mr and Mrs. Coïsson, Mr. Emilio Ganz and the three mentioned earlier. However, at the beginning of the thirties, only the two couples, Coïsson and Tron, were still at work in Eritrea.[770]

In Closing

This chapter has given us a picture of an Evangelical community that was slowly trying to find its place, to establish a spiritual home, and develop forms for the practice of its faith. Here we have a community seeking to define and grow into its new identity, without appearing to be rebellious or prone to compromises.

The Kenisha had ties in many directions and on many levels in Eritrea. They carried fresh memories from their immediate, ancestral societies. All these relationships required a measure of redefinition and adjustment. They called for different modes of co-existence. Since the Kenisha were a more or less ostracized group, at least in the countryside, they felt obliged to win back their place in society, at least spiritually and psychologically. They were quietly engaged in attempting to establish a new living space for themselves, under the guidance of seasoned missionaries and older Kenisha. The official founding of an Evangelical Church of Eritrea, about which K. J. has written, took place in a context marked by these challenges. In spite of the fact that the Kenisha had their spiritual and social networks in place long before the establishment of an official church, it cannot be denied that the establishment of a church as a legal body, a public institution with its own structure and official representatives, strengthened the self-image of the Evangelical community.

It is striking that the ECE chose to use the designation *Sinodos* (Synodos) for its highest decision-making body. The word *Sinodos* means, *way together* and goes back to two Greek words: *syn* a prefix meaning *with* and *hodós* (meaning "way"). To be engaged in a *Sinodos* is to be engaged in a common undertaking, a common journey. Synodical meetings reflect or should reflect the joint mode of operation of a religious body. The

---

770   Reported by Bruno Tron in May, 2000.

Synodical way of deliberations and decision-making is a centralized or centralizing mode of leadership, though consensus was the goal.

Who or what influenced the ECE in its choice of this pattern of leadership? Its mentors, the SEM and, by extension, the Church of Sweden, do not use the term for their highest decision making bodies. I would presume that the ECE borrowed the word and the practice connected with it from the Orthodox Tewahdo Church. It is to be remembered that the OTC calls its highest decision-making body *Qiddus Sinodos* (the Holy Synod).

If our suggestion is right, the move would amount to a confirmation of the attitude that lay behind the decision of the ECE to follow the Orthodox (Julian) Calendar as a guide for the celebration of its solemn Church feasts.[771] The choice of the term *Sinodos* and the mode of operations implied by it seem to be expressions of the fact that the ECE too had a heritage on which it could fall back, also in matters of church polity and decision-making.

The summaries from the minutes of the eleven Synodical meetings which have been lifted forth in this chapter by K. J. are far too short to help us to capture the moods in which the different deliberations were held. However they do provide us with footprints from the common journey of those who were given the responsibility of leading the ECE. The minutes bear records of some recurring discussions and recommendations.

These minutes from the various synodical meetings, reflect the growing pains of an indigenous church. They actualize burning issues and lift forth recurring problems. In this sense they provide an agenda for both long and short range measures. (Ed.)

---

771   The decision to follow the Julian or Ge'ez calendar in this regard was taken at the Fifth Synod of the ECE held in Tse'azzega from October 12–15, 1929.

Missionaries evicted from Eritrea and Juba, in Italian Somaliland, here after arriving in Sweden 1936. Picture taken in the Chapel of Johannelund. Sitting from left: Brita Edlund, Anna Ström, Selma Göransson, Rosa Holmer, Vilma Nyström, Signe Berg. Standing: Einar Thurfjell, Ruth och Herbert Uhlin, Mikael Holmer, Herman Lundin, Ellen Gustafsson

Chapter Twenty one

The Storm Broke Loose – Swedish Mission Evicted 1935

Introduction

As war with Ethiopia came closer and closer, the government displayed an increasing measure of suspicion and lack of good will towards the mission. [...] Padre Fabiano let the Kunama understand, "When the political situation is ripe, we are going to drive out the Swedes, with the help of the government, and take over their stations."[772]

These are the words of Missionary Olle Andersson (later known as Olle Hagner), recorded in his book *Stormen Bröt Lös* (The Storm Broke Loose), which came out in 1947 and whose title we have used as the title of our chapter. Whether these words are verifiable or not, they are an expression of a sentiment which was evidently shared by other missionaries and Kenisha. It will be remembered that Olle Andersson was in Eritrea when Italy invaded Ethiopia in 1935 and again from 1939 to 1945, when he had to negotiate about confiscated mission property with both Italian and British military authorities.[773]

One thing is clear: It was the eleventh hour. "By now," writes K. J. "much of the work of the Evangelical Church and the Swedish Mission had been closed down."

The schools were closed by order of the colonial authorities in 1932. Olle Andersson maintains that this and similar measures taken against the SEM and the ECE were the Italian Government's way of rewarding the Vatican for its cooperation with Mussolini. In support of his claim, Andersson cites a certain "well initiated and fully reliable" person, a so-called *Gerarca* (presumably one who belonged to either the political or religious hierarchy) in Milan and a "kommendör (rear admiral) B." in Rome. Both of these persons knew, according to Andersson, the SEM and appreciated its work in Eritrea.[774] Once again, regardless of the debatable nature of the charges against the Vatican, Swedish missionaries and not a few Kenisha were of the same mind as Andersson on this question.[775]

Italy's colonial ambition was now ready for its next leap. All

772　O. Andersson 1947, 47, 49. See also A. Andersson 1948, 198 ff.
773　His wife Greta spent many a lonely year in Sweden, taking care of her children and waiting for her husband to return. Olle returned to Sweden in 1945, after six years in Eritrea. In her book *I Didn't Do it For You. How The World Betrayed A Small African Nation* (2005), Michela Wrong gives a fascinating account of the Battle of Keren, where Commonwealth troops defeated the Italians and their colonial troops after pitched battles in which both armies displayed great courage. Wrong 2005, ch.4. (Ed.)
774　O. Andersson 1947, 54
775　In a Master's thesis on "Italian Educational Activities in Colonial Eritrea 1890–1941" defended at the University of Tromsoe, Norway, in November 1997, Christine Smith-Simonsen takes up the background and eventual fate of the schools of the Swedish Mission in Eritrea. See especially pp. 131–135. She admits her strong dependence on the works of Father Ezechia da Iseo (Da Iseo 1914) and particularly Tekeste Negash (T. Negash 1987). (Ed.)

potential eyewitnesses to the unfolding of the coming move, parties whose loyalty to Italy was questionable, had to vacate the scene or be effectively silenced. Among these were the missionaries of the SEM and the leaders and members of the ECE. However, these two bodies had become part and parcel of Eritrean society. In fact there were Italian, Waldensians missionaries sharing the life of this Evangelical community and contributing actively to it. It is possible that the presence of these Waldensians contributed to the blunting of the edge of the increasingly aggressive censorship of the colonial administration. How did a minority church continue to breathe in a period that, at the risk of some exaggeration, can be characterized as the eleventh hour?

K. J. gives us glimpses into the day to day struggles of a church trying to keep afloat on the eve of Italy's next step in colonial expansion, the invasion of Ethiopia. His text follows. (Ed.)

Increased Strain on the SEM after Iwarson's Departure

By now, much of the work of the Evangelical Church and the Swedish Mission had been closed down by the colonial authorities, with the tacit support of the Roman Catholic Mission in Eritrea. All educational activities had been curtailed, staff from abroad had been prevented from coming (with a few exceptions) and many constraints had been placed on the remaining few. There was also the fear of war. The Italian military build up had been in progress for a number of years and even if this was kept secret, preparations had been made for an attack on Ethiopia. In Eritrea tension was mounting.[776]

On the development of the Catholic Mission, Da Nembro reports,

> The new direction which Governor Riccardo Astuto (1930–1934) was following brought about a remarkable expansion of schools entrusted to the Catholic Mission on the Abyssinian highlands. Thus, in the period 1932–1934, the Catholic mission appropriated the schools in Tse'azzega and Beleza, previously run by the Protestant Swedes.[777]

Jonas Iwarson had been the head of the Mission since 1913 and president of the indigenous church since its establishment. He was

---

776   T. Negash 1987, 130 note 66.
777   Da Nembro 1953, 193. On the movement of former Swedish *Eritrea* missionaries to Ethiopia see Halldin-Norberg 1977, 110–112 and Arén 1999, 182–188. (Ed.)

well known in missionary circles and had attended the Jerusalem Mission Conference in 1928.

He was concerned about mission work not only in Eritrea but also in Ethiopia. Already before the establishment of the Italian colony of Eritrea, Swedish missionaries had been active in Tigrai. One of these was Rev. Anders Svensson. A more permanent contact with Tigrai was established through *Haleqa* Tewolde-Medhin Gebru. From the time he took over as Director of SEM, Iwarson continued to assist the development of Evangelical activities in Northern Tigrai.

As many Evangelicals in Eritrea had immigrated to Ethiopia, especially to Addis Ababa, Iwarson maintained close contact with what he called "the Southern Field". Furthermore, there were many former Eritrea missionaries who had not been granted permission for re-entry to Eritrea by the Italian colonial government, and had therefore been sent to Ethiopia. The tightening of restrictions on the Mission in Eritrea subjected Iwarson to much stress.

Since his early years in Eritrea, Iwarson had made it a point to concentrate on the training of indigenous personnel. This training was given on different levels. One phase consisted of shorter courses, intended particularly for village teachers and Orthodox Christians who wanted to find out more about what the Bible taught on specific issues. Other courses were of longer duration and prepared the students to serve as teachers in mission schools. No other indigenous pastors had been ordained until 1920, with the exception of Tewolde-Medhin Gebre-Medhin and Teklé Tesfa-Kristos [1909 and 1910], respectively.[778] By the time Iwarson was preparing to leave for good, the number of ordained pastors had reached 18. Among these pastors, only two, Girma-Tsion Gebre (1877–1934) and Gebre Sillassé Habtu (1901–1979), had advanced beyond the basic theological education that they had received. The former had served together with Dr. Winqvist as he was well versed in Ethiopian languages, while Gebre-Sillassé had been tutored by Rev. Anders Svensson. Both spoke Swedish and Italian fluently and had also visited Sweden. Gebre Sillassé was there in 1927 together with his mentor and Girma-Tsion visited the country in 1931, when he participated in the celebration of the 75th Anniversary of the SEM.[779]

---

778   A. Kolmodin 1909, 207.
779   Hofgren 1956, 319.

Girma-Tsion, who had served as vice president of the Church during his latter years, died in 1934.

Iwarson's age, long experience and wide contacts had made him a prominent figure. There was no missionary or Eritrean Church leader who could match him. The election of the pious and soft-spoken Mikael Holmer as president of the Church in 1933 introduced a new tone and style of leadership.

Glimpses from Here and There

The school in Asmara was a showpiece of the SEM. Its closure in 1932, the culmination of a long process of intentional tightening of the screws, was a blow to the mission. Now that the schools were closed and some of the other activities curtailed, it was all the more important that pastors and nurses and the few remaining missionaries maintain personal contacts and vital services. Coïsson reported about a visit he had made along the Anseba River together with *Qeshi* Yohannes Emilios. At Boggu they had visited a woman who was sick. They moved on to Salaba, Raptu, Schi'ib and Quenne, where five Kenisha families lived and where a family waited to have their child baptized. The visitors finally moved on to Muschia.[780]

Qeshi Hezqiel Gulai reported about ten boys and ten girls who came together for instruction.

Early in 1933 Rev. Iwarson paid a visit to Geleb. He was impressed by the development that had taken place there. Well-constructed stone houses, green plantations, trees and a fine church met his eyes. He stated,

> The Kantiba, Oqba-Mikael, is a member of our Church, and so are the majority of the members of the village. The Muslim sub-chief came to greet me, and he too expressed his gratitude. However, perhaps the most moving experience was Kantiba Oqba-Mikael's speech, in which he expressed his gratitude for all that the Mission had accomplished. The members of the congregation now numbered 432.[781]

---

780 SEM/MTBB 1933, 80.
781 SEM/MTBB 1933, 155–156. This is a summary by K. J., not a direct quotation.

Elsie Winqvist when she celebrated her 70th birthday in Asmara. She died in 1957 at the ripe old age of 94 and was buried in Beleza.

Reporting from Kunama where the heat in late April was oppressive, Signe Berg writes,

> Schools were not permitted but we arranged a Bible Course for the Christians. This was held at Ausa [Awsa] Konoma but some Evangelical families came also from Tendar and Ouganna. We divided them into two groups each, meeting 4 hours a day.

Olle Andersson had completed the first two sections of the Catechism in Kunama and had them printed before he left. These were now put to use. As the course progressed, interest grew.[782]

Work on the Translation of the Scriptures

Elsie Winqvist celebrated her 70th birthday on September 4, 1933. The translation team which worked under her, had just completed the revision of the New Testament in Tigrinya and was now working on the Old Testament.[783] In her task of translating the Scriptures, she had

782 SEM/MTBB 1933, 378.
783 SEM/MTBB 1933, 530.

faced several problems owing to the differences in the dialects in the northern and southern parts of the country. Finally the team agreed to use the dialect of Serayé, in the south of Eritrea.[784] One example of the problems they encountered was the rendition of the Tigrinya word for *but*. They had previously used *inte khwoné* (even if), but now found it preferable to use the word *gina* (but).

> Another imperfection which we encountered, she wrote, was the sentence structure. We felt that we were bound by the division of verses. However, Ethiopia's Semitic languages require that a subordinate clause precede the main clause, contrary to the Greek. A long sentence may be divided into several verses. It was thus impossible to follow this rule, and we were obliged to try to join the verses.

She continues,

> We decided to invite our pastors, elders and teachers to a conference which would last for two days and where these proposals would be discussed. There were some discussions as to the right way of spelling words. There are some sounds for which we do not have a sign and others that have several. We agreed to follow the traditional Ethiopian spelling, using two points after each word, even if this is both troublesome and expensive. A consistent pattern of spelling would certainly be much better, but we will have to hasten slowly.[785]

In November 1931, Bairu Uqbit became Winqvist's assistant. His knowledge of Italian, Amharic and Ge'ez was of great help. The team would sit together at the same table under the direction of *Haleqa* Tewolde-Medhin, while Winqvist listened to their discussions. In April 1932, when *Haleqa* had to leave Eritrea and return to Tigrai, Bairu was already initiated into the procedures of their work. The team would sit together working on a section. They would then call upon *Qeshi* Girma-Tsion to assist them with the final wording.

> At times we called Pastor Holmer to assist us, for which task he might take off a couple of days. Our youngest co-worker, the teacher Embaye, was in charge of checking the manuscripts, particularly with regard to orthography, punctuation and preliminary proofreading. He became a

---

784 Memhir Melles Sahle has in fact told the editor that it was the dialect of *Tsillima* in Serayé which was selected. (Ed.)

785 When the complete Bible was published in 1957 Winqvist's proposals were implemented.

Committee for the revision of the Tigrinya New Testament. From left: Bairu Uqbit, Embaye Habte-Egzy, Girma-Tsion Gebre. Right: Elsie Winqvist and Mikael Holmer. Picture from 1933.

Qeshi Mezgebe Woldu with Pastor Mikael Holmer inside the Church of Tse'azzega They worked together as part of a larger team of translators of the Tigrinya Bible. The picture must be from the period after A. Svensson's death in 1928.

valued co-worker.[786]

Rev. A. Tron was also responsible for the printing press. In 1934 John Bunyan's classical work, Pilgrim's Progress, was published in a Tigrinya translation with the title *Mägäddi Kristian,* basically the fruit of Bairu Uqbit's efforts.

Staff

In 1934 it was decided that the large congregations be subdivided into smaller units. The following geographical divisions and assignments were suggested,

Asmara: Rev. Tron (Superintendent) and *Qeshi* Gebrehet Mihtsintu, Assistant.

Addi Gwa'idad and its surroundings: *Qeshi* Gebre-Mikael Tesfa-Lidet

Beleza: *Qeshi* Gebre-Yesus Medhin

Shimanigus La'ilai: *Qeshi* Gebre-Sillassé Habtu,

Zagir: *Qeshi* Tesfu Zeré

Geshinashim: *Qeshi* Tesfu Bairai

Deqqi Mehari: *Qeshi* Kifle Gila-Mikael

Tse'azzega: Rev. Mikael Holmer and *Qeshi* Yihdeggo Desta

Himbirti: *Qeshi* Kahsai Gebre

Ad-Dequ-Tsin'a: *Qeshi* Wolde-Yesus Kinfé

Addi Ugri: *Qeshi* Ande-Mikael Wolde-Menqerios

Quolla Serayé and surroundings: *Qeshi* Gebre-Sillassé Gebru (Addi Hizbai) and *Qeshi* Fisseha (Addi Mana)

Geleb: Mr. E. Coïsson and *Qeshi* Yosef Hemmed

Keren: *Qeshi* Yohannes Emilios Musa

Kunama: *Qeshi* Daniel Luli (Awsa Konoma), *Qeshi* Yosef Mati (Kulluku) and *Qeshi* Hezqiel Gulai (Annalé).[787]

Besides the two ordained missionaries mentioned above there were a few other missionaries in service. The following were responsible for

---

786   SEM/MTBB 1933, 530.
787   SEM/Annual Report 1934, 201–202.

A class in home-making in Tse'azzega. Notice that the names of the girls have been embroidered on the aprons. From the left: Vorka, Katarina, Dahab, Rebka, Gooj, Heddega.

Dolls made by Hanna Holmer as Christmas gifts for children at the Children's home in Tse'azzega. Picture published in 1930.

different tasks in Asmara: Velia Danesi, wife of Alessandro, (she had arrived in Eritrea in 1926) was in charge of the work among women and girls in the congregation. Elsie Winqvist worked on Bible translation and Thérèse De Pertis was responsible for medical work and training. Britta Edlund was in charge of the Beleza station. Mrs. Rosa Holmer took care of the running of a Children's Home at Tse'azzega and her daughter, Signe Holmer, was in charge of the education of youth. In Geleb, Ida Mathieu, wife of Enrico Coïsson (she had arrived in 1928) assisted with the work on the station. Finally, Signe Berg was stationed in Kunama but, as she was also in charge of the Central Treasury, she had to make occasional trips to Asmara.[788]

Andersson to Adwa

When Rev. Olle Andersson and his wife returned to Eritrea in 1934 their main intention was to take up educational work in Tigrai Province. However, Andersson first paid a visit to Kunama with the aim of studying the possibilities of continuing work on Christian literature in the Kunama language. He had hoped that he could work with Kassala as his base, just inside the Sudanese boarder, but this proved impossible. He could remain in Eritrea for only a limited period, and was therefore obliged to move on to Tigrai to take up work as an advisor for the province in matters of Education. He had been called to pay a visit to Addis Ababa for plans on his work and, on his return to Asmara, he was ready to move to Adwa.[789] The Italians had built a paved road from Asmara down to the Mereb River. The rest of the road was, however, only a dirt track, not negotiable by his car. He therefore dismantled the car, whose parts were then carried by Ethiopian soldiers into Adwa, where Andersson reassembled the parts.[790] He had hoped to establish a working system of schools and to serve the Evangelical community. He found, however, that the Governor, Ras Siyum, and particularly his wife, often solicited his services as a driver to places that they wanted to visit. The local army was put on the alert and within a short time a road was constructed from Adwa to Axum.[791] Relations between Andersson

---

788   SEM/Annual Reports 1934, 202–204.
789   SEM/MTBB 1934, 275–276.
790   Puglisi 1952, 158.
791   Hagner to Author.

Olle Hagner and his cherished Ford on a visit to Tse'azzega The car had traveled 15,000 (Fifteen thousand) kilometers without causing too much of a problem! Picture from early nineteen-thirties.

and *Haleqa* Tewolde-Medhin were not the best. The latter was trying to work within the Orthodox Church, a policy that Andersson found difficult to accept. However, Andersson never needed to resolve this predicament since he and his family had to leave when conflict started looming between Italy and Ethiopia.[792] The family returned to Asmara.

The End of the Swedish Mission?

The situation on the Eritrea–Ethiopia boarder was getting more and more tense. In a letter written to the Mission Director in Sweden in May 1935, Olle Andersson reported that he had applied in writing to and received permission from Emperor Haile Selassie for a leave of absence. The reason he had given was that his wife and children were not able to stand the climate. However there was also the question of Italy's preparations for war. The Anderssons therefore returned to

792   SEM/MTBB 1935, 138–140 See also Arén 1999, 455.

Eritrea and settled in Keren.[793]

The situation was tense when the Synod of the ECE met in September 1935. The minutes of the meeting are not extant, except for some short notices that were retrieved later.

Preparations for and the Launching of the War

Italy was preparing for war against Ethiopia. It had transported some 200,000 men to its colonies and another 140,000 were preparing to move to the front. On finding out that Italian troops had crossed the frontier at Awsa, on October 2, 1935, Emperor Haile Selassie called up his forces located some 30 kms from the Eritrean border.

On October 3, 1935, the Italians had crossed the Mereb River separating Eritrea from Ethiopia, launching a three-pronged invasion.[794] There were soon engagements on five key battlefronts, most of which were in Tigrai Province. The Italians captured Adwa on October 6. (Ed.)

Dr Harald Nyström, son of Missionary Karl Nyström, writes,

> Never was a colonial war organized in such a thorough manner. Everything was prepared. All that hundreds of thousands of soldiers needed to do, was to embark on board ships at Naples and Genoa, only to march up to the Eritrean highlands some days later, where rows of tents, beds already made and food already prepared awaited them. The only things the soldiers needed to carry were their rifles and 200 rounds of ammunition each. The rest of their things were brought after them by car, in good order. Nothing was lacking. On the contrary, there was an overabundance of everything, at least during the first six months of the war.[795]

Both De Bono, who arrived in Eritrea in the autumn of 1934, and Badoglio who replaced him at the end of 1935, carried out the final

---

793 SEM/MTBB 1935, 244.

794 There is ample literature on Italy's invasion of Ethiopia, a body of writings which says a lot about Eritrea as a base of operations and about Eritreans as manpower at home and as soldiers abroad. Examples of such books are General Emilio De Bono's *La Preparazione e le Prime Operazioni* (Roma 1937), The Preface and first chapter of Pietro Badoglio's *The War in Abyssinia* (1937), General Quirino Armellini's *Con Badoglio in Etiopia* (With Badoglio in Ethiopia), 1937, especially the chapter entitled "Durante La Preparazione", 61–72, Anthony Mockler's *Haile Sillassé's War* (1985), especially pp. 46–47, 53–54 and Chapter Two of Angelo Del Boca's book *The Ethiopian War. 1935–1941* (1965). (Ed.)

795 Nyström 1937, 188. Nyström served with the Ethiopian forces as a Medical doctor. See also Olle Andersson 1947, 58–59. According to him, Massawa was awash with incoming ships, equipment and goods in the autumn of 1934. (Ed.)

stages of their planning and preparations in Eritrea. Both the SEM and the Kenisha followed these preparations with a growing sense of anxiety. Not a few of the Kenisha must have succeeded in becoming employed in the vast network of preparations, which had become a labour market, although the Kenisha were apparently singled out for discrimination.[796]

That there were a number of Kenisha soldiers in the colonial army is suggested by some small hints in the literature of the time. In his diary entry for December 14, 1939, Olle Hagner writes,

> Gebreselassie [Gebru] told me about our friends in Quolla Serayé, that they were spread out right now and that they could not gather as usual because of the harvest but that they were nevertheless firm in their faith. He said, "The soldiers who are out in the world write often to me and I pass on their news to the recipients concerned."[797]

The war was on and soon the SEM was to find its freedom of movement and action severely curtailed.

The mission in Eritrea had been hit by bitter disappointments on many occasions before. The missionaries felt that, before long, the Government would deliver the final blow and cut them off completely from their mission activities and install Catholic missionaries in their place.[798]

Expulsion Order from Colonial Authorities

The order of expulsion directed at the Swedish missionaries was written on December 6, 1935 but was handed over to the Mission three days later. Rev. Alessandro Tron was requested to present himself at the office of the Government at 12 o'clock on December 9, where he was directed to inform the Swedish missionaries about the content of the ruling, orally. On the 15th of the month they were expected to be ready to hand over all immovable property to the Government and to see to it that all movable property was delivered for safekeeping.

---

796 Olle Andersson 1947, 47–49. See also what Gustavo writes on page 69.
797 OHD/K.J.S. Book 2, 18b. In 1939, as a young man of about 18, a paternal uncle of the editor, [the present Qeshi Elias Habte-Egzy], was whisked away for military service from his home village of Amadir, at the end of a day of farming. He was not even given time to remove the yoke from his oxen. He fought in several battles during the period of Italy's declining military fortunes and witnessed the collapse of the Mettemma Front in northern Ethiopia in 1941 under General Guglielmo Nasi." (Ed.)
798 SEM/Annual Report 1935, 198–200.

It was first believed that the expulsion order included the Waldensian missionaries, the Trons and Coïssons. However, Rev. Alesandro Tron was later informed that these two families would not be expelled but that they would have to cease to have any connections with the Swedish Mission and its congregations. Tron maintained that he already belonged to the pastoral body of the Waldensian Church and that he had been authorized to assist Italian soldiers of Evangelical persuasion in Eritrea. He also stated that his services would be salaried by his Home Church. The answer he received was,

> As Italians you will, of course, not be expelled, but it would probably be better, from our point of view, if you served your Church in Italy and if we could assign some other pastors, who are unknown here, to serve Italian Evangelical soldiers.[799]

The authorities denied that the expulsion of the missionaries had anything to do with religion.

The result was that the churches buildings were not closed. They were transferred to the Evangelical congregations and became their property.

In Closing

The period 1933–1935, with which K. J. has dealt in this chapter, was a time in which a small community struggled, quietly, to maintain the routines of preaching, teaching, serving and healing, under growing pressure and anxiety. The main concern of the SEM and the ECE seems to have been to hold their positions, not to initiate big plans or move on to new areas of activity. The ECE was a house trying to do its best with diminishing resources and shrinking elbowroom. "Business as usual." was the message that the SEM and the ECE wanted to communicate to the colonial authorities. Worship, pastoral work in town and country, the distribution of Christian literature, encouraging the faithful to contribute even more to the financial upkeep of their congregations: these were some of the activities which were carried out at the grass roots level. The training of deaconesses, continuing work on the translation of the Bible to Tigrinya, printing edifying literature and contributing to evangelistic work in Tigrai, were important areas of responsibility of the church at large.

---

799   SEM/Annual Report 1935, 201.

Visit to Geleb, 1934.
Sitting in front: Signe
Holmer with the Coïsson
children, Mario to the
left and Anna Lisa to the
right.
Seated: Girma-Tsion,
Dawit, Ida Coïsson.
Back row: Mikael
Holmer, Yosef Hemmed,
Gebre-Yesus.

However, the church was never given a respite. In 1935, Italy struck from Eritrean soil and the invasion of Ethiopia was a fact. Eritrea, which the SEM and their Kenisha colleagues had once conceived as a bridgehead for a missionary outreach to the Oromo, now became a spring board for a military invasion. With this phase of Italy's colonial venture, the curtain fell on the SEM and, to a certain extent, on the ECE. A new period of *exile* descended on the Kenisha, an experience of isolation and homelessness in their homeland.

At the time of writing, the ECE [read ELCE], once worried about its very existence under Italian rule, is still alive and working in Eritrea, almost seventy years after the collapse of the Italian colonial administration. K. J.'s brief but compact treatment of the period has given us instructive glimpses into the life of a struggling minority church, at the end of five decades of an ambitious Italian colonial adventure. (Ed.)

Chapter Twenty two

The Price They Paid

Introduction

The ageing kes Gebra Medhen, now wracked with pain [...], he who was once beaten mercilessly for the sake of the Gospel at the time of persecution when Lager died a martyr's death [...] made a deep impression on me. There was warmth in the look of the old man.[800] I had the same impression when I met the aged Indrias, the widow of Hailab [Haile-Ab] the priest, who stood by Lager's side in a confession which held fast to the very gates of death. When I visited her in her simple but orderly hut the day after and brought her greetings from Mrs. Lundahl, her face shined. In the course of our conversation I asked her, among other things, how old she was. "Who can know that?" she

---

800 I must admit that I can't identify the "kes Gebra Medhen" who is named in this connection. He can't possibly be *Qeshi* Gebre-Medhin Tesfai, the father of Qeshi Tewolde-Medhin Gebre-Medhin, who died in the battle between Tse'azzega and Hazzega at Wekki Dibba already in July 1876. In a letter written on November 22, 1873, Lager states that "[...] four of our brothers in the faith in Hamasen have been recently arrested by the authorities." Among them he mentions the deacons 'Habta Georges' and 'Madhan'. Could Kolmodin be referring to the latter? See Hellström 1989, 15. (Ed.)

broke out, with hands stretched out and a smile on her face? She then continued, "It is 31 years since my husband died."[801] (Ed.)

These words are part of the description of the reception given to Adolf Kolmodin when he arrived in Asmara from Massawa on October 7, 1908. Indeed, Indrias didn't remember exactly how old she was. After all, what did that matter? There were more important things to remember. The death of her husband, *Qeshi* Haile-Ab Tesfai, to take one example![802]

Indrias was not alone on this journey of sorrow and adjustment to life without one's life companion. She had a fellow pilgrim, a comrade in arms from a far away country. The name of this fellow pilgrim is Bengta Lager, the widow of Per Erik Lager who was put to the sword with Haile-Ab outside the Church of Qiddus Miki'el in Addi Qontsi on July 17, 1876. On the day when Indrias met Kolmodin in Asmara, Bengta Lager was in the USA, an immigrant from both Eritrea and Sweden, perhaps a fugitive from the places and people who would remind her of the great sorrow in her life.

A section of a letter by her, dated August 15, 1876 and written in Geleb about a month after her husband fell to the sword, reads,

> For the first four days and nights after Lager's death I was confined to such a difficult prison that I can't describe [my situation] with words. Sometimes, as many as eight soldiers would be in my room, besides a number of soldiers riddled by bullets and mutilated by the sword. I was ordered to apply bandages to their wounds. As I did so, I thought in my heart, "Oh! If only my friend [meaning her late husband] would be here, regardless of the seriousness of his wounds! How wonderful that would have been! But, no! He lay there, food for birds and wild animals, until Wednesday, when they buried him. Several times I had begged to be allowed to approach Woldo Mikael, for permission to bury him. Impossible!"[803]

801 A. Kolmodin 1909, 48. Lager and Haile-Ab were killed on July 17, 1876.
802 Indrias was apparently hesitant to commit herself fully to the Evangelical cause while her husband lived. Soon however her commitment to the faith for which her husband had given his life became obvious. In her biography on Per Eric Lager, Rosa Holmer writes, "From a notice written in 1879, we can read that she and four other women came to Månssons and said, "We want to be in deep fellowship with our Saviour and eat His body and drink his blood for the forgiveness of sins in Holy Communion, and give our hearts to him." Holmer 1937, 173–174. (Ed.)
803 See Beskow 1884, 235–238. Bengta Lager's name is found in the official register of "legally qualified doctors" of the State of Illinois, published by the health board of the State in 1902. There it is recorded that she was a registered doctor as of 1885 (i.e. one year before the first Swedish female doctor in Sweden, Karolina Widerström, graduated!). According to the same source she died in Chicago in 1913. (Ed.)

On the day when Kolmodin met Indrias in Asmara, perhaps Bengta too, then a medical doctor in Chicago, Illinois, said to herself, "It is 31 years since my husband died."[804]

The Different Faces of Persecution

In September 1874, Emperor Yohannes was ready to round up the *Bible Readers* (the Kenisha) who had been accused before him of heresy. Gustav Arén writes,

> The thing leaked out. A friend of the reformers made for Tse'azzega as fast as he could and warned them of the impending arrest. They gathered immediately in their church for secret counsel. The same night in early September 1874, over thirty people, old and young, followed Haile-Ab's advice by making a voluntary exodus into Egyptian-held territory to avoid certain death. Aged and handicapped people and others, went into hiding instead. In recalling the event Selomon and Zer'a-Tsion saw God's wonderful mercy in the concord that they experienced: Whether fleeing or hiding "not one wife opposed the will of her husband." Some of their friends in Hamasen could not be warned in time or neglected to put themselves out of harm's way before the persecution broke out towards the end of 1874. Then everyone found in possession of a copy of the printed Scriptures was imprisoned and had his property confiscated.[805] (Ed.)

The narrative entitled *Nai Wängel Birhan ab Hamasen kämäy ilu käm z'aton käm itägältsen* (How the Light of the Gospel Entered and was Revealed in Hamasen), written in *Birhan Yikun* by *Qeshi* Selomon and *Qeshi* Zer'a-Tsion in 1912, contains records of some of the earliest cases of persecution and martyrdom among the Kenisha. There is also an interesting account on the difficulties faced by Evangelical Christians at the station at Geleb at this time, and of how some of them were helped to escape. A section of the said account reads,

---

804   Lager and Haile-Ab were killed on July 17, 1876. Bengta Lager left Eritrea for Sweden on November 4, 1876. In 1881 she immigrated to the USA and settled in Chicago where she worked as a medical doctor, married and took the surname Carlson. The last sign of life from her was an article written about her in 1911 in a periodical entitled *Korsblomman* and published by EFS (The SEM) in 1911. See also SEM/MTBB, nr 23, 2003. (Ed.)

805   Arén 1978, 179–180. (Ed.)

Indrias (the widow of Qeshi Haile-Ab Tesfai) and her disciples. Picture taken on October 20, 1908 in connection with the visit of Professor A. Kolmodin.

There was a generous handmaiden of the Lord by the name of Mrs Beata Carlsson. Those who could not flee, the ones like Segid Zemouy, Debbas Negasi, Gebre-Mariam Medhin and his brother Zer'é, Gebre-Ab Girmai, and Yosef Zer'a-Tsion, she tucked in, like lambs, under the bed. Others, who were a little older, she hid in her home, having dressed them to conceal their identity. She became deeply worried when Bashai Habtu came to her home. To dissuade him from searching her house, she gave him a shotgun with two barrels. When better times came, she sent her protégés to Imkullu.[806]

One of the things to which the fathers of the Kenisha reacted was dependence on the type of literature known as *gädl* (the *contendings*

---

806 *Birhan Yikun* 1912, 195. For more details on the death of Lager and Haile-Ab, the two first martyrs of the SEM/ECE, see BY 1912, 193, Rosa Holmer 1937, 170–172 and A. Kolmodin 1909, 245 ff. On their flight to the coast not a few Kenisha died of Malaria and other causes of exhaustion and debility. BY 1912, 193. (Ed.)

of the saints and martyrs, as it has been described).[807] There is no pressing need to reintroduce this category of literature into the Evangelical tradition in which the Kenisha stand. However, it should be pointed out that those who did suffer for their faith among the Kenisha are in fact remembered with admiration and reverence. K. J. was fully aware of this sentiment within the ECE. His text, which has been compiled from different, longer references to this subject, follows. (Ed.)

Persecution in the District of Addi Ugri

Early in 1926 the Holmers reported on the situation in their area, particularly in view of the increased pressure on the Evangelical Church and the SEM. They wrote,

> For some of our people, this year has been a period of severe pressure from the enemies of the Gospel, spearheaded by a powerful local ruler, Dedjach Kidane-Mariam Gebre-Mesqel, who lives in Areza, some forty kms west of Addi Ugri.[808] Some of those who had embraced the Gospel and joined us were made to feel his heavy hand. He is particularly keen on being known as one who keeps his area free from Tséré Mariam, the enemies of St Mary. At the beginning of March one of our members was put in prison and kept in detention for three weeks. The ruler was clever enough to give not religion but a different pretext for the arrest, and it was therefore impossible to plead the cause of the prisoner either before the commissioner or the government. On releasing the prisoner, he sentenced him to high fines and ordered him to leave his village. However, later the commissioner allowed him to return home. Another member, who ran the risk of being imprisoned, succeeded in fleeing and was later allowed to return.
>
> Once again the faithful have been threatened with deportation from their home areas. After a long delay, the commissioner opened the case. The reasons given by the ruler was that a member of the Evangelical Church had defamed the Ark of the Covenant [tabot] and that another one had visited some priests and misled them. Both of the accused were

---

807   Wallis Budge's translation of *Mätsehafä Gädlä Hawaryat* has, precisely, the title *The Contendings of the Apostles!* (Budge 1901). (Ed.)

808   Kidane-Mariam Gebre-Mesqel was born in 1862 and was considered to be the most faithful local ruler by the Italians, up to 1941. In 1938 he was appointed *Ra'si* by Vice King Amadeo d'Aosta. Puglisi 1952, 82.

Church and congregation in Addi Ugri. Picture taken after the dedication on April 13, 1925, in the presence of Mission Director Nils Dahlberg.

Qeshi Yihdeggo Desta, teacher i Adu Ugri, with his wife Abrehet and their first son.
Picture published 1938.

given strict orders by the commissioner not to propagate their faith. They were, however, allowed to return to their home villages.[809]

Persecution in Quolla Serayé

The actions against the Kenisha in Quolla Serayé continued as *Ra'si* Kidane-Mariam renewed his accusations. Three leading members of the Evangelical Church in that area were arrested and sent to forced-labour camps for a lengthy period. They were Kebté Selomon from Addi Gaba, Uqba-Mikael from Deqqi Werasi and Yohannes Imnetu from Deqqi Taez. Uqba-Mikael went through an especially gruesome time as he suffered from leprosy and was incapable of engaging in hard labour, to which he was assigned at the salt mines. However, as he was found to be literate, he was given the task of teaching the other inmates and thus found an opportunity to witness about Christ.[810]

One of the first Evangelical Christians in Quolla Serayé was a woman, by the name of *Addei* Amleset, from Addi Belsäy, a village close to Debre-Merqorios. After having embraced Evangelical Christianity, she was forced to leave the district of Afelba, but had no place to go to. She was summoned to court and came there alone. She was then told that she should bring a male advocate who could speak on her behalf. She answered, defiantly: "I have no man as my advocate. Christ is my advocate!" As a result, she was immediately expelled from the district. She then went to Addi Ugri where she found a refuge in the compound of the Swedish Mission. She stayed there for several years with her two children.[811]

---

809   SEM/MT 1926, 63.

810   Yosef Gebre-Wold to Gustav Arén, September 9, 1971, also reported in Arén 1999, 224–225. At a meeting where the *Qeshi* Elias Habtezgy and the author as well as the leadership of the Mahbere Hawariat were present in April 1998, a former associate and worker with *Ra'si* Kidane-Mariam stated rather emphatically that it was the Italian commissioner who was responsible for the violations against the members of the Evangelical Church, not Kidane-Mariam as such.

811   Report by *Qeshi* Elias Habtezgy to author, May 8, 2002.

Persecution in Himbirti

Another story was reported from Himbirti. The local Church Register carries the name of a lady by the name of Hiriti Hidru, born in 1897.[812] The Church elders retold, vividly, the story of the life of this woman, a narrative that had been kept alive for more than 75 years. Early in 1926 Mrs. Louise Iwarson had written an article in the mission paper describing the story in question,

> This woman had attended the school at Beleza. She was the daughter of the chief in her home village and had been married to a man from Tsilima. After some time, however, her husband abandoned her. Later she was happily married to a man of Evangelical persuasion in Himbirti. The Abyssinian priests had tried to persuade him to return to the Orthodox Church, but he had refused. Her husband died, however, suddenly and the priests refused to bury him as he was considered to be an unbeliever. Hiriti then dug a grave near their hut and buried him there, reading portions of Scripture and laying him to rest with three shovels of earth. This made a very deep impression on all present.[813]

Some Gratifying News

In 1929 Iwarson again expressed his concern for the men who had been expelled from their homes already in March 1927, because they had conducted prayer meetings.[814] Early in May 1930 Mrs. Iwarson writes,

> We have some gratifying news. Three of our imprisoned brethren from Addi Ugri district have been released. According to the Government, the fourth one has been ordered to remain in custody, for some unknown reason, but we trust that he too will be released. He has a wife and seven children who are dependent on him. The local ruler, Ra'si Kidane-Mariam who arrested them three years ago, has now changed his attitude.
>
> Rev. Iwarson, *Qeshi* Gebre Sillassé Gebru from Addi Hizbay, *Haleqa* Kahsay and *Abba* Haile Mariam visited the ruler a week ago. They were exceedingly well received, and the ruler even asked *Qeshi* Gebre Sillassé Gebru for forgiveness for the way he had mistreated him. Iwarson felt that, from an Abyssinian point of view, this was something

812   Shown to the author, December 2, 2001 in Himbirti church.
813   SEM/MT 1926, 155–156.
814   SEM/MTBB 1929, 477–478.

unprecedented. In the words of Mrs Iwarson,

> The ruler made a return visit the following Saturday and we invited him to dinner together with his men. He has given a solemn oath that he shall no longer persecute our Christians and that they would be free to hold their meetings and confess their faith.[815]

Aboy Kebté – A Sturdy Kenisha of the Old Stock

Aboy (Father) Kebté won a name for steadfastness under trials and tribulations. Karl Johan Lundström met him in person in the nineteen-fifties at the lowland village of Addi Gaba where he and *Qeshi* Yihdeggo from Mendefera were to hold a Bible Week. Kebté had a chance to reminisce with K. J. and *Qeshi* Yihdeggo.

In an article entitled *On a Bible Week in Addi Gaba*, K. J. writes,

> The village is not exactly centrally located! [...] The path descended almost without interruption, for three hours. And down there, a glorious Kunama heat awaited us![816]

> [...] There is an old man in the village and his name is Kebte. He was the first Evangelical Christian in the village, having come to faith through a study of the Bible. Ras Kidane-Mariam, the head of the province, was not happy about this and reported the case to the current government, which put Kebté in prison. *Abboy* [Father] Kebté had to do forced labour for four years at Adi Qeyih. That was 25 years earlier. Ras Kidane-Mariam is dead. But as Kebté sat there with the large group of Evangelical Christians around him, and sang so that the mountains reverberated with echoes, his face shined and he said, "Imagine if the *Ra'si* had lived to see this!"

In Closing

It is to be remembered that the title of the present chapter reads *The Price They Paid*. To whom does the word *they* refer? Thus far we have let it apply primarily to Swedish missionaries and their Kenisha colleagues. However we are also justified in asking the question: Were the Swedish missionaries and the Kenisha the only ones who paid a price in the course of the planting and growth of the ECE? Or was the preaching of

---

815   SEM/MTBB 1930, 275.
816   "Kunama heat" in this connection simply means *intense heat*.

Memhir Gobezé Goshu, from Tigrai, with members of his family after his release from a stay of some months in prison in 1923, for the sake of his Evangelical faith.

the Gospel, as the Swedish missionaries and their Kenisha colleagues understood it, a venture in which other parties too paid a price?

Our answer to this question must face the fact that the preaching of this Gospel resulted not only in joy and freedom for many a conscience, but also in sorrow, bitterness and alienation among the members of many a family in Eritrea. At least for a time. The parents of *Qeshi* Gebre-Ewostatewos (*Qeshi* Ze-Mikael and Woizero Wolete-Tatios), whose story we have already narrated, paid a bitter price for the decision made by their only son. To quote Gustav Arén,

> Derision and contempt befell his (Gebre-Ewostatewos) parents. The disgrace of having his son branded as an apostate was hard for them to bear. Ze-Mikael said that he would rather be told that his only son had died than hear people say that he had become a *Tserä Mariam* (Mary's enemy).[817]

817   Arén 1978, 376.

Permit me to insert a short anecdote, with personal connections. My father, Ato Gebremedhin Habte-Egzy (1900–1980), was a young deacon and cantor (singer) at the Orthodox Church of *Arba'te Inssissa* (The Four Beasts) in the village of Amadir, in Serayé, before he became an Evangelical Christian. The move that he took (by undergoing Confirmation in Tse'azzega under Pastor Anders Svensson), was regarded as a scandal both in his family and in the Church community in which he was loved and appreciated. His mother, a woman of strong will and deep emotions, felt that she had lost her first born. Often she sighed, "*Wai wädei! Wai wädei!*" (O my son! O my son!). However one day something happened which made her decide that there was a limit to the price that she was prepared to pay in grieving the loss of her son to another faith, as she conceived the move taken by her son. Some of her female friends came to her and urged her to take her son to the monastery of *Abunä Buruk* [Enda Abunä Buruk Amlak], which was believed to possess powers to heal diseases and drive out demons. There was, in all likelihood, some well-engineered irony behind their suggestion that her son was demon-possessed. If so, the stratagem did succeed. Their words caused my grandmother to react with anger. She had paid the price of deep sorrow when her son left the church of his forefathers. She was not prepared to pay the unthinkable price of concluding that he had become demon-possessed. She answered defiantly,

> How dare you suggest that my intelligent son has become demon-possessed? I told you that he had erred, not that he had lost his mind!

Her friends then answered, "Well then, stop murmuring!" In time our grandmother became reconciled to the painful fact that her husband, her eldest child, (and later all of his brothers) had become Evangelical Christians. But none of them had become despisers of father and mother, of home and hearth, of clan and tribe, of country and folk. The price that Orthodox parents and relatives in Eritrea had paid, in shock and pain, when their kith and kin became Kenisha, eventually evolved into a tacit truce, a mutual understanding which bestowed a good measure of harmony upon everyday life.

Such an evolution underlines the truth that even difficult decisions rarely lead to a permanent state of estrangement among human beings, when motivated by a sober and responsible conscience. In the

Per Eric Lager killed outside of the Church of Qiddus Mikael, Addi Qontsi, in 1876.

Gustaf Arrehnius died in Khartoum in 1882, in connection with the Second Oromo Expedition.

vast majority of cases, this happy state of affairs eventually prevailed among the Kenisha and their kith and kin as well as other Eritreans. They found a *modus vivendi*, a way of living together.

No one can claim exclusive credit for the efforts made to bring about such a sate of things. Many a Kenisha would surely recall St. Paul's words in First Corinthians 1:31 "Let him who boasts boast in the Lord." That, after all, is the liberating truth that they had heard through the preaching of the Gospel of unmerited grace. (Ed.)

Epilogue

The Evangelical Vision:
Renewal without Revolt

By Ezra Gebremedhin

Introduction

K. J. Lundström didn't get a chance to write a final epilogue to this book. Nevertheless, I would like to give him the privilege of the last word, at least in part. He used to flavour his conversations with occasional doses of Tigrinya sayings. One of them reads: *Säb ammami, Izgi fetsami!* (Man proposes but God disposes!)

He had hoped to complete the writing of the history of the ECE. His plans and labours were, however, cut short by a mortal sickness. When he started working on his assignment, neither he nor I had the slightest notion that I would be involved in its completion. If he were to be given the opportunity to say something now, K. J. would probably quote the same Tigrinya saying again: *Säb ammami, Izgi fetsami.* (Man proposes but God disposes), as a commentary on the final shape that his book on the history of the ECE took.

The saying has created some associations within me. For many a Tigrinya speaking person, the words quoted above imply that the realization of man's dreams and efforts are dependent, in the last analysis, on God's will. For a Kenisha, the saying may even strike a special chord on the harp of the Gospel understood as Good News (Tigrinya: *Bishirat or Bisirat*). It suggests, in effect, that man's destiny, his salvation, depends, in the last analysis, not on man's intentions and resolve but rather on God's undeserved grace and mercy. This was the core of the message of the missionaries from far away Sweden. This was the Good News that had captured the hearts of the priests of the Church of Qiddus Giorgis in Tse'azzega. The Evangelical Lutheran (read: Kenisha) cry, *soli Deo gloria* (glory to God alone), can be regarded as a confirmation and maximization of the popular saying: *Säb ammami, Izgi fetsami!* Many a guilt ridden soul has found peace of conscience through this message.

The second association that I have in mind has to do with the attitudes of Swedish missionaries to the traditions and cultures of Eritrea. K. J.'s use of this saying (and it was not the only one that he used) was a *"Yes"* to both language and culture in an Eritrean setting. For him too, the aim of Evangelical mission in Eritrea was spiritual renewal without revolt against history and culture. In this regard, he was an heir to a time-honoured Swedish missionary tradition.

Respect for Tradition

The effort to maintain harmony between faith and tradition is, in a sense, a reflection of the ethos out of which the Swedish mentors of the Kenisha came. Sweden was a country with a history of powerful kings, a state church, jealously preserved historical landmarks, and a national/regional heritage held with pride. In short, the Swedish missionaries reinforced some of their own values among their Eritrean coreligionists. The Kenisha never became iconoclastic (i.e. radically destructive) of the tradition of their forebears.

Let us take some examples. The Kenisha don't follow any calendar of angels and saints as a matter of religious conviction or obligation. Nevertheless, in their associations with other Christians in Eritrea, they felt at home in the popular aspects of the *Orthodox* calendar of angels and saints within the framework of the Julian calendar. A Kenisha of the old stock could very well say,"So and so was born on Hidar Mikael", meaning, that the person in question was born on Hidar 12, according to the Julian [Ge'ez], calendar (ca. November 20 according to the Gregorian calendar). And other Kenisha would understand him or her, without raising eye-brows at the use of the name of an angel in everyday life.

Traditional marriage practices pertinent to specific areas in Eritrea were followed strictly among the Kenisha, as long as they did not contradict the norms of Evangelical faith and practice.[818] Though ascetic in their general life-style, the missionaries of the SEM did not prevent their children in the faith from drinking *ssewa* (traditional beer) and *mes* (a fermented variant of *honey mead*). What the missionaries and Eritrean pastors pleaded for was moderation. In this respect too, the Kenisha maintained an important link with traditional Eritrean culture.

Neglect of Local Musical Heritage

There is one issue related to culture about which the Swedish missionaries (and perhaps those Kenisha who helped them) could have displayed more insight. They and their Eritrean co-workers translated a great number of hymns, lock, stock and barrel, from Swedish and Italian hymn books. The contents of these hymns are often profound and generations of Kenisha have received both instruction and comfort from them. Those groomed, from childhood, in the melodies to which the hymns are set, sing them very well. However, Olle Hagner, a missionary and an accomplished musician, writes something to the effect that many Kenisha scream forth rather than sing these songs.[819]

Olle Hagner was somewhat astonished to discover that a hymn sang at funerals among the Kenisha was actually set to the melody of the Swedish national anthem.[820] Hardly any chance seems to have been given to Eritreans to compose music and texts on the basis of their own culture. For the Swedish and Italian missionaries, translating church documents from Swedish or Italian into Tigrinya or Tigré was the quickest and surest way of promoting congregational worship. Nevertheless the fact remains that the formation of the hymnody should have paid far greater attention to the musical heritage of the

---

818   For an excellent presentation of the customary laws of Highland Eritrea (H'ghin s'rAtin endabba) see the article by Gebre H. Tesfagiorgis in *Traditions of Eritrea. Linking the Past and the Present*, [Tesfa Gebremedhin, editor]. 2008, 1–36. (Ed.)

819   (OHD/K.J.S. October 29, 1939, Book 1, p.5). See Mezmur Selam 241. (Ed.)

820   (OHD/K.J.S. April 15, 1940, Book 2, p. 34). (Ed.)

A feature of Swedish culture on Eritrean soil! Kenisha youth 'mobilized' into celebrating the Swedish festival of Santa Lucia, which falls on December 13, according to the Gregorian calendar. The young man to the far left looks very much like the late Dr Emmanuel Gebre-Selassé!

people among whom the hymns were to be used.

We also have the question of the traditional dances, generally known as *gwaila*. Guardians of the spiritual wellbeing of the Evangelical

Church of Eritrea and the Lutheran Church of Eritrea maintain that the prohibition of *gwaila* was introduced for fear that the combination of alcoholic beverages and youthful competition around the coveted *koboro* (drum) on festive occasions, would lead their children in the faith into fights and immoral behaviour. Their fears were justified and the prohibition of *gwaila* has had its protective functions among generations of Kenisha. However, the fact remains that this prohibition has created a measure of estrangement from a widespread, and culturally relevant, feature of the life of the rest of Eritrea. This is especially true of the Post World War II development in the cultural practices of Eritreans, in the country and abroad.

The SEM may have contributed to making the Kenisha a "non-dancing" people. However, in return, they groomed them into a singing community. Singing was, for decades, the distinguishing mark of members the ECE and LCE–a heritage which permeated their lives and followed them through thick and thin. At least those of the old stock among the Kenisha sang at their own homes, often both morning and evening. They sang at work, at the grinding stone, at the steaming earth-oven, at the water-well or at the river where one washed clothes or watered cattle. They sang while walking or sitting. They sang their hymns as lullabies to their sleepy children. They sang at their weddings and baptisms. They sang by the bedside of the sick and dying and, above all, at their funerals, the funerals of others and in houses of mourning. Kenisha of all ages and of both sexes sang together, in groups or individually. If we may say so reverently, their singing became a way of entertaining, encouraging and socialising with their fellow Eritreans of other religious convictions. What the Kenisha had lost by way of social contact with their fellow Eritreans, through abstaining from *gwaila*, they gained through becoming a singing community. Kenisha hymns are on the whole soft and inclusive. These hymns cover all situations in life. In this respect, the hymns have had something of a centripetal effect on their surroundings. They pull in and embrace.[821]

---

821 For more details in the treatment of this and similar topics see the editor's article in Ezra Gebremedhin 2005, 119–213.

The Orthodox Church of Qiddist Maryam in Asmara. Picture published 1926.

Lasting Respect for Fellow Eritreans

Most of the older pastors and lay people in the ECE had their roots in the Orthodox Tewahdo Church and maintained their respect for it. This is reflected by the attitude of a well known Kenisha pastor. In 1889 *Qeshi* Marqos Girmai, a Kenisha graduate from the Institute of Theology at Johannelund in Stockholm, gave a highly sophisticated lecture on the Orthodox Tewahdo Church, a church which he defended passionately before a Swedish audience as *our church*, without thereby absolving this ancient church of what he felt were its shortcomings.[822]

The Kenisha shared the joys and sorrows of their Orthodox, Catholic and Muslim relatives and compatriots. They took part in baptisms, weddings, funerals and other social and family events. Through mission

822 Markus Germei 1889, 191–219.

schools and clinics opened with the help of the Swedish mission and sponsored by the Kenisha, rural Eritrean communities were able to benefit from the availability of education and medical care for their children and families. In this sense, the Kenisha became mediators of benefits to the society of which they were a part. When all is said and done, the return and reintegration of the Kenisha into the highlands and other parts of Eritrea, was to the benefit of all parties involved. To this very day, the Kenisha remain a basically well-integrated part of Eritrean society.

This fact called forth the respect of Eritrean communities. The dramatic reception that was given to Adolf Kolmodin on his visit to Geleb in 1908 was a reflection of this truth. Almost the entire male population of the town came out to receive him, led by their chief *Kentiba Tesfamkel*. Kolmodin's approach to the town was welcomed by a fanfare of flutes, and by Evangelical hymns.[823] The town gave Kolmodin a big ox as a welcome present. About this ox Kolmodin writes,

> I heard later on that there was a little story around this ox. As a calf, it had been set aside as a gift to the former governor Di Martini, who was expected to pay the town a visit just before his departure from the colony. He never came and the young calf grew up to become a big ox. And now, I (i.e. the Mission) received him instead.[824]

Which Way Forward?

Having observed the work of both the Catholic missionary order known as the Capuchins and the Swedish Mission in Eritrea, Renato Paoli, an Italian Catholic traveller in the colony in 1906, was impressed by the affluence and orderliness of the Swedish Mission. He expressed his admiration, but nevertheless criticized the Protestants and their methods,

> Your religion seems to me, personally, antipathetic and unsuitable for the colony. A cold and white religion, just like your churches, speaks, if it speaks at all, to the head and not to the heart. This is surely not for us Latins. [825]

823　A. Kolmodin 1909, 135. (Ed.)
824　A. Kolmodin 1909, 137. (Ed.)
825　Jonathan Miran 2002, 126, quoting, in translation, a text from Renato Paoli 1908, 182. (Ed.)

A meeting of teachers in Beleza, December 30, 1908, during the visit of A. Kolmodin.

It was not the last time that similar challenges would be hurled at the SEM and the Kenisha by other Christians in their surroundings. One can of course question if the picture of Swedish Protestantism in Eritrea, painted by Paoli, provides the reader with a fair evaluation of Evangelical spirituality and indigenous Kenisha worship at the time. However, the question remains: Can Kenisha in the twenty-first century afford to be indifferent to the challenges directed at them by honest people like Renato Paoli, challenges which are still voiced by kindred spirits among both Eritreans and expatriates?

Having taken upon myself the task of editing and partly adding to this work on the history of the Kenisha, I realize that I cannot also put on, with any convincing sense of modesty, the mantle of a prophet. However, as a stakeholder in the fortunes of the community whose story I too have tried to tell, I hope that I would be forgiven for expressing a wish or two on the future of this community. In his two books, *Exclusion and Embrace* (Abingdon 1996) and *Free of Charge* (Zondervan 2005), the brilliant Yale theologian, Miroslav Volf, has developed the theme of the primeval, unconditional love of God. Ours is a world in which people inflict wounds and suffer wounds. It is a planet which creates and cultivates divisions, gradations, classifications, and categorizations with far reaching implications. Miroslav Wolf, who writes out of his own firsthand experience of teaching in Croatia during the war in former Yugoslavia, is not a stranger to this reality. What is striking is that he cites Martin Luther's teaching on God's unmerited love and grace as a potent source for the healing of sores, bitterness and alienation even in the twenty-first century. He writes,

> [...] as Luther stated, because God's love isn't caused by its object, it can love those that are not lovable, "sinners, evil persons, fools, and weaklings in order to make them righteous, good, wise, and strong". Luther concluded, "rather than seeking its own good, the love of God flows forth and bestows good." Such divine love is supremely manifested on the cross on which Jesus Christ took the sin of the world upon himself.[826]

To work out the everyday implications of this kind of love at home, at work and in one's larger community, is a tall order. But it is evidently the life-programme to which Kenisha are called.

Maintaining respect for history and a sound cultural heritage, while longing and working for an ongoing spiritual renewal, are two sides of one and the same coin. In a healthy spiritual community, the two factors interact with and correct each other. Dynamic life always implies preservation and innovation. One is reminded of the words of Jesus in Matthew 13:52,

> Therefore every teacher of the law who has been instructed about the kingdom of heaven is like the owner of a house who brings out of his storeroom new treasures as well as old.

To learn to know one's own store-room of historical and spiritual values and to use both the old and new treasures within this storeroom is the challenge facing the Evangelical Lutheran Church of Eritrea. In a sense, this book by Karl Johan Lundström is a modest invitation to look into one's own store room. The still pending study of the history of the ECE for the period after 1935 is an important part of the acquisition of further knowledge about the same store-room. It will, hopefully, also contribute to sound innovation, to the shaping of the future of a small but significant Eritrean religious community. One would hope that the continuation of the recording of this history would be the concern of the Swedish Evangelical Mission, the Evangelical Lutheran Mission

– Bibeltrogna Vänner (ELMBV) and all Kenisha who now belong to the one Evangelical Lutheran Church of Eritrea. (Ed.)

826   Volf 2005 38–39. (Ed.)

Portraits of six boys whose education was financed by different mission groups in Sweden. Front row: Gebre-Ab, Gebre-Giorgis, Daniel and Wolde-Mikael. Back row: Gebre-Egziabher and Birhané. Portraits published in the SEM Periodical in 1883.

Six young students from the school of Lundahl in Imkullu, 1884. Front row from left: 1. Bihil 2. Petros 3. Kidane-Mariam. Back row: 4. Mehari 5. Habte-Mariam 6. Natnael.

Appendix I

On Eritrean Staff by the End of 1924 and 1930

Staff by the end of 1924

Local staff: Serving as Pastors, Teachers and Evangelists

ASMARA: *Qeshi* Girma-Tsion Gebre, Firezgi Gebre-Mikael, Afeworqi, Gebre-Mikael Teodros, Mihtsintu, Berhe Zemmu, Redda-Tsadiq, Gebrat Giliat, Yishaq Tewolde-Medhin, Tesfu Derso, Sebhatu Daniel (?), Bahlibi Garza (medical), Indrias Haile-Ab (female)[827], Hanetsa Mebrahtu (female).

TSE'AZZEGA: Debbas Negasi, *Qeshi* Fisseha-Tsion Fisseha (?), *Qeshi* Wolde-Yesus Kinfé, Mezgebe Woldu, Gebre-Le'ul Tirfé, Segid Zemui, Kahsay Gebre, Gubsa Tikwabo, Bekhit Habelom, Habte-Mariam Tesfa-Mariam, Beyin Dafla, Gebre-Sillassé Tesfa-Gabir, Abba Gebre-Sillassé Mengistu (Abba Ma'asho), Wolde-Gabir Habte-Tsion, Tekle-Haimanot Gebre, Wolde-Kristos, Mebrahtu Samuel, Yohannes Fitiwi, Gebre-Sillassé Habtu, Indrias Gebre-Le'ul, Tek'a Lidet (?) (female), Tibé Tessema (female).

BELEZA: *Qeshi* Tewolde-Medhin Gebre-Medhin, Zeré Kafil, *Qeshi* Selomon Atsqu (retired), *Qeshi* Zer'a-Tsion Musé, Teklu Uqbai (retired), Tesfu Bairai, Gebrehet Mihtsintu, Gebre-Yesus Medhin (?) Teklé Ristu, Yosef Selomon, Debesai Mengesha, Kifle Gila-Mikael (?), Tesfa-Mikael Gebru , Sereqé (?) Tesfu Zeré, Simret Bihil (Retired) Beyin Ristu, Gedel, Tesfazgy, Kidane Zer'u, Amlesom, Gebre-Mesqel, Nigusé, Woldenki'el, Yfter Tesfa-Egzy, Simret, (retired), Jemmer. Female workers: Tsehaitu Ni'amin, Lette-Tsion Gebre-Mariam, Aster Woldemariam, Elsabet Habte-Tsion, Hagosa Mengis.

---

827 If the name refers to the widow of the well-known *Qeshi* Haile-Ab Tesfai, then the
     surname Haile-Ab cannot apply to her.

ADDI UGRI: Tewolde-Berhan Gebre, Yihdeggo Desta, Uqba-Mikael, Sebhat-Le'ab, Haile Mariam, Tekié, Berhane Gishen, Tesfanki'el Gebre. Female workers: Bitchir, Lette-Birhan Habtu.

GELEB: Dawit Amanuel, Alazar Hemmed, Yishaq Hemmed, Yosef Hemmed, Natnael Negasi, Abraham Etel, Tesfa-Le'ul Hibtes, Iyassu Be'imnet, Yishaq Be'imnet, Timotewos Faid, Samuel Etman, Yohannes Emilios Musa, Uqba-Gabir Zer'u (?), Marta Barnabas (female).

KUNAMA: Yosef, Yaqob Sada, Stefano Badi.

Staff by the end of 1930

Local staff: Serving as Pastors, Teachers and Evangelists

ASMARA: *Qeshi* Girma-Tsion Gebre, Firezgi Gebre-Mikael, Berhe Zemmu. Gebrat Giliat, *Qeshi* Yosef Hemmed, Haleqa Tewolde-Medhin Gebru, Gebrehet Mihtsintu, Ande-Mikael Wolde-Merqorios, Yishaq Tewolde-Medhin, Afeworqi, Bahlibi Garza (medical), Alazar Hemmed, Alazar Hailu (?) (medical), Ezra Awalom (medical), Wolde-Aregay (medical), Zewdi (female).

TSE'AZZEGA: *Qeshi* Wolde-Yesus Kinfé, Kahsay Gebre, *Qeshi* Gubsa Tikwabo, *Qeshi* Mezgebe Woldu, Segid Zemui (retired), Bekhit Habelom, (retired) Beyin Dafla, Habte, Negassi, Bahlibbi Semere, Abba Gebre-Sillassé Mengistu (Abba Ma'asho, retired), Wolde-Kristos, *Qeshi* Yihdeggo Desta, Amete-Tsion Gebre-Mariam (female), Kibirti Tekle-Haimanot (female).

BELEZA: *Qeshi* Gebre-Sillassé Habtu, *Qeshi* Gebre-Yesus Medhin, *Qeshi* Zer'a-Tsion Musé, Teklu Uqbai (Retired), Tesfu Bairai, *Qeshi* Kifle Gila-Mikael, Tesfa-Mikael Gebru, Tesfu Zeré, Simret Bihil (retired), Beyin Ristu, Habtu, Lette-Tsion Gebre-Mariam (female), Tsehaitu Ni'amin (female), Ellen Kahsai (female).

ADDI UGRI: *Qeshi* Gebre-Sillassé Gebru, *Qeshi* Fisseha-Tsion, *Haleqa* Kashsay, Uqbanki'el, Haile Mariam, Negasi Kahsay, Bitchir (female) Elisabeth Kahsay (female).

GELEB: *Qeshi* Dawit Amanuel, Alazar Hemmed, Timoteos Faid, Samuel Etman, Tesfa-Le'ul Hibtes, Eyassu Be'imnet, Ellen Kahsay (female).

KEREN: *Qeshi* Yosef Hemmed, Yohannes Emilios.

KUNAMA: Yosef Mati, Hezqiel Gulai, Yoel Fafi, Simon Natnael, Musa Torti, Daniel Lulu.

Appendix II

Sources for a History of the ECE

By Ezra Gebremedhin

Early Periodicals and Historical Records

Though not the subject of a full-dress history, the story of the roots and development of the ECE has been told by many different people, Swedes, Italians and Eritreans, at different times, since the arrival of the first Swedish missionaries in Massawa in 1866.

Already in 1834, C. O. Rosenius, one of the founders of EFS/SEM, started giving out a paper entitled *Missions-Tidning,* SEM/MT, (Mission Paper or Mission News). In 1862 he handed over the paper to the SEM and the periodical became the official organ of the foreign mission activities of the SEM. The paper is still going strong under the name *EFS Missionstidning Budbäraren.* (The Mission News of the SEM. The Messenger). This periodical has included occasional articles on the mission of the SEM in Eritrea and on the ECE, although its coverage of the ECE diminished drastically after 1974. Older issues of *Budbäraren* are a significant source of information on the SEM and the ECE.

From 1893 to about 1963 the SEM gave out an annual periodical called *Varde Ljus* (Let there be Light!), something of a gold mine of information on Eritrea and Ethiopia.

G. E. Beskow's two volumes with the title *Den svenska missionen I Ost-Afrika* (The Swedish Mission in East Africa), published in 1884 and 1887 respectively, abound in quotations from first-hand missionary sources and provide a rich background to the early history of the SEM and the ECE.[828] So do H. B. Hammar's *Evang. Fosterlands-Stiftelsens Ost-Afrikanska mission 1856–1900,* (SEM:s East Africa Mission 1856–1900) published 1901. Beginning with the year 1856, EFS (The Swedish Evangelical Mission)

---

828 Beskow 1884 and 1887.

gave out *Annual Reports* with detailed accounts on its activities both at home and abroad. These yearbooks are a rich source of information on the history of the SEM and the ECE.

In 1906, the board of *Evangeliska Fosterlands-Stiftelsen* (The Swedish Evangelical Mission) gave out a commemorative book on the fiftieth anniversary of the SEM. It was entitled *Evang. Fosterlands-Stiftelsens 50-åriga verksamhet 1856–1906.* (The Fifty Years of Activity of the Swedish Evangelical Mission 1856–1906.) This work too contains a section (pp. 123–165) with information on the life and activities of the SEM at home and of its mission work in Eritrea. Eskil Levander's (Ed), *Evangeliska Fosterlands-Stiftelsen genom 75 år (I–II). Jubileumsskrift,* (The Seventy-Five Years of Activity of the Swedish Evangelical Mission 1856–1931) came out in two volumes in 1931.

Professor Adolf Kolmodin's account of his visit to the mission field of the Swedish Mission in Eritrea from October 16, 1908 to March 15, 1909 (a work entitled *Några Minnen från min Resa till Ost-Afrika 1908–1909,* i.e. Some Reminiscences From My Journey to East Africa 1908–1909) is a very rich and enjoyable source of information on Eritrea, the SEM and the prehistory of the ECE. Kolmodin writes with heart and mind and his notes radiate personal involvement. He gives a review of the history of the SEM in Eritrea to date and a detailed description of current events and trends in mission and church in the colony at the turn of the last century. It also outlines visions for the future of the mission and the ECE.[829] I have made extensive use of his book.

The material for Johannes Kolmodin's work *Zanta Tsazzegan Hazzegan* (Story of Tse'azzega and Hazzega) was collected and compiled through the facilities made available by missionaries of the SEM in Eritrea and their Eritrean colleagues among the Kenisha.[830] The book is not specifically on the ECE but it does give us a rich picture of the historical and cultural context within which the ECE came into being and developed in Hamasen. It is no wonder that Johannes Kolmodin dedicated the book to the Swedish missionary, Anders Svensson, a

829 A. Kolmodin 1909.
830 Johannes Kolmodin, "Traditions de Tsazzega et Hazzega. Textes Tigrinya" (Preface in French), *Archives d'etudes Orientales* 5:1, Uppsala, 1912. J. Kolmodin, *Zanta Tsazzegan Hazzegan,* edited by Fre Woldu Kiros, Stockholm: African Triangle, 1989. It is to be remembered that J. Kolmodin, the eldest child of A. Kolmodin, accompanied his father on the latter's journey to Eritrea in 1908–1909, after having received his Master's degree in Linguistics at the University of Uppsala. (Ed.)

patriarch among Evangelical Christians in Eritrea. Svensson and other informants from the Eritrean Evangelical community had helped Kolmodin to collect the material for the book.

The organ of the ECE and the LCE, *Mel'ichti Selam*, (Message of Peace) is a source of history in its own right. There are some rare copies of bound editions of this periodical. The first issue of this Tigrinya language periodical of the SEM and the Evangelical community came out in March 1909.[831] One such example is a bound copy for the years 1909 to 1913, according to the Julian calendar.[832] These issues cover the period between 1917 and 1921 according to the Gregorian calendar, a period which coincides with the last part of the First World War. This bound edition of *Mel'ichti Selam* gives us an engaging picture of the spiritual life and concerns of the Evangelical community during these crucial years.[833] It is now several years since *Mel'ichti Selam* was discontinued.

Historical Surveys for the Period after World War I

In 1918, the Swedish Mission in Eritrea published a book in Italian, entitled *Notizie Storiche e Varie sulla Missione Evangelica Svedese Dell' Eritrea. 1866–1916* (Historical and Sundry Notes on the Swedish Evangelical Mission of Eritrea. 1866–1916).[834] The authors were the Swedish missionary Jonas Jwarson (Iwarson) and the Italian, Waldensian missionary, Alessandro Tron. The purpose of the book was to enlighten the Italian colonial authorities on the history and goal of the SEM. In spite of its modest size (51 pages of text and almost 90 pages of pictures), this book can very well be regarded as the first book on the roots and development of the ECE.[835] It is surprising that it has not been translated into Tigrinya or English.

Allan Hofgren's *Med Gud och hans vänskap. Evangeliska Fosterlands-Stiftelsen genom 100 år* (With God and His Mercies. The Swedish Mission

---

831 For further details on the history of this periodical see the article by Ezra Gebremedhin on the subject *Mel'ichti Selam* in *EAE*, Vol. 1, 2007, 695. (Ed.)
832 Printed at Bet Mahtem Missione Swedese (sic.), Asmara. No date given.
833 I am grateful to Yohannes Tesfa-Mariam for lending me his copy of the bound edition of *Mel'ichti Selam* for the years mentioned. (Ed.).
834 The editor is very grateful to Professor Sven Rubenson for giving him his own copy of this rare and highly valuable book. (Ed.)
835 Iwarson-Tron 1918.

through 100 Years), which came out in 1956 for the 100ᵗʰ anniversary of the EFS and which Allan calls "A book film", is literally a mission lexicon on the work in Eritrea and other mission fields of the SEM. It is an effective shortcut to vital information on the SEM and the ECE for the period up to 1956.

In 1974 the SEM published a work entitled *Ut I All Världen. Evangeliska Fosterlands-Stiftelsens mission I Afrika och Asien 1866–1973*. (Out into the Whole World. EFS Mission in Africa and Asia 1866–1973). The work was edited by Thore Tafvelin and Gustaf Lundmark. Pages 47 to 152 deal with Eritrea, Ethiopia and Jubaland. This work too is a useful source of information on the SEM and the ECE, not least on the period after 1935.[836]

Booklets, Pamphlets and Monographs

There are, apart from monographs and bigger books, a great number of pamphlets or booklets as well as diaries on the work of the SEM. Though many of these pamphlets deal with the lives and services of specific missionaries or Eritreans, they also provide descriptions of the times and circumstances under which these missionaries and their Kenisha colleagues worked. They provide us with revealing glimpses into conditions in different parts of Eritrea and its people, during the period between 1866 and the end of the 1940's. Examples are works on Eritrea in the series called *D.U.F: s Missions bibliotek för våra Juniorer* (The Mission Library for Our Juniors in the Association for Youth), or the series *Missionsskrifter utgifna av Evangeliska Fosterlands-Stiftelsen* (Mission Publications Issued by The Swedish Evangelical Mission).

K. G. Rodén and R. Sundström carried out their studies in Tigré literature within the same Evangelical community, even though their sources were not exclusively Evangelical. Naffa wod Etman (1882–1909), who initiated Sundström and the German explorer Enno Littmann into Mensa folklore and cultural heritage, was a son of the Evangelical community in Eritrea.[837]

The study of Tigré, Tigrinya and Kunama opened the way for research into cultural history, folklore, Ethnology, and literature. Eritreans, who co-operated with the missionaries in the translation of the Scriptures

836 Tafvelin-Lundmark 1974.
837 Arén 1978, 356–359.

and/or hymns into Tigrinya, or those who wrote different types of work on their own, can be said to have made their contributions as members of the ECE or its forerunners, directly or indirectly. Their individual contributions are also a part of the history of the ECE.

The two books by Mrs. Elsie Winqvist, with the titles *Livsbilder från Eritrea* (Life-Glimpses from Eritrea) which came out in 1921 and 1927, and *Med livet som insats. Läkaremissionen i Eritrea* (At the Cost of One's Life. Medical Mission in Eritrea), which came out in 1945, are also narratives about the Kenisha even though their main actors are Swedish missionaries.[838]

Rosa Holmer's book *Per Eric Lager* (1937), the beloved missionary and close friend of *Qeshi* Haile-Ab Tesfai, both of whom were killed outside the Church of *Qiddus Miki'el* in Addi Qontsi, in July 1876, is also the story of the Evangelical community to which these two kindred spirits belonged.[839] So is her book *Twoldo Medhin*, a biography of the well known pastor of the ECE, *Qeshi* Tewolde-Medhin Gebre-Medhin.[840]

The series of three collections of articles in book form, under the title *Bortom Bergen* (Beyond the Mountains), edited by F. Hylander and published between 1953 and 1960, are a useful source on the history of Swedish missionary efforts in both Eritrea and Ethiopia. The material on Eritrea is found in Volume I.

In a section entitled "The Early History of Tigrinya until the 1890's" in his book *A History of Tigrinya Literature. The Oral and the Written 1890–1991*, Ghirmai Negash mentions some of the earliest literary productions of the SEM and the Lutheran Church in Eritrea (LCE). He refers to the contributions made in this regard by the SEM and the forerunner of the ECE.[841]

There are pamphlets or longer writings by the Lundahls of Imkullu, Karl Winqvist, the doctor of Beleza fame and his wife, the linguist

---

838   E. Winqvist 1921, 1945. The latter book is basically a salute to the persons and labours of Dr. Winqvist and Dr. De Pertis. (Ed.)

839   R. Holmer 1937. Arén 1978, 197–201.

840   R. Holmer 1938.

841   Ghirmai Negash 1999, 69–74, 89, 102–103; Joseph Gabra-Woldi's B.A. thesis *The Origin and The Early Development of The Evangelical Church of Eritrea 1866–1917* (Addis Ababa 1972) contains lists of books in Tigrinya issued under the auspices of the SEM between 1896 and 1917, (p 51), books in Tigré issued between 1889 to 1917, (p 56), books in Amharic issued between 186 and 1907, (p 58), books in Galligna (Oromiffa) issued between 1893 and 1899, (p 59), and books in Kunama issued between 1903 and 1914, (p 67). (Ed.)

Elsie Winqvist, K. G. Rodén of Mensa and Geleb, August Andersson of Kunama, Pastor Anders Svensson of Tse'azzega, Britta Edlund, of the Girls Home in Beleza, and Mikael and Rosa Holmer, with their many years of service in Addi Ugri, to take a few examples. Olle Andersson's *Stormen bröt lös* (The Storm Broke Loose) from 1947 is a short, spirited, and comprehensive book on the history of the SEM and the ECE. The last chapters in the book which deal with the Italian invasion of Ethiopia and the war years between 1935 and 1940 in Eritrea, are both provocative and instructive.

Even translating the available Swedish material on mission and church in Eritrea into English and/or Tigrinya, would give the ECE a sizeable library on its history and background.[842]

History of Mission in Eritrea and Ethiopia

Material connected with the topic that K. J. took up lies embedded in a number of more recent works on Eritrea and Ethiopia. Gustav Arén's first book on the history of the Ethiopian Evangelical Church Mekane Yesus (EECMY), *Evangelical Pioneers in Ethiopia. Origins of the Evangelical Church Mekane Yesus* is also a history of the origins of the ECE or its forerunners.[843] Arén's second book, *Envoys of the Gospel in Ethiopia. In the Steps of the Evangelical Pioneers,* which came out in 1999, has also sections which touch upon Eritrea or activities initiated in Eritrea. This is especially true of parts of chapters one and five in the book.[844]

Gustav Arén is, without any doubt, the giant among the writers on the history of the early Evangelical communities in Eritrea and Ethiopia. However, he is not the only actor in this arena of literary work. A look into the sources and bibliographical material used in sections of Gustav's *Evangelical Pioneers,* points to the availability of a wealth of material in this field.[845] The City Archives of Stockholm and the Archives of the Swedish Evangelical Mission in Uppsala are sources of rich background information on the ECE.[846]

The work of the translation of the Bible into Tigrinya, a task which

842   For references to sources leading to these works see Arén 1978, 457 ff.
843   Arén 1978.
844   Arén 1999.
845   Arén 1978, 19–22.
846   Arén 1978, 458.

mobilized both Swedes and Eritreans, over several decades, was a task carried out, to a large extent, in the very bosom of the Evangelical community which gave birth to the ECE.[847] The Tigrinya Bible has become a source of inspiration not only in Eritrea but also among Tigrinya speaking people in the Diaspora. K. J. has narrated the story of this venture in the present book.

In one of the notes that he has left, K. J. writes,

> An Eritrean teacher, Yosef Gebre-Woldi had, after several years' work, with the Eritrean Evangelical School, got the opportunity of further studies at Addis Ababa University in Ethiopia. History was his subject and he chose to write his BA treatise on the early history of the Eritrean Evangelical Church. This was in 1972.

> [...] After many years as an instructor at a Teachers' Training Institute and following the liberation of Eritrea Yosef Gebra-Wold returned to his home country. He began publishing articles from his church history in the ECE magazine Melechti Selam.

> When I was asked to continue the studies on the history of the ECE, on the request of Dr. Arén, I felt it was natural that I would do that in co-operation with my friend Yosef. We planned for this work during a month-long stay I had in Asmara April 1998, but later the same year he died.

Joseph (sic) Gabrawold wrote his thesis in 1972. The title of the thesis is *The Origin and Early Development of the Evangelical Church of Eritrea 1866–1917*. His thesis is in fact the first work in English devoted specifically to the history of ECE. The thesis (a 93-page essay with notes and bibliography) builds on written sources and interviews. These interviews (31 in number, out of which 28 were interviews with Kenisha) can be counted as Yosef's special contribution to the history of Eritrea.

Qeshi Alazar Menghestu's book, *Bakgrunden och Framväxandet av en luthersk kyrka i Eritrea, 1912–1932. Eritreanskt-svenskt initiativ* (The Background and Coming into being of a Lutheran Church in Eritrea, 1912–1932. An Eritrean-Swedish Initiative), which was also published in a Tigrinya version by Admas Publishers in Sundbyberg, Sweden in 2003, is a story of part of the background of the ECE and of the history of The Lutheran Church of Eritrea. The work builds around a theological

---

847 Winqvist/Janér 1958, 140-161. Arén 1978, 336-337.

conflict that engaged Swedish missionaries in Eritrea and, to a lesser extent, their Eritrean followers, and with the consequences of this conflict among the Kenisha.[848] What I found particularly interesting in the Tigrinya version of the book is the account on the life and work of *Qeshi* Marqos Girmai, a life story that could very well be the subject of a novel.[849] The story of *Qeshi* Marqos, up to the time of the split between SEM and Bibeltrogna Vänner (BV), is also the story of the ECE.

In 1994, Anders Joëlson published a typewritten work entitled *Peter Andersson från Ornakärr, missonär i Kunama.* (Peter Andersson from Ornakärr, A Missionary in Kunama).[850] Peter Andersson, a colorful messenger of the Gospel, and an uncle of A. Joëlson, was born in 1868. He came to Kunama in 1903 and left for good in 1929. He was in Eritrea during a critical period in the relationship between the SEM and the Italian colonial authorities. His biography too gives us glimpses into the history of both the SEM and the ECE.

In 2006, Tore Bergman came out with his *August Bergman och hans familj i Ostafrika och Sverige. Sammanställning av Tore Bergman.* (A. Bergman and His Family in East Africa and Sweden. A Compilation by Tore Bergman).[851] This work, printed in a limited number of copies, contains a good number of letters from A Bergman's (1855–1923) stay in both Eritrea and Sweden. A. Bergman was an uncle of the writer. Both of these typewritten works, given out privately, make further material on Eritrea, the SEM and the Evangelical community in Eritrea available to those who can read Swedish. They contribute directly or indirectly, to a history of the ECE.

Records from Symposiums, Conferences and Seminars

On February 20–23, 1993, an International Symposium on the Tigrinya Language (the first of its kind) was held in Asmara. Speaking on the topic *Abbotat Tigrinya* (Fathers of Tigrinya), Memhir Feqadu Gebre-Sillassé, a Kenisha, names and comments on *Qeshi* Marqos Girmai, *debtera* Rufaél, *Qeshi* Tewolde-Medhin Gebre-Medhin, *Qeshi* Alessandro

---

848 A. Menghestu, 2003.
849 The books in both the Tigrinya and Swedish versions contain a lot of valuable information, on both missionaries and their Kenisha colleagues.
850 Joëlson 1994.
851 Tore Bergman 2006.

Tron, *Qeshi* Gebre-Ewostatewos, Memhir Bairu Uqbit, *Qeshi* Embaye and others as representatives of the Kenisha among such fathers. Memhir Yishaq Tewolde-Medhin, the educator, is also mentioned. I would like to add the name of Memhir (now *Qeshi*) Musa Aron, teacher and author, not least because his novels have an underlying message. At the same symposium, *Qeshi* Elias Habte-Egzy gave a lecture on Ato Woldeab Woldemariam's contributions to the Tigrinya language. These people are or were all members of the ECE.[852]

Dr. LarsOlov Eriksson has written an article entitled "The Swedish Evangelical Mission as a Background to Johannes Kolmodin's Life and Work" in the publication *The Last Dragoman. The Swedish Orientalist Johannes Kolmodin as Scholar, Activist and Diplomat*. In the article, he describes the extent to which knowledge of the Swedish Mission in Eritrea and contacts with Eritrean Evangelical Christians during his youth in Sweden had influenced J. Kolmodin's thinking and contributed to his knowledge of the Tigrinya language and the culture of highland Eritrea.[853]

The editor of the present work has recently published an article (whose main title is "Let There Be Light! Aspects of the Swedish Missionary Venture in Eritrea and their Implications for Political Awareness (1866–1962)" in a book of essays entitled *African Identities and World Christianity in the Twentieth Century*, edited by Professor Klaus Koschorke of the University of Münich.[854] This article too touches on several aspects of the history of the ECE.

Renato Paolo's *Nella Colonia Eritrea*, which came out in 1908, Metodio Da Nembro's *La Missione dei Minori Capuccini in Eritrea*, which came out in 1953, Alexander Nati's B.A. thesis from 1982, *The Impact of Euro-Christian Missions on Kunama Traditional Culture. Senior Essays in Applied Anthropology*, presented at the Addis Ababa University, Jonathan Miran's "Missionaries, Education and the State in the Italian Colony of Eritrea" in *Christian Missionaries & the State in the Third World*, which came out in 2002, and Gianni Dore's "Chi non ha una parente Andinna?", *Ethnorêma. Donne e possessione come archivio storico ed esperienza dell'alterità tra i Kunama*

---

852 The proceedings from this symposium have not, to the knowledge of this editor, been published yet.
853 See LarsOlov Eriksson 2006, 71–82. See also Ezra Gebremedhin "Zanta Tsazzegan Hazzegan. Johannes Kolmodin's Contributions to an Understanding of Eritrean Highland Culture", in the same publication, especially pages 84 to 92. (Ed.)
854 See Ezra Gebremedhin 2005, 119–213.

d'Eritrea, which came out in 2007, all contain material which contribute, in some measure, to the history of the SEM and the ECE.

Material from the Archives of Bibeltrogna Vänner (BV) and the Lutheran Church of Eritrea

The archives of the Swedish Mission BV after 1912 and those of the Lutheran Church of Eritrea (LCE) cannot be regarded as a first hand source for the history of the ECE. However, it is not unreasonable to argue that these archives contain material which can corroborate or throw further light on events and developments recorded in the archives of the SEM and the ECE for the period after 1912. To my knowledge, the archives of BV and the LCE are not among the sources that K. J. has used in any significant measure in the writing of the history of the ECE. These sources cannot be neglected in a serious study of at least the latter part (i.e. the period after 1912) of the history of the ECE.

In this regard, Dr. Bereket Yebio has pointed out the importance of private archives, among which we have Axel B. Svensson's private archives, stored at the Landsarkivet in Lund.

Encyclopaedia Aethiopica

An excellent source of up to date information on the political, cultural histories of Ethiopia and Eritrea is the series known as *Encyclopaedia Aethiopica, (EAE)* given out under the auspices of Hamburg University and the editorship of Professor Ulrich Uhlig. The series, published by Harrassowitz Verlag, is so far available in three volumes. Volume 1, which covers subjects under the letters A-C, came out in 2003. Volume 2, which covers subjects under the letters D-Ha, came out in 2005. Volume 3, which covers subjects under the letters He-N, came out in 2007. Volume 4, which covers subjects under O-X, is expected in 2010. These volumes contain a number of short but solid articles on a number of the individuals, places and literary sources connected with the SEM and the ECE.

From left: Uqbai Kiflé, Gebre-Medhin Habte-Egzy, Kifle-Egzy Yihdeggo, Gebre-Amlak Rufael. Kenisha who moved to Ethiopia in 1927.

Appendix III

Some of the Evangelical Christians who Moved to Ethiopia

Among those who fled from Eritrea or moved to Ethiopia in the Nineteen-twenties, there were several members of the ECE. The majority of these sought the fellowship of the Evangelical Lutheran Community in Addis Ababa and became the nucleus of what is now the Addis Ababa Mekane Yesus congregation. Among those who were received into the Evangelical Congregation in Addis Ababa on October 16, 1927 (according to Gustav Arén's list) were,

> Araia Aberra from Addi Quntsi, Gebre-Egziabher Goytom, Tse'azzega Congregation, Tewolde-Berhan Gebre-Sillassé and his wife Kidan, Tesfa-Egzy Gebre-Sillassé and his wife Senait, Zekarias Teklé, Tesfu Derso,

Yehidego [Yihdeggo] Zigta, Habte-Sillassé Uqba-Yohannes and his wife (Tiblets Tekle-Giorgis), Isaias Tekle-Haimanot and his wife (Hiriti Wolde-Mariam), Zekarias Mebrahtu, Gebrenkiel [Gedefa/Godefa?], Yosef Tewolde Mariam [Tewolde Birhan?], [from] Shimanigus and his wife, Uqbai [Kiflé], Stefanos (Idris) from Geleb, Fisseha Kiflé, Deqemahré, Oqba Sillassé [Gebre], mason, arrived together with the previous one, Yosef Selomon, carpenter, Gebre-Sillassé [Mengistu], Misgginna Bairai, Gebre-Medhin [Habte-Egzie], Gebre-Amlak [Rufael], Paulos Teklé, Tesfa-Mariam Zer'é, Geshinashim, Selomon Baraki, gardener and his wife [Zennebetch] Tseggai Medhin, Wolde-Mariam, [...] Shumbash Mekonnen, Tse'azzega, and his family and his son Iyasu and his daughter-in-law, Redda Tsadiq and his family, Abrehet Gebre-Medhin."[855]

Olle Hagner, who visited *Mission Gibbi* in Addis Ababa in January 1943 writes,

All those who lived in the mission compound are Eritreans and my acquaintances from former days. The former teacher, Tesfazghi (incidentally the son of *Qeshi* Gebre-Sillassé from Addi Hizbai!) still lives in the compound with his family. Others who live in the compound of the former school for girls are Gebremedhen [Gebremedhin, father of the editor of this work], Hedego, Sakarias [Zekarias], Berechet, Gejim [Gayim] and Gomesh [Gumesh, wife of the late *Qeshi* Gebre-Ewostatios, missionary to Wollega]. Most of them are poor and can hardly pay rent (sic) but each of them is responsible for his house. Inside, their homes are orderly.[856]

Not a few of Emperor Haile Selassie's Eritrean civil servants (diplomats, high ranking officers in the Ethiopian army and Police Force, businessmen and craftsmen) had their spiritual roots in the ECE. So were some of the very first trained nurses who manned the Teferi Makonnen Hospital, which was established in 1926, and was originally known as Betä Saida.[857]

The coming of Dr. Knut Hanner and the two nurses Vera Boström and Verna Hagman from Sweden to Betä Saida, was the result of Mission Director Nils Dahlberg's response to a request by Ras Teferi.[858] Kenisha nurses trained in Eritrea were sent to Ethiopia to reinforce the Swedish personnel.

855 See Arén 1999, 231–232. The list is based on a letter written from Addis Ababa by Rev. Nils Nilsson to Rev. Iwarson in Asmara on October 18, 1927. See also Launhardt 2004, 37–38. (Ed.)
856 OHD/K.J.S. Book 5, entry for January 1943, 75. (Ed.)
857 For a fairly detailed description of the role of these Eritrean Christians in the Ethiopian Diaspora, see Launhardt 2004, 24–38. (Ed.)
858 On these Swedish staff see also Adamson 1987, 187–189. (Ed.)

Appendix IV

Important dates in the History of the SEM and the ECE

1856	The Swedish Evangelical Mission (SEM) founded in Sweden.
1866	March 15, Arrival of first missionaries at Massawa.
1866	July, Arrival of first missionaries in Kunama.
1869	April 17–18, Kjellberg and Elfblad murdered in Tika,Kunama.
1870	January, Missionaries withdraw from Kunama to Massawa.
1870	July 26, Bengt Petter Lundahl arrives at Embaderho.
1872	March 31, Nesib baptized as Onesimos.
1872	Lundahl celebrates Holy Communion in Massawa with the assistance of Onesimos.
1872	Hedenström starts work in Beleza.
1873	SEM starts work in Geleb, Mensa.
1873	May, First confrontation between Tse'azzega Reformers and monks from Debre Bizen.
1876	July 17, Lager and Haile-Ab killed at Addi Qontsi.
1877	General Charles Gordon buys and gives a plot of land to the SEM at Imkullu.
1877	Dawit Amanuel baptized by Lundahl at Geleb.
1877–1884	First Oromo Expedition.
1879	SEM moves its station from Massawa to Imkullu.
1881–1882	Second Oromo Expedition.
1883	Karl and Elsie Winqvist arrive in Imkullu.
1884–1886	Third Oromo Expedition.
1885	Lundahl dies of small pox.
1889	Filippo Grill, first Waldensian missionary to Imkullu.
1889	Return of the SEM to Mensa.
1891–1895	Fourth Oromo Expedition.
1889	First reader published in Tigré.
1890	Italy declares a crown colony called Eritrea.

1890   SEM given a site at Beleza. A. Bergman from Imkullu to Beleza.

1891   Headquarters of SEM removed from Imkullu to Tse'azzega.

1891   SEM establishes station in Asmara.

1893   Karl Nyström arrives in Eritrea.

1897–1898 Fifth Oromo Expedition. Gebre-Ewostatewos Ze-Mikael and Gumesh Wolde-Mikael to Oromo land.

1897   J. M. Nilsson returns to Kunama.

1902   NT printed in Tigré.

1908–1909 A. Kolmodin's visit to Eritrea.

1909   January 1, first ordination in Eritrea. Kolmodin ordains Tewolde-Medhin Gebre-Medhin in Asmara.

1909   December, NT printed in Tigrinya.

1909   December 6, K. Winqvist dies, two days after publication of NT in Tigrinya.

1909   March, first issue of *Mel'ichti Selam*, the Tigrinya periodical of the ECE.

1912   Bibeltrogna Vänner begin mission work in Debarwa.

1912   *Birhan Yikun* published in Asmara.

1913   Board of SEM decides to sell Imkullu.

1913   K. Rodén publishes *The Tribes of Mensa*, both in Tigré and in Italian.

1913   R. Sundström publishes *History of the Mensa People in Tigré.*

1913   Alessandro Tron of Waldensian Church arrives as teacher.

1913   Dr. Nicola De Pertis comes to Beleza.

1914   A. Andersson publishes Kunama hymnbook.

1915   October, Expulsion of August Andersson and Johannes Eriksson från Kunama.

1920   A. Svensson authorized to ordain pastors locally.

1921   Peter Andersson, first Swede to be ordained in Eritrea.

1925   First visit of Mission Secretary Dahlberg to Eritrea.

1926   September, the Evangelical Church of Eritrea (ECE) constituted.

1927   NT printed in Kunama.

1928   June 1, Anders Svensson dies in Tse'azzega.

1929   Decision to adopt the Ethiopian (Julian) Calendar in ECE.

1930   September, Qeshi Tewolde-Medhin Gebre-Medhin dies.

1932   Schools of SEM and ECE closed by order of colonial government.

1933   Elsie Winqvist and team ready with revision of NT in Tigrinya.

1935   December, missionaries of SEM expelled from Eritrea.

Appendix V

The Story of My Life – In Brief

By Qeshi Zer'a-Tsion Musé (written ca 1933)

(To begin with) as far as my upbringing was concerned, I grew up studying to become a deacon and a priest. And in conformity with the general practice of the country, they ['my parents'] saw to it that I entered the state of marriage at a very young age. However, my bride and I were bound by love. Up to 1874, I lived according to the ways of our fathers, with my partner in the covenant of holy matrimony, fasting and receiving Holy Communion. We lived as we were expected to, in close relationship and in harmony. In our hearts there was nothing which could separate us.

From 1874 however, I completely relinquished the practices of the church, within the tradition (rules) of the Fathers, in which I had been brought up, i.e. the honour which I had enjoyed as a priest and father-confessor among many, and the respect with which my status as priest was regarded by others. By the grace of Jesus Christ, his word continued to be revealed to me. I continued to relish it increasingly and it became firmly established in my heart. I still live in the full realization of the meaning of the words in Second Corinthians 5:21 and on the basis of the grace that has been bestowed upon me: "God made him who had no sin to be sin for us, so that in him we might become the righteousness of God." Love to our Saviour Jesus Christ became increasingly fervent and strong in my heart. Praise to God for his glorious grace.

The following is what led me to this state of things. We used to receive, free of charge, a book written in the form of questions and answers (called a book of questions), by Maier Johannes, published in Chrischona in 1866 and made available in Asmara. They [Maier's colporteurs?] also brought many books in Ge'ez and left them in Tse'azzega at the [town-] square of Dedjiat Hailu. [The books] didn't lie there in vain but rather struck root [in our hearts] and bore fruit. The way God's grace is bestowed [to mankind] is wonderful. We picked up the books casually, without any prior knowledge, but they led us to an imperishable gift. They introduced us to the One who gives life, so that we would become heirs of his kingdom. I and several friends, bound in love, used to meet at a certain place and eventually arrived at an understanding of God's Word, by reading together.

In this entire process, there was no ferendji (European) in our circle of acquaintances. We were individuals with our families and lived independently, according to our means. We didn't expect anything from them ['the ferendji']. Neither were there any rumours to the effect that they [the ferendji'] doled out money. However, we became diligent and were granted openness as a result of our reading of some books in Amharic, printed by Otto Flad in 1875. The titles of these books were: *Wädä zel'aläm dähninät yämiwäsd mängäd* (A Way Which Leads to Eternal Salvation), *Mäglächa* (Explanation), *Kristos hulu bähulum näw* [Christ is All in All]. We had no craving for money. At that time there was no one to whom the ferendji doled out money. Neither was there anyone among us who received money. And at that time there was no lamba (kerosene).

But in the course of time, we became acquainted with the Swedish missionaries of the Gospel, Mr. Lager [1837–1876]) and Mr. Hedenström [1844–1904]. These two had settled in Beleza with the permission of Niburä Id (later Waqshim) Gebru. The two [missionaries] used to visit us in Tse'azzega, and we used to receive them with love. However, enemies of the Gospel kept accusing us maliciously and caused turbulence among all the people. Three years passed in this state of turbulence, after which a time of persecution began. Then, the missionaries received us in love. Prior to that, they hadn't done anything on our behalf or for us. However, the fact that they received us with love is a source of wonder. While our brothers and relatives hated us and persecuted us, these people, who were not related to us biologically, became closer to us than our relatives and parents. This most wonderful and astonishing experience is a result of the love of Christ and his Gospel, his wisdom and his bounty. We render him our praises.

At that time we did that which has been narrated in Matthews 13: 44, "The kingdom of heaven is like a merchant looking for fine pearls. When he found one of great value, he went away and sold everything he had and bought it." We too bought the treasure [i.e. the Gospel of Grace], and this treasure is with us until this very day. May God richly reward those who once received [welcomed] us. I shall not cease to say so until the day of my death. Neither shall I forget it [this favour] in my prayers. It is in my heart to stay.

To come back to my story, my partner in holy matrimony had not yet received instruction. However, I reasoned with her about the Word of God, and she expressed her willingness to be banished with me. She did not want to be separated from me. She said, "Let your fate be mine!" Her father and mother did not want to work against her resolve, but rather approved of her decision to go.

First, the whole of our region entered [moved to] Adwa for fear of Ra'si Wolde-Mikael. We then took counsel with each other and came to the decision to move to Massawa with merchants. We had come to the conclusion that it would be better for us to be at a place where we would have access to God's Word and where we could study about the salvation of the soul, morning and evening. Having coming to know the date on which we would leave with merchants, we made ourselves ready and departed.

I then prayed to God with the following words, "Please spare for me these three children whom you have given me, [i.e.] Ametou, Yosef and Tsiriha. I don't bother about other matters."

He did for me according to my prayers. Two boys and two girls who were born there were also buried there. We believed that one son, who had reached the age of six and was healthy and handsome, would survive to ascend [to the highlands] with us, since the government of Italy had already come by then. However, he died of a disease which strikes children and was left behind [i.e. buried in Imkullu] with his brothers and sisters.

Our exile was of great benefit for us. My wife, who hadn't had any education, previously, was given the opportunity to study and receive the kind of knowledge which led to the salvation of her soul. She witnessed about her faith before the congregation. Even though she grieved because of the death of her children, she was comforted by the [knowledge of the] salvation of her soul and by the fact that she had acquired knowledge of the Word of God.

Menkullo had a shining, beautiful church, in the midst of Muslims, visible to all eyes. It also had a school for boys and girls. There we lived for 14 years. But when we left it [we thanked God] in the words of

Ephesians 3:20, "Now to him who is able to do immeasurably more than all we ask or imagine, according to his power that is at work within us, to him be glory in the church and in Christ Jesus throughout all generations, for ever and ever! Amen"

From the three to whom we gave birth, we have been able to see the fourth generation, and God has given us 83 years, by his grace. But now we entreat him to let us depart in peace.

Preface

I was born in 1850 [Gregorian calendar]. And this can be divided into two [periods]. From 1850 to 1874 was the period during which I lived according to the tradition of the fathers. But from 1874 I have lived according to the Gospel until now. And behold, this has now been written briefly.

Qeshi Zer'a-Tsion Musé

Some Observations

Our text is a narrative about the life of one of the pioneers of the Evangelical Church of Eritrea, Qeshi Zer'a-Tsion Musé, for the period between 1850 and 1933. The narrative must have been written in or around 1933. Qeshi Zer'a-Tsion states that he was 83 at the time of writing. Since he died in 1940 at the age of 90, he must have been 83 in 1933. In another document, the writer maintains that he was born in 1842 (in Ge'ez numbers, i.e. according to the Julian calendar), and then goes on to write that this corresponds to 1850 [i.e. in numbers used to indicate the Gregorian calendar.] The sentence in the original of our present text reads, "From the date of my birth up to 1873 (in Ge'ez numbers), I lived according to the ways of our fathers, with my partner in the covenant of holy matrimony, fasting and receiving the Eucharist." Nevertheless, this dating must be Gregorian, since a Julian dating would imply that his "Evangelical" period started in 1880 or 1881. And such a dating would be far too late. The story is a flashback, a backward glance. We chose the text, which we found among the documents which the late Karl Johan Lundström had left behind, because it was short, comprehensive and readily available here in Sweden. Our narrator is one of the three pioneers of the Evangelical Church of Eritrea. The other two, Qeshi Haile-Ab Tesfai (1846–1876), Qeshi Selomon Atsqu (1848–1926) have equally interesting stories. In substance, their stories are the same. Theirs are tales of spiritual seeking and discovery. (Ed)

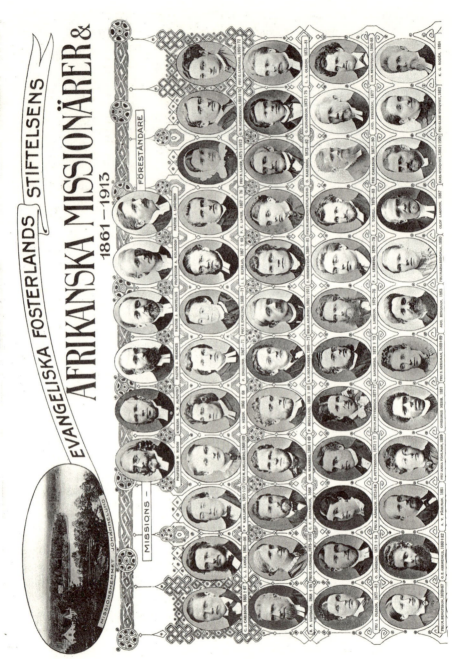

The Swedish Mission. Missionaries to Africa, 1861-1913.

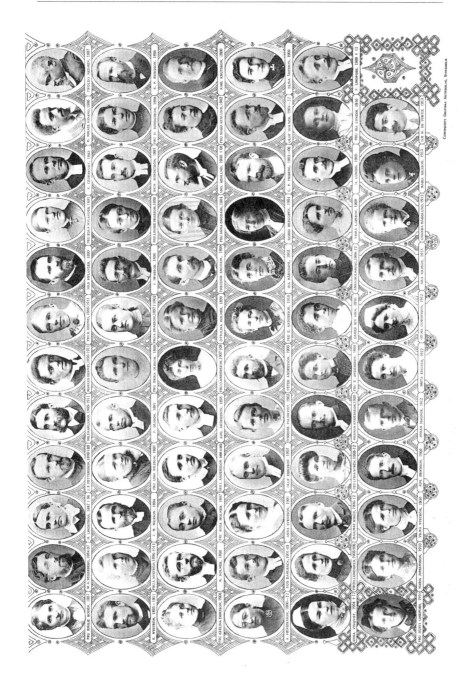

Appendix VI

List of Missionaries of the SEM in Eritrea 1866 upto 2008

In the list of missionaries to Eritrea we have included all those who laboured in Eritrea from 1866 to the present, as well those who went to Somalia, to the small locality of Natal in South Afria and those who served in Ethiopia up to ca. 1936. The reason for this is that Swedish missionary activity in all these three areas was regarded as a unit.

Ahlborg, Wilhelm, ★1841–09–11, †1911–08–02. Commercial Agent in Massawa 1870–1872 and later treasurer at the headquarters of the SEM in Stockholm 1873–1904.

Andersson, August, ★1868–10–24, †1952–02–09. Pastor in Agordat, Kulluku 1898–1901, Kulluku 1902–1906, Awsa Konoma 1908–1915. Married to Lydia Thorsell 1901–10–17. Married a second time to Octavia Lindström 1907–10–15 and a third time to Sigrid Pettersson 1927–03–14.

Andersson (Öst), Elisabeth, ★1880–06–28. Worked in Kismayu, Somalia 1909–1914. Married to Herman Andersson 1909–12–07.

Andersson (Hansson), Emma Charlotta, ★1869–10–01, †1948–07–27. Teacher and nurse in Kulluku 1910–1911, Awsa Konoma 1912–1915, Kulluku 1916–1929. Married to Peter Andersson 1910–09–02.

Andersson, G W, †1870–07–01. Served in Massawa and Tendar 1868–1870. Died in Massawa.

Andersson, Herman, ★1881–08–19. Pastor in Kismayu, Somalia 1908–1914. Married to Elisabeth Öst 1909–12–07.

Andersson (Thorsell), Lydia, ★1872–03–12, †1902–02–21. Teacher at School for Girls in Beleza 1896–1901. Moved to Kulluku where she died in 1902. Married to August Andersson 1901–10–17.

Andersson, Märta, ★1889–04–14, †1922–11–16. Teacher. In Asmara for language studies 1921, then worked as a visitor of the sick. Died in Asmara 1922.

Andersson (Lindström), Octavia, ★1874–08–01, †1909–03–29. Teacher in Awsa Konoma 1908–1909. Died of dysentery

865   In 1873, the SEM initiated a mission project in Natal, South Africa. The intention was to establish mission colonies which would eventually be economically self-sufficient. The person who took the initiative was C L Flygare a missionary with the Herrmannsburg Mission. A total of four missionaries were out on the field. The project was, however, not feasible and had to be interrupted in 1874. The Mission Ship Ansgarius was used to transport both missionaries and equipment.

in Awsa Konoma 1909. Married to
August Andersson 1907-10-15.

Andersson, Peter (Petter), ★1868-08-20,
†1947-08-03. Pastor in Kulluku
1903-1904, Awsa Konoma 1905-1915,
Kulluku 1916-1929. Married to Emma
Hansson 1910-09-02.

Armand-Hugon, Augusto, ★1901, †1963.
Italian teacher sent by the Waldensian
Church. Teacher in Asmara 1919-1920.

Arrhenius, Gustaf Emil, ★1850-02-04,
†1882-05-30. Medically trained and
Pastor in Massawa 1880. Leader of
Second Oromo Exp. 1981-1982. Died in
Khartoum on May 30, 1882.

Bengtsson (Cassel), Fredrika Wilhelmina
(Mimmi), ★1848-02-17, †1887-03-30.
Teacher at the School for Boys in
Imkullu 1879-1887. Died in Imkullu
after giving birth to a son on February
14, 1887. Married to Samuel Bengtsson
1881-10-11.

Bengtsson, Samuel, ★1851-06-07.
Teacher of handicraft and trainee
in Imkullu 1881-1888. Developed
heart problem in the summer of 1888
and returned to Sweden. Married to
Fredrika Cassel 1881-10-11.

Berg, Daniel, ★1887-04-26, †1922-08-25.
Pastor who waited long to come out
as a missionary. In Asmara 1921-1922.
Buried in Asmara 1922. Married to
Signe Linder 1916-12-21.

Berg (Linder), Signe, ★1886-05-10,
†1979-12-06. Nurse sent out by
organization known as "Barnens vän"
(Childrens' Friend, SEM). Matron and
head of Children's home. Asmara 1921-
1930. Awsa Konoma 1931-1933, Asmara
1934-1935, when she was expelled.
Married to Daniel Berg 1916-12-21.

Berggren, Sigrid, ★1874-05-19, †1967-
03-18. Worked among women, in the
areas of education, health care and
evangelization. Tse'azzega 1904-1921,
Beleza 1922. Addis Ababa from 1926
until her expulsion in 1936.

Berglund (Nilsson), Aina, ★1925-03-31.
Nurse in Asmara 1952-1955, Tse'azzega

1955-1964. Married to Ivar Berglund
1951-03-24.

Berglund, Axel, ★1912-01-19, †2005-
07-12. Pastor also engaged in medical
work in Asmara 1945-1946, Geleb
1946-1962, Addi Ugri 1963-1972.
1978-1986 in Nairobi. Engaged in
the translation of the Bible to Tigré.
Married to Linnea Fällman 1943-06-16.

Berglund, Ivar, ★1925-04-17, †1985-
12-01. Pastor in Asmara 1952-1955,
Tseazzegga 1955-1964. Married to Aina
Nilsson 1951-03-24.

Berglund (Fällman), Linnea, ★1914-12-06,
†1999-06-23. Worked with sewing
groups, taught handicraft to girls,
evangelism, home visits in Asmara
1945-1946, Geleb 1946-1962, Addi Ugri
1963-1972. Nairobi 1978-1986. Married
to Axel Berglund 1943-06-16.

Berglund, Per (Petrus), ★1840-01-30,
†1869-07-31. Pastor. Came to Imkullu
1868. Died in Tendar, Kunama 1869.

Bergman, August, ★1855-01-13, †1923-
04-23. Medical assistant in Imkullu
1883-1889, Beleza 1890-1897. Took
part in Third Oromo Exp. 1884-1886.
From 1898 travelling representative
for SEM's Foreign Mission, Sweden.
Married to Sarah Sidey 1889-01-08.
Married a second time to Maria
Hallendorf 1891.

Bergman (Hallendorf), Maria, ★1865-
03-25. Matron in Beleza 1890-1897.
Married to August Bergman 1891.

Bergman (Sidey), Sarah, †1889-02-18.
Missionary in Imkullu 1888-1889.
Died in Imkullu one month after her
marriage in 1889. Married to August
Bergman 1889-01-08.

Boberg-Menghestu (Boberg), Lisbeth,
★1941-03-07. Nurse and midwife in
Keren 1969-1971 and Barentu 1972-
1974. Worked among Eritrean refugees
in Khartoum, Sudan, 1978-1979. Married to Alazar Menghestu 1976-06-26.

Borgström Ebba, ★1900-10-01. Teacher at
school for the deaf in Keren 1962-1963.
Sent out by DAM.

Carlsson, Carl Johan, ★1836–06–17, †1867–10–02. Pioneer missionary, layman. Came out to Kunama in 1866. Tendar 1866, Ouganna 1867. Died in Frida.

Carlsson (Hellgren), Hulda, ★1850–04–26, †1929–11–26. Missionary in Imkullu 1879–1880. Then missionary in India 1880–1909. Married to Per Carlsson 1880–05–05.

Carlsson, Per, ★1849–08–31, †1909–01–08. Pastor in Imkullu, Adwa in 1877–1878, Geleb 1879–1880. Then missionary in India 1880–1909. Buried in Betul, India. Married to Hulda Hellgren 1880–05–05.

Cederqvist, Karl, ★1854–10–28, †1919–11–11. Seamen's pastor in Hamburg, Liverpool and Grimsby. Came as pastor to Imkullu, Aden, Lamu 1893–1895, Geleb 1896–1897, Kismayu 1898–1902. From 1904–1919 the only missionary in Addis Ababa. Buried in Addis Ababa.

Coïsson, Enrico, ★1900–05–17, †1941. Italian teacher sent by the Waldensian Church. Teacher in Beleza 1924, Shimanigus, 1925–1926, Geleb, Keren 1927–1938. Married to Ida Mathieu 1929.

Coïsson (Mathieu),Ida ★1897, †1990. Italian teacher sent by the Waldensian Church. Worked among women in Geleb, Keren 1928–1938. Married to Enrico Coïsson 1929.

Dahlbäck, August, ★1875–10–23. Pastor in Kulluku, Kunama 1901–1903. Pastor for Seamen from 1903.

De Pertis, Nicola, ★1884–09–10, †1931–06–03. Italian Medical doctor in Asmara 1913–1914, Beleza 1914–1916. Military service in Segeneyti, Massawa, Eritrea, 1917–1918, Asmara 1918–1931. Died in Italy. Married to Therese Palmqvist 1915–10–14.

De Pertis (Palmqvist), Therese, ★1876–01–22, †1961–02–25. Nurse and midwife in Beleza 1903–1916, Segeneyti 1917–1918, Asmara 1918–1934. Helped with translation of Bible in Rome

1937–1939. In Asmara 1939. Married to Nicola De Pertis 1915–10–14.

Edlund, Brita, ★1883–03–18, †1972–10–24. School teacher and teacher in Needlework in Beleza 1912–1932, 1934–1935, when she was expelled. Asmara 1948–1951, 1954–1957, Addi Ugri 1956–1957.

Edsinger (Eriksson), Hans, ★1894–10–01, †1974–10–27. Pastor and teacher in Addis Ababa 1924–1928. Married to Karin Rudolphi 1926–11–20.

Edsinger (Eriksson, Rudolphi), Karin, ★1896–12–07, †1984–08–28. Teacher and midwife. Addis Ababa 1926–1928. Married to Hans Eriksson 1926–11–20.

Elfblad, Johan Leonard, ★1839–12–07, †1869–04–18. Pastor with education in Medicine. Massawa 1867, Kunama 1867–1869. Murdered in the Tika region in Kunama 1869.

Engdahl (Johansson), Anna, ★1875–10–03, †1920–08–03. Teacher in Kismayu, Somalia 1904–1909, 1913–1919, Mofi 1910–1912. Married to Teodor Engdahl 1904–08–17.

Engdahl (Nilsson), Gustaf Teodor, ★1874–02–03, †1921–01–09. Pastor in Kismayu 1899–1909, Mofi 1910–1912, Kismayu 1913–1919. Married to Anna Johansson 1904–08–17.

Englund, Petrus, ★1836–05–05, †1916–06–06. Pastor, teacher and language scholar. Tendar 1867, Ouganna 1868–1869, Massawa 1870. Missionary among Seamen in Alexandria 1871–1873. Married to Sofia Löwendahl 1869–02–08.

Englund (Löwendahl), Sofia, ★1836–07–06. Teacher who came out as a missionary bride. Massawa 1867, Ouganna 1868–1869, Massawa 1870. To Alexandria with her husband in 1871–1873. Married to Petrus Englund 1869–02–08.

Eriksson (Norrby), Axelina, ★1875–12–04, †1965–02–20. Teacher in Asmara 1906–1909. Married to Erik Eriksson 1906–08–31.

Eriksson, Erik Petter, ★1869–08–18, †1930–01–22. Sent out to be head of printing press in Asmara 1898–1909. Married to Axelina Norrby 1906–08–31.

Eriksson, Johannes, ★1877–09–08, †1951–12–04. Pastor with training in Medicine. Kulluku 1909–1915. Later some years Travelling Secretary in Sweden.

Eriksson, Olof, ★1878–09–17, †1962–02–05. Pastor, translator, head of printing press. In Kulluku 1903–04, Beleza 1905–1910, Asmara 1911–1915 (as head of printing press). Addis Ababa 1920–1936. Pastor for seamen in Calcutta, India, 1936–1952.

Erking (Eriksson), Torsten, ★1921–05–22. Pastor in Kulluku, 1955–1964. Married to Gertrud Sjunnesson 1954–05–17.

Erking (Eriksson, Sjunnesson), Gertrud, ★1926–07–01. Teacher in Kulluku, 1955–1964. Married to Thorsten Eriksson 1954–05–18.

Forslund, Eskil, *1935–04–20. Teacher in Beleza 2006. Earlier missionary in Mendi, Nedjo, Neqemte and Addis Ababa 1963–1976, 1978–1981, 1993–1996 and Mission Secretary at SEM in Sweden 1984–1993. Married to Gertrud Edström 1962–06–02.

Forslund (Edström), Gertrud, *1935–03–17 Social worker in Beleza 2006. Earlier nurse in Mendi, Nedjo, Neqemte and Addis Ababa 1963–1976, 1978–1981, 1993–1996. Married to Eskil Forslund 1962–06–02.

Forsman, Mats, ★1947–08–22. Teacher in Asmara 1971–1973.

Frangullis, Antonio, ★1898–09–18. Originally from Greece. Teacher and pastor in Asmara 1946–1963. Ordained 1960.

Friberg, C P, ★1869–01–06. Medical Doctor in Kismayu, Somalia 1904–1906.

Ganz, Emilio, ★1898–08–15, †1990. Italian teacher sent by the Waldensian Church. Teacher and head of Printing press in Asmara 1919–1930.

Germei (Johansson), Regina, ★1857–01–30, †1943–07–17. Teacher, matron and Bible-woman. Imkullu 1888–1889,

Beleza 1890–1896, Geleb 1896–1897, Asmara 1897–01, 1905–1911. Went into the service of BV in 1911. Wife of Qeshi Marqos Girmai 1899–12–06.

Giselsson, Febe, ★1909–03–27. Teacher for the deaf, Keren 1961. Sent out by the DAM (Deaf Africa Mission).

Giudici, Benedetto ★1862, †1926. Italian teacher sent by the Waldensian Church. In Asmara 1909–1913. Married to Dircea Veneri 1901.

Giudici (Veneri), Dircea ★1875, †1966. Italian teacher sent by the Waldensian Church. In Asmara 1909–1913. Married to Benedetto Giudici 1901.

Gomér (Karlsson), Ethel, ★1936–11–17. Nurse in Keren 1972–1977. Addis Ababa 1978–1981. Married to Gunnar Gomér 1963–08–17.

Gomér, Gunnar, ★1938–09–24. Teacher for the deaf in Keren 1972–1977. Addis Ababa 1978–1981. Married to Ethel Karlsson 1963–08–17.

Grill, Filippo ★1859, †1945. Italian teacher sent by the Waldensian congregation in Florens, Italy. Teacher in Imkullu 1889–1891.

Gustavsson, Boris, ★1946–04–15. Teacher in tailoring in Keren 1970–1977. Later social worker among refugees in Wad El Hillewa, Sudan 1977–1980.

Gustavsson, Ellen, ★1890–10–24, †1982–06–21. Teacher in Awsa Konoma 1921–1931, Kismayu, Somalia 1934–1935, when she was expelled.

Göransson, Selma, ★1881–10–31, †1954–09–28. Nurse in Kismayu and Mofi, Somalia 1912–1935.

Hagner (Andersson, Sjölin), Greta (Margareta), ★1901–02–02, †1986–02–09. Missionary in Awsa Konoma 1925–1931, Asmara 1933, Adwa 1934–1935, Keren 1935–1936, 1954–1957, 1959, Awsa Konoma 1960, 1962–1970, Keren 1961. Married to Olof Hagner (Andersson) 1926–01–15.

Hagner (Andersson), Johan, ★1888–12–08, †1963–05–18. Teacher and later pastor in Kulluku, Kunama 1912–1914. Later secretary for Foreign Mission for SEM 1935-1955. Married to the nurse Svea Hammar 1917-12-09.

Hagner (Andersson), Olle (Olof), ★1895-08-27, †1978-04-07. Teacher and later pastor. Awsa Konoma 1922-1931, Asmara 1933, Adwa 1934-1935, Keren 1935-1936. Asmara 1938-1946, 1948-1950, Keren 1953-1957, 1959, Awsa Konoma 1960, 1962-1970, Keren 1961. Married to Greta Sjölin 1926-01-15.

Hedenström, Erik Emil, ★1844-03-13, †1904-04-08. Came as a homesteader to Ailet 1870-1872. Geleb 1873-1879, Imkullu 1880-1881. Later engaged in mission work in Zanzibar and British East Africa. Married to Mina Karlsson on 1874-05-28, on the ship Ansgarius, in Massawa.

Hedenström (Karlsson), Mina, †1902, Missionary in Geleb 1874-1879, Imkullu 1879-1881. Died 1902 in Kolesa, by the shores of Lake Tana, some years before Emil. Married to Erik Hedenström 1874-05-28.

Hedin, Olof, ★1839-04-25, †1868-06-10. Pastor and pioneer missionary. Came out 1866. Tendar 1867-1868. Died in Tendar, Kunama.

Henoch, Maria, ★1890-12-18, †1978-05-06. Nurse in Geleb 1921-1928. Later missionary among seamen in Bremen, Germany.

Henriksson, Augusta Henrika, ★1867-04-13. Teacher in Beleza 1900-1906, Shimanigus 1907-1909, Beleza 1910-1912.

Hitchcock (Filer), Esther, ★1941-08-09. Teacher in Geleb 1968-1970. Married to John Hitchcock 1964-08-29.

Hitchcock, John, ★1937-11-04. Teacher in Geleb 1968-1970. Married to Esther Filer 1964-08-29.

Hjalmarsson-Stjärne (Stjärne), Ingrid, ★1931-05-09, †2009-01-12. Teacher in Barentu 1994-1996. Earlier work among refugees in Umrakuba, Sudan 1988-1990. Married to Per-Gunnar Hjalmarsson 1959-06-19.

Hjalmarsson, Per-Gunnar, ★1930-10-03. Agronomist in Barentu 1994-1996. Earlier work among refugees in Umrakuba, Sudan 1988-1990. Married to Ingrid Stjärne 1959-06-19.

Holmberg, Anna Viktoria, ★1881-12-07, †1949-08-25. Teacher in sewing, knitting and handicraft in Beleza 1908-1912.

Holmer, Mikael, ★1869-01-08, †1944-01-04. Pastor in Asmara 1898-1906, Addi Ugri 1907-1916, Asmara 1919-1922, Addi Ugri 1922-1926, Tse'azzega 1928-1935, when he was expelled. Engaged in translation of the Bible 1937-1939. Married to Rosa Solem 1901-10-17.

Holmer, Olof, ★1874-04-09, †1945-02-07. Pastor. Became sick on his way to the mission field in 1903 and stayed in Aden 1904, after which he returned to Sweden the same year.

Holmer, Ottolina, ★1876-01-11, †1961-02-18. Matron and teacher in Asmara 1899-1909, Shimanigus 1911-1916, Addi Ugri 1916-1917, Asmara 1918-1919.

Holmer (Solem), Rosa, ★1872-08-17, †1949-03-27. Nurse in Beleza 1897-1900, Asmara 1901-1906, Addi Ugri 1907-1916, Asmara 1919-1922, Addi Ugri 1922-1926, Tse'azzega 1928-1935. Married to Mikael Holmer 1901-10-17.

Holmer, Signe, ★1906-11-04, †1989-10-31. School teacher and teacher in needlework, Tse'azzega 1933-1935, when she was expelled. Then missionary in India 1937-1944. Came back to Asmara 1950, head of station at Addi Ugri 1951-1961, Asmara 1963-1967.

Holmgren, Anders Vitalis, ★1848-01-20. Layassistant in Massawa 1870.

Holmgren (Stefansson), Aina, ★1946-02-26. Teacher in Awsa Konoma (Barentu) 1973-1975, Asmara 1975-1977, 2000, 2004-2007. Worked also among refugees in Gedaref in Sudan 1980-1983. Married to Bertil Holmgren 1970-06-27.

Holmgren, Bertil, 1947-02-08. Pastor, builder, and district missionary.

Kulluku 1969–1970, Awsa Konoma (Barentu) 1973–1975, Asmara 1976–1977, 1985, 2000, 2004–2007. Worked also among refugees in Gedaref in Sudan 1980–1983 and Khartoum 2007. Married to Aina Stefansson 1970–06–27.

Hylander (Hedberg), Edla, ★1860–05–14, †1948–01–19. Midwife in Lamu, East Africa, 1893–1894. Harer 1894–1895. Married to Nils Hylander 1893–11–12.

Hylander, Nils, ★1861–02–21 †1929–02–23. Pastor in Imkullu 1890, Geleb 1891–1892, Lamu 1893, Harer 1894–1895. Took part in Fourth Oromo Expedition 1893–1895. Later Assistant Secretary for Foreign Mission for SEM, Editor of the Mission Periodical. Married to Edla Hedberg 1893–11–12.

Hägglund, Amanda, ★1888–02–04, †1961–06–11. Nurse and midwife in Geleb 1913–1921.

Härndahl, Ida, ★1869–04–05, †1942–04–10. Nurse and work among women in Geleb 1903–1922, Keren 1923–1928, Geleb 1929–1931. Head of home for girls in Geleb.

Iwarson (Sahlström), Anna, ★1872–08–22, †1902–08–10. Matron, Asmara 1897–1901, Tse'azzega 1901–1902. Died in Tse'azzega. Married to Jonas Iwarson 1897–11–05.

Iwarson, Jonas, ★1867–08–28, †1947–07–26. Pastor and teacher in Asmara 1897–1901, Tse'azzega 1901–1902, Asmara 1903–1929, Asmara 1930–1933. Married to Anna Sahlström 1897–11–05. Married a second time to Louise Lindfors 1905–06–24.

Iwarson (Lindfors), Louise, ★1874–03–24, †1942–03–09. Teacher in Geleb 1899–1905, Asmara 1905–1929, Beleza 1930–1933. Married to Jonas Iwarson 1905–06–24.

Joëlson, Per–Olof, ★1943–05–16. Construction engineer, Keren 1969–1970 and Neqemte 1971–1975. Married to Birgitta Johansson 1969–05–24.

Johannesson, Alma, ★1888–12–07, †1929–06–20. Teacher, trained in Medicine.

Served in Jonti, Alessandra and Mofi Somalia, 1920–1929. Died i Kismayu, Somalia.

Johansson, Carl Fredrik, ★1840–08–09, †1928–01–28. Lay missionary to Eritrea, became ordained later. Massawa 1867, Ouganna 1868, Tendar 1869, Massawa 1870. From 1873 seamen's missionary in Boston.

Johansson, G, †1875–04–09. Homesteader and farmer. Missionary to Natal 1873 and Massawa 1874–1875. Died in Geleb 1875.

Johansson, Maria, ★1883–02–21, †1952–07–09. Nurse and midwife who also worked as head of the home for girls and of the work among women in Geleb 1910–1919.

Jonsson, Axel, ★1890–02–08, †1959–10–30. Pastor in Geleb 1919–1926. Bible translator (Old Testament) to Tigré, 1920–1932. Addis Ababa 1933–1936. Asmara 1946–1948. From 1950 to retirement, Mission Secretary at headquarters of the SEM. Married to Gertrud Lundh 1921.

Jonsson (Lundh), Gertrud, ★1886–08–11, †1958–03–10. Matron in Geleb 1921–1926. Addis Ababa 1933–1936. Asmara 1946–1948. Married to Axel Jonsson 1921.

Jonsson, Simon, ★1940–08–24. Agronomist in Kulluku 1970–1974. Married to Vera Stefansson 1969–05–17.

Jonsson (Stefansson), Vera, ★1945–01–21. Teacher, education of women. Kulluku 1970–1974. Married to Simon Jonsson 1969–05–17.

Karlsson (Andersson), Beata, ★1843–02–27. Deaconess and nurse in Ailet 1875, Massawa 1876–1878, Geleb 1879, Imkullu 1879–1882. Married to Olof Karlsson in November 1876.

Karlsson, Nils, ★1851–09–16. Carpenter in Imkullu 1889, Beleza 1890–1891, Asmara 1902–1910, when he went into the service of BV.

Karlsson, Olof, ★1833–04–19. Teacher in Carpentry. Massawa 1874–1877,

Adwa 1877–1878, Imkullu 1879–1882. Married to Beata Andersson in November 1876.

Kauppinen, Anni, ★1926–01–19. Teacher at School for the Deaf, Keren 1962–1971. Sent out by DAM.

Kinell, Axel Herman, ★1885–08–24, †1962–01–26. First practical missionary as engineer and 1931 ordanied as Pastor. Jonti 1920–1923, Allessandra 1924–1933. Married 1927 to Gerda Kinell.

Kjellberg (Carlsson), Maria, ★1845, †1869–06–11. Teacher who came out as a missionary bride to Per Eric Kjellberg. They were married on February 8, 1869. Died in Tendar (Kunama) after the birth of a son to her and P E Kjellberg. The son too died.

Kjellberg, Per Eric, ★1837–02–27, †1869–04–17. Pioneer missionary who was both a craftsman and blacksmith in Tendar. Died in an ambush in the Tika region, Kunama. Married to Maria Karlsson 1869–02–08.

Knutsson, Karl, ★1863–06–14, †1936–06. Lay missionary and builder in Kismayu, Mofi och Jonti 1900–1928.

Kågebo (Karlsson, Malm), Sally, ★1902–11–29, †1986–02–25. Nurse and teacher in Nedjo and Neqemte 1931–1934. Later in Bijori, India. Married to Uno Karlsson 1931–06–14.

Kågebo (Karlsson), Uno, ★1901–09–19, †1985–02–27. Pastor in Nedjo and Neqemte 1931–1934. Later missionary in Bijori India. Married to Sally Malm 1931–06–14.

Lageard, Eraldo, ★1905, †1982. Italian teacher sent by the Waldensian Church. Teacher and worker at printing press. First in Geleb, and then in Asmara, 1924–1930.

Lager (Nilsson), Bengta, ★1842–05–14, †1913. Deaconess and nurse in Ailet 1875–1876, married to Per-Eric Lager 1875–11–22. Bengta gave birth to a daughter, Erika, in Sweden on March 4, 1877, who died the same year.

Emigrated to USA 1880 where she became a registered doctor in 1885. Died in Chicago 1913.

Lager, Per Erik, ★1837–11–10, †1876–07–17. Pioneer missionary, teacher and dresser (medical orderly) from 1866–1876. Murdered in Addi Qontsi, Eritrea. Married to Bengta Nilsson 1875–11–22.

Lange, Lars Johan, ★1836–07–11, †1911–02–07. Pastor and one of the first three missionaries. In Kunama only the year 1866, then pastor in the diocese of Växjö diocese. From 1887 vicar in Pjätteryd, Sweden.

Larsson, Adolf, ★1842–08–07. Carpenter who was sent out 1875 as a homesteader, stayed in Alexandria, Egypt, due to disturbances caused by war. Returned to Sweden 1876.

Larsson, Barbro, ★1930–11–09, †2000–02–06. Teacher at Swedish School in Asmara 1972–1974.

Larsson, Erika, ★1872–10–31, †1930–02–23. Nurse and midwife, most of the time in Awsa Konoma 1909–1925.

Larsson, Olof, ★1859–09–27, †1949. Came out 1887 as medical assistant but returned due to sickness. Assistant with seamen's mission in Hamburg 1889. Seamen's pastor in Bremen and Lübeck until 1939.

Larsson-Alsén (Larsson), Signe, ★1926–11–11. Nurse and midwife in Geleb from 1954 to 1969. In Asmara from 1970–1974. Medical Coordinator in Gedaref 1981–1983. Married to Stig Alsén 2000–03–31.

Lennse (Eriksson), Agneta, ★1959–05–13. Theologian and teacher in Barentu 1997–1998. Married to Anders Lennse 1989–04–28.

Lennse, Anders, ★1962–05–20. Pastor and teacher in Barentu 1997–1998. Married to Agneta Eriksson 1989–04–28.

Lexberg, Frans Ludvig, ★1852–10–25. Came as "Homesteader" to Massawa 1875–1877.

Lindén, Gudrun, ★1942–04–26. Teacher for the deaf in Keren 1969–1971.

Lindfors, Frans Johan, ★1884-01-18, †1912-06-22. Pastor in Beleza 1909-1912. He died a month after his marriage to Gusti Steinvall 1912-05-01.

Lindfors, Gusti, see Söderström.

Lindfors, Louise, see Iwarson

Lindström, Hulda, ★1854-07-13, †1898-08-21. Deaconess and matron. In Imkullu 1887, Tse'azzega 1891, Asmara 1892-1898. Died in Asmara after being struck by thunder.

Ljungdahl, Karin, ★1921-12-31. Teacher in Asmara 1963 and Adwa 1964-1965.

Lundahl, Bengt Peter, ★1840-03-17, †1885-12-11. Came out 1868 as pastor. Mission pioneer. Promoter of translation of hymns, order of worship, and portions of Scripture. Promoter of Oromo expeditions. Died in Imkullu 1885. Married to Gustava von Platen 1870-08-31. Married a second time to Emelie Cassel 1875-05-13.

Lundahl (Cassel), Emelie, ★1842-11-21, †1929-12-29. Teacher in Massawa and Imkullu 1875-1889 and Beleza 1890-1894. Thereafter service at the headquarters of SEM. Married to B P Lundahl 1875-05-13.

Lundahl (von Platen), Gustava, ★1839-07-01, †1872-12-20. Gustava come out as a missionary bride to Bengt Petter and they started the first school in Massawa 1871. She was also a gifted artist. Died in child birth at Ajun Musa in "Arabia" Egypt 1872. Married to B P Lundahl 1870-08-31.

Lundgren, Frida, ★1877-10-29, †1906-05-12. Nurse and midwife in Kulluku 1905-1906. Died in Kulluku.

Lundholm, Anders, ★1842-08-23, †1918. Pastor who came to Massawa 1868, then Tendar in Kunama 1869. 1870 seamen's pastor in Alexandria. Married 1876-05-30.

Lundin, Herman, ★1881-12-25, †1954-08-25. Pastor in Kismayu 1909, Jonti 1910, Mofi 1911-1916, Kismayo 1920-1935, when he was expelled. Married to Ida Fogelin 1911-10-28. Married a second time to Julia Lundberg 1928-10-06.

Lundin (Fogelin), Ida, ★1883-10-28, †1926-04-16. Teacher in Jonti 1910, Mofi 1911-1916, Kismayu 1920-1926. Died in Kismayu. Married to Herman Lundin 1911-10-28.

Lundin (Lundberg), Julia, ★1890-06-09, †1974-04-03. Teacher in Kismayu 1928-1935, when she was expelled. Married to Herman Lundin 1928-10-06.

Lundström, Karl Johan, ★1927-10-30, †2003-12-09. School Director and teacher Asmara 1952-1964. In Ethiopia 1964-1979, Torit in Sudan 1981 and Nairobi, Kenya, 1990-1995. Married to Maj-Britt Mannervik 1949-06-11.

Lundström (Mannervik), Maj-Britt, ★1915-08-11, †2010-06-09. Teacher for nurses and deaconesses in Asmara 1952-1964. In Ethiopia 1964-1979, Torit in Sudan 1981 and Nairobi, Kenya, 1990-1995. Married to Karl Johan Lundström 1949-06-11.

Mila, Jerker, ★1932-01-13. Teacher in Asmara 1973-1975. Married to Ulla Andersson 1965-04-17.

Mila (Andersson), Ulla, ★1930-10-13. Teacher in Asmara 1973-1975. Married to Jerker Mila 1965-04-17.

Månsson, Olof, ★1845-01-17, †1894-07-15. Pastor and teacher. Missionary in Imkullu, Geleb, Massawa, Asmara and Beleza, 1874-1894. Died in Beleza 1894. Married to Rosa von Hagen 1875-05-15.

Månsson (von Hagen), Rosa, ★1841-09-28, †1885-07-29. Director for Girls' School in Imkullu 1875-1885. Died there. Married to Olof Månsson 1875-05-15.

Nilsson (Gustafsson), Elsa Maria, ★1886-01-14, †1921-11-13. Nurse and Matron at the Children's home in Beleza 1919-1921. Died in child birth in Asmara. Buried in Beleza. Married to Nils Nilsson 1919-11-01.

Nilsson, Inga, ★1924-01-14. Teacher at Swedish school in Asmara 1958-1960 and in Beleza 1963-1966.

Nilsson (Hallendorf), Lina, ★1866-07-27,

†1942–06–14. Matron in Agordat 1897–1902, Geleb, Kulluku 1902–1905. Married to J M Nilsson 1897–11–05.

Nilsson, Johan Magnus, ★1865–12–20, †1949–11–28. Pastor in Geleb 1895–1896, Agordat and Kulluku 1897–1910, Geleb 1911–1913, Kulluku 1913–1915, Konoma 1921–1924. Married to Lina Hallendorf 1897–11–05.

Nilsson, Maria, ★1879–10–06, †1930–03–12. Nurse in Kulluku 1913 and 1923–1930, and Awsa Konoma 1914–1921. Buried in Kulluku.

Nilsson, Marianne, ★1941–12–29. Teacher in Asmara 1963–1965, Adwa 1970–1973. Music teacher in Addis Ababa 1973–1976.

Nilsson, Nils, ★1881–09–17, †1953–11–23. Pastor in Beleza 1913–1923. Addis Ababa 1924–1936. Married to Elsa Maria Gustafsson 1919–11–01. Married a second time to Tekla Frisk 1924–11–27.

Nilsson, Tekla, ★1884–06–16, †1974–07–07. Teacher at Children's home in Eritrea 1921–1930, Ethiopia 1931–1937. Later missionary in Tanzania 1940–1949.

Nilsson (Frisk), Thekla, ★1889–11–25, †1984–12–13. Nurse in Beleza 1921–1924, Addis Ababa 1925–1936. Married to Nils Nilsson in 1924–11–27.

Nilsson, Thilda. Nurse who became sick on her way out to Kunama in 1907 and had to return.

Nordfeldt (Ericsson), Ingeborg, ★1898–05–28, †1985–04–11. Teacher at Children's home in Beleza 1922–1924. In Ethiopia and Neqemte 1924–1926 and Nedjo 1927–1936. Then missionary in Tanzania 1938–1954. Married to Martin Nordfeldt 1924–09–02.

Nordfeldt, Martin, ★1898–11–29, †1976–12–20. Pastor i Neqemte 1924–1926, Nedjo 1927–1936. Later in Tanzania, Ilula 1938–1940, Kidugala 1941–1942, Ilembula 1942–1948, Kidugala 1949–1954. Married to Ingeborg Ericsson 1924–09–02.

Nordlander, Agne, ★1939–07–24. Dr. of Theology. Teacher at Beleza 2005.

Missionary in Ethiopia 1992–1996. Married to Karin Öberg 1968–06–21.

Nordlander (Öberg), Karin, ★1945–06–29. Teacher. Worked among women in Asmara 2005. Missionary in Ethiopia 1992–1996. Married to Agne Nordlander 1968–06–21.

Norelius, Hanna, ★1912–04–20, †2004–10–15. Teacher of homemaking in Beleza 1967 and Addi Ugri 1968–1972.

Normark (Lundgren), Ruth, ★1940–06–19. Teacher in Beleza 1964–1965, Kulluku 1965–1970, Addi Ugri 1972–1975. Missionary in Khartoum 1981–1982, teacher in Beleza 2006. Secretary for recruitment of personnel for international service for SEM, SCM and CSA 1988–1996, and Mission Secretary for the Horn of Africa 1996–2001. Married to Sture Normark 1961–06–10.

Normark, Sture, ★1937–07–19. Pastor in Beleza 1964–1965, Kulluku as district missionary 1965–1970, Addi Ugri as district missionary 1972–1975. Later Mission Secretary at SEM in Sweden. Khartoum 1981–1982, Teacher in Beleza 2006. Married to Ruth Lundgren 1961–06–10.

Nylander (Johansson), Ester, ★1897–09–18, †1992–05–01. Nurse in Kismayu 1928–1929, Mofi 1930–1933. Later missionary in Tanzania 1949–1964. Married to Gustav Nylander 1930–11–28.

Nylander, Gustav, ★1901–01–17, †1984–12–25. Pastor in Alessandra, Somalia 1926, Kismayu 1927–1929, Mofi 1930–1933. Later missionary in Tanzania 1949–1964. Married to Ester Johansson 1930–11–28.

Nyström (Palmér), Agnes, ★1870–10–10, †1957–12–15. Missionary in Imkullu 1897–1898, Beleza 1898–1911 when she joined BV. Missionary in Eritrea until 1932. Married to Karl Nyström 1896.

Nyström, Greta, ★1905–11–05. Nurse and midwife in Nedjo 1934–1936, when she was expelled.

Nyström, Karl, ★1866–04–01, †1946–09–29. Nurse who later became educated as a medical doctor in London 1895. Lamu 1893, Harer 1894, Imkullu 1896–1897, Beleza 1898–1911, when he joined BV. Missionary in Eritrea until 1932. Married to Agnes Palmér 1896.

Nyström, Vilma, ★1883–04–12, †1961–05–05. Nurse and midwife in Awsa Konoma 1910–1911, Beleza 1912–1913, Addi Ugri 1913–1920, Asmara 1923–1925, Tse'azzega 1925–1931, Awsa Konoma 1931–1932.

Olivetti,Germana ★1899, †1969. Italian teacher sent by the Waldensian Church. Teacher in Beleza 1924–1925.

Olsén (Tåquist), Eva, ★1947–06–12. Nurse and midwife at clinics in Asmara 1975–1977. Work among refugees in Sudan 1977–1978, 1985–1987 and in Somalia 1988–1990. Married to Ulf Olsén 1993–02–27.

Olsson (Waller), Anna, ★1906–09–24. Missionary, educated in language and management. In Nedjo 1932. Later missionary in India 1936–1952. Married to Josef Olsson 1932–05–19.

Olsson (Andersson), Erika, ★1863–11–21, †1942–02–25. Teacher and matron at Children's home in Kismayu and Jonti 1899–1935, when she was expelled. Married to Per Olsson 1899–10–05.

Olsson, Hilma, ★1896–12–08, †1970–07–18. Nurse in Neqemte Ethiopia 1926–1927 and Nedjo 1927–1930, 1933–1936, when she was expelled.

Olsson, Håkan, ★1920–05–15, †2003–11–24. Head Master and Teacher and later Pastor. In Asmara 1948–1953, 1957–1959. Married to Siri Jönsson 1947–12–06.

Olsson (Olsson), Ingeborg, ★1843–09–09, †1888–11–11. Missionary in Geleb and Imkullu 1877–1880. Married to Lars Anders Olsson 1877–03–10.

Olsson, Josef, ★1904–04–13, †1974–03–09. Pastor in Nedjo 1931–1932. Later missionary in India 1936–1952. Married to Anna Waller 1932–05–19.

Olsson, Lars Anders, ★1840–12–29, †1916–10–15. Missionary to Natal

1873–1874, then Pastor in Massawa, Geleb and Imkullu 1874–1880. Thereafter seamen's pastor in Gloucester, Hamburg and then pastor in Sweden. Married to Ingeborg Olsson 1877–03–10.

Olsson, Per, ★1864–12–13, †1926–04–05. Pastor in Geleb 1895–1898, in Kismayu and Jonti 1899–1927. Buried in Africa. Married to Erika Andersson 1899–10–05.

Olsson (Jönsson), Siri, ★1917–03–17, †2002–04–01. Nurse in Asmara 1948–1953, 1957–1959, Zazega 1960. Married to Håkan Olsson 1947–12–06.

Perman, Ruth, ★1897–11–03. Nurse in Neqemte Ethiopia 1930–1931 and Nedjo 1932–1936, when she was expelled.

Persson, Gunilla, ★1941–11–07. Teacher at the Swedish school in Asmara 1965–1967, later missionary in Tanzania.

Persson, Inger, ★1949–01–13. Teacher in Keren 1974–1977. Later missionary among refugees in Umgurgur, Sudan.

Pettersson, Gustaf, ★1849–11–03, †1877–08–04. Missionary to Natal 1873. Worked as teacher in carpentry in Massawa 1874–1877. Died in Geleb 1877. Married to Hulda Nyberg 1877–03–10.

Pettersson (Nyberg), Hulda, ★1839–01–07. Teacher in Masawa 1877. Returned some time after the death of her husband in 1877. Married to Gustaf Pettersson 1877–03–10.

Pettersson, Johan Emanuel, ★1860–02–15, †1888–11–19. Practical person and teacher in carpentry who arrived in Imkullu on Oct. 28, 1888 and died of dysentery on Nov 19, 1888.

Påhlman (Söderblom), Anna, ★1861–12–18, †1925–08–16. Missionary in Imkullu 1889–1890, Geleb 1891–1892. Married to Axel Påhlman 1889–09–22.

Påhlman, Axel Wilhelm, ★1852–10–01, †1928–04. Teacher in Imkullu. Took part in the 2nd Oromo Exp. 1881–1882 and the 3rd Oromo Exp. 1884–1886. In

Geleb 1891–1892. Travelling preacher in Sweden 1892–1899. Married to Anna Söderblom 1889–09–22.

Renlund, Anders, ★1870–03–25, †1908–04–15. Pastor in Imkullu 1900–1906, Geleb 1907–1908. Died in Geleb 1908. Married to Maria Söderlund 1902–11–24 in Imkullu.

Renlund (Söderlund), Maria, ★1876–03–19, †1952–01–02. Teacher in Imkullu 1902–1906, Geleb 1907–1908, when her husband died. After coming home, she served at the headquarters of the SEM. Married to Anders Renlund 1902–11–24.

Riggers, Heinrich ★1864–08–24. American of German origin. Took part in Fourth Oromo Expedition to Lamu 1893–1894. Left for Germany 1894.

Rodén (Nilsson), Emelie, ★1865–09–13, †1925–03–14. Nurse in Arkiko 1887–1888, Geleb 1899–1920. Married to Karl Gustaf Rodén 1887–10–06.

Rodén, Karl Gustaf, ★1860–08–27, †1943–11–23. Pastor in Massawa 1884–1886, Arkiko 1887–1888, Geleb 1889–1911, 1913–1920. Published literature in Tigré. Married to Emilie Nilsson 1887–10–06. Married a second time to Anna Nilsson 1926.

Roos, Elsie, ★1900–04–26, †1967–06–02. Teacher for the deaf in Keren 1955–1965. One of the founders of the school. Sent out by DAM.

Rostan, Nora, ★1896, †1979. Italian teacher sent by the Waldensian Church. Teacher in Asmara 1924–1925.

Rönnbäck (Holmström), Elisabeth, ★1937–11–19. Teacher in Geleb 1962–1965, Beleza 1966–1969, Addi Ugri 1970, Asmara 1971–1973. Married to Inge Rönnbäck 1960–08–13.

Rönnbäck, Inge, ★1937–11–19. Teacher and Pastor in Geleb 1962–1965, Beleza 1966–1969, Addi Ugri 1970, Asmara 1971–1973. Married to Elisabeth Holmström 1960–08–13.

Rönnbäck (Persson), Märta, ★1939–11–18. Teacher. Asmara 1968–1974. Later missionary in Nairobi 1977–1982, partly with Christian Council of Kenya. Married to Nils Rönnbäck 1967–05–27.

Rönnbäck, Nils, ★1939–09–11. Teacher and School Director in Asmara 1968–1974. Work with National Christian Council of Kenya 1977–1982. Later Mission Secretary at SEM/CSM in Sweden. Married to Märta Persson 1967–05–27.

Sandberg, Lars, ★1844–06–04, †1875–04–08. Lay Missionary to Natal 1873. Massawa 1874–1875. Died in Geleb 1875.

Sand-Björkman (Björkman), Ingrid, ★1941–01–12. Nurse in Neqemte Ethiopia 1970–1973 and Asmara 1974–1976. Married to Stig Sand 1991–07–05.

Segerberg (Nicander), Anna, ★1856–08–16, †1886–12–05. Teacher at school in Massawa 1884–1888. Died of TB at a hospital in Asab. Married to Wilhelm A. Segerberg 1886.

Segerberg, Wilhelm Alfred, ★1856–09–27. Head of printing press in Imkullu 1884–1894, Asmara 1895–1896. Married to Anna Nicander 1886.

Sköld, Stina, ★1893–09–03. Teacher in Neqemte 1926–1936, when she was expelled. Married to Emil Karlsson 1937.

Slotte (Edholm), Iris, ★1919–03–18, †2000–07–09. Teacher in Asmara 1946–1948, Addi Ugri 1948–1951, Sweden 1951–1953, Beleza 1953–1959. Married to Wilhelm Slotte.

Slotte, Wilhelm, ★1917–10–17, †1991–07–02. Pastor in Asmara 1946–1948, Addi Ugri 1948–1951, Sweden 1951–1953, Beleza 1953–1959. Married to Iris Edholm.

Stjärne, Per, ★1895–10–07, †1984–04–29. Teacher and pastor in Addis Ababa 1921–1933. Came back to Ethiopia after the war 1945 and served up to 1969. Married to Valborg Olsson 1921–01–23.

Stjärne (Olsson), Valborg, ★1895–02–07, †2000–03–28. Teacher in Addis Ababa 1921–1933. Came back after the war in November 1945 and served up to 1969.

Married to Per Stjärne 1921-01-23.

Stolpe, Isabella, ★1885-02-03, †1973-11-14. Nurse in Asmara 1921-1930. Then worked at SEM Headquarter in Sweden 1931-1949.

Ström, Anna, ★1892-04-08, †1975-04-20. Deaconess in Somalia, Mofi 1921-1923, Jonti 1924-1928, Kismayu 1929-1933, Jonti 1934-1935, when she was expelled. Later missionary to Tanzania 1939-1948.

Ståhlberg (Olsson), Ingrid, ★1937-10-27. Teacher in Asmara 1966-1975. Married to Ingvar Ståhlberg 1965-07-31.

Ståhlberg, Ingvar, ★1936-03-10. Teacher, School Director in Asmara 1966-1975. Married to Ingrid Olsson 1965-07-31.

Sundin, Anna-Lisa, ★1934-01-07. Teacher in Asmara 1967-1977.

Sundström, Gustaf Richard, ★1869-08-18, †1919-06-16. Pastor, nurse, language scholar, archeologist. Italy 1897, Geleb 1898-1907, 1910-1911, Keren 1913-1919. Died in Keren 1919. Married to Hanna Broberg 1898-11-06.

Sundström (Broberg), Hanna, ★1871-04-01, †1963-12-24. Matron at Children's home in Geleb 1898-1907, 1910-1911, Keren 1913-1921. Married to Gustaf Richard Sundström 1898-11-06.

Svennas, Doris. Teacher for the deaf in Keren, 1959-1960. Sent out by DAM. Married to Ivar Svennas.

Svennas, Ivar. Teacher and pastor for the deaf in Keren, 1959-1960. Sent out by DAM. Married to Doris Svennas.

Svensson, Anders, ★1849-04-07, †1928-06-04. Pastor. Missionary in Massawa 1877, Adwa 1877-1879, Imkullu 1879-1883. Shewa 1884, Imkullu 1885-1890,Tse'azzega 1891-1928. Field Director 1886-1913. Buried in Tse'azzega. Patriarchal figure in SEM and ECE.

Svensson, Anna, ★1866-05-23, †1960-12-05. Teacher in Beleza 1901-1909, 1917-1919 and Geshinashim 1910-1916.

Svensson (Larsson), Astrid, ★1922-03-09. Nurse and midwife in Awsa Konoma

1950-1956, Asmara 1957-1967. Refugee work in Khartoum, Sudan 1980. Married to Gunnar Svensson 1949-12-31.

Svensson, Gunnar, ★1923-09-03. Pastor and district missionary in Awsa Konoma 1950-1956, Field Representative in Asmara 1957- 1967. Later Mission Secretary at SEM in Sweden. Refugee work in Khartoum, Sudan 1980. Married to Astrid Larsson 1949-12-31.

Säfström, Kerstin, ★1942-04-07. Teacher at the School for the Deaf in Keren 1969-1971.

Söderström, Erik D., ★1890-09-26, †1945-11-10. Doctor in Addis Ababa 1920-1923 and Neqemte 1924-1936, when he was expelled. Later missionary in South Africa and Ethiopia. Married to Gusti Lindfors 1919.

Söderström (Lindfors, Steinwall), Gusti, ★1884-09-26, †1947-04-05. Nurse and teacher in Tse'azzega 1910-1911, Beleza 1912-1914, Addis Ababa, Neqemte 1920-1936, when she was expelled. Later missionary in South Africa and Ethiopia. Married to Frans Lindfors 1912-05-01 but became a widow already after June 22. Married a second time to Erik Söderström 1919.

Söderström, Karin, ★1893-01-14,1967-11-30, Nurse in Addis Ababa 1920-1923 and Neqemte 1924-1936, when she was expelled.

Thorell, Johan Fredrik, ★1846-07-18, †1893-06-26. Sent to Beirut for language studies 1873-1874, then to Massawa 1876-1877. Seamen's pastor in Alexandria 1877-82. Married to Rosalie Fougelberg 1879-10-10.

Thurfjell, Einar, ★1902-10-29, †1988-04-10. Pastor in Jonti, Somalia 1933-1935, when he was expelled. India 1937-1948. Teacher at Johannelund 1948-1953, Assistant Secretary for Foreign Mission 1953-1955, Secretary for Foreign Mission 1956-1959, Mission Director 1959-1969. Married to the teacher Karin Dahl 1937-01-12.

Torpstad, Emmy, ★1919–03–21, †2002–07–24. Nurse in Kulluku 1948–1970.

Tron, Alessandro , ★1887–09–02, †1966–10–05. Italian teacher sent by the Waldensian Church. Teacher and later Pastor in Asmara 1913–1923, Beleza 1924–1929, Asmara 1930–1949, Keren 1950–1951, Asmara 1952–1954. Married to Dina Danesi 1911. Married a second time to Velia Danesi 1926.

Tron, Bruno, ★1930–06–03. Italian Teacher and later Pastor in Asmara 1949, 1953–1955, Addi Ugri 1958–1959, Beleza 1959–1967, Asmara 1967–1977. Married to Paola Nisbet 1962–01–31.

Tron (Danesi), Dina, ★1881–10–07, †1921 Italian teacher sent by the Waldensian Church. Teacher in Asmara 1915–1921. Married to Allessandro Tron 1911.

Tron (Nisbet), Paola, ★1934–06–26. Teacher in Beleza 1962–1967, Asmara 1967–1977. Married to Bruno Tron 1962–01–31.

Tron (Danesi), Velia, ★1888–04–20, †1968. Italian teacher sent by the Waldensian Church. Teacher and women secretary in Beleza 1924–1929, Asmara 1930–1935, Beleza 1936, Asmara 1937–1949, Keren 1950–1951, Asmara 1952–1954. Married to Allessandro Tron 1926.

Törnkvist, Rune, ★1943–03–25. Advisor in Economic matters in Asmara 1993–1994. Later Mission Secretary at SEM in Sweden.

Uhlin, Herbert, ★1898–11–04, †1976–03–16. Pastor in Jonti Somalia 1926–1935, when he was expelled. Later missionary in Tanzania, Dongobesh 1938–1942, teacher in Kinampanda, Lwandi, Makumira up to 1963. Married to Rut Johansson 1929–03–31. Married a second time to Greta Johansson 1943–07–18.

Uhlin (Johansson), Ruth, ★1906–04–29, †1942–02–07. Teacher in Jonti, Somalia 1928–1935, when she was expelled. Missionary in Tanzania, Dongobesh 1938–1942. Married to Herbert Uhlin 1929–03–31.

Vanberg, Johannes, ★1835–04–09, †1869–11–11. Lay assistant. Massawa 1867, Ouganna 1968, Tendar 1969, where he died of fever.

Wallin (Högberg), Gerd, ★1947–07–07. Nurse in Asmara 1970–1977. Married to Olle Wallin 1968–08–10.

Wallin, Olle, ★1945–03–27. Construction Engineer in Asmara 1970–1977, 1996. Married to Gerd Högberg 1968–08–10.

West, Arvid, ★1890–12–17, †1967–12–23. Pastor in Mofi, Somalia 1921–1926. Married to Inez Karlsson 1922–01–22.

West (Karlsson), Inez, ★1895–06–08, †1966–01–10. Teacher in Mofi, Somalia 1921–1926. Married to Arvid West 1922–01–22.

Winqvist, Anna, ★1878–12–05, †1912–04–26. Nurse and head of Home for Girls in Geleb 1904–1912. Died in Geleb.

Winqvist (Hefter), Elsie, ★1863–09–04, †1957–12–22. Teacher in Imkullu 1883–1895, Beleza 1897–1909, Asmara 1930–1936, when she was expelled. Translated Bible in Eritrea and later in Rome from 1937. Back in Asmara 1946–1957. Died in Asmara. Married to Karl Winqvist 1883–11–15.

Winqvist (Karlsson), Karl, ★1847–10–14, †1909–12–06. Seamen's pastor in Grimsby 1878–1879. From 1880–1883 medical studies in Edinburgh. Mission doctor in Imkullu 1883–1895 and in Beleza 1897–1909. Promoted translation of Bible and other devotional literature. Died in Beleza. Married to Elsie Hefter 1883–11–15.

Wirén, Hjalmar, ★1876–09–03. Lay missionary and teacher of handicraft in Asmara 1906–1912. Married to Lydia Nordbrandt 1908–10–16.

Wirén (Nordbrandt), Lydia Kristina, ★1875–10–22. Missionary in Asmara 1908–1912. Married to Hjalmar Wirén 1908–10–16.

Åkesson, Elina, ★1873–12–25, †1938–03–28. Nurse, midwife, teacher and missionary among women in Kismayu 1904–1912.

Appendix VII

List of Eritrean and Ethiopian Colleagues for the Period upto ca. 1935

This list of Eritrean and Ethiopian colleagues is by no means complete. It is based on names (often only forenames) and facts found in annual reports for SEM and on the lists of those who received regular support from Swedish friends of the mission. In other words the list is heavily dependent on Swedish sources. In many cases the spelling of names and places is defective. In this list we have included those who have laboured in Somalia and Ethiopia up to ca. 1936. The reason for this is that Swedish missionary activity in Eritrea, Ethiopia and Somalia, was regarded as a unit.

Abraha. Assistant at the printing press in Asmara, 1908.

Abraham Etel. Teacher and Evangelist in Geleb 1905–1924. Co-worker with Karl Gustaf Rodén.

Afeworqi. Teacher and Evangelist in Beleza 1910–1911, Asmara 1914–1937.

Alazar Hailu. Dresser in Asmara, 1929–1937.

Alazar. Evangelist and assistant at the printing press in Imkullu 1887–1893, Geleb 1894–1904, Keren 1905–1908, Geleb 1909–1955.

Almaz Selomon. Completed the Teacher Training Course at Beleza in 1932 .

Amanuel Gebre-Mikael. Co-worker at the Home for Children at Addi Qeyih 1913–1915, Asmara 1916–1920 and Tse'azzega 1921–1922.

Amanuel Hemmed. Former Muslim Oromo. Ailet/Geleb 1877. Took part in the First Oromo Expedition 1877–1884.

Was in Jimma 1885–1891. Died on November 16, 1891.

Amanuel. Assistant at the printing press in Imkullu 1892–1894, Asmara 1895–1907.

Amete-Tsion Girma-Tsion. Bible woman and nurse in Beleza 1921–1924.

Amleset Selomon. Bible woman in Himbirti, district of Tse'azzega 1913–1920.

Amlesom. Farmer-teacher in Beleza district, 1914–1924.

Andemikael Wolde-Merqorios (Menqeres). Teacher and pastor in Asmara 1930, Beleza 1931–1932, Tse'azzega 1933 and Addi Ugri 1934–1945.

Aster Ganno Salbana, 1859–1964. Oromo translator and Bible woman in Imkullu 1892–1894, Geleb 1895–1897, Asmara 1898–1903, Nedjo 1904–1905, and Neqemte 1905–1955.

Aster Woldemariam. Trained in Addi Ugri and Beleza. Served in both Addi Ugri and Asmara, not least in connection with the Spanish Flu. Bible woman and teacher in Tse'azzega 1926. Teacher at a school for girls in Addis Ababa 1927–1935, and in other capacities from 1936–1944. Died in 2000 in USA.

Bahlibbi Semere. Born in Beleza July 1891. Died Jan. 1, 1988. Farmer, teacher and builder. "Protected" mission property in Beleza under Italian/Catholic period as tenant. Made head of administration of the Beleza station by SEM.

Bahlibbi Garza. Nurse and Evangelist. Deda, 1914–1915, Asmara 1924–1929, Tse'azzega 1930–1945.

Bahta. Evangelist, Tse'azzega 1908–1909.

Bahtu (Haleqa). Former Orthodox scholar who became an Evangelical Christian. Served as an evangelist and teacher in Addi Ugri 1919–1924.

Bairu Uqbit. Teacher and translator. Active in Asmara, from around 1920. Prominent member of Synodical Council. Translated Pilgrim's Progress to Tigrinya in 1926. Also took part in translation of the Bible to Tigrinya.

Barnabas. Evangelist and teacher in Wasentat 1911–1920. Died in 1920.

Beftu. Teacher in Geshinashim, Beleza district, from 1916, 1920–1921. Died in 1922.

Begashet Ingida. Received into the congregation in Tse'azzega in 1901. Teacher in Asmara from 1906–1913. Also assistant to Olle Eriksson in the production of literature.

Bekhit Habelom. Assistant at the printing press in Asmara 1907–1908. Teacher in Addi Ni'amin 1910–1916, and Tse'azzega 1917–1944.

Berhe Zemmu. Teacher in Addi Ugri 1914–1922, Asmara 1923–1931. Later moved to Ethiopia.

Beyin Dafla. Assistant Printer and then farmer-teacher. Asmara 1904–1909, Shimanigus 1910–1922, Tse'azzega 1923–1930.

Beyin Ristu. From the village of Shimanigus La'ilai. Evangelist and teacher in Beleza district 1923–1945.

Bihil Mahrai. Teacher and Evangelist already from Imkullu days. In Beleza 1900–1913, Kwazen 1914–1916, Beleza 1917–1944. In Wollega on several occasions to teach and preach. Built a home-church at Addingoda, Kwazen.

Birhane Gishen. Teacher and Evangelist in Addi Zarna 1913–1916, and Addi Ugri from 1917–1930.

Birikhti. Female co-worker, Beleza 1920.

Birritu. Bible woman and teacher in Beleza 1910–1913, Addi Ugri 1914–1915, Beleza 1920.

Birru Tirfé (Qeshi). Teacher, later ordained. Imkullu 1897, Asmara 1898–1899, Beleza 1900–1920. Died in 1922.

Bitchir. Female co-worker from the village of Berrakh, near Addi Ugri. Served in Addi Ugri district 1924–1937, 1945–1955.

Boru Siba. Evangelist and teacher in Bojji Kerkero, (Wollega), Ethiopia, 1904–1908, Siban 1909–1922.

Daher Bin Abdi. Born 1884 in Somalia. Educated at Imkullu and at Johannelund in Stockholm 1903–1908. Trained in Medicine in London 1908. Kismayu and Jonti 1909.

Dafla Hosabai. Dresser in Geleb 1925 and later.

Damte. Dresser in Tigrai 1928–1937.

Daniel (Debela). Baptized in Imkullu 1881, received the name Daniel at baptism. Teacher in Imkullu 1887–1891, Tse'azzega 1891–1896. To Neqemte via Jimma and Gojjam. Neqemte 1897–1901, Leqa 1902–1904. Died in 1904.

Daniel Luli. Imkullu 1881. Ordained in Asmara 1932, Teacher in Asmara district 1932–1937, pastor in Kunama 1953–1955. Helped with translation of the Bible into Kunama.

Daniel. Guard in Imkullu 1908–1909.

Dawit Amanuel. 1862–1944. First convert of Mensa stock. Baptized by Lundahl by immersion in the Geleb River on July 8, 1877. A pillar of the church. Evangelist in Imkullu 1888-1889, then in Geleb district 1890–1944. Ordained in 1925. Very important contribution to translation of the New Testament to Tigré.

Debbas Negasi 1869–1927. In 1888 sent to the Waldensian Seminary at Firenze, Italy for teacher training. Teacher and Evangelist in Tse'azzega 1894–1897, Asmara 1898–1915, Tse'azzega 1921–1925. Tutored some of the first Oromo converts who were on a visit to Eritrea in 1911.

Debesai Mengesha. Teacher in Beleza 1921–1924.

Debre Sillassé. Teacher in Asmara 1900–1905.

Djämer. Teacher in Beleza 1910–1911, Tigrai 1912, Shimanigus 1913, Addi Ugri 1914–1919, Beleza 1920–1924.

Efrem Tewolde-Medhin. Son of *Qeshi* Tewolde-Medhin Gebre-Medhin. Dresser and teacher. Ghinda 1905. In 1913 he and his brother Yishaq studied in Beirut with Bahta Gila-Mikael. Served in Beleza 1916–1920, Asmara 1921–1922. He then moved to Ethiopia as a teacher, where he eventually became a diplomat of rank.

Elias. Baptized 1889. Assistant at the printing press in Imkullu 1894, Asmara 1895–1896.

Ellen Kahsai. Among the first women trained as nurses in Asmara. Nurse in Geleb 1927–1928, Beleza 1929–1947.

Elsabet (Ajané). Massawa 1875–1877. Received name Elsabet at baptism in 1877. Went to Wollega as Evangelist 1878. Jimma 1888–1889. Died in 1889.

Elsabet Bekhit. Bible woman in Tse'azzega 1916.

Elsabet Habte-Tsion. Bible woman in Beleza 1924–1926, Tse'azzega 1929, and Addi Ugri 1945–1955.

Elsabet Kahsai. Bible woman in Addi Ugri 1928–1937.

Embaye Habte-Egzi. Bible translator, dresser, teacher, pastor, and translator of a number of books on the spiritual life. Asmara 1927–1931, Bible translation in Rome 1940–1944 in cooperation with Elsie Winqvist. In Asmara 1945–1955. Translated several books. Died Jan. 9, 2000.

Ezra Awalom. Well-known dresser in Asmara 1926–1945. Moved to Ethiopia.

Filippos Feraja. An Oromo baptized as a young man in Imkullu. Took part in the Second Oromo Expedition 1881–1882. Died in Khartoum 1882.

Firezgi Gebre-Mikael. Teacher and Evangelist in Tselot 1913–1915, Asmara 1916–1945.

Fisseha-Tsion Gebre-Giorgis. From Addi Manna in Guhtsi'a. Evangelist and teacher in Asmara 1905–1906, Addi Manna 1907–1913, Addi Ugri 1914–1922. Ordained 1922. Pastor in Tse'azzega 1923–1924 and in Addi Ugri 1925–1946.

Gebrat Giliat. Teacher/Evangelist, Asmara 1916–1931. Moved to Ethiopia.

Gebre-Egziabher Kiflom. Dresser/Evangelist, Asmara 1925–1926, Tigrai 1927–1945.

Gebre Kristos Tekle-Haimanot. Son of *Qeshi* Tekle-Haimanot Mihirka of Hatsebo near Axum. Teacher at the school for boys in Asmara and Weki Dibba from 1910–1920. Moved to Addis Ababa. Appointed director of Ras Teferi's new printing press Birhan ena Selam (Light and Peace). Died in Addis Ababa in October 1932.

Gebre-Egziabher Kokebe-Worq, (*Abba*). Monk and colporteur (seller and distributor of books). Massawa 1887–1896, Jimma 1897–1898, Gojjam 1899–1901, Leqa 1902–1909, Amhara 1913–1919, Wollega 1920–1922, Addis Ababa 1926–1944.

Gebre-Ewostatewos Ze-Mikael. Orthodox priest, who later served as an Evangelical pastor in Tse'azzega, 1892–1896. Felt a call to the Oromo. Pioneer among Kenisha missionaries outside of Eritrea. Proceeded to Jimma 1897–1898, Neqemte, 1899–1901, Leqa 1902–1903, Bojji Kerkero 1904–1905. Died in a fire at Bojji 1905.

Gebre-Georgis Baryaw. A refugee from the highlands who replaced Habte-Giorgis Tesfai (after the latter's death) as evangelist and teacher at the school at Imkullu. Served from 1887–1890 and in Beleza 1891–1895.

Gebre-Georgis Tirfé. Son of *Qeshi* Tirfé from Tse'azzega, who was employed in 1877 to teach boys at the boys' school in Imkullu. Translated *Pilgrim's Progress* to Amharic. Served until 1887 and sent to Italy by Anders Svensson in 1888 for further training as teacher.

Gebrehet Bilon. Teacher/Evangelist in Addi Ugri 1928–1929.

Gebrehet Goshu. Brother of Gobezé Goshu. Teacher and Evangelist in Tigrai 1913–1920. Died in 1921.

Gebrehet Mihtsun (*Qeshi*). From the village of Zagir. Teacher who later became pastor. Beleza 1908–1912, Zagir 1913–1917, Beleza 1918–1926, Asmara 1927–1944, Beleza 1945–1955.

Gebre-Le'ul Tirfé. Son of *Qeshi* Tirfé from Tse'azzega. Attended the boys' school in Imkullu with his brother Gebre-Giorgis in the late 1890,s. Studied in Italy for a year. Evangelist in Misgwag, in the district of Tse'azzega 1901–1902, 1910–1924.

Gebre-Mariam. Evangelist and teacher in Ta'ireshi, Beleza district 1913–1919.

Gebre-Mesqel. Teacher in Beleza 1916–1924.

Gebre-Mikael Tedros. Assistant at the printing press at Asmara 1890–1955.

Gebre-Mikael. Evangelist in Addi Qontsi 1899–1912, Addi Gulgel 1913–1916, Tse'azzega 1917–1920. Died on September 16, 1920. Buried by the side of the Swedish missionary Lager.

Gebre-Mikael. Evangelist in Tigrai 1927–1945.

Gebre-Selassie Mengistu (*Abba* Me'asho). From Addi Baro. Former priest in the Orthodox Church. Evangelist in the district of Tse'azzega 1917–1922.

Gebre-Sillassé Gebru (*Qeshi*). From the village of Addi Hizbai. Spent some

years in Italy in his youth. Pastor in Addi Ugri 1906–1912, Addi Hizbai 1913–1916, Addi Ugri 1917–1945.

Gebre-Sillassé Habtu. A disciple and protegé of Pastor Anders Svensson in Tse'azzega. Pastor and president of the ECE for a long period after the 1940,s. Served in Tse'azzega 1924–1929, Shimanigus, in the district of Beleza, 1930–1944, Asmara 1945–1955.

Gebre-Sillassé Tesfa-Gabir. From Himbirti. Son of an Orthodox priest. Sent out to Bojji Kerkero in Wollega, Ethiopia, as an evangelist, where he served 1905–1909. Was in Neqemte from 1910–1913. Returned to Eritrea for some years because of ill health. Ordained and placed in Addis Ababa 1922–1931. Died on October 2, 1932 in Eritrea.

Gebre-Yesus Medhin. Evangelist and later pastor in Kwandebba, 1913–1915, and Beleza district 1916–1945.

Gebre-Yesus Tesfai. Assistant at the printing press in Imkullu, 1892–1893, 1899. Served as evangelist and teacher in Misgwag 1902–1904. He then left for Kerkero, Wollega (Ethiopia) where he served as teacher and evangelist 1905–1922. He played a leading role as evangelist, teacher and guide in the difficult period after the tragic death of *Qeshi* Gebre-Ewostatewos Ze-Mikael. He died 1925.

Gebru. Teacher and Evangelist in Tigrai 1924.

Gedel. Evangelist in Beleza 1924.

Getahun. Evangelist in 'Amhara' (Begemdir) 1913–1922, Addis Ababa 1923–1944. Co-worker with *Aleqa* Tayelinj.

Gezahegn. Evangelist and teacher in Tigrai 1914–1929.

Gidei. Bible woman in Geshinashim 1911.

Gila-Giorgis. Assistant at the printing press in Imkullu 1903.

Girma-Tsion Gebré. Evangelist and later pastor. One of the early leaders of the ECE following its establishment in 1926. Involved in the translation of the Bible. Visited Sweden. Served in Asmara 1898–1909, Beleza 1910–1912, and Asmara 1913–1933, for a while as vice-president of the ECE.

Gobezé Goshu. 1883–1951. Native of Nai'der, Tigrai. Evangelist and teacher in Beleza 1909–1911, Adwa 1912–1915. Close colleague of *Haleqa* Tewolde-Medhin Gebru. Was persecuted and once imprisoned for his faith.

Goitom. Farmer-teacher in Beleza district 1910–1911.

Gubsa Tekhlu. Teacher in Misgwag 1910–1945.

Gömesk (?) Bayou. Female co-worker in Wollega, Ethiopia, 1920–1922.

Habte-Ab Woldemariam. Teacher and musician who was trained at the Teacher Training School at Beleza and graduated in 1931. Younger brother to Woldeab Woldemariam. Moved to Ethiopia soon after graduating from Beleza, hoping to continue his musical studies abroad.

Habte-Giorgis Tirfé. 1854–1885. From Tse'azzega. Wounded severely in July 1876 in connection with the murder of Lager and Haile-Ab outside of the church of Qiddus Mikael in Addi Qontsi. He survived and was nursed at the mission clinic in Ailet until 1877. Served in Imkullu 1882–1883.

Habte-Mariam Kasa. Evangelist and teacher, a "convert" of Onesimos. Served in Asmara 1903. Neqemte 1904–1906, Sayo 1907–1909, Hamaja 1910–1922 in Wollega.

Habte-Tsion. Teacher in Addi Ugri 1914–1918, Tse'azzega 1919–1922.

Habte-Tsion. Evangelist and teacher in Hadish Addi, in the district of Addi Ugri 1907–1916, and Beleza 1917–1921.

Habtih-Yimer. 1872–1920. An Oromo resident of Asmara and a friend of Onesimos. Made a quick trip to Bojji and back in six months in April 1903. Reported on the mission to Oromo and accompanied Onesimos back to Wollega as an evangelist in 1904.

Habtu (Habté?). Teacher and evangelist who served in Haddish Addi, within the district of Addi Ugri 1910–1923.

Habtu (*Haleqa*). Evangelist and teacher in Beleza district 1930–1955.

Habtu. Evangelist and teacher in Beleza 1916–1929.

Hadji. Guard at the mission station in Imkullu 1912.

Hagosa Mengis. Female co-worker in Beleza 1921–1924.

Haiki. Assistant at the printing press in Asmara 1907.

Haile-Ab Tesfai. One of the three Evangelical pioneers. A former Orthodox priest, and spokesman for the . Begun in Ailet 1873. Put to the sword with Lager outside the church of Qiddus Mikael in Addi Qontsi on July 17, 1876.

Haile-Mariam (*Abba*). Former Orthodox priest, a monk of the monastery of Abune Merqorios. Became an Evangelical Christian and served as an evangelist and teacher in Addi Ugri 1914–1955.

Haile-Mikael Kidanu. 1856–1919. Teacher and Evangelist. On a mission to Adwa in 1877. Attended the Theological Institute at Johannelund, Stockholm, 1881–1886. Served in Imkullu 1886–1889. Teacher in Beleza 1901–1917.

Hailu. A young 'highlander', trained at Imkullu and commissioned as an evangelist. Married Sema'itu, a girl from Axum Tsion. They joined the Second Oromo Expedition 1881–1882 but had to return to Imkullu due to ill health.

Hanetsa Mebrahtu. Female co-worker in Asmara 1924–1925.

Hanna. Female co-worker in Addis Ababa 1935–1944.

Haron. Teacher and Evangelist within the Tigré-speaking area 1922–1923.

Hezqiel Gulai. Evangelist and later pastor in Kunama 1927–1955.

Hiddego (Yihddego?) Desta. Evangelist and teacher who was later ordained. Served in and around Addi Ugri 1910–1913, 1917–1924, 1945–1955, Asmara 1913–1916 and Tse'azzega 1925–1944.

Hiddego. Farmer-teacher in Addi Deqi Tekhlu, in the Addi Ugri district 1916–1920.

Hiriti. Bible woman in Asmara 1921–1937.

Imiru (Qes). Former Orthodox priest, later a teacher and evangelist in the tradition of Aleqa Tayye, in 'Amhara' (Begemdir) 1913–1917. Died in 1920.

Indirias. Widow of Qeshi Haile-Ab Tesfai. Bible woman in Beleza 1891–1896, Asmara 1897–1926. In Beleza she ran the first day school for girls which had been established as an extension of the regular school for girls. Met Adolf Kolmodin when he visited Eritrea in 1908. Died in 1926.

Indreas Gebre-Le'ul. Teacher in Tse'azzega 1924–1928.

Isaias. Teacher in Imkullu 1902–1907, Agordat 1908, Ouganna 1901–1911, Raptu 1912–1916. Kunama 1917.

Iyasu Mezengi'i. Evangelist and teacher in Tse'azzega 1908–1920.

Iyasu Be'imnet. Evangelist and teacher in Geleb 1924–1932.

Joel Fafi. Evangelist and teacher in Kunama 1930–1937.

Kafil. Assistant at the printing press and teacher at Imkullu 1887–1894, Asmara 1895–1901, Dirko 1901–1916, Addi Ugri 1916–1920, Beleza 1921–1954.

Kahsai (Haleqa). From the village of Addi Mongonti. Former Orthodox scholar who became an Evangelical Christian. Evangelist and teacher in Addi Ugri 1907–1945.

Kahsai Gebre (Qeshi). Teacher, Evangelist and later pastor in Tse'azzega district, mainly in Himbirti, 1914–1945, 1953–1955.

Kahsai Habte-Mariam. Evangelist and teacher in Tse'azzega district from 1923–1925.

Kibirti Tekle-Haimanot. Nurse, Bible woman and teacher in Tse'azzega 1929–1945.

Kidan. Farmer-teacher in Beleza area 1910–1911.

Kidane Zeru. Evangelist and teacher in Adtekelezan in Beleza district, 1913–1924.

Kidane-Mariam (Debtera). Former Orthodox scholar. Worked as evangelist in Karneshim 1895–1910. As of 1895 supported the Evangelicals. In Tigrai 1911–1912.

Kiflé Gila-Mikael. Printer at Imkullu 1896, teacher training and teaching in Asmara until 1907. Ordained 1919 and pastor in Deqqi Mehari in Beleza district.

Lette-Birhan Bahtu. From the village of Addi Felesti, Sef'a. Bible woman in Addi Ugri 1924.

Lette-Hiywet. Bible woman and nurse in Tigrai 1934–1952.

Lette-Tsion Gebre-Mariam. Nurse in Belleza 1927–1930, Asmara 1931–1951.

Lettinkiél. Bible woman in Geleb 1912.

Mahlet. Female teacher in Beleza 1892 and later.

Marqos Girmai (Germei). 1862–1924. Trained at Lundahl's school in Imkullu and then sent to Sweden where he finished his theological studies with distinction. Ordained in Uppsala in 1889. Pastor and teacher. Imkullu 1890, Tse'azzega 1891–1893, Asmara 1894–1902, 1905–1910. Went into the service of BV in 1911. Died in Sweden on April 24, 1924.

Marta Ali. Dresser in Imkullu 1889–1891, Geleb 1902 and Nurse in Keren 1934–1951.

Marta Barnabas. Teacher in Geleb 1924.

Matias. Evangelist who went with Onesimos from Asmara to Neqemte in 1904.

Me'asho. Teacher in Addi Ugri 1912–1916.

Mebrahtu Samuel. Evangelist and teacher, later ordained. Served in Hazzega 1904–1915, Tse'azzega 1916–1924.

Mekonnen Nigusé. A disciple of Aleqa Tayye who travelled from Asmara to Wollega on Febr 11th 1897 in the company of Gebre-Ewostatewos and Gumesh, Daniel and Tiru.

Mengesha Birru. "Aboy Mengesha", one of the Kenisha who moved to Ethiopia. Worked at printing press in Imkullu 1888. Sent by Emperor Minilik to Europe in 1907 to buy equipment for a printing press.

Mengesha. Teacher and Evangelist in Beleza 1921–1924.

Meshesha Lulu. Took part in Fifth Oromo Expedition 1897–1898.

Mezgebe Woldu. Teacher and Evangelist and later pastor in Abarda 1910–1925, Asmara 1925–1929, and later within the district of Tse'azzega 1930–1955. Co-operated with Pastor Mikael Holmer, Svensson's successor in Tse'azzega, in the work of Bible translation, after the death of the latter.

Mihret. Female co-worker (nurse?) in Addis Ababa 1923–1924.

Mihret. Wife of Onesimos. Took part in the Second Oromo Expedition which went via Khartoum, 1881–1882. Those who survived returned to Imkullu. Mihret died on November 20, 1888.

Mihretu. Graduated from Teacher Training School in Beleza 1931, became a teacher in Addis Ababa. Son to *Haleqa* Tewolde Medhin Gebru.

Mihretu. Teacher and Evangelist in Addis Abeba 1927–1944, Addi Ugri 1953–1955.

Mikael Nagosch. Evangelist who was with *Qeshi* Selomon in Sahati 1889.

Mikael Uqba-Gabir. Teacher within Asmara district 1916–1922. Later moved to Wollega 1922 and Addis Ababa 1923.

Musa. Teacher and Evangelist in Juba 1919–1929, Kunama 1930–1945.

Naffa wod Etman. 1882–1909. From Geleb. An Evangelical Christian, knowledgeable in matters of language and culture. Was in Germany 1907–1909 as an advisor to Enno Littmann. Disappeared between Genoa and Massawa, from the boat on which he was travelling back o Eritrea.

Natanael (Natnael) Hagena Djigo. A Kunama from Tika, admitted to Lundhahl's school in Massawa, baptized on November 11, 1877. Studied Theology in Sweden but died in May 1888, just before he could graduate. Died at Ersta Hospital in Stockholm and was buried at Bromma Cemetery in Stockholm.

Natnael Negassi. Evangelist and teacher in Imkullu, 1903–1904, Massawa 1905–1907, Geleb from 1908 into the 1920,s.

Negasa Silga. Teacher and Evangelist in Nedjo, Wollega 1934–1944.

Negassi Kahsai. Teacher in Addi Ugri and Asmara from around 1930. Director tax-office in Eritrea during The Federation. Teacher of Amharic and Morals at the Bet-Gergish government school, Asmara.

Nigusé Tashu. Ethiopian merchant who became an Evangelist and a teacher primarily among the Oromo but also others. Took part in the First Oromo Expedition, 1877–1884. Laboured in Jimma 1885–1899, the settlement known as Djiren 1903–1916, and among the Oromo 1917–1919 providing for the spiritual and physical well being of his protegés.

Nigusé. Co-worker in Wara, Beleza district 1914–1924.

Nitsiha. Female worker at the school for boys in Imkullu.

Onesimos Nesib. Born i Illubabor 1850. "First Fruits" of work of SEM. Baptized on Easter day, May 31 1872, in Massawa. Studied Theology in Sweden between 1876 and 1881. Took part in 2nd and 3rd Oromo Expeditions (1881–1882, 1884–1886). Laboured in Geleb and Asmara as an evangelist and translator of the Bible into the language of the Oromo (then known as Galligna). He returned to Wollega in 1903–1904 and laboured in Nedjo and Neqemte. Married to Mihret, who died in November 20, 1888, married a second time to Lidia Dimbio. Onesimos died in Neqemte June 21, 1931.

Pertros Reziq. Worked at printing press in Asmara 1904–1908, Geleb 1912, Juba 1923–1925. Died in 1926.

Petros Chibsa. Took part in The Third Oromo Expedition 1884–1886.

Qelati. Farmer-teacher in Beleza district 1910–1911.

Rahel Isaias. Nurse in Kunama and Geleb 1929–1955.

Reda-Ezgi. Teacher in Addi Sherefeto, in the district of Tse'azzega 1914–1916.

Redda-Tsadiq (Haleqa). Teacher and Evangelist in Tse'azzega 1904–1909, Tsa'ida Kristian 1910–1916, Tse'azzega 1917–1922, Asmara 1923–1924. Moved to Addis Ababa.

Samra. Evangelist and teacher in the Tigré-speaking regions 1914–1920.

Samuel Danki. Evangelist and teacher who opened the Alle Ambalto School in Wollega 1902. Also laboured in Kerkero 1904–1906, and in other Oromo areas 1917–1922.

Samuel Etman (Faid). Baptized and received into the congregation in Geleb 1896. Teacher in Geleb, Keren and other Tigré-speaking regions 1901–1944, and Beleza 1921–1924.

Samuel Manna. Teacher in Tse'azzega from 1933–1935.

Samuel Meshesha. Dresser in Neqemte 1923–1931.

Sebhat Le-Ab. Teacher and Evangelist in Addi Ugri district 1914–1924.

Segid. Blind teacher in Imkullu in 1887 and then in Tse'azzega up to 1930.

Selomon (Josef ?) Worked at the printing press in Imkullu 1891–1894, Asmara 1895–1896, "Hamasen" 1899, Tse'azzega 1900, Geleb and Beleza 1906–1912, 1926, Addi Kolom 1914–1916.

Selomon Atsmai. Evangelist and teacher in Addiké 1913–1915.

Selomon Atsqu. Former Orthodox priest, and one of the fathers of the Evangelical Church of Eritrea. Pastor

and teacher in Geleb 1877, Imkullu from 1881, Addi Daso from 1890, Addi Kolom 1891–1892, and later on in Asmara and Beleza 1901–1925. Died in 1926.

Selomon Hemmed. Evangelist and teacher in Geleb 1906–1920.

Sema'tu. Wife of Hailu. Took part in the Second Oromo Expedition 1881–1882 which had to return to Imkullu. She seems to have been in Asmara 1913–1944.

Semoet (Simret?). Evangelist and teacher in Addis Ababa 1923–1929.

Sereqé. Evangelist and teacher in Guritat, Beleza 1916–1924.

Showhat. Bible woman in Tse'azzega from 1916.

Sibhatu Birru. Evangelist and teacher in Addi Nifas, Asmara district 1916–1927.

Simon Oddi. Evangelist and teacher in Kunama 1927–1944.

Stefano Baddi. Evangelist in Kulluku 1924–1929.

Stefanos Bonaya. Took part in the Fourth Oromo Expedition 1893–1895. In Geleb 1896–1897.

Stifanos Tebedje. Evangelist and teacher in Addis Ababa 1934–1944.

Sälela. Bible-woman in Tse'azzega 1901–1920 (1914–15 in Addi Ugri), and Tigrai 1921–1922.

Tackalat (?). Evangelist and teacher in Tse'azzega 1924.

Tadewos. Evangelist and teacher in Tigrai 1924–1931.

Taha (Zaha?). Female teacher at the school for girls in Beleza until 1890–1892.

Tamrat. An evangelist with an Orthodox background, a disciple of Aleqa Tayye. Served in Addis Ababa 1927–1944.

Tayyelign (Tayye) Gebre-Mariam (Aleqa). 1898–1924. An Ethiopian Orthodox scholar from Begemdir in Northern Ethiopia, who became an Evangelical Christian in Imkullu in 1887. Served in Tse'azzega 1891–1898, Gojjam 1899–1904. Teacher, preacher, author.

Was research assistant in Germany 1905–1906. Imprisoned for his faith in Addis Ababa (1910–1911).

Tebedje. Evangelist and teacher in Amhara 1913–1944. A disciple of *Aleqa* Tayye.

Tedla Aflei. Evangelist and teacher in Beleza 1980–1910, Addi Diblai 1911, Geshinashim 1913–1916, Beleza 1917–1923. Moved to Ethiopia.

Teferra. Evangelist and teacher in Oromo country 1918–1919.

Tegenye (*Aleqa*). Teacher and Evangelist in Bojji Kerkero. In Addis Ababa 1924–1941.

Teka. Bible woman in Geleb 1929.

Teké. Evangelist and teacher in Addi Ugri 1913–1916, 1924, Tse'azzega 1917–1923.

Tekh'a. Evangelist in Asmara from 1904.

Teklé (*Qeshi*). Pastor in Shimanigus and Beleza district 1914–1923.

Teklé Ristu. Evangelist and teacher in the district of Beleza 1921–1925.

Teklé Tesfa-Kristos. Evangelist and teacher, later ordained 1909 Served in Asmara 1899–1902, Himbirti 1903–1915, Tse'azzega district 1916–1919.

Teklé Tetehany. Evangelist and teacher in Oromo country 1920–1922.

Tekle-Haimanot Mihirka (*Haleqa*). Former Orthodox priest from Hatsebo, near Axum in Tigrai. He became a teacher in Beleza 1900–1911, Dekemhare 1913–1914, Beleza 1915–1920, Tigrai 1921–1931, Beleza 1934–1937.

Tekle-Haimanot Gebre. Teacher in the districts of Tse'azzega and Addi Ugri: Addi Sherefeto 1911–1916, Addi Ugri 1917–1920.

Tekle-Mariam (*Abba*). A learned theologian from Axum. Received as member 1891 in Tse'azzega. Became an Evangelist and teacher in Tigrai 1928–1929.

Teklu Uqbit. Evangelist and dresser in Imkullu 1888–1897, in Asmara 1898–1899, and in Beleza 1900–1934. The "right hand" of Drs. Karl Winqvist and Nicola De Pertis.

Tesemma Hailu. Evangelist in Gojjam

1900–1902, Amhara 1903–1906, Girmajer 1907–1910. Died in 1912.

Tesfa-Ezgi Gebre-Sillassé. Teacher, son to *Qeshi* Gebre-Sillassé Gebru. Served in Tse'azzega 1916–1922, Beleza 1923–1924, 1926, Addi Ugri 1925. Moved to Addis Ababa where he served as a teacher from 1927 to 1944.

Tesfa-Gabir Gidé. Former Orthodox priest (1846–1940) from Himbirti. Became an Evangelical Christian. Father to *Qeshi* Gebre-Sillassé Tesfa-Gabir (1881–1932), who was sent to Ethiopia in 1905 and was to serve in Ethiopia for several decades. Tesfa-Gabir, who had also moved to Ethiopia, died at the age of 102 years.

Tesfa-Leul Hibtes. Evangelist and teacher in Geleb 1914–1932.

Tesfa-Mariam. Received as a member in Tse'azzega 1899. Evangelist and teacher in Raptu 1908–1909, Geleb 1910, and Tse'azzega 1923–1924.

Tesfa-Mikael Gebru. Evangelist and teacher in Addi Ugri 1914–1919, Beleza 1920–1945.

Tesfankiel Gebre (*Qeshi*). Pastor in Addi Ugri 1920–1924.

Tesfu Bairai (*Qeshi*). Evangelist and teacher who was later ordained. Served in and around Asmara 1916–1920, in Beleza 1921–1951. Died in 1952.

Tesfu Derso. Evangelist in Asmara 1923–1924. Registered in the Evangelical congregation in Addis Ababa 1927.

Tesfu Zeré. Teacher, later ordained. Served in Beleza 1908–1912, Dequ-Zer'ou 1913–1915, Emba Derho and Beleza district 1916–1954.

Tewold-Birhan Gebré. Teacher and carpenter under Anders Svensson in Tse'azzega. Was in Asmara 1923 and in Addi Ugri after 1924 as a carpenter working with Pastor Holmer.

Tewolde-Medhin Gebru. Orthodox priest and scholar originally from Mai Misham in Tigrai. First came to Beleza for treatment in 1899. Came to Evangelical conviction. Worked with translation of Tigrinya NT which was published in 1910. Back in Mai Misham, Tigrai, 1910–1929, as teacher and evangelist. Asmara 1930–1931 and Tigrai 1932–1955.

Tewolde-Medhin Gebre-Medhin (*Qeshi*). Deacon in Orthodox Church. Came to mission school in Geleb 1876. After studying Theology at Johannelund in Stockholm, back in Imkullu 1887. In Arkiko 1888–1890, Geleb 1891–1900, Asmara 1901–1910. Ordained in 1909. Tse'azzega 1914–1920, Sweden 1922, Asmara-Beleza areas 1923–1928. The first vice-president of the ECE at its establishment in 1926. Visited Sweden. Died in February 2, 1930.

Ti'bé. Dresser who worked with Winqvist in 1888. Asmara 1903. Neqemte 1904 (?)

Tiblets. Bible woman in Ta'ireshi from 1913–1915.

Timoteos Faid (Yohannes) Evangelist in Mihlab 1901–1916, and later in Geleb 1917–1955.

Tirfé (*Qeshi*). From Tse'azzega. In Massawa in 1877. Employed as a teacher for boys. Translated "Pilgrim's Progress" into Amharic. Later ordained. Died in 1880 and succeeded by his son Habte-Giorgis.

Tiruneh, *Qeshi*). Former Orthodox priest (1870–1930) who became an Evangelist in the tradition of *Aleqa* Tayye. Mainly at Dera in "Amhara" 1913–1918. Served in Addis Ababa 1927–1930.

Tirunesh. Female teacher at the school for girls in Addis Ababa 1923–1924. Apparently the daughter of John John, (The well-known traveller Mansfied Parkyns). She was the second wife of *Aleqa* Tayye.

Tsegai Medhin. Printer in Asmara 1904–1908. Registered in the Evangelical congregation in Addis Ababa 1927.

Tsehaitu Ni'amin. Teacher at the home for children in Beleza 1920–1937. Came to Asmara and was in active service as a teacher 1938–1955.

Uqba-Egzi. Teacher in Asmara from 1898–1915.

Uqba-Gabir. Farmer-teacher in Beleza district from 1910–1918.

Uqba-Gabir Zeru. Teacher and Evangelist in Raptu 1911–1924.

Uqba-Mikael. Teacher and Evangelist in Addi Ugri 1914–1937. Died in December 1938.

Wolde-Medhin. Night time guard in Ailet 1877.

Woldeab Woldemariam. Teacher, school director, one of the key leaders and advocates of the ECE during the turbulent years of Second World War. Journalist, beginning in the 1940,s. Asmara 1930, Kunama 1931–1935, Asmara 1944–1955.

Wolde-Aregai Abreha. Dresser and evangelist, in Asmara 1930, Tigrai 1932.

Wolde-Gabir Habte-Tsion. Evangelist and teacher from Addi Belih, and served in the district of Tse'azzega, 1923–1924.

Wolde-Gabir Selomon. Evangelist and teacher in the district of Tse'azzega 1923–1924.

Wolde-Gabriel. Asistant at the printing press in Imkullu, 1903–1904, then an evangelist in Addi Zarna from 1905–1912, in Tse'azzega 1916–1918, in Addi Ugri 1919–1920, and Massawa 1921–1923.

Wolde-Gerima. Evangelist and teacher in Tigrai 1923.

Wolde-Kidan. Evangelist and teacher in Tembien, Tigrai 1913–1915.

Wolde-Kristos. Teacher in Wekki Dibba 1908–1913, Tse'azzega 1914–1932.

Wolde-Mariam. Received as member in Tse'azzega in 1900. Well-read Orthodox scholar

Wolde-Mariam Shuba. Dresser in Beleza 1920 (?) Neqemte, Wollega 1927–1932.

Wolde-Mikael. Assistant at the printing press in Imkullu, 1887–1891, and then evangelist in Beleza 1906–1911, Tigrai 1912–1913, Kwanddebba 1914–1916, and Beleza 1917–1922.

Wolde-Sillassé Kinfu. A *debtera* who lived

1841–1876. Contacts with The British and Foreign Bible Society. Attended Gobat's school in Jerusalem for a year. One of the disciples of J. Martin Flad, (1831–1915) missionary to the Felasha. Teacher in Massawa 1874.

Woldenki'el. Evangelist and teacher in Beleza 1923–1924.

Wolde-Tinsaé (*Abba*). A former Orthodox monk. Later Evangelist and teacher in Tse'azzega and Tsa'ida Kristian 1907–1910.

Wolde-Yesus Kinfé. Former Orthodox priest. Pastor in Dequ Tsin'a 1914–1915, Tse'azzega 1916–1955.

Wolde-Yohannes (*Abba*). Former Orthodox, head priest in Beleza. Received into the Evangelical congregation in Beleza in 1891. Evangelist and teacher in Hamasen and Tigrai. Died in 1914.

Wolette-Birhan. Female co-worker in Neqemte, Wollega 1927–1952.

Yaqob Sada. Evangelist and teacher in Kunama 1919–1924.

Yfter Tesfa-Egzy. Evangelist and teacher in Shimanigus Tahtai, in the district of Beleza from 1914–1924.

Yishaq Be'imnet. Teacher and Evangelist within the Tigré-speaking area 1924.

Yishaq Hemmed. Evangelist and dresser in Imkullu 1888–1891, Geleb 1892–1926.

Yishaq Tewolde-Medhin. Educated in Beirut. Teacher in the Tigré-speaking region 1914–1922, Asmara 1923–1924, Beleza 1927–1929, Asmara 1930–1932. Director for schools under the British Administration in Eritrea.

Yohannes Emilios. Evangelist and teacher and later pastor. Served in Qanna 1911–1924, Asmara 1925–1929 and Keren 1930–1950. Died in 1952.

Yohannes Faraja. Interpreter on First Oromo Expedition 1877–1884. In Massawa 1877, Shewa 1878–1884, Jimma 1885–1896. Died in 1896.

Yohannes Fetur. Evangelist and teacher in Tse'azzega 1916–1924.

Yohannes Teklu. Dresser in Beleza 1929–1940, later in Tigrai 1941–1944. Son of the well-known Teklu "Hakim" who was a close co-worker of Drs. Karl Winqvist and Nicola De Pertis.

Yohannes Wolde-Mariam. Co-worker in Wollega 1920–1924.

Yohannes. Taylor's assistant in Geleb 1903.

Yokabed (Jockebed). Bible woman in Tse'azzega 1910–1913.

Yosef Hawariat (?). Beleza 1931.

Yosef Hemmed. Co-worker in Imkullu and Massawa 1903–1910, Geleb 1911–1925. Ordained 1920. Pastor in Addi Ugri 1926, Keren 1927–1929, Asmara 1930–1932, Geleb 1933–1955.

Yosef Mati. Teacher and later pastor in Kunama 1925–1937.

Yosef Selomon. Evangelist and teacher in Addi Kolom 1914–1916, Beleza and Asmara 1917–1924.

Yosef. Teacher in Tailoring. Imkullu 1901, Geleb and Beleza 1906–1914, Kunama 1919–1924.

Zafu Tewolde-Medhin. Evangelist and teacher in Tigrai 1924–1929. Son of *Haleqa* Tewolde-Medhin Gebru.

Zaha (See Taha).

Zekarias Teklé. Evangelist and teacher in Asmara 1925–1926. Moved to Addis Ababa in December 1926. Among those who were received into the Evangelical congregation in Addis Ababa in 1927

Zemhret. Evangelist and teacher in Beleza 1920–1924.

Zer'a -Tsion Musé. Former Orthodox priest and one of the fathers of the ECE. Massawa 1877, Imkullu 1881–1889, Teacher in Addi Qontsi 1890–1891, 'Hamasen' 1892–1899, Beleza 1900–1910, Geremi 1913–1915, Beleza 1916–1940.

Zer'e Kafil. Evangelist and teacher in the district of Beleza 1913–1931. (Asmara 1928–1930).

Zer'e-Mariam. Evangelist and teacher in the district of Beleza 1920.

Zewdi Girma-Tsion. Female dresser in Asmara 1929–1931 and in Tigrai from 1932–1933.

Bibliography

Books Used and Recommended

MISSION PERIODICALS, MINUTES, AND REPORTS

MT -MISSIONS TIDNING. A Swedish Mission Periodical.

ANNUAL REPORTS OF THE EFS/SEM.

BOARD MINUTES, Reports from Field Conferences.

REPORTS FROM MISSION CONFERENCES.

U14. STOCKHOLM ARCHIVES. Special Archives with Letters from missionaries.

OTHER SOURCES

ADAMSON, CAROL A.
1987 Sweden and the Ethiopian Crisis, 1934–1938. Madison.

ALAZAR MENGHESTU
2004 Bakgrunden och framväxten av en luthersk kyrka i Eritrea, 1912–1932. Eritreanskt-svenskt initiativ. Sundbyberg.

ALEMSEGED TESFAI
1991 Kilitä Qinä Ab Difu'at (Tigrinja: Two Weeks in a Trench). Hidri Publishers. Asmara.
2001 Aynifälalä 1941–1950. Hidri Publishers. Asmara.
2002 Two Weeks in a Trench. Red Sea Press. Trenton.
2006 From Anze Matienzo to Tedla Bairu. Asmara.

ANDERSSON, AUGUST
1903 Ett och annat om kunamaerna, (Some Facts about the Kunama People). EFS-förlaget. Stockholm.
1908 Eko från Kunama. (Echoes from Kunama). EFS-förlaget. Stockholm.
1941 Från gravarnas och blodssåddens land. (In the land of graves and the seeds of blood). EFS-Bokförlag. Stockholm.
1947 På gamla återställda stigar I. (On old and restored paths). EFS-förlaget. Stockholm.
1948 På gamla återställda stigar II. EFS-förlaget. Stockholm.

ANDERSSON, NORMARK, ET AL.
2006 Så, skörda och så vidare. EFS Uppsala. (Sew, Reap ,Etc.)

ANDERSSON, OLLE
1947 Stormen bröt lös. (The Storm broke loose.) EFS-Bokförlag. Stockholm.

ARÉN, GUSTAV
1978 Evangelical Pioneers in Ethiopia. Origins of the Evangelical Church Mekane Yesus. Stockholm. Addis Ababa.
1999 Envoys of the Gospel in Ethiopia. In the Steps of the Evangelical Pioneers 1898–1936. Stockholm.

ATIYA, AZIZ
1968 A History of Eastern Christianity. (146–166). Indiana.

BADOGLIO, PIETRO
1937 The War in Abyssinia. New York.

BAHRU ZEWDE
1991 (2002) History of Modern Ethiopia. Oxford, Addis Ababa.

BANDRÉZ, JOSÉ L. AND ZANETTI, UGO
2003 "Christology" in EAE. Vol.1, A-C, pp. 728-732. Wiesbaden.

BAUSI, ALLESSANDRO AND LUSINI, GIANFRANCESCO
1999 "Appunti in Margine a una Nuova Ricerca sui Conventi Eritrei" (Marginal Notes on a New Research on Eritrean Monasteries) in Rassegna Di Studi Etiopici Vol XXXVI, Roma-Napoli.

BAUSI, ALESSANDRO
1995 Il senodos etiopico. Peeters, Louvain.
1997 "Su alcuni manoscritti presso le communità monastiche Dell'Eritrea." Parte Seconda, in Rassegna Di Studi Etiopici. Volume XXXIX 1995, 25–48. Roma-Napoli.
2005 "Didesqelya" in EAE, Vol.2, D-Ha, pp.154-155. Wiesbaden.

BAUSI, DORE AND TADDIA (ED.)
2001 Anthropological and Historical Documents on "Rim" in Ethiopia and Eritrea, Torino.

BENDER, LIONEL
2007 Kunama Language in *EAE*, Vol 3, pp. 451–453. Harrassowitz, Wiesbaden.

BEREKET HABTE-SELLASSIE
1989 Eritrea and the United Nations. The Red Sea Press. Trenton.
2007 The Crown and the Pen. The Memoirs of a Lawyer Turned Rebel. Red Sea Press.
2009 "State, Religion and Ethno-Regional Politics". In *awate.com* for March 02, 2010.

BERDAL-JACQUIN, D AND PLAUT, MARTIN
2005 Unfinished Business. Ethiopia and Eritrea at War. Red Sea Press. Trenton.

BERGLUND, AINA
1959 Varde Ljus 1959. Stockholm.

BERGMAN, TORE
2006 August Bergman och hans familj i Ostafrika och Sverige, sammanställning av Tore Bergman. (August Bergman and His Family in East Africa and Sweden, Compiled by Tore Bergman). Uppsala. (Typewritten essay)

BERHE Y
2001 Tarikh Ortodoks Tewahdo Betäkristian Ertra (A History of the Orthodox Tewahdo Church of Eritrea). Asmara.

BESKOW, GUSTAF EMANUEL
1884 Den svenska missionen i Ost-Afrika, I. Stockholm.
1887 Den svenska missionen i Ost-Afrika, II. Stockholm.

BRANT, PETER
2003 "Bible Canon" in *EAE*. Vol.1, A-C, Wiesbaden.

BRAW, CHRISTIAN
1993 Nåden och Världen (Grace and the World). Verbum. Stockholm.

BRODD, SVEN-ERIK
1992 Diakonatet, in Tro och Tanke 1992:10. Klippan.

BUONAIUTI, CESARE MARGONGIU
1982 Politica e religioni nel colonialismo italiano, 1882–1941. Varese.

BUDGE, WALLIS (TRANSLATOR)
1901 Mätsehafä Gädlä Hawaryat. The Contendings of the Apostles. Vol. II. (Translation). London.

CHAILLOT, CHRISTINE AND BELOPOPSKY, ALEXANDER
1998 Towards unity. The Theological Dialogue between the Orthodox and the Oriental Orthodox Churches. Geneva.

COHEN, LEONARD AND MARTINEZ, ANDREU
2007 "Jesuits", in *EAE* Vol. 3, He-N. Wiesbaden.

COÎSSON, ROBERTO
1963 I valdesi e l'opera missionaria. Torre Pellice.

COLLINS, ROBERT O (ED.)
1994 "Educating The African" in Historical Problems in Imperial Africa. Princeton.

COLLINS, ROBERT O
1962 The Southern Sudan 1883–1898.

CRUMMEY, DONALD
1972 Priests and Politicians. Protestant and Catholic Missions in Orthodox Ethiopia 1830–1868. Oxford.

DAHLBERG, NILS
1932 Från slav till översättare (From Slave to Bible Translator). Stockholm.
1953 Under Högre Befäl. En Minnesbok om Prins Oscar Bernadotte. (Under Higher Command. A Commemorative Book about Oscar Bernadotte). Norrköping.

DA ISEO, EZECHIA
1916 La Colonia Eritrea. Manuale d'istruzione italiano-tigrai ad uso delle scuole indigene. Asmara. (Smith-Simonsen has translated this work, or parts of it for use in her doctoral thesis. See Smith-Simonsen 1997).
1922 I Capuccini in Eritrea: Dieci anni

di Apostolato. Asmara.

DA NEMBRO, METODIO
1953 La Missione dei Minori Capuccini in Eritrea. Roma.

DAWIT WOLDE GIORGIS
1989 Red Tears. War, Famine, and Revolution in Ethiopia. Trenton.

D'AVRAY, ANTHONY
1996 Lords of the Red Sea. The History of a Red Sea Society from the Sixteenth to the Nineteenth Centuries. Aethiopische Forschungen. Harrassowitz Verlag, Wiesbaden.

DEL BOCA, ANGELO
1969 The Ethiopian War, 1935–1941. Chicago.

DE BONO, EMILIO
1937 Anno XIII: The Conquest of an Empire. Cresset Press. London.

DORE, GIANNI
2007 "Chi non ha una parente Andinna?". Donne e possessione come archivio storico ed esperienza dell'alterità tra i Kunama d'Eritrea. Ethnorêma. Tortona.
2007 Kunama Etnography, EAE, Vol 3, pp 453–455. Harrassowitz, Wiesbaden.

DORESSE, JEAN
1967 (1959) Ethiopia. (Translated from the French by Elsa Coult). London.

EDLUND, BRITA
1961 Minnen ur dagböcker och reseanteckningar (Reminiscences from diaries and travel notes). Östersund.

EMMANUEL ABRAHAM
1995 Reminiscences of My Life. Oslo.
2010, Reminiscences of My Life. African World Press, Inc. & The Red Sea Press. Inc.

ENGBLOM, ULRICA RISSO
2003 Images of Poverty in Colonial Eritrea as Portrayed by Swedish Missionary sources. (An Abstract for the Nordic African Days 3–5 October 2003). Uppsala.

ENGLUND, PETRUS
1873 Litet prof på kunama-språket. (Some exampels from the Kunama language). Stockholm.

ERIKSSON, OLOF (OLLE) (ED.)
1912 (Sia la Luce!). Birhan Yikun. Asmara.

ERIKSSON, JOHANNES
1936 Nya färdvägar i Ostafrika (New Paths in East Africa). Stockholm.

ERIKSSON, LARSOLOV
2006 "The Swedish Evangelical Mission as a Background to Johannes Kolmodin's Life and Work" in the Last Dragoman. The Swedish Orientalist Johannes Kolmodin as Scholar, Activist, Diplomat. E.Özdalga editor. Pp. 71–82. Istanbul.

ERITREA-NYTT:
1993 "Eritrea från koloni till fri nation" (Eritreagrupperna i Sverige nr. 2–3)

EYASSU GAYIM
1993 The Eritrean Question. The Conflict between the Right of Self-Determination and the Interests of the States. Uppsala.

EZRA GEBREMEDHIN
1977 Life-Giving Blessing. An Inquiry into the Eucharistic Doctrine of Cyril of Alexandria. Uppsala.
1997 "Searching for Mäzgäba Haymanot (MH= The Treasury of Faith) at Däbrä Bizän, Eritrea" in Amidst Crosses and Minarets. Reports from a Field Study in Ethiopia and Eritrea. 1997. Helena Andersson, Anne-Mari Arthursson etc. Uppsala University.
1998 "Aleqa Taye: The Missionary Factor in his Scholarly Work", in The Missionary Factor in Ethiopia (pp. 101–120), Haile, Lande, and Rubenson (eds.) Peter Lang, Frankfurt am Main.
2003 Review of Alessandro Bausi, Gianni Dore and Irma Taddia's Anthropological and Historical Documents on "Rim" in Ethiopia and Eritrea, L'Harmattan Italia.

"Il Politico e La Memoria". Torino, 2001, in Aethiopica. International Journal of Ethiopian Studies. 6, 236–240.

2005 "Let There Be Light!" Aspects of the Swedish Missionary Venture in Eritrea and Their Implications for Political Awareness, in African Identities and World Christianity in the Twentieth Century, Klaus Koschorke (Ed.) Wiesbaden.

2006 "Zanta Tsazzegan Hazzegan: Johannes Kolmodin's Contribution to the Understanding of Eritrean Highland Culture" in the Last Dragoman. The Swedish Orientalist Johannes Kolmodin as Scholar, Activist and Diplomat. (Swedish Research in Istanbul Transactions Vol.16) pp. 83–95. E. Özdalga (Ed.) Istanbul.

2007 "Mel'ichti Selam" in *EAE* Vol.1, p. 695.

FEKADU GURMESSA
2009 Evangelical Faith Movement in Ethiopia. Origins and Establishment of the Ethiopian Evangelical Church Mekane Yesus. Translated and Edited by Ezekiel Gebissa. Lutheran University Press. Minneapolis.

FICQUET, ELOI
2003 "Boru Meda" in *EAE* Vol.I, A-C, p. 609. Wiesbaden

FISSEHA BAHTA (MERIGETA)
1985–1986 "Tefesihi Be'igziabher ze red'ané " (Rejoice in God who has helped us!). A poem composed in 1938 in honour of Abuné Marqos (1877–1953, Julian Calendar) a monk of Debre Bizen and the first Eritrean bishop. Published in Quaderni di Studi Etiopici. 6–7, 158–165.

GEBRE H. TESFAGIORGIS
2008 "Customary Laws in Eritrea" in Traditions of Eritrea. Linking the Past and the Future, 1–36. The Red Sea Press. Trenton.

GETATCHEW HAILE
1991 "Ethiopian Monasticism" in Coptic Encyclopedia, Aziz S. Atiya, Editor in Chief. Vol. 3, pp. 992–993. New York.

2000 Bahra Hassab. Our Heritage with Regard to Reckoning Time, with Historical Notes (In Amharic). Collegeville, Minnesota.

2004 Deqiqä Istifanos. "Behigä Amlak". (Translation). Collegeville, Minnesota.

GHIRMAI NEGASH
1999 A History of Tigrinya Literature in Eritrea. The Oral and Written. 1890–1991. Leiden.

GREENBERG, JOSEPH
1963 Languages of Africa. The Hague.

GUDMUNDSEN, G
1936 Fjorton år bland kopter och hedningar i Abessinien (Fourteen Years among Copts and Pagans in Abyssinia). Stockholm

GUIDA D'ITALIA
1938 Guida D'Italia Della Consociazione Turistica Italiana. Africa Orientale Italiana. Milano, 1938 XVI. Roma.

HAGNER, OLLE
1939–1943 Dagböcker (Diaries). In possession of Olle's son, Olle Hagner. A typed summary of these diary entries was made by K. J. Lundström in xxxx.

1953 " Till Galla eller dö" in Bortom Bergen, (F. Hylander. Ed.) Stockholm.

HAILE, LANDE, RUBENSON (EDS)
1998 The Missionary Factor in Ethiopia. Frankfurt am Main.

HALLDIN-NORBERG, VIVECA
1977 Swedes in Haile Selassie's Ethiopia, 1924–1952. Stockholm.

HAMMAR, H. B.
1901 Evang. Fosterlands-Stiftelsens Ost-Afrikanska mission 1856–1900, Stockholm.

HAMMERSCHMIDT, ERNST
1967 Äthiopien: Christliches Reich
     zwischen gestern und morgen.
     Wiesbaden.

HASTINGS, ADRIAN
1994 The Church in Africa: 1450–1950.
     (Ch 1, 4, 6). Oxford.

HELLSTRÖM, IVAN
1989 Bland faror och nöd i Kunama.
     Stockholm. (Second edition 1996)

HENRIKSSON, ALF
1963 Svensk historia I, Stockholm.

HEYER, FRIEDRICH
1971 Die Kirche Aethiopiens. De Gruyter.

HOFGREN, ALLAN (ED.)
1956 Med Gud och hans vänskap.
     Evangeliska Fosterlands-Stiftelsen
     genom 100 år. (With God and His
     Goodness. The Swedish Evangeli-
     cal Mission and Its One Hundred
     Years of Mission). Stockholm.

HOLMER, ROSA
1937 P E Lager. Stockholm.
1938 Twoldo Medhen. Stockholm.

HUSEIN AHMED
2007 History of Islam in Ethiopia. EAE
     3, 2007, 204–205.

HYLANDER, FRIDE (RED)
1953 Bortom bergen. Stockholm.

HYLANDER, NILS (RED)
1916 Jubileums-album. Stockholm.

HYLANDER, NILS
1893 Ökenröster (Desert Voices). Lands-
     krona.
1917 Morgonljus, EFS förlagsexpedi-
     tion. Stockholm.

ISICHEI, ELISABETH
1995 A History of Christianity in Africa:
     From Antiquity to the Present.
     London

IWARSON, JONAS
1935 På färdvägar i Ostafrika. Stock-
     holm.

IWARSON, JONAS AND TRON, A
1918 Notizie storiche e varie sulla
     Missione Evangelica Svedese
     dell'Eritrea 1866–1916. Asmara.

JEWFIMISZYN, ANNA
2006 "Doctor Anna i nöd och lust"
     interview of Anna Jewfimiszyn
     by Liselotte Rogberg in SEM/MT
     Budbäraren, nr 23, 2006. Uppsala.

JOËLSON, ANDERS
1994 Peter Andersson från Ornakärr,
     missionär i Kunama. (Private
     publication, typewritten essay)

JOHN ABRAHA
2005 "Kunama Dialects and Morpholo-
     gy" in Journal of Eritrean Studies.
     Vol. IV, 1&2, pp. 28–44.

JONES, ARNOLD H M AND MONROE, ELISABETH
1935 (1970) A History of Ethiopia.
     Oxford.

JOSEPH GABRAWOLD
1972 The Origin and Early Develop-
     ment of the Evangelical Church
     of Eritrea 1866–1971 (Machine-
     typed thesis for the degree of
     B.A. in Education. Haile Selassie I
     University. Addis Ababa.

KAPLAN, STEVEN
1998 Fils d'Abraham. Les Falashas.
     Brepols.

KEBEDE HORDOFA-JANKO AND PETER UNSETH
2003 "Aster Ganno" in EAE, vol.1, (2003),
     pp. 387–388. Wiesbaden.

KELLY, JOHN NORMAN
1980 Early Christian Doctrines. London.

KIROS FRE-WOLDU (ED.)
1989 J. Kolmodin's Zanta Tsazzegan
     and Hazzeggan. Tigrinya version.
     Stockholm.

KNIBB, MICHAEL
2003 Bibel Vorlage Syriac Hebrew, Cop-
     tic, Arabic in EAE, Vol 3, p 565

KOLMODIN, ADOLF
1885 Carl Johan Carlsson. Stockholm.
1909 Några Minnen från min Resa till
     Ost-Afrika 1908–1909. (Some Remi-
     niscences from my Journey to East
     Africa 1908–1909). Stockholm.

KOLMODIN, CARL GUSTAF
1999 Johannes Kolmodin i Brev och
     Skrifter. (=Filologiskt arkiv 41.
     Kungl. Vitterhets Historie och

Antikvitets Akademien.) Stockholm.

KOLMODIN, JOHANNES
Traditions de Tsazzega et Hazzega. Archivs d'Études Orientales,
5:1–3.
1912 Vol. 5:1, 'Textes tigrigna'. Rome.
1914 Vol. 5:3, 'Annales et documents'.
Uppsala.
1915 Vol. 5:2, 'Traduction francaise.'
Uppsala.
1914 Traditions de Tsazzega et Hazzega.
Annales et Documents. Upsal.

LANGE, LARS JOHAN
1965 Utdrag ur missionär L. J. Langes
Dagbok. Klippan.

LATOURETTE, KENNETH SCOTT
1975 A History of Christianity, 2 vols.
San Francisco.

LAUNHARDT, JOHANNES
2004 Evangelicals in Addis Ababa,
(1919–1991): With Special Reference to the Ethiopian Evangelical Church Mekane Yesus and the
Addis Ababa Synod. (Studien Zur
Orientalischen Kirchengeschich-
te.) Münster.

LEVANDER, ESKIL (ED)
1931 Evangeliska Fosterlands-Stiftelsen
genom 75 år (I-II). Jubileumsskrift.
Stockholm.

LEVI, CARLO
1945 Christ Stopped at Eboli. (Cristo
si è fermato a Eboli). English
translation by Francis Fernaye.
Strasbourg and New York.

LITTMANN, ENNO
1907 Preliminary Report of the Princeton University Expedition to
Abyssinia. Berlin
1931 Deutsche Aksum-Expedition.
Band 1. Berlin.
1910–1915. Publications of the Princeton Expedition to Abyssinia.
Vol.1.4. Leiden.

LONGRIGG, STEPHEN HEMSLEY
1945 A Short History of Eritrea. London, Oxford University Press.

LUNDSTRÖM, KARL JOHAN
1990 The Lotuho and the Verona Fathers. A Case Study of Communication in Development. Uppsala.
2003 Dagboksanteckningar av Olle Hagner 1939–1943 (sammanställda av
Karl Johan Lundström= Diary Notes compiled by K. J.Lundström).
1999 Kanisha, a stenciled section of a
history of the Evangelical Church
in Eritrea.

LUSINI, GIANFRACESCO P
2005 "Däbrä Bizän" in EAE Vol. 2, 15–17.
Harassowitz.
1993 Studi Sul Monachesimo Eusta-
ziano. (secoli XIV-XV). Napoli

LUSSIER, DOMINIQUE
1997 "Local Prohibitions, Memory and
Political Judgment among the Ku-
nama: An Eritrean Case Study," in
Ethiopia in a Broader Perspective,
Papers of the XIIIth International
Conference of Ethiopian Studies,
Kyoto, 12–17 December 1997, ed.
Katsuyoshi Fukui, Eisei Kurimoto,
and Masayoshi Shigeta, vol. 2,
441–455, Kyoto.

LÖFGREN , OSCAR
1970 "The Necessity of a Critical Edition of The Ethiopian Bible" in
Proceedings of the Third International Conference Of Ethiopian
Studies, Addis Ababa 1966, ii
157–161. Addis Ababa.

MARKUS GERMEI
1889 "Abessinska kyrkan förr och nu"
i Meddelanden från Student-
missionsföreningen i Uppsala.
Häft 1, 2 årg. häft 3. (191–219).
Upsala, Almqvist & Wiksell .1890,
Studentmissionsföreningen i
Uppsala.

MASTRANTONIS, GEORGE
1982 Augsburg and Constantinople.
The Correspondence between
the Tübingen Theologians and
Patriarch Jeremiah II of Constantinople on the Augsburg Confession. Brookline.

MEINARDUS, OTTO FRIEDRICH AUGUST
2000 Two Thousand Years of Coptic Christianity. Cairo.

MERID WOLDE-AREGAI
1998 "The Legacy of Jesuit Missionary Activities in Ethiopia from 1555 to 1632" in Haile, Lande, Rubenson (Ed.) The Missionary Factor in Ethiopia. 31–70. Frankfurt am Main.

METSIHAFÄ QIDDASÉ (THE HANDBOOK OF THE ORTHODOX MASS)
1964 E. C. (= 1972, according to the Julian Calendar). Addis Ababa.

MIKAEL HASAMA RAKA
1984, Future Life and Occult Beings. New York.
1992, Zanta Eretra, 'The Story of Eritrea'. Asmara.

MIRAN, JONATHAN
2002 "Missionaries, Education and the State in the Italian Colony of Eritrea" in Christian Missionaries & the State in the Third World. Edited by Holger Bernt Hansen & Michael Twaddle. Oxford. Athens.
2005 "A Historical Overview of Islam in Eritrea," Die Welt des Islams 45 (2), 177–215, Koninklijke Brill NV, Leiden. [Republished in an anthology: Andrew Rippin (Ed.), World Islam: Critical Concepts in Islamic Studies, Volume III. (London and New York: Routledge, 2008), pp. 195–224.]
2009 Red Sea Citizens. Cosmopolitan Society and Cultural Change in Massawa. Indiana University Press.

MOCKLER, ANTHONY
1985 Haile Selassie's War. New York.
1998 "The Catholic Mission and the Catholic Community in Eritrea, 1894–1950" in the Missionary Factor in Ethiopia (pp.121–134), Haile, Lande, and Rubenson (eds.) Frankfurt am Main.

MUNRO-HAY, STUART
2003 "Christianity", in EAE Vol. 1, A-C, pp 717–723. Harrassowitz.
2003, "Ark of the Covenant", EAE, vol.1

(2003), pp 340–341. Wiesbaden.

MUNZINGER, WERNER
1883 Ostafrikanische Studien. Basel. Even Schaffhausen, 1864.

NATI, ALEXANDER
1982 The Impact of Euro-Christian Missions on Kunama Traditional Culture. Senior Essays in Applied Anthropology. Addis Ababa University.
1982 "Elders and Juniors in Kunama Society", in International Symposium of History and Ethnography in Ethiopian Studies, Addis Ababa.

NIKODEMOS IDRIS,
1987 The Kunama and Their Language, (BA diss.), Addis Ababa University.
1993 Phonology of Kunama, Addis Ababa, September (mimeographed).

NILSSON, NILS
1921 Mäzgäbä Haymanot - Trons Skattkammare (A Treasury of Faith) in Varde Ljus. (48–77). Stockholm.

NORDLANDER, AGNE
1999 "The Missiological Strategy of Niguse Tashu, Gebre-Ewostatewos Ze-Mikael, and Onesimos Nesib in Reaching the Oromo with the Gospel" in Missiology and Linguistics. Papers Presented at the First Institute of the Centennial of the Bible Translation into Oromo. (36–52). Addis Ababa.

NORMARK, STURE
1972 Social Changes in the Kunama Society. Sociologiska institutionen på Uppsala Universitet.

NYSTRÖM, HARALD
1937 Med S:T Giorghis på Dödsritt. (With St.George on a Death Ride). Stockholm.

O'MAHONEY, KEVIN
1982 The Ebullient Phoenix. A History of the Vicariate of Abyssinia. Vol. I Asmara.

PAICE, EDWARD
1966 Guide to Eritrea. Bradt Travel Guides. Buckinghamshire.

PANKHURST, RICHARD
1968   Economic History of Ethiopia 1800–1935. Addis Ababa.

PAOLI, RENATO
1908   Nella Colonia Eritrea. Milano.

PAULOS, TZADUA (ABBA) (TR.) AND STRAUSS, P.L. (ED.)
1968   The Fetha Negast: The Law of The Kings. Addis Ababa.

POLLERA, A
1913   Il regime della proprietà terrierra in Etiopia e nella Colonia Eritrea. Roma.
1935   Le Popolazioni Indigine Dell' Eritrea, Roma.
1935   Annali del Regio Istituto Superiore Orientale di Napoli, 8:1.

PUGLISI, G
1952   Chi é ? dell´Eritrea. Dizionario biografico. Agenzia Regina. Asmara.

QERLOS ABBA
1976, 1983/1984. Firé Haymanot (The Fruit of Faith). Asmara.

REDIE BEREKETEAB
2000   Eritrea. The Making of a nation 1890–1991. Uppsala.

REINISH, L
1880   Die Kunama Sprache. Wien.

RETA ZEWDE
1987   (Ethiopian Calendar) 2000. Ye Ertra Gouday (The Case of Eritrea). Addis Ababa.

RODÉN, K. G.
1907   Mensa. Något om dess land och folk, samt missionsverksamheten därstädes, EFS Stockholm.
1911   "Den gamla flämtande kristendomen i Mensa" i Varde Ljus 1912, pp. 56–71, EFS-förlaget Stockholm.
1913   Le Tribù dei Mensa. Storia, Legge e Costumi. A: Tigré text; B; Italian translation. Asmara.

ROHLFS, GERHARD
1883   Meine Mission nach Abessinien. Leipzig.

RODÉN, NILS
1938   Johannelunds Missionsinstitut genom 75 år. Stockholm.

ROUAUD, ALAIN
2007   "Jerome, Abba"in EAE 3, p.272. Harrassowitz

RUBENSON, SAMUEL
1998   "The Interaction between the Missionaries and the Orthodox: the Case of Abune Selama" in the Missionary Factor in Ethiopia, (71–84), Haile, Lande, and Rubenson (eds.) Peter Lang, Frankfurt am Main.

RUBENSON, SVEN
1966   King of Kings Teodros of Ethiopia. Addis Abeba - Nairobi.
1976   The Survival of Ethiopian Independence. London.
1998   "The Missionary Factor in Ethiopia. Consequences of a Colonial Context" in the Missionary Factor in Ethiopia (pp. 57–70), Haile, Lande, and Rubenson (eds.) Frankfurt am Main.

RYMAN, BJÖRN
2005   Nordic Folk Churches: A Contemporary Church History. Grand Rapids.

SAMUEL, V. C.
1964   "One Incarnate Nature of God the Word" in Greek OrthodoxTheological Quarterly. 10, 1964. 37–53. Crestwood, New York.

SANDSTRÖM, ALLAN
1988   Per Stjärne missionären. Uppsala.

SAPETO, GIUSEPPE
1857   Viaggio e Missione Cattolica fra i Mensa, I Bogos e gli Habab. Roma.

SHACK, WILLIAM
1974, The Central Ethiopians. Amhara, Tigrina and Related Peoples. London.

SMITH, DENIS MACK
1969   (1982) Garibaldi. A Great Life in Brief.

SMIDT, WOLBERT
"Wäldä Selase Kinfu", in S.Uhlig (ed): EAE, vol. 4. Harrassowitz, Wiesbaden.

SMITH-SIMONSEN, C
1997 "... all'Ombra della Nostra Band-
iera." (In the Shadow of our Flag).
A Study on Italian Educational
Activities in Colonial Eritrea
1890–1941. Tromsoe.

SPENCER, JOHN
1984 Ethiopia at Bay: A Personal Account of the Haile Selassie Years.
Reference Publications. Algonac,
Michigan.

STENHOUSE, PAUL LESTER (TRANSLATOR),
2003 Futuh Al-Habasha (The Conquest
of Abyssinia) [16th century], a
translation of the Arabic original
by Sihab ad-Din Ahmad bin Abd
al-Qader bin Salem bin Utman.
Tsehai Publishers, Los Angeles.

STERN, HENRY AAR
1862 (1968), Wanderings Among the
Falashas in Abyssinia.

STIFTELSENS STYRELSE
1906 1856–1906. Evangeliska Foster-
lands Stiftelsens 50-åriga verksamhet. En minnesskrift utgifven av
Stiftelsens Styrelse. Stockholm.

SUNDKLER, BENGT AND STEED, CHRISTOPHER
2000 A History of the Church in Africa.
Cambridge.

SUNDSTRÖM, RICHARD
1910 "Martyrerna i Nagran. Översätt-
ning och bearbetning av det
Etiopiska Originalet" (= The
Martyrs of Najran. Tr. and ed. of
the Ethiopic original) in Missionsskrifter utgifna af Evangeliska
Fosterlands-Stiftelsen 17. Stockholm.

TADESSE TAMRAT
1998 "Evangelizing the Evangelized.
The Root Problem between Missions and the Ethiopian Orthodox
Church", in the Missionary Factor
in Ethiopia (pp.17–30.) Haile,
Lande, and Rubenson (eds.) Frankfurt am Main.

TADDIA, IRMA(ED)
2001 Anthropological and Historical

Documents on "Rim in Ethiopia
and Eritrea". L'Harmattan, Italia.
Torino.

TAFVELIN, THORE - LUNDMARK, GUSTAF (EDS.)
1974 Ut i all världen. Evangeliska
Fosterlands-Stiftelsens mission I
Afrika och Asien 1866–1973. (Into
the Whole World. The Mission of
the Swedish Evangelical Mission
in Africa and Asia. 1866–1973).
EFS-förlaget. Stockholm.

TAPPERT, T
1959 The Book of Concord. The Confessions of the Evangelical Lutheran
Church. Fortress Press. Philadel-
phia.

TEKESTE FEKADU
2002 Journey from Nakfa to Nakfa. Back
to Square One 1976–1979. Asmara.

TEKESTE NEGASH
1987 Italian Colonialism in Eritrea,
1882–1941. Policies, Praxis and
Impact. Uppsala.
1997 Eritrea and Ethiopia. The Federal
Experience .Transactions Publis-
her. Piscataway, N. J.

TEKESTE NEGASH AND KJETIL TRONVOLL
2001 "The Rise and Fall of Rim in Eritrea" in Anthropological and Historical Documents on << Rim>>
in Ethiopia and Eritrea. (Edited
by Alessandro Bausi, Gianni
Dore and Irma Taddia) 93–114.
L'Harmattan Italia. Torino.

TERGEL, ALF
1973 Från Jesus till Moder Teresa. 5[th]ed.
Stockholm.

TESFA GEBREMEDHIN
2008 "Traditional Agricultural Sustenance in Eritrea" in Traditions
of Eritrea. Linking the Past and
the Future, 131-154. The Red Sea
Press. Trenton.

TESFA G. GEBREMEDHIN & GEBRE H. TESFAGI-
ORGIS (EDITORS)
2008 Traditions of Eritrea. Linking
The Past and The Future. Red Sea
Press. Trenton.

TESFATSION MEDHANIE
1986 Eritrea: Dynamics of a National Question. Amsterdam.

TONINI, EZIO (ED.)
1985–1986 Quaderni di Studi Etiopici, Asmara. (6–7, Centro Studi Etiopici). Asmara.

TOURN, GIORGIO
1989 You Are My Witnesses. The Waldensians Across 800 Years. Torino.

TREVASKIS, G.K.N.
1960 Eritrea. A Colony in Transition 1941–1952. Oxford University Press.

TREVELYAN, GEORGE MACAULAY
1911 Garibaldi And The Making of Italy. Longmans, Green & Co.

TRIMINGHAM, G. SPENCER
1952 Islam in Ethiopia. London.

TRONVOLL, KJETIL
2009 The Lasting Struggle for Freedom in Eritrea. Human Rights and Political Development, 1991–2009. Oslo Center.

TUQUABO ARESSI (ED.)
1995 Mirutsat Anketsat Ato Woldeab 1941–1991 (Selected Articles by Ato Woldeab. 1941–1991) Asmara.

UHLIG, SIEGBERT (ED.)
2003 Encyclpaedia Aethiopica (EAE), 1, A-C. Harrassowitz, Wiesbaden.
2005 EAE 2, D-Ha. Harrassowitz, Wiesbaden.
2007 EAE 3, He-N. Harrassowitz, Wiesbaden.
2010 EAE 4, O-X. Harrassowitz, Wiesbaden.

ULLENDORF, EDWARD
1968 Ethiopia and The Bible. The Schweich Lectures of the British Academy 1967. London.
1973 The Ethiopians. An Introduction to Country and People. Oxford University Press.

VOLF, MIROSLAV
1996 Exclusion and Embrace. Abingdon.
2005 Free of Charge. Zondervan 2005.

VOLKER-SAAD, KERSTIN
2007 "Mänsa", EAE, Vol 3. Harrassowitz, Wiesbaden.

WALLIN, SOPHIE
1914 Mitt Lifs Hitoria (The Story of My Life). Nordiska Boktryckeriet. Stockholm.

WENGELAWIT BETE-KRISTIAN ERTRA (THE EVANGELICAL CHURCH OF ERITREA)
1974 Mezmur Selam (Hymnal). Asmara.

WINQVIST, ELSIE
1921 Livsbilder från Eritrea. Stockholm.
1927 Ett liv i i tro, kärlek och utgivande för Abessinien. Missionär Johan Martin Flads självbiografi. (A Life in Faith, Love and Sacrifice. The Autobiography of Missionary Johan Martin Flad). Stockholm.
1945 Med livet som insats. Läkarmissionen i Eritrea. Stockholm.
1953 "Plantskolan i öknen" in Bortom Bergen, Vol 1. (F.Hylander, ed.) Stockholm.

WINQVIST-JANÉR, ELISABET (ED.)
1958 Under heligt tvång. Till minne av Elsie Winqvist, missionär i Eritrea. Stockholm.

WITAKOWSKI, WITOLD
2007 "Council of Nicaea", in EAE, Vol.3, pp 1175–1177.
2003 Council of Chalcedon, in EAE, vol. 1, pp. 709–711. Harrassowitz, Wiesbaden.

WONDIMAGEGNEHU, A AND MOTOVU, J (EDS)
1970 The Ethiopian Orthodox Church. Addis Ababa.

WRONG, MICHELA
2005 I Didn't Do It For You. How the World Betrayed A Small African Nation. London.

WOLDEAB WOLDEMARIAM
1935 Vår mission i Kunama. Av infödde medarbetaren Woldealb Woldemariam" in Varde Ljus! Svensk Missionskalendern för 1936. Edited by Nils Dahlberg. Stockholm.
1949, 1995 "Mot Grazmatch Zer'e Berakhi" (The Death of Grazmatch

Zer'e Berakhi) published by Tuquabo Aressi 1995, in Merutsat 'Anqetsat Ato Wolde-ab 1941-1991, pp. 315-317. Hidri Publishers. Asmara 1995.

ZACH, M
2001 "Onesimos Nasib": His Life and Work" in Missiology and Linguistics. Papers Presented at the First Institute of the Centennial of the Bible Translation into Oromo 1999. (4–20). Addis Ababa.

ZEWDE GEBRE SELLASSIE
1975 Yohannes IV of Ethiopia: A Political Biography. Oxford.

YACOB TESFAY
1994 The Scandal of a Crucified World. Orbis Books. Maryknoll. N.Y.

1997 Liberation and Orthodoxy: The Promises and Failures of Inter Confessional Dialogue. Orbis Books. Maryknoll. N.Y.
2010 Holy Warriors, Infidels and Peacemakers in Africa. Palgrave Publishing House, New York.

YOHANNES OKBAZGHI
1991 Eritrea. A Pawn in World Politics. University of Florida Press.

YEBIO WOLDEMARIAM
2008 Italy: The Unpaid Debt. Awate.com

ÖZDALGA, ELISABETH (ED.)
2006 The Last Dragoman. The Swedish Orientalist Johannes Kolmodin as Scholar, Activist and Diplomat. (=Swedish Research in Istanbul Transactions Vol. 16) Istanbul.

Nine students from the school of Lundahl in Imkullu 1884.
Front row from left: 1. Kifle, 2. Yohannes, 3. Mohammed, 4. Sahle, 5. Sayid.
Back row: 6. Gebre-Giorgis, 7. Kidanu, 8. Ayana, 9. Retta.

GENERAL INDEX

In this index, Eritrean and Ethiopian names of authors begin with forenames.

Basic Facts on the Evangelical Lutheran Church of Eritrea (ELCE), 2010

(Taken from data for 2010 and modified on the basis of current estimates)
- Official name: The Evangelical Lutheran Church of Eritrea
- President: *Qeshi* Yosef Araya
- General Secretary: Temesghen Brhane
- Central office: Asmara
- Districts with locations of central offices: Maekel (Asmara), Deboub (Mendefera), Anseba (Keren), Gash Barka (Barentu)

Structure

The Synodical Convention, which normally meets annually, has the following functions:

- Elects the Synodical Council and Auditors
- Approves some of the boards
- Approves budgets
- Receives and discusses annual reports
- Takes steps to revise the constitution, should the need arise.

The Synodical Council has 9 (nine) members, including the President, Vice-President and the General Secretary. In the set up which was in force in the ECE, women and youth were represented. How this matter will be handled in the new ELCE is yet to be decided. The General Secretary is an ex-officio member and secretary of the Council. Members serve for a three-year term. The members can be re-elected for a further three-year term.

Departments

- Parish Work Department
- Programme Department
- Department of Finances
- Department of Communications
- Beleza Church Study Centre

Statistics

- Baptized members: ca. 15,000
- Pastors in active service   26
- Evangelists   11
- Lay leaders   26
- Congregations   41
- Preaching places   30
- Missionaries   None
- Primary Schools   2
- Schools for the deaf   2
- Clinics   3
- Preschools/kindergartens   4

1. Gabra Mariam Tinno.   2. Barafi.   3. Elias.   4. Gabra Leul.
5. Woldo Georgis.   6. Gabra Kristos.   7. Kefflei.   8. Berru.   9. Geberahiet.

Nine young students from the school of Lundahl in Imkullu. Front row from left: 1 Gebre-Mariam Tinno, 2 Berakhi, 3 Elias, 4 Gebre-Le'ul. Back row: 5 Wolde-Giorgis, 6 Gebre-Kristos, 7 Kifle, 8 Birru, 9 Gebrehet (Gebre-Hywet) Portraits sent for the benefit of the supporters in Sweden. Published in the SEM paper in December 1884.

The Editor

The editor of this book, Ezra Gebremedhin (B.A., M.A., B.D., D.Th.) was born and brought up in Ethiopia, where he was also ordained into the ministry of the Ethiopian Evangelical Church Mekane Yesus (EECMY). From his Kenisha parents, who had moved to Ethiopia from the Italian Colony of Eritrea in the latter half of the Nineteen-twenties, he and his siblings received a deep and lasting impression of the Evangelical faith which had nourished their parents in the Eritrea of their youth. A retired Assistant Professor of Theology at the University of Uppsala, the editor has also served as pastor among Diaspora Eritreans and Ethiopians of Evangelical Lutheran persuasion. He has three children and seven grandchildren. He and his wife, Gennet Awalom, are residents of Uppsala, Sweden.